OPEN FOR BUSINESS

AN INTRODUCTION TO THE *REAL WORLD*

Brock Williams
Metro Community College

Dane Galden
Columbus State Community College

with Contributions from Idalene Williams

Kendall Hunt
publishing company

Book Team
Chairman and Chief Executive Officer Mark C. Falb
President and Chief Operating Officer Chad M. Chandlee
Vice President, Higher Education David L. Tart
Director of Publishing Partnerships Paul B. Carty
Product/Development Supervisor Lynne Rogers
Vice President, Operations Timothy J. Beitzel
Project Coordinator Sara McGovern
Permissions Editor Tammy Hunt
Cover Designer Mallory Blondin

Kendall Hunt
publishing company

www.kendallhunt.com
Send all inquiries to:
4050 Westmark Drive
Dubuque, IA 52004-1840

Copyright © 2015 by Kendall Hunt Publishing Company

ISBN 978-1-4652-7652-0

Printed in the United States of America

BRIEF CONTENTS

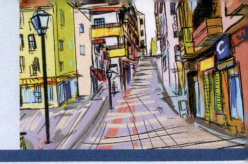

BRIEF CONTENTS

CONTENTS

ABOUT THIS BOOK

This is an introductory text to be used for what is normally a student's first business class. Each chapter introduces a subject that might become a full class or even a full business focus in a student's continuing education.

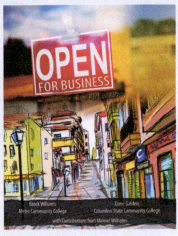

The idea behind this textbook was to write it especially for community college students. Every teacher has found themselves, at some point, explaining what the author really meant. In writing this text, we wanted to create a work written in a plain, flowing, and easy to read format that would encourage students to read and learn from the text to supplement what the teacher does in class. All of the college level rigor is here but in an easily read format.

The textbook authors and contributors are long-time community college educators. They each understand the huge diversity of students that take college classes at this level. Students at this level are frequently parents, often work full or part time, are often returning students with many years since their last classroom experience, and often attend more than one college at a time. Students need a textbook that will provide all of the necessary information in an easily readable and retainable format.

That is what we have attempted to do with this book.

PREFACE

From the title, you should be able to tell that this textbook is different. Our focus on "the real world" means that you get practical, usable advice in addition to high-end concepts and theories. But most of all we realize that you want to know how all of this applies to *you.*

Whether you work at a large company, are employed by a small business, or want to start your own venture, we will walk you through what you need to know. We cover the basics but also include enough examples and practical advice so that you can start using what you learn right away.

Our approach and our style make the material fun and effortless. You can easily see how ideas build on one another, and have a good foundation to understand more advanced concepts also if you choose to continue your education. Business itself is an education, and together we can get you off to a great start.

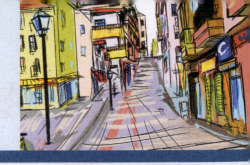

Brock Williams teaches a variety of business and economics classes at Metropolitan Community College in Omaha, Nebraska. This college of about 15,000 students has seven campus locations and serves eastern Nebraska. Brock has been teaching full time since 1999 and has also taught at other community colleges and four-year institutions. Brock served in the U.S. Air Force for 29 years, primarily in joint special operations and counter terrorism roles. After retiring from the service, he owned and operated two small businesses before he began his teaching career. As a private pilot, his hobby is flying his small airplane. He writes articles for a quarterly journal called Fine Lines and does some business and academic consulting.

Courtesy of Adam Williams.

Dane Galden is beginning his fourth year of teaching in the Business Programs Department at Columbus State Community College in Columbus, Ohio. He teaches courses in Management, Negotiation, and other business disciplines. Galden's current consulting work outside the classroom deals with product development, logistics, management efficiency, and computer/Internet development. His latest project has him overseeing the design and implementation of a web-based learning platform.

Galden has an MBA from Duke University, where he focused on Global Business and traveled all over the world to learn about and study companies and culture in Asia, India, Eastern Europe, South America, and more. Before that, Galden earned a B.A. in Economics from the University of Notre Dame, and received a concentration in Asian Studies from Sophia University (Jo-chi Daigaku) in Tokyo, Japan.

Galden's first job out of college was working for the Merchandise Services division of American Express, focusing on logistics. After that, he worked for a Nintendo licensed company, where he did engineering design work on video game products and traveled overseas to manage the production in Asia. He has since been involved in product development and manufacturing throughout Asia for electronics, computer parts, toys, and many other products using microcomponents, metal, and plastics. Working at large corporations and mid-sized companies, as well as being involved with several start-ups, has given him a unique perspective on how businesses work at all levels. Galden has also written and edited several college textbooks on various business topics and related disciplines.

Pastor William Williams
Dr. Idalene Williams, Ph.D

INTRODUCTION

INTRODUCTION

1

Foundations of Business

LEARNING OBJECTIVES

1. Define business and relate its importance to our country
2. Trace the key historical events in the development of modern business
3. Identify the important historical figures in world and American business
4. Identify the basic rights we enjoy as Americans

© bikeriderlondon/Shutterstock, Inc.

OPENING STORY

Paul and Linda are two remarkably self-sufficient people. They live in the Northeast and farm for a livelihood. They live in the house they built. While many people have a house built, they actually built their house and the furniture in it. They also built the outdoor kitchen, the swimming pool, and even Paul's airplane. If their cars or farm equipment need repairs, they repair them. The crop needs bee pollination, so Linda raises bees. In addition to their cash crop, cranberries, they raise the vegetables and animals they eat as well. They can spend weeks on their land without any need to go to a store, since they

have practically everything they need right there. In spite of this self-sufficiency, they do go to the store occasionally to purchase the things they either are unable to produce themselves or do not wish to. Of course, as farmers, they also run a business to earn money to purchase what they do not produce.

Most of us are not this way. We specialize in doing one or a few things that earn us money and then we trade that money for other things we cannot or do not want to create for ourselves. We are all more or less in business and dependent on businesses for the things we need and want.

WHAT IS BUSINESS?

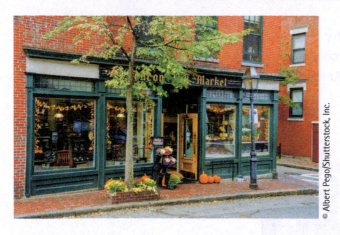

One way to define business is to say a **Business** is an organized effort intended to earn a profit. So how does a business earn a profit? Businesses provide goods, services, or information to satisfy identified needs, for which people, governments, or other businesses will pay. Business, or an enterprise, then is the profit-seeking organization or activity. **Goods** are tangible things we can hold or see. A house, television, and cell phone are examples of goods. **Services** are things we do for other people or businesses, which are not tangible. **Information** is useful correlated data that can inform or allow decision-making. Since we are not all as self-reliant as Paul and Linda in the opening story, we do what we are good at or what we can to earn money.

Businesses can be very small, many are just a single person working alone, or they can be large with tens of thousands of workers, conducting their activities all over the world. Without regard to the size, every business conducts some interchange between a buyer and a seller. The buyer exchanging money, or something of recognized value in exchange for the good, service, or information, with the seller.

Business is an organized effort intended to earn a profit.

Goods are tangible things we can hold or see.

Services are things we do for other people or businesses, which are not tangible.

Information is useful correlated data that can inform or allow decision making.

It is important to note the profit-seeking aspect of business. Profit serves many purposes. From a financial aspect, **profit** is the leftover revenue after expenses have been deducted. Profit can also be seen as the reward to the business owner or entrepreneur who has taken the risk of investing his or her time and money and setting up a business in the hopes of earning a living. Profit is also like a signal that tells the owner whether they are doing the right thing or not. If the business owner is unable to make a profit or enough of a profit to keep the enterprise going, the consumer is signaling that the business owner's efforts are not valued enough. If the business is earning profits, however, the consumer is signaling that those efforts are valued and the owner is doing the right thing. Consumers, in a sense, vote with their dollars on whether the business should continue.

Profit is the left over revenue after expenses have been deducted.

Businesses are everywhere; the large department store at the mall, the mall itself, the corner gas station, the automobile dealership, a lemonade stand, the grocery store, and even the 12-year-old that cuts your grass each week in the summer. Businesses can take on many forms and serve thousands of purposes. They are both part of our economy and the chief driver of that economy. They provide the things we need, the jobs we need, and the direction we need to continue growing our country.

Nonprofit Organizations are not businesses in a classical sense, but they may well be organized and operate like businesses. In a business, at the end of the day, or accounting period, if there is a profit, it belongs to the owner. In a nonprofit organization, there is no profit and at the end of the day, or accounting period, no one takes any money home. That is not to say there is no money involved. Many nonprofits have considerable budgets and handle lots of money. People that work there are employees and can earn good salaries. However, any net operating funds are generally returned to the public or some entity. For example: Let's look at two similar entities to compare how a

business differs from a nonprofit organization; a bank is a business and people open them to earn a profit. The banks attract depositors and then use those deposits as the banks' assets for lending or investment purposes. The difference between the earnings from those loans or investments and the deposit interest and other operating expenses represents the owner's profit. A credit union, on the other hand, is a nonprofit organization. They operate just like a bank except the net operating proceeds are returned to the depositors usually in the form of greater interest on their deposits or lower interest on loans. Both a business and a nonprofit organization may use net operating funds for growth and expansion. There are many examples of nonprofit organizations, from churches and charities to national organizations like the American Red Cross or local organizations like the city public swimming pool. Nonprofits and for-profit business enterprises operate alongside each other, and from the consumer's perspective, they may appear very much alike.

© Scott Prokop/Shutterstock, Inc.

FACTORS OF PRODUCTION

In one sense, we can say that everything we produce is made of exactly the same things, the four inputs, or **factors of production**. Whether we are discussing goods or services, we need the same inputs to conduct business. For everything we produce, we need Land/Natural Resources, Labor, Capital, and Knowledge/ Entrepreneurship. Different businesses will use different types and relative amounts of those resources, but every enterprise requires them all. A Walmart Supercenter may require 120 acres of land for building and parking, while a freelance writer may only need 16 ft^2 for a small desk and chair. Each, however, requires some physical space in which to operate.

Land/**Natural Resources** are the things produced in nature that are used to produce goods and services. The most obvious example is the **land** on which a business operates. However, the water, air, iron ore, wood, and many other resources are also necessary for many businesses to operate.

Labor is the physical or mental effort of the people that work in the business. Every business, even highly automated enterprises, needs someone doing something. Many businesses consist of a single person doing everything. Like the freelance writer mentioned before, the labor and the owner may be the same person. Other large businesses may have thousands of people doing labor and there is frequently separation between the owners and the workers.

In the case of publically traded corporations, the shareholders, who are the owners, may have nothing to do with the operation of the business. Labor can be a physical thing such as the landscaper that digs holes to plant trees and shrubs, or it can be a mental task, such as the designer that mentally creates new clothing concepts. In most cases, labor involves both physical and mental tasks.

Many businesses consider their staff the most important asset of the company. Not only is the labor, or human resources, doing the job, but they are also frequently the face of the company seen by the consumer and a valuable source of new ideas and innovation. The human resource staff is a factor of production but also a major stakeholder in the success of the company.

Capital is the machines and equipment used in the production of the goods or service. It is the money and material things money buys that are used to make things. For example: At the big department store, the capital includes computers, cash registers, shelving and carts, mops and buckets for cleaning, the building, and many other necessary pieces of equipment. For the independent writer, it might just be a computer and printer along with some reference materials. Regardless, all businesses need capital.

Knowledge/Entrepreneurship is the owner's efforts in risk-taking to set up a business and also the **knowledge** used in the efforts to organize and manage the other factors of production in the pursuit of profit. Although there are obviously no historical records of the times, business probably started as soon as people began to communicate. Entrepreneurs come in all ages and from all walks of life. The United States has always had a strong entrepreneurial spirit, and many Americans would like to someday own their own business. This entrepreneurial spirit, to be your own boss, to depend on yourself, and to reap the benefits of whatever you produce, is a strong driver of business development. In 2005, a group of economists from three Eastern European countries, Latvia, Lithuania, and Estonia, former Soviet Republics, toured the United States to try to understand the dynamic U.S. entrepreneurial spirit that was much less evident in their countries. According to these economists, 90% of Americans at least consider owning their own business someday. In their countries, the number was 40%. This lack of risk-taking was holding back the growth in their countries.

THE CHANGING NATURE OF BUSINESS

Every business must face the reality that the marketplace is constantly evolving. Any business that is static, that is, unchanging over a period of time may begin to fail because the circumstances that drove their business practices change constantly. This changing nature of business is certainly not new. We identify several broad eras in business during our history (Table 1.1).

The **Colonial Period** was a time of small towns with a few small businesses and mostly agriculture. Town's people traded among themselves or occasionally ordered something from a catalog. Only rarely did someone purchase anything produced more than 50 miles from their home. Relatively few large businesses existed, although notably the Dutch East India Company became the first truly **multinational company** during this period.

The **Industrial Revolution** changed the nature of work. Beginning in the middle of the 1700s, owners brought together groups of unskilled or

Capital is money or the things money can buy, like machines and buildings, which are used in the production of goods and services. The initial money used to start an investment.

Knowledge/Entrepreneurship The most important factor of production, since it combines skill with risk-taking to maximize innovation and efficiently use the other factors of production to increase output or productivity.

Knowledge The skill required as a factor of production to maximize innovation and efficiently use the other factors of production to increase output or productivity.

© Everett Collection/Shutterstock, Inc.

Colonial period was a time of small towns with a few small businesses and mostly agriculture.

Multinational company multinational company: a business that has operations or functions in more than one country.

Industrial revolution Industrial Revolution: an era beginning in the middle of the 1700s which changed the nature of work as business owners brought together groups of unskilled or semi-skilled workers to mass produce consumer goods.

TABLE 1.1   Broad Eras of Business in US History

Colonial	Agricultural	Before the 1760s
Industrial revolution	Mass production began along with the use of machines	1760–1850
Industrial entrepreneurs	New technologies were developed, along with transportation and consumers had access to manufactured goods. Great wealth was concentrated in a few entrepreneurs	1850–1880
Production era	Assembly lines developed as emphasis became mass production	1880–1950s
Marketing era	Focusing on the consumer to understand buying habits	1950s–1990s
Relationship era	Partnering with suppliers, producers, employees, consumers, and other businesses	1990s–present

Mass-produce the method by which companies produce large quantities of identical or very similar products.

Productivity the amount of output generated from given inputs.

Industrial entrepreneurs Individual risk takers who started business enterprises in the late 1800s that continued advances in technology which increased demand from consumers and brought opportunities for large business to develop, especially in steel, oil and automobiles.

semiskilled workers to **mass-produce** consumer goods. Instead of a craftsman producing one complete item at a time, less skilled workers could be trained to build a single part that could later be assembled along with other parts to complete the products. The use of production machines was introduced during this time. This allowed greater **productivity**, lower wages, (since skilled craftsmen were not needed), and greater buying power for the consumer since prices fell from these advances in mass production. This period greatly expanded the reach of the producer. Since more products were being produced than were needed locally, shipping products to distant markets became important as well.

Industrial Entrepreneurs rose late in the 1800s. Continued advances in technology and increased demand from consumers brought opportunities for large business to develop. Most notable among them were three industrial giants. Andrew Carnegie built the Carnegie Steel Company. Located in Pittsburgh, the company produced the steel that was necessary for the development of the country's infrastructure. Henry Ford not only developed the automobile industry into what it is today, he is also generally credited with developing the assembly line. Although some assembly lines existed before then, Ford Motor Company developed the concept of separating complicated production into simple steps. This greatly increased production and lowered price, and in Ford's case, brought automobiles to the common person for the first time. John D. Rockefeller created the Standard Oil Company and in so doing, became the first American billionaire ("Brief History of Business," 2014).

The **production era** followed with a focus on mass production of consumer goods using lots of labor as well as machines to drive down price and drive up the quantity of goods produced. Rather than focusing on what the consumer wanted, the production era was a time when

© filmfoto/Shutterstock, Inc.

companies focused on what they wanted to produce. This led to comments like "What is good for General Motors, is good for America" (Ino.com, 2014). This quote from Charlie Wilson, Chairman of General Motors, was indicative of the attitude that companies were the experts in their products and services and could determine what the consumer wanted without bothering to ask.

The **marketing era** brought about change in focus to consumers and what they wanted. Marketing became a science with scientific studies on consumer buying behavior to determine how the buying decision-making process works. Research has led to bright packaging, catchy television advertisements, product positioning in movies, paid "slotting fees" for special placement in stores, and any other tech-

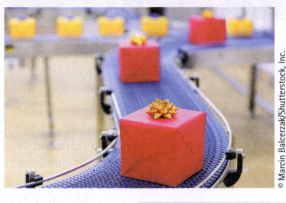

nique to draw your attention away from competitors and on to a company's own products or services. The newest trends are to use the locating features on mobile phones and similar devices to provide real-time ad notices as you walk around in a mall or drive along a street. Using the Internet not only brings a wealth of information to you, it also provides a wealth of information to marketers about what interests you. This allows companies to download product information to you, which matches your search history.

The **relationship era** is another change of focus. The intent in this era is to establish and maintain long-term, close relationships between suppliers, producers, trans-porters, and customers. You can hardly purchase anything anymore without being asked for your email address. The company doesn't just want to sell you something, they want to communicate with you as well. They want to get surveys done to find out if they are meeting your needs, and they want to correct any failings so they can generate repeat business.

Sustainability may be the next era of business. Sustainability is the pursuit of strategies that help preserve natural resources. It is hard to see the future, but many business experts as well as scientists and policymakers worry about a future crisis in sustaining the Earth's resources. From the business perspective, there is both the need to ensure that valuable resources are available in the future and the chance to take advantage of a shift in consumer tastes and interests.

Commercial fishing was one of the first industries to recognize significant risks associated with continuing to operate without restraint. For hundreds of years, fishers simply caught as many fish as they could. In the last of half century,

Production era   an era from 1880 - 1950s when companies focused on mass production of consumer goods using lots of labor as well as machines to drive down price and drive up the quantity of goods produced, rather than focusing on what consumers wanted.

Marketing era   an era from about the 1950s – 1990s which focused on the consumer to understand buying habits and what consumers wanted, as Marketing became a science with scientific studies on consumer buying behavior to determine how the buying decision making process works.

Relationship era   an era from 1990s – present, when companies focused consumers to understand their buying habits, with an intent to establish and maintain long term, close relationships between suppliers, producers, transporters, and customers.

Sustainability   is the pursuit of strategies that contribute to long-term preservation of natural resources. Reduction of pollution and emissions and recycling.

© docstockmedia/Shutterstock, Inc.

however, overfishing had taken a huge toll and several species were on the verge of collapse as a widespread food source.

Climate change, while still wildly debated as to the cause, is having an impact on agriculture in the United States and around the world. In the last 15 years, global warming had eased, and the debate now is whether this represents a pause in a continuing problem or a peak in global temperatures that will now decline. Even without rising global temperatures, however, change in rainfall has brought widespread drought in some areas and tragic flooding in others. It may be a while before science can sort out all the factors and come to conclusions that will lead to solutions.

Meanwhile, business is both a potential solution and a part of the problem. For instance, the global increase in demand for energy has pushed the oil industry to pursue more production to satisfy the demand. At the same time, industry has improved automobile efficiency while some other companies are switching to Compressed Natural Gas, and these two efforts have reduced the dependency on oil in our country.

© Colwell Photography/Shutterstock, Inc.

Another concern is the sustainability of the American workforce. With global communication and transportation along with reduced trade restrictions, companies producing goods in the United States must compete with lower labor costs enjoyed by companies that produce abroad. The U.S. cost of living and minimum wage laws preclude lowering labor costs by simply paying workers less in wages. However, labor cost per product can sometimes be lowered by increasing the worker's productivity. Instead of trying to use many unskilled or semiskilled workers, sometimes a better approach is to use fewer workers that are highly paid, very skilled.

Focusing on sustainability in the future business and industry helps provide solutions to global problems as well as earn and enjoy the benefits of successful satisfaction of consumer needs.

THE BASIS OF OUR FREE MARKET SYSTEM

The United States has a free market system that allows individuals and businesses to make decisions that benefit themselves the most as long as they also respect other's rights. People are rewarded when they provide the goods and services others are willing to buy. In a true free market, there might be no government involvement and everything would be driven purely by individual decision. We do have government involvement to some extent. Governments are providers of services and demanders of services as well. In some instances, the government operates alongside and in competition with private businesses. For instance, the government-sponsored U.S. Postal Service operates in competition with

© Stephanie Frey/Shutterstock, Inc.

UPS and FedEx in shipping packages around the country and the world.

For the most part, however, private businesses make up our economic system and operate in a profit-seeking competitive environment. These businesses must also operate within the laws passed at the local, state, and national levels. The historical basis for our legal system of codified law comes from the U.S. Constitution and the various state constitutions. These documents set up legislatures that create laws and court systems that rule on those laws and also make law by interpreting what the legislatures do. The combined legal system in practice in our country today is constantly evolving as our needs, culture, and technologies change.

These legal systems establish the basic rights we enjoy in our economic system. For instance, we have the right to own **private property** and the right to **freedom of choice**. These two rights allow an individual to decide for themselves what they want to do for a living and to start and own their own business if that is their choice. This gives them the right to keep all profits as personal compensation for their efforts. We have no right to success, but we definitely have the right to try to succeed.

Although individuals do have substantial freedom of choice in our legal system, there is some abridgement of those rights to provide for public safety and to allow for differences in local culture. For instances, some locations have at times decided they did not want to have alcohol sales in the city limits. Some states allow casino gambling and others have decided that is not in the best interest of their citizens and have banned casinos. Some states or cities have strong gun control laws that severely limit who can own a firearm, whereas other states and cities leave it up to the individual and have few restrictions. Pornography is another area where there is considerable variation around the country in what is allowed.

In addition to what may be allowed, many cities also set up zoning laws to control what goes into specific areas. For instance, you would not expect to find a gas station between houses in a neighborhood. It might be convenient to get gas two doors down on your way out of the neighborhood, but zoning laws do not allow commercial businesses to mix in areas intended to be residential. The zoning laws and city planning can help reduce noise and light pollution in areas where people live and combine shopping areas to provide greater convenience for consumers.

OPEN FOR BUSINESS IN THE REAL WORLD

There are tens of thousands of stories of great success in our marketplace. One such great story is of people like Bill Gates, who turned a business started in his garage to an international power and made him the richest person in the world. There is also Warren Buffet, who borrowed money from personal friends and

Private property things that an individual owns, derived from a basic right in the legal system of the U.S. which says that people have the right to own things, including the fruits of their labor or profits from a business.

Freedom of choice right that allow individuals to decide for themselves what they want to do for a living and to start and own their own business if that is their choice, derived from a basic right in the legal system of the U.S.

© JStone/Shutterstock, Inc.

© Rob Byron/Shutterstock, Inc.

© Bocman1973/Shutterstock, Inc.

created Berkshire Hathaway. Also, there is Sam Walton, who went from a small-town department store to an international business that is the world's largest retail concern.

However, it is important to note that most businesses do not succeed. Many of our most famous and richest entrepreneurs became successful not on their first try, but in some cases they failed several times before finding the right formula. In fact, most businesses fail. Over 50% fail in the first seven years. Even large businesses can be fragile. During the 2007–2009 recession, both General Motors and Chrysler needed both government loans and bankruptcy protection to survive. Several financial institutions did not survive. Many large and successful companies of the 1960s and 1970s are gone if not forgotten. Several large automobile manufacturers that were fixtures as recently as the early part of this century have gone out of business. Pontiac and Oldsmobile were some of the original car companies but have recently passed into history.

Not very many companies survive over a hundred years. Notably, some of the oldest companies are firearms companies like Winchester and Distilleries like Jack Daniels, both of which have been operating for well over a 100 years. The Pinkerton Agency, a private detective and security company, has been in business since before the Civil War. That high failure rate does not deter people from trying, however, and it should not. Even when a business closes, that does not necessarily mean failure. Each attempt is also a learning opportunity. As noted, many people fail several times before becoming a success.

LOOKING AHEAD

This textbook will introduce many subjects in the remaining chapters. Each of the subjects is an important aspect of the business discipline. Chapters on accounting, economics, human resources, marketing, law, information technology, and much more will become future courses you may take in your study of the business area. You may decide to major in one of these subject areas as well. Although the chapters can be studied in isolation, together they represent the major subject areas in a business degree program.

Chapter Summary

A business is an organized effort to produce a good, service, or information that people will buy and hopefully provide a profit for the owner. Owners or entrepreneurs create a business enterprise and offer their services, hoping to satisfy a need and demonstrate the value of their efforts. If people do recognize the value and reward the owner with sufficient revenue to create a profit, that is the market's signal that the entrepreneur is doing the right thing.

Nonprofit organizations are very similar to businesses in structure and organization and sometimes operate in competition with businesses. They are different only in their lack of profit motive and sometimes in their mission.

All businesses must have resources, which are known as the factors of production. These factors, land/natural resources, labor, capital, and knowledge/entrepreneurship, are common to and necessary for all businesses. Although different businesses will use different amounts of the factors of production, all enterprises must have all of them to succeed.

The marketplace in which a company must compete is constantly evolving, and to continue operating successfully, a firm must change as well. Although the change is constant, we generally recognize six distinct eras of business in the United States: the colonial period, the Industrial Revolution, the Industrial entrepreneur era, the production era, the marketing era, and the relationship era.

The basis of our business and economic system comes from three legal sources. Constitutional Law drives from the U.S. Constitution. Civil Law comes from the legal system in effect in Great Britton during and prior to our colonial days. Civil Law is based on the legal system in France during the colonial period and is used in Louisiana. These three legal systems provide the basic rights that establish our free market, capitalistic system. Those rights, the right to private property and the right to freedom of choice, are fundamental to our economic success in the United States.

Review Questions

1. How would you define a business enterprise?
2. Identify the factors of production.
3. What was the first truly multinational company?
4. What were the most common types of businesses in the colonial period?
5. How are a bank and a credit union different?
6. What are zoning laws?
7. Where is civil law used in the United States?
8. What are the factors of production, and how can it be said that everything we produce is made from the same things?
9. How are Carnegie, Ford, and Rockefeller important in U.S. business history?
10. What is "Entrepreneurial Spirit?"

Discussions Questions

11. Distinguish between a business enterprise and a nonprofit organization. How are they alike, and how are they different?
12. How do private property rights and freedom of choice contribute to our free enterprise system?
13. How does the relationship era of business lead to more permanent business agreements and repeat business?
14. What must a business do to deal with a constantly evolving marketplace?
15. How does profit send signals to entrepreneurs on what to produce?

Key Terms

- Business
- Capital
- Colonial Period
- factors of production
- freedom of choice
- Goods
- Industrial Entrepreneurs
- Industrial Revolution
- Information
- knowledge
- Knowledge/Entrepreneurship
- Labor
- land

- Natural Resources
- marketing era
- mass-produce
- multinational company
- Nonprofit Organizations
- private property
- production era
- productivity
- profit
- relationship era
- Services
- Sustainability

Works Cited

Brief History of Business (2014). Retrieved July 5, 2014, from http://www.briefhistory.net/?q=node/70

Ino.com (2014). Traders Blog. Retrieved July 12, 2014, from http://www.ino.com/blog/2008/06/what-is-good-for-general-motors-is-good-for-america/#.U8GCPLAo5Ms

CHAPTER

2

Forms of Business Ownership

LEARNING OBJECTIVES

1. Explain the different forms of business ownership
2. Explain the advantages and disadvantages of each type of ownership
3. Discuss corporate ownership and governance
4. Detail how some forms of ownership combine the advantages of multiple types
5. Discuss the different types of organizational structure

© mangostock/Shutterstock, Inc.

OPENING STORY

Sydney Sheffield is thinking about turning her lifelong hobby into a commercial enterprise. She has been an amateur photographer for years and has even sold a few examples of her work to the local newspaper. Several of her friends have encouraged her to open a photo studio and go professional. She gets requests for photographing weddings and events already, because the only other photographer in her small town can't handle all the business. He has even passed on a couple to her in the past.

Talking it over with Rick, her husband, she said "I worry about the risk of going into business myself, but I think the demand is there to make a go of it. I already have most of the equipment I would need and I think I have the skills. What I don't have is a place; a studio and I can't continue to do everything out of what we intended to be our guest bedroom." Rick asked what type of ownership she would choose and with a quizzical look, she replied "Well, I would be way too small to be a corporation so that would only leave being in business for myself wouldn't it; are there any other options?" Rick said "I think you are talking about owning a sole proprietorship. I think there are several options, but I think we need to call someone and get a little advice."

What are her options when it comes to business ownership?

Does she need a separate place to conduct business or can she operate from her home?

The next day, she and Rick checked with the Small Business Administration (SBA) and discovered there were three basic options of ways to organize or set up a business and a couple of subcategories and the size of the business was not important. Note: The **SBA**, the Chamber of Commerce, and SCORE, The Service Corp of Retire Executives are all excellent resources for helping new and small businesses.

© lightpoet/Shutterstock, Inc.

INTRODUCTION

One of many decisions a business owner has to make is the form of ownership. It is important to understand that this decision should be made based on the advantages and disadvantages of each form of ownership, not based on the size or type of business. Most, but not all, large, well-known businesses are **corporations**, but not just because they are large. Most, but not all, small businesses are sole proprietorships—but not just because they are small.

The decision on ownership form is independent of the size or type of business.

There are three primary forms of business ownership: Sole Proprietorship, Partnership, and Corporation.

Corporations a business that is incorporated and is separate from its owners.

Sole proprietorship A business that is owned and usually operated by a single person and is not incorporated.

SOLE PROPRIETORSHIP

A business entirely owned by a single person, which is not incorporated, is a **sole proprietorship**. These firms are normally also operated by the owner, although absentee ownership is possible as well. Some people decide to own a business but hire someone else to manage it. Most businesses in the United States are sole proprietorships because they are the least complicated to start, the least complicated to close, and the least complicated to operate.

Advantages of Sole Proprietorships

Easy to Start and Stop   Many sole proprietorships do not even need a business license or
permission from anyone to start. Although that
depends on local laws, there are no artificial barriers to entering the market with this form of
business ownership. They also require much less
paperwork and record-keeping compared to other
forms. If an owner wishes to end the business, by
closing or selling the business, that is simple as
well. A business that operates inside a city may
need a business license and may face limits on
those licenses. For instance, many communities
may limit the number of liquor license. If there are
employees, the business will need an account to withhold and
forward taxes, and if there is a product sold, the firm will need
a taxpayer identification number with which to pay sales tax.

© Tyler Olson/Shutterstock, Inc.

Single Taxation   The profits of a **sole proprietorship** belong
entirely to the owner. In this form of business ownership, there
is no legal separation between the business and the owner,
therefore all profits are the owners and are taxed a single time
as regular income. At the end of each accounting period, whatever profits exist automatically become the owner's income.

© mangostock/Shutterstock, Inc.

Flexibility of Operations   The owner of a sole proprietorship may establish his or her own operating hours and days
within the customs and laws of the local area. **For example:**
Local laws may prohibit selling alcohol on Sunday or after
a certain hour at night, but otherwise, the operating hours are set by the owner.
The owner may also accept or reject work, as long as discrimination laws are not
violated, determine his or her own goals, hire whomever he or she wishes, again
within the laws, and generally run their business as she or he see fit.

Privacy   With the exception of tax returns, there is no requirement to inform
anyone about how much the business earns, nor its net profits, expenses, contracts, or any other aspect of operations. As long as no laws are broken, the owner
may operate her business as she wishes and without informing anyone.

Self-Determination and Satisfaction   There can be great personal satisfaction
in being your own boss. There is perhaps no greater example of tying personal
success to individual effort. If the business succeeds, the owner succeeds, and the
greater the success, the greater the reward. Of course, that works in reverse as
well. Ultimately, many sole proprietorship owners list the idea of being their own
boss as the best part of owning their own business.

Disadvantages of the Sole Proprietorships

Unlimited Liability   Since the business and the person are not legally separate,
neither are the liabilities of the business. If the business owes money, the owner
owes money and the assets of the owner, even those not part of the business, may
be forfeited or liquidated to satisfy debt. This unlimited liability also includes
liability for accidents that may happen on the property or related to the business.

This could be to either customers or employees. **For example:** A delivery driver who has an accident on the way to drop off products may sue the owner if he or she is injured. So could anyone else that is injured, even if the driver was personally at fault.

Limiting the Problem: One way to mitigate the issue of unlimited liability is to purchase insurance. For many owners, their greatest worry is a lawsuit that would wipe out not only the business assets, but their personal assets as well, such as their home. A liability or umbrella insurance policy can protect an owner, at least to the limits of the policy. In addition, it enlists the aid of the insurance company, and their legal staff, which does not want to pay out on a lawsuit if it is avoidable.

Limited Management Experience

An individual business owner may be an excellent manager, and many start businesses based on their expertise in a field. However, the skill set necessary to run a business is frequently different than the skills that lead a person to a particular field. Being an excellent plumber, for instance, does not necessarily prepare a person to be an excellent plumbing company owner and manager.

Limiting the Problem: Although an owner is limited to whatever experience and expertise he or she brings to the business, this does not prevent him or her from hiring experts. Not only can business hire professionals, some can be retained part-time. For instance, many businesses might have an attorney on retainer or use the services of an accountant monthly or quarterly. Businesses may also hire a consultant for specific purposes or time periods.

Benefits

In the modern business environment, people have come to expect employee benefits and some of these are now required by law. Some common benefits a person might routinely expect to be provided by the business include Workmen's Compensation, paid time off, and medical coverage. None of these benefits, however, are due to the owner unless the owner pays for them himself or herself and payment for those come out of what would otherwise be profit. Whereas an employee of the company would get a wage or salary plus benefits, the owner gets profit minus benefits.

Funding Limitations

An individual owner may or may not have excellent credit, but the situation of having a single person liable for all debts of the business limits the access to funding. Many small businesses fail, and lending institutions are well aware of this.

© Tyler Olson/Shutterstock, Inc.

Lack of Continuity

Since the business and the person are the same, the death or serious illness of the owner may end the business. An owner may leave the business to heirs as part of their estate, but if this is not done, the business ends upon the owner's death. Operations might also be suspended if the owner is seriously ill for a period of time.

Limiting the Problem: A married couple that files taxes jointly and jointly owns a business can elect to consider the business a Qualified Joint Venture, essentially a co-owned sole proprietorship. The death of one owner then does not end the company. This type of business ownership may not be available in all states.

Risk of Failure   The risk of failure in a sole proprietorship is great; in fact, most of them do fail. However, failure does not necessarily mean bankruptcy, just that the business was closed or discontinued. It may simply mean the profits were not great enough to keep the owner interested in continuing the enterprise.

Independent Contractors—One-Person Companies

Many people work in companies that have no name and consist of just the owner as the sole person in the firm. Many people working as **independent contractors** do not even think of themselves as company owners. Photographers like in the opening case, sports officials working on high-school athletic contests, freelance writers, designers, construction workers, motivational speakers, actors, artists, musicians, consultants, models, house cleaners, and many others work on a contract basis for the length of that contract, which might be for only a few hours or for many months or sometimes even longer. For people in these situations, the business name often is simply the name of the individual and the rules of a sole proprietorship apply. Any money earned by the company is the owner's money and taxes are paid on profits as regular income. Liability is still unlimited. In an independent contract position, a person who wants to discontinue operating can simply not accept any more contracts.

Open for Business in the Real-World Issue   Some companies attempt to save on employee benefits and taxes by recategorizing their employees as independent contractors, thus making the individual responsible for taxes and withholding and eliminating benefits. Independent contractors can choose to work or not, how much they will work, and when they will work. They can accept a contract or not. Employees can be directed to report to work at the company's discretion and employment has no time limit.

PARTNERSHIPS

When two or more people share ownership of the business, both the assets and the liabilities, the business is a partnership. Two or more means just that. There is no legal limit to the number of partners and some businesses have hundreds. **For example:** Large law firms, medical practices, and accounting firms may be set up as partnerships and well-performing employees may achieve partnership status, gaining access to partnership profits as well as management responsibilities. Partnerships come in two basic forms, general partnerships and limited partnerships. One thing that is important to note is that ownership does not have to be equal. It is entirely possible for one person to own half a business and three others to share ownership in the other half. It is also possible for each of several partners to own different amounts of equity in the firm.

Independent contractors
A company that consists of a single person.

Of the three primary forms of business (Sole Proprietorship, Partnership, and Corporation), the partnership is the least common form.

Advantages of Partnerships

Easy to Start and Stop   For the most part, partnerships are just as easy to start or stop as a proprietorship except for the need of a partnership agreement. In addition, in many states, partnerships must be registered with the state or local government and the taxes are more complicated.

Single Taxation   The profits of a partnership belong entirely to the owners. Once distributed, they become personal income in the same way as any other earned income and in the same way as the profit of a sole proprietorship.

Flexibility of Operations   The owners of a partnership have the same flexibility as a proprietorship, plus they have the advantage of having individual flexibility for time away from the business.

Privacy   Again, with the exception of tax returns, there is no requirement to inform anyone about how much the business earns, net profits, expenses, contracts, or any other aspect of operations.

Self-Determination and Satisfaction   Just like the Proprietorship, partners are working for themselves and enjoy the self-satisfaction that comes with it.

Access to Funding   Although multiple owners may have poor credit or limited funds just like a proprietorship, having more than one person responsible for liabilities increases the likelihood of borrowing funds.

Disadvantages of Partnerships

Unlimited Liability   Just as in proprietorships, all liabilities of a partnership are the liabilities of the partners. In one way, the liability is greater in that creditors may seek complete compensation from any partners without regard to how much of the company they own. **For example:** If three people jointly own a partnership and two of the partners skip town, the remaining partner can be held liable for all business debts although they may have only owned a third of the business or even less.

Problems between Partners   Good friends do not necessarily make good business partners. There is no requirement to have a formal partnership agreement, but they are a good idea. The agreement can describe the percentage of ownership, the responsibilities of owners, the decision-making process, the addition or departure of partners, the sale of the business by the group or each partner's share, and what to do about the death of a partner or the inheritance of that partner's portion of the firm, the divorce of a partner, and adding more partners.

Different Types of Partnerships

General Partnership   In a general partnership, all partnerships have full ownership and authority. All partners are general partners and have unlimited liability and management authority. One thing to note: ownership in a partnership does not have to be equal. For instance, one partner may own half the business and two more my each own a quarter.

Limited Partnerships   In a limited partnership, the business has one or more General Partners who have unlimited liability and one or more limited partners who have a liability equal to their investment. In a limited partnership, the limited partners own a share of the business, but may have limited management authority. You might think of limited partners as separate investors that invest by buying a portion of the business, but without full liability or authority. **For example:** Often used for real-estate development, limited partnerships might have a general partner that seeks several investors as limited partners. These limited partners will own their share of the business, but not have any management authority or responsibility and their liability is just what they invested in the business.

Limited Liability Partnerships   The Limited Liability Partnership (LLP) can help protect one partner from the mistakes of another. This limits a person's liability to what they have invested in the firm. LLPs are not legal in every state, and in some states, only certain types of businesses can establish this type of business ownership.

Master Limited Partnerships   Master Limited Partnerships are a special type of business that is actually a partnership of businesses and, according to U.S. law, can only be set up for companies that are involved in the production and transportation of natural gas and oil or similar natural resources. Ownership shares are traded just like stock in a corporation, but because they are not corporations, they avoid corporate taxes.

CORPORATIONS

A corporation is a business that is separate from its owners. Sometimes, corporations are referred to as C-Corps, to distinguish them from S-Corps, which we will discuss later. It is incorporated, that is, legally set up according to state law. The corporation is considered a separate entity and has many of the same legal rights as an individual. Corporations can own assets and have liabilities, sign contracts, sue or be sued, raise funds through a variety of means, operate for profit, and pay taxes.

© Ljupco Smokovski/Shutterstock, Inc.

© Adnresr/Shutterstock, Inc.

Corporations are chartered, or set up according to state law, in any state they wish. The charter simply establishes the home of record for the company, which can then operate in any state as long as they comply with the local law. Some states are known as "Corporate Friendly," and many firms will incorporate there to take advantage of easy rules or lower taxes. Delaware and Nevada are two such friendly states.

Advantages of a Corporation

Limited Liability   The primary advantage of the corporate form of ownership is the limited liability enjoyed by owners. When someone invests in a corporation, they risk only what is invested. There is said to be a corporate veil that separates a person's assets from the assets of the corporation. Piercing the corporate veil generally only happens with personal wrongdoing or violation of regulations, such as that happened with Enron. Courts have ruled that the corporate veil is pierced when the owner does not maintain separate checking accounts. Commingling of personal and business funds can mean the commingling of personal and business liability.

Raising Funds   Corporations can raise funds by borrowing money from banks just like other businesses. However, two other means of raising funds are available to corporations. Corporations can issue bonds, essentially borrowing from potentially thousands of investors. **For example:** The company might issue 5,000 bonds, each with a face value of $10,000, a 10-year period, and 4% interest. If the company sells all the bonds, they will raise $50 million in borrowed funds. The company can also issue stock in two classes and sell shares of ownership to thousands or even millions of people that want to own small portions of a large publically traded corporation. Selling of shares or bonds is tightly controlled by the Securities Exchange Commission, and sale of bonds or shares of stock normally requires the involvement of a licensed stock broker or investment banker. **Initial Public Offerings**, the first time stock is available for sale, is also handled through an investment bank or financial institution.

© Africa Studio/Shutterstock, Inc.

Initial public offerings
The first offering of a typically large number of shares of stock to the public.

Continuity of Operations   Since corporations are an entity separate from the owners, they live on without regard to the life or illness of the person that started them. Ownership and management may change over the years, with no impact on the company.

Transfer of Ownership   A person owns all or part of a corporation by owning shares of stock. These shares may be sold or transferred over the counter or on the open stock market. Ownership in a corporation transfers as the shares transfer. Once on the market, the company cannot control who purchases the stock or then who owns part of the company.

Tax Benefits   The initial corporate tax rate is lower than individual income tax rates, and capital gains that are passed on to owners also get favorable tax rates. At some income levels, the taxes might be lower in this form of ownership. Corporations can also keep capital in the organization by simply not distributing the after-tax income. Stockholders are not taxed personally on corporate income until they receive it as a dividend. This capital, or retained earnings, can be used for ongoing operations, expansion, buildings or equipment, or for any other business purpose.

Disadvantages of a Corporation

Double Taxation   Most people consider the double taxation of corporations as the chief disadvantage. Corporate profits are taxed; since the corporation is an entity, it pays taxes on profits based on corporate tax rates to both the federal government and the state in which they are chartered. If after-tax profits are then distributed to the owners in the form of dividends, these realized returns on their investment are then taxed again.

Government Regulations   Although all businesses may have regulations that impact their operations, this is especially true of corporations. Many government regulations apply only to corporations, at least publically traded corporations, and most government regulations occupy significant time and resources to ensure compliance. Publically traded corporations must have an annual shareholder's meeting, file financial reports with several government oversight agencies and publish it for the public to view, send every shareholder required information like annual reports and numerous other regulations that can cost the company a lot of money to comply.

Lack of Privacy   Because corporations are potentially owned by anyone, the financial details of the corporations are made available to the public. Sales of assets and stock, mergers and acquisitions, revenue and profit are all part of the public record. Corporations are not allowed to withhold information or publish misleading data. Privately held corporations, however, can limit such information to the owners and government oversight agencies.

As you can see from the chart, by far, most businesses are proprietorships and partnerships are the least common (Figure 2.1).

Corporate Ownership

Publically Owned versus Closely Held versus Privately Held: People own a corporation by owning the shares of the corporation. Each share of stock is a piece of ownership. **For example:** Signet Jewelers has almost 81 million shares issued. So, each share of stock represents 1/81,000,000 of the total ownership of the company. Ownership can be widespread with thousands or millions of corporate owners. Or, it may be just a few owners. A publically traded company has ownership, or stock, sold on the open stock market, and anyone who chooses to may purchase stock and become part owner. Other companies may use the corporate

Sole proprietorships	Partnerships	Corporations
71.5%	10%	18.5%

Figure 2.1   US Businesses by Ownership Type.
Source: U.S. Census Bureau, Statistical Abstract, accessed June 17, 2013

form, but keep ownership to one or a few owners. Closely held corporations limit ownership to a few stockholders. These shares are sometimes traded on the stock market, but usually only after getting the agreement of the other stockholders. Privately held corporations are essentially corporations owned by a family or a few friends that do not trade on the stock market. Ownership is limited just to the few members. **For example:** Mars Incorporated, the third largest privately held U.S. Corporation, is one of the world's largest food companies, although they also have pet care and health industries.

Shareholders People may purchase shares of stock in publically traded corporations. Sometimes, these shares are purchased directly from the company or "over the counter," or they may be purchased on the open stock market through a broker. Over-the-counter sales are normally part of employee stock option or profit sharing plans. Over-the-counter sales to the public are rare but may occur with companies that have not listed on a stock exchange. Stock transactions in the stock market generally come from previous owners. Shares of stock come in two classes: common stock and preferred stock. A corporation may issue either or both classes.

Common stock is the most common form of shares. Common stock owners not only own a piece of the company and share in the profits, but they also generally get a vote on large matters such as the members of the board of directors. Common stock holders share in the success and the failure of the company. They are not guaranteed any return on their investment. In fact, if a company goes out of business and the assets are sold off, the common stock holders are last in line for any leftover assets.

Preferred Stock is a much less used form of equity ownership that lies somewhere between stock and bonds in how they work. Preferred stock is similar to common stock in that it is equity, receives dividends, those dividends can be withheld by the board of directors, and there is no guaranteed repayment of principle. They are similar to bonds in that there is normally a regular return on investment, the return is usually based on a fixed value, known as par value, and if the company goes out of business, the preferred shareholders have a claim on assets before common stock holders, but behind bond holders. Each company can determine the exact characteristics of preferred stock, and those characteristics may include convertibility to common stock and required return on investment, which is again, much like bonds.

Shareholder Rights When a person owns even a single share of a company's stock, they are part owner of the company. Shareholders generally get a vote on important matters and may attend the required annual shareholder's meeting. Each share of stock gets one vote; therefore the more shares one owns; the more he or she has and the more important the important the decisions become, because of the extent of a shareholder's investment. Although minor shareholders may not be interested in the annual meeting, some companies draw considerable interest among even minor shareholders. **For example:** Tens of thousands of shareholders, many with as little as one share, attend the annual Berkshire Hathaway meeting in Omaha Nebraska each year, in part to hear the annual report by Warren Buffet. A shareholder my vote their shares, or they may give up their right to someone else. This is called proxy voting and for most holders of small amounts of shares, this is the most common way to vote.

For a publically traded company, anyone with the money and a brokerage account may own a share of the company. The free right to purchase also comes

Common stock is the most common form of shares, equity in a corporation that includes voting dividends rights.

Preferred stock a much less used form of equity ownership that lies somewhere between stock and bonds in how they work. Equity in a corporation with preferential status to receive dividends over common stockholders.

with the free right to sell. Since each share of stock includes a voting right, the more shares of stock a person owns, the greater their influence over the company. If a person acquires one share more than 50 percent of the stock, they control the company. Because company stock is so widely dispersed, effective control can be gained by far less than 50 percent. For example: Bill Gates, is one of the riches people in the world and is the largest single shareholder of Microsoft, but he only owns about 4.5% of the company. Purchasing significant percentages of stock can be done on the open market or can be done as a single transaction by convincing shareholders to sell in mass. Sometimes a major investor or another corporation attempts a **hostile takeover** of a company by purchasing the shares even against the wishes of the Board of Directors, the executives, or major shareholders.

Hostile takeover   When a company is acquired or forced to merge, against the wishes of the current owners or managers.

Going Public   When companies initially sell stock to the public, called an initial public offering, or IPO, they are said to be going public, or offering the shares up for public purchase. This is one way for a corporation to draw in funds for further growth. In essence, the firm sells off some of itself in exchange for cash. **For example:** Google went public in April of 2004, raising billions. Corporations sell millions of shares of stock through these public offerings, earning the money for their founders and for additional growth. Once purchased, these shares then become part of the open stock market, usually after a waiting period, and are then available for anyone to buy. When people buy shares in the open market, that money goes to the existing stock owner; not the company that issued the stock.

Going Private   A corporation becomes a publicly traded company by going public, thus sharing ownership with whoever wishes to buy the stock. Sometimes a publically traded company wants to reverse the process and return itself to a closely held or privately held company. In these cases, the company's stock is bought up by someone, typically the founder or their family and returned to its original family owned firm. This is sometimes done to limit interference or control from shareholders or government oversight. Sometimes it is done simply because the original owners want to go back to private ownership. **For example:** Dell Computer went private to return it to its original form and owners.

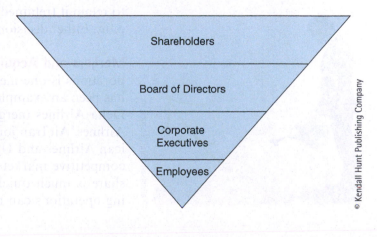

© 360b/Shutterstock, Inc.

Boards of Directors   Corporations are owned by the shareholders, but since ownership is widespread, with hundreds of thousands of shareholders, the management of the corporation and the decision making process must be in the hands of a smaller number of people. Shareholders elect a board of directors, typically from nine to nineteen members, who then appoint the senior executives of the company who run operations.

The share holders elect the board of directors, who appoint the corporate executives, who

Shareholders

Board of Directors

Corporate Executives

Employees

© Kendall Hunt Publishing Company

hire the employees. However, since stock ownership is open to anyone, members of the board, corporate executives, employees and the general public may be and frequently are all shareholders.

Different Types of Corporations

S–Corporations   Subchapter S Corporations, or S-Corps as they are commonly known, are a means of combining the advantages of a sole proprietorship or partnership, while avoiding the disadvantages of a corporation. The S-Corp avoids the double taxation of regular corporations but retains the limited liability. S-Corporations are chartered companies like regular corporations but have certain limitations while they enjoy the single taxation. These limitations include a limit of 100 shareholders, and in some states, the operations must take place entirely inside the state. Shepphudd's Corporation is a financial planning business, organized as an S-Corporation in the Houston area.

Nonprofits   Not-for-Profit Corporations take in revenue, produce a product or service, have expenses, pay their employees, and in many ways, operate like any other business except that they do not do so for profit. They must spend or otherwise divest themselves of all excess money. Many nonprofits are religious-based or sponsor some civic organization. Some nonprofits, however, compete in the market place along with for-profit businesses. **For example:** Credit unions, which are nonprofit and member-owned, compete with banks, which are for-profit businesses.

© new photo/Shutterstock, Inc.

Business Growth   Once established, companies generally attempt to grow. A larger share of the market, greater revenue, more sales and customers, usually bring greater reward for the owners. Growth comes in two primary forms; growth from operations during the normal course of business activities or mergers and acquisitions, essentially combining forces among companies.

Operational Growth   If a company operates successfully and earns a profit, the owner, or the board of directors, in the case of a corporation, then must decide what to do with that profit. The profit belongs to the owners or shareholders, but the board must decide whether to send it to them in the form of dividends or whether to retain it (retained earnings) and use the profits to grow the company. Either decision may enrich the shareholders.

© alphaspirit/Shutterstock, Inc.

Mergers and Acquisitions   Combining forces by merging of corporations is one method of quickly growing. The airline industry has been an example in the last few years. Northwest Airlines and Delta Airlines merged, Continental Airlines merged with United Airlines, AirTran joined forces with Southwest Airlines, and American Airlines and US Airways are in the merger process. In highly competitive markets with limited profit margins, gaining market share is much quicker through mergers. In some cases, combining operations can make a company more efficient by eliminating duplicate operations. Mergers must get the consent of the shareholder and the government oversight organizations like the Federal Trade Commission and the Justice Department. Mergers are normally allowed as long as they do not unjustly limit trade or violate antitrust legislation.

When a merger occurs, the companies involved generally operate as a single company under the previous name of one of the companies. **For example:** United Airlines and Continental Airlines operate together as United Airlines. In other cases, companies may combine but continue to operate under separate names. **For example:** Ginsu Knives continues to operate under their separate name although they are part of Berkshire Hathaway. These are usually referred to as acquisitions, as one company, a parent company if you will, acquires another as an asset. The acquiring company gets all the assets and liabilities of the acquired company, and one of those assets may, in fact, be the name of the company itself.

Mergers among competing companies working at the same level in the industry are described as **Horizontal mergers**. **For example:** Southwest Airlines and AirTran Airlines conducted a horizontal merger. A **Vertical merger** takes place when companies operating at different levels in an industry combine forces. **For example:** If a company building deep water oil and gas drilling platforms like Transocean were to merge with an oil production company like Shell Oil, that would be a vertical merger. Sometimes companies merge that have little relationship or common interest and this is known as a **Conglomerate merger**. **For example:** When Fox Jewelers merged with Fred Meyer Jewelers, who later merged with Kroger, the parent company, Kroger, wound up with grocery stores, warehouses, big box stores, and jewelry stores.

Horizontal merger   When competing companies working at the same level in the industry combine forces.

Vertical merger   When companies operating at different levels in an industry combine forces.

Conglomerate merger   When companies that have little relationship or common interest combine forces.

Limited liability company   A type of ownership that limits the liability of the owner to the amount of his or her investment.

OTHER FORMS OF BUSINESS

Limited Liability Companies   One way to enjoy the advantages of a sole proprietorship, while avoiding the primary disadvantage (unlimited liability) is to form a **Limited Liability Company** (LLC). As its name suggests, the owner's liability is limited by separating the business assets from those of the owner. **For example:** As companies grow, the original owner is sometimes forced to move away from direct contact with the work and the workers and take on more of a managerial role. Without direct supervision, the owner may increase his or her risk for regulation violations or lawsuits. OSHA inspections at work sites can assess severe penalties for safety violations that might not have occurred had the owner been on site. A $30,000 penalty can eat up the business assets and encroach on the owner's personal assets if he or she is not protected by an LLC form of ownership.

Forming an LLC is somewhat more complicated than a sole proprietorship and may require the assistance of an attorney. However, the extra time and expense necessary may be worth it.

OPEN FOR BUSINESS IN THE REAL WORLD

Rhone Booth, the owner of Alegent Restorations in Omaha, has recently seen his general contractor firm grow from a small but successful operation in and around Omaha, Nebraska, to a three-state operation that spans from Iowa to Colorado. The size of the business may soon triple, and Mr. Booth is questioning whether he can risk the personal liability inherent in the sole proprietorship form he currently uses. Taking on multiple projects in different locations will limit his ability to manage them closely, and he may need to hire supervisors and that will put a layer of management between him and the work. Since he also owns rental homes, he is considering reorganizing his business as a Limited Liability Company (LLC). This would protect his personal assets from any business debts or lawsuits that target the assets of the business. He could even separate the rental homes from the general contractor business.

© littleny/Shutterstock, Inc.

Cooperatives   Cooperatives, or Co-ops as they are sometimes called, are actually separate businesses but act as a single business in cooperation with each other. A common example of a co-op is a farmer's market where the various businesses agree on a common time and location for operation and share certain expenses like location rent and advertising expense.

Joint Ventures   Another combining of separate businesses is a Joint Venture, which combines the activities of two or more businesses acting as a single company for a specific project or period of time. In many ways, a joint venture can appear much like a merger of companies, except there is no combining or change of ownership, and furthermore, when the project or time period is over, the separate companies simply return to their separate operations. Joint ventures are also known as strategic alliances. Joint ventures are formed when companies need to partner with another to share expertise. **For example:** When Japan wanted to buy F-16 fighter aircraft from General Dynamics, they wanted to produce the aircraft in Japan. The Japanese aircraft industry formed a Joint Venture with General Dynamics to produce the aircraft domestically.

Chapter Summary

Business ownership takes on three basic forms—sole proprietorships, partnerships, and corporations—although there are specialized forms of each. The type of ownership is independent of the type or size of a business, and the decision on the type of ownership should be one based on the advantages and disadvantages of each form. The simplest and by far the most common type of business is the sole proprietorship, which is a company owned and generally operated by a single owner. They are easy to start, simple to operate, and all profits belong to the owner. However, they have unlimited liability. Partnerships have a lot of appeal, but in fact are the least common form of business ownership. Partners may be general partners or limited partners, and there can be any number of partners sharing ownership. Corporations are separate legal entities, that is, the ownership and the owner are separated by law. This limits the liability of individual owners to the value of their investment. Corporations are much more complicated to establish and may require legal assistance. They also are encumbered by more government regulations than other forms of business. However, the limited liability and easy change of ownership make them an attractive form of ownership.

Review Questions

1. What are the three basic forms of business ownership?
2. Is the size of a business significant when it comes to determining the form of ownership?
3. Describe the difference between a Limited Partnership and a General Partnership.
4. What options does a small business owner have to protect herself from unlimited liability?
5. Why should a partnership create a partnership agreement?
6. Which form of ownership is the most complicated to create?
7. Is a person that works entirely by and for themselves really a business owner?
8. If you move and rent your home out to someone else until you decide whether to sell the home or not, are you a business owner?
9. What type of merger results when two competing businesses operating at the same level in the industry decide to combine operations?
10. Why are relatively few businesses started as partnerships?
11. What are the three ways a corporation can raise funds?
12. Why might a corporation choose to be closely held instead of privately held?
13. What does it mean when a corporation goes private?
14. What happens if a nonprofit organization winds up with excess funds from operations? What do they or can they do with the money?
15. In most proprietorships and partnerships, the owners are also the managers. Why is this not always true? What about in a corporation, who are the owners and who are the managers?

Discussion Questions

16. Let's say you were going to operate as a home cleaning service, offering to clean private homes in your area at the going rate of about $25 an hour. You hope to work hard and get referrals so you can grow the business until you have three houses a day for six days a week. Knowing the advantages and disadvantages, which form of business ownership would you choose? Would your answer change if you became very successful and needed to hire a couple of employees to take on some of the cleaning?
17. What advice would you give about ownership form to a friend who is a freelance writer, doing columns for the local newspaper and a couple of magazines? Would your advice change if the friend was operating as an independent delivery truck driver for hire?

Key Terms

- Common stock
- Conglomerate merger
- Cooperatives
- corporation
- General Partnership
- Going Private
- Going Public
- Horizontal merger
- hostile takeover
- independent contractors
- Initial Public Offerings
- Joint Ventures
- Limited Partnerships
- Limited Liability Company
- Master Limited Partnerships
- Mergers
- Partnerships
- Preferred Stock
- S-Corporations
- SBA
- SCORE
- Shareholders
- sole proprietorship
- Vertical merger

CHAPTER
3

Business Law

LEARNING OBJECTIVES

1. Explain basic business laws, both at the Federal and at the State level, protecting the consumers, the environment, and so on.
2. Discuss company transactions and competitive behavior, both legal and illegal.
3. Detail types of contracts, requirements for enforcement, and liability for breach.
4. Discuss labor laws that impact businesses, including equal employment opportunity, compensation, and safety.
5. Explain relevant tax, accounting, and bankruptcy law implications for business.

OPENING STORY: LEGALZOOM

Legal advice has never been cheap, and the prospect of an expensive office visit to hear advice you may not fully understand kept many people from seeking legal advice. That can be dangerous for business owners. The simple act of incorporating a business or forming an LLC can have tremendous benefits, yet many were not doing it. That started to change in 2001 with the founding of LegalZoom. com. Although the site and its advertising are careful to point out that they offer self-help legal services and don't offer legal advice, making forms available online and demystifying the process once thought to be expensive or complicated have proven to be a good business model.

While self-help services will never replace guided legal advice answering questions about a specific situation, online availability is getting things started for many small business people who might otherwise think that legal services were unnecessary or out of reach. "LegalZoom is poised to significantly broaden the range of services it offers consumers and small businesses." Asking for advice is always a good thing.

(Source: http://www.abajournal.com/magazine/article/latest_legal_victory_has_ LegalZoom_poised_for_growth).

INTRODUCTION

You just formed your business, carefully following the suggestions and requirements laid out in the previous chapter. You may think that you're ready to start transacting business now, but there are many more areas where you need to be in compliance with the law. You may be thinking: "If I pay my taxes and am honest with people, isn't that enough?" That's a good start, but you still have to comply with Labor Laws, Competitive Laws, Intellectual Property Laws and even rules for the environment, accounting, and many more business regulations. There are specific laws for the Internet, taxes, and countless other areas. We won't turn you into a legal expert, but we can help you know where to look for help and give you some of the right questions to ask the lawyer who should be part of your business team.

GENERAL BUSINESS LAW

© Africa Studio/Shutterstock, Inc.

Business law is the study of the regulations and rules companies must follow to comply with various federal, state, and local statutes put in place by governments at all levels. In addition, there are some good practices you should follow to keep you out of trouble as a business owner. We'll discuss some of these as well. Keep in mind that although some of these laws only apply to large corporations, the federal government's Small Business Administration website at www.sba.gov points out that many laws and regulations must be followed by all businesses regardless of size.

Federal Permits?

Business law the study of the regulations and rules companies must follow to comply with various federal, state, and local statutes put in place by governments at all levels.

In the last chapter, we discussed the laws for forming a business. Next, you'll need to see if there are any special permits or licenses required for the type of business you've chosen. There are some very specific business areas where you must register with the federal government before transacting business, sometimes to ensure that you are complying with federal laws and other times so that the government can collect any taxes or user fees associated with that type of business. Everything from farming to firearms may be subject to extra requirements. For example, if you are selling plants or animals across state lines, you must have a permit from the U.S. Department of Agriculture. Selling weapons or ammunition or explosives requires registering with the Bureau of Alcohol, Tobacco and Firearms (ATF). Even starting a simple transportation company that uses highways needs to abide by the U.S. Department of Transportation guidelines (and often requires additional filings at the state level).

Some other businesses that require permission or compliance at the federal level include alcohol, aviation, fishing and maritime, mining and drilling, nuclear-related industries, and broadcasting for TV, radio, or other uses of the public airwaves. There's a convenient tool you can use to investigate these areas and any changing requirements by visiting the U.S. government's Small Business Administration website link for licenses and permits: http://www.sba.gov/licenses-and-permits. There you can also input information about your business to find out state-by-state requirements as well.

© T.W. van Urk/Shutterstock, Inc.

Licensed, Bonded, Insured

At the state level, you will often need to be licensed for many common businesses that deal with the public, particularly if they involve the public trust where you might be perceived as an "expert" with specialized knowledge upon which the public would rely. This involves things like selling insurance, representing others as an agent in real-estate transactions, or offering to repair or install many home improvement items. The various states want you to be licensed so that you can prove that you have a certain minimum level of competence in helping the public. In fact, many of these professions require that you are **licensed**, **bonded**, and **insured**.

As mentioned, a **license** is the state's acknowledgement that you have demonstrated a minimum level of competence either through passing a test, providing education credentials, or in any number of other ways, which vary by state and/or by profession. **Bonded** means that you have deposited a certain amount of money with a recognized authority that will pay out cash to any of your customers in the event that you are not able to complete a job as promised, in this way ensuring that the customer is "made whole" and not left with unfinished repair work. **Insured** is an additional protection for yourself and your company should anyone be injured while you are working on an assignment, a job, or any other contracted work such that the insurance company will pay out any valid claims resulting from covered incidents. This is just one more way you can attempt to limit your liability in the event that there's an accident or things do not go as planned.

There are additional Federal and State laws protecting the buying public, other people, and the environment—all before you start transacting business.

License the state's acknowledgment that you have demonstrated a minimum level of competence either through passing a test, providing educational credentials, or in any number of other ways that vary by state and/or by profession.

© Bonita R. Cheshier/Shutterstock, Inc.

Bonded you have deposited a certain amount of money with a recognized authority which will pay out cash to any of your customers in the event that you are not able to complete a job as promised, in this way ensuring that the customer is "made whole" and not left with unfinished repair work.

Insured an additional protection for yourself and your company should anyone be injured while you are working on an assignment, a job, or any other contracted work such that the insurance company will pay out any valid claims resulting from covered incidents.

Federal and State Laws on Advertising

If you publicly advertise your business products or services across the country, chances are that you will come under the purview of the Federal Trade Commission (FTC), which monitors business activity, including advertising. According to the FTC website, http://business.ftc.gov, the Federal Trade Commission Act states that:

- Advertising must be truthful and nondeceptive;
- Advertisers must have evidence to back up their claims; and
- Advertisements cannot be unfair.

An ad is deemed "deceptive" if it is likely to mislead a "reasonable consumer"; thus, the government is particularly stringent and vigilant with health claims made in advertising, as well as for product claims that consumers would have trouble evaluating themselves. Evidence to back up claims typically must be in the form of actual studies rather than simple testimonials. *You* can say yours is the best (often referred to as "puffery"), but as soon as you make it look like someone in a position of authority is endorsing your product, then you are held to a higher standard.

Finally, specific unfair advertising examples are documented on the website, but one common tactic that garners special attention for enforcement is **"bait and switch."** This is where a business advertises a product at a very low price to lure customers, but in reality has no intention of selling the advertised product—or may not even have it—instead trying to push something more expensive on consumers who respond to the ad. The FTC primarily focuses on national advertising campaigns and refers other regional ad concerns to the appropriate state or local authorities.

© z576/Shutterstock, Inc.

Another way government promotes trust between businesses and the public is through enforcement of various marketing provisions so that people can trust the origin of goods. These include federal **Intellectual Property** (IP) laws, which confirm that trademarked and copyrighted material is being sold by, or under the authority of, the true owner. Selling counterfeit goods is a serious offense investigated by the Federal Bureau of Investigation (FBI). If you want protection for your own goods, placing a small "™" (for **trademark**) on your physical product names, symbols, and so on, or a "©" (for **copyright**) on printed matter, software, and so on, is a good start, but full protection under the law is only guaranteed by registration with the appropriate U.S. government agency. (**Patents**, on the other hand, MUST be filed and granted to provide any type of protection for utility or design of products; so, contact the U.S. Patent & Trademark Office or an attorney specializing in patent law.)

Certain federal laws require a statement of contents and/or origin for various products, including items made of cloth or textiles and most toys. A separate division of the **Federal Trade Commission (FTC)** is charged with monitoring much of this activity, since the public good depends on honest and true claims. In addition, public safety may be impacted when goods from an "un-safe" country are mislabeled. To claim the origin of goods as being "Made in the USA," all (or virtually all) of the product's significant parts and processing must originate in the United States, with no (or negligible) foreign content. Details can be found at the FTC's website, http://business/ftc/gov, which contains a link explaining the standard entitled: Enforcement Policy Statement on U.S. Origin Claims (http://www.ftc.gov/os/1997/12/epsmadeusa.htm).

"Bait and switch"   when a business advertises a product at a very low price to lure customers, but in reality has no intention of selling the advertised product—or may not even have it—instead trying to push something more expensive on consumers who respond to the ad.

Intellectual Property (IP)   copyrights, trademarks, and patents owned as intangible assets and covered by specific laws.

Trademark   name, design, or trade dress protection afforded by law to physical products if designated as protected by placing a small "™" on your physical product names, symbols, and so on, or a small "SM" as "servicemark" for service-related protection claims. (Once Federal protection is granted a ® can be used instead.)

Copyright   printed matter, software, and so on, that is protected under the law from unauthorized duplication since it was designated as such by the owner placing a "©" on the matter. (Full protection under the law is only guaranteed by registration with appropriate U.S. government agency.)

Patents   formal protection under the law for products' functionality ("utility patent") or appearance ("design patent") which have been filed and granted such protection by the U.S. Patent & Trademark Office. Companies are granted a monopoly on producing a new product that is deemed sufficiently innovative to be protected from competition for and exclusive period of time.

Federal Trade Commission (FTC)   an agency of the U.S. federal government charged with monitoring business and advertising activity, since the public good depends on honest and true claims. The FTC's mission is to promote competition, protect consumers from anti-competitive mergers, and stop other unfair business practices.

© Ribah/Shutterstock,Inc.

Federal and State Laws on Privacy, Telemarketing, and Email Marketing

Other ways people are protected include various federal and state laws protecting privacy, restricting telemarketing activity, and prohibiting "spam" email campaigns. For example, consumer privacy must be protected when collecting personal information and additional guidelines for data security are also put forth by the FTC. In fact, the FTC takes this so seriously that they offer free resources for businesses of all sizes at its website. Additional precautions must be taken for any mobile apps produced or used by your business, and there are even more stringent rules when dealing with children's data on a website. The Children's Online Privacy Protection Act (COPPA) was updated in July 2013 to clarify the Six-Step process that all website operators must use when dealing with children under the age of 13. This includes things like verifying age, getting parents' permission, notifying parents, and honoring their wishes when it comes to their kids' information.

As far as restricting sales over the phone, the FTC has posted complete guidelines for the **Telemarketing Sales Rule** on its website, covering things such as prohibiting unsolicited "cold calls" to consumers where a prior relationship does not exist, requiring immediate disclosures of certain facts and warning against misrepresentations. Certain types of calls are exempt, notably charitable organizations, political-related activities, outbound business-to-business calls, and incoming calls in response to consumer advertising. A national **"Do Not Call" Registry** has also been established where consumers can submit phone numbers, which the telemarketers are prohibited from calling under any circumstances or risk facing a fine and other penalties. Similarly, there is a list maintained of email addresses, which cannot receive unsolicited emails. This is part of the **"CAN-SPAM" Rule** designed to prevent marketers from sending emails in bulk to random people in the hopes of obtaining business or other responses. Among the law's many provisions, subject lines cannot be deceptive, headers must not be altered to hide the true source of the email, and there must be specific instructions for the recipient to "opt out" of receiving any future communications. Each email that violates the CAN-SPAM Act is subject to penalties of up to $16,000.

Telemarketing sales rule
FTC rule that covers things such as prohibiting unsolicited "cold calls" to consumers where a prior relationship does not exist, requiring immediate disclosures of certain facts, and warning against misrepresentations.

"Do not call" registry
national list established where consumers can submit phone numbers which telemarketers are prohibited from calling under any circumstances, or risk facing a fine and other penalties.

"CAN-SPAM" rule
national rule providing establishment of a list of consumer provided email addresses that cannot receive unsolicited emails, thus designed to prevent marketers from sending emails in bulk to random people in the hopes of obtaining business or other responses.

© Andreas Baba Crailsheim/ Shutterstock,Inc.

Federal and State Laws on the Environment

Environmental laws are also made and enforced at the federal, state, and local levels. Businesses must be in compliance with regard to land usage, waste disposal, pollution, and handling of hazardous materials, among other things. The best information on these laws can be found at the **Environmental Protection Agency's (EPA)** website: http://www.epa.gov. Among the areas where regulatory compliance is a hot topic include mold, asbestos, and toxic substances. Some industries impacted by these rules include agriculture, automotive, construction, and transportation. Federal rules can be found at the EPA site, as well as links to specific state information. Regulations are very specific under the Clean Air Act and Clean Water Act regarding discharge of any substances determined to be pollutants.

The EPA at the federal and state level offers various programs and certain types of help. For example, compliance assistance is offered at the federal level (and some states) by providing training and tools to help businesses meet environmental requirements. Various incentives are in place to reduce or eliminate some penalties if violations are voluntarily disclosed, and collaboration with the government is encouraged to bring businesses into compliance. EPA investigators at the federal and state levels are charged with monitoring submitted information, providing site inspectors, and checking for possible violations. There are also small business programs listed on the federal EPA site.

Environmental Protection Agency's (EPA) federal, state, and local agencies that establish rules with regard to land usage, waste disposal, pollution, and handling of hazardous materials.

Biodegradable when the "entire product or package will completely break down and return to nature within a reasonably short period of time after customary disposal" . . . which is defined by the FTC to be within one year.

Recycled "materials that have been recovered or diverted from the waste stream during the manufacturing process or after consumer use."

© WvdM/Shutterstock, Inc.

© Studio_G/Shutterstock, Inc.

The government also gets involved when businesses include environmental claims on their products or in their advertising. All such claims should be specific and supported with scientific evidence. For example, simply stating that a product is "green" or "eco-friendly" is too general and hard to substantiate. Instead, a package might say that it is **"biodegradable,"** meaning according to the FTC that the "entire product or package will completely break down and return to nature within a reasonably short period of time after customary disposal," which they define as within one year. The business must have evidence to this effect as well. **Recycled** content claims must also be specific, stating the percentage of "materials that have been recovered or diverted from the waste stream during the manufacturing process or after consumer use." All of these claims should ensure that they are not designed to mislead the public. Furthermore, any connection that a business has to entities offering "certification" or a "seal of approval" must also be disclosed. This is just a sample of the rules put in place to protect the public. The FTC has a comprehensive Green Guide for Marketers available to download on its website.

Additional Federal and State Laws

Most of the advertising, privacy, and environmental standards apply to all businesses. There are special rules for companies that sell automobiles, franchises, funerals, nonprofits, and certain other businesses as detailed on the FTC website. Furthermore, there are additional guidelines, restrictions, and laws for any and all businesses offering loans as their main product or providing financing for the products they sell. Provisions of the **Truth-in-Lending Act** state that, among other things, a business cannot simply advertise a low monthly payment to entice consumers without making additional disclosures about the other costs of obtaining the money, conditions of the loan, and credit terms. Again, all of this information is available on the FTC website, http://business.ftc.gov, or from your legal counsel.

Truth-in-lending act federal law which states that a business cannot simply advertise a low monthly payment to entice consumers without making additional disclosures about the other costs of obtaining the money, conditions of the loan, and credit terms.

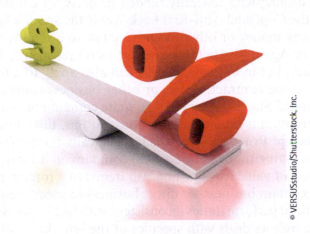

© VERSUSstudio/Shutterstock, Inc.

COMPANY TRANSACTIONS AND COMPETITION

When companies transact business with each other, there are still laws that must be followed for various reasons. In general, the law offers less protection to businesses since people who operate a business are viewed by the law as being more sophisticated. Still, taking unfair advantage of business relationships may impact consumers, and so the law takes this into account when creating various rules and regulations that must be followed or in prohibiting certain activities. Here, we discuss kickbacks, collusion, and the **Uniform Commercial Code (UCC)**. The large topic of contract law follows in the next main section of this chapter.

Uniform Commercial Code (UCC)   rules and guidelines for businesses to follow in various detailed transactions and adopted by most states in order to make business transactions go smoothly.

Kickbacks and Bribes

One of the most important things in business is to be honest and ethical. But if you are and everyone else isn't, you can feel like you're at a disadvantage. To that end, there are a number of laws that help keep things more fair for everyone. In general, laws prohibit individuals or businesses from paying any additional money or gifts or incentives that are not disclosed in order to win business, orders, sales, or contracts. You are also not allowed to pay bribe money to government officials "to get things done." The idea behind these laws is that any

© Jan S./Shutterstock, Inc.

Kickback   any money (or other thing of value) paid to an individual or a business in exchange for granting a contract, placing an order, and so on.

Copeland anti-kickback act   the specific law that applies to federally funded projects for construction of other public works.

Bribe   any money or other incentive given to an individual to influence his or her behavior.

Foreign corrupt practices act   law that specifically prohibits any U.S. citizen or other person acting on behalf of a U.S. company in a foreign country from offering anything of value (cash or non-cash items) to a foreign public official to obtain business, retain business or direct business to specific entities or further to have that official perform duties inconsistent with local laws.

secret compensation leads to an unfair advantage for one business and does not create a level playing field for all businesses to compete. In that environment, it is unlikely that consumers will get the best prices or governments will get the best deal for taxpayers. This can also lead to other distortions of free market enterprise and an overall mistrust of the system.

A **kickback** is any money paid to an individual or a business in exchange for granting a contract, placing an order, and so on. The implication is that the money is exchanged secretly, without the knowledge of the larger company, government, or organization that the person works for. Thus, this is prohibited because it means that the person making the decision is not doing so solely based on price, service, qualifications, and so on, but rather because of receiving the kickback money. Although "money" is typically used in the definition, a kickback can actually be anything of value received, which is not disclosed to all parties. When dealing with federally funded projects for construction or other public works, the **Copeland Anti-Kickback Act** is the specific law that applies.

A **bribe** is any money or other incentive given to an individual to influence his/her behavior. Again we are talking about secret payments. This is very similar to a kickback, but in business, a bribe can also apply to a third person who is not a party to the contract, order, or other business transaction. Although illegal in the United States, bribery can be quite common in some foreign countries where corruption is rampant. In response to this, the United States passed the **Foreign Corrupt Practices Act,** which specifically prohibits any U.S. citizen or other person acting on behalf of a U.S. company in a foreign country from offering anything of value (cash or noncash items) to a foreign public official to obtain business, retain business, or direct business to specific entities, or further to have that official perform duties inconsistent with local laws. The U.S. Department of Justice website deals with specifics of the law along with examples and commentary. (http://www.justice.gov/criminal/fraud/fcpa/)

© Kamil Macniak/Shutterstock, Inc.

Collusion, Antitrust, and Anticompetitive Behavior

There are some additional ways where consumers or honest businesses could be at a serious disadvantage, and again there are laws to try and prevent these situations from occurring. For example, if businesses work together, then their **collusion** could set prices higher than they otherwise could by simply reacting to market forces. Any "deal" that is reached would force consumers to pay inflated prices, with no possibility of relief from normal competitive forces in the economy. Thus, the U.S. government has passed laws that prohibit companies from getting together and setting prices. Collusion of this sort to fix prices is illegal—and can even result in jail time—however, there is nothing stopping companies from following a price leader based on open actions in the marketplace if they so choose. This is why you often see gas stations on opposite corners appearing to raise and lower their prices in

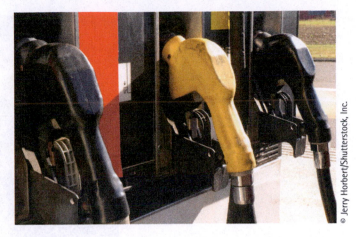

© Jerry Horbert/Shutterstock, Inc.

unison; they can't sit in a room and discuss it, but they can follow each other's prices posted on the gas station signs.

In addition to setting prices at higher levels, there are other ways that businesses could conspire to harm consumers. In order to stop these **anticompetitive** actions that distort competitive forces in the marketplace, the government uses its regulatory authority and police power to stop abuses and protect consumers by passing **antitrust laws**. The federal and state laws dealing with these issues began with passage of the Sherman Antitrust Act in 1890 by the federal government.

The provisions of the **Sherman Antitrust Act** prohibit companies from conspiring together to restrain trade, which would in effect raise prices for consumers because of lesser competition in the marketplace. Without businesses competing to offer the best prices, quality, and service to consumers, it would have the same effect of raising prices as if one company were a **monopoly** and thus the sole provider of certain products or services. Specific actions forbidden by the law include conspiring to set prices, colluding to divide a market into territories where certain companies would enjoy exclusive sales, or any number of other activities, which would tend to grant or extend monopoly power to certain market participants.

The **Clayton Act** passed in 1914 took this a step further and also prevents companies from joining forces in circumstances where doing so would limit competition or consumer choice. The idea was to prevent monopoly behavior before it could even occur, since combining business entities could give them the power to raise prices without alternatives for customers to choose. Under this law, large businesses who wish to merge must get permission from the U.S. government first. If they hope to gain approval, they must demonstrate that their newly combined company will not be so dominant that they will be able to control prices and that the remaining competitors will have enough market share to prevent any monopoly behavior.

About that same time in 1914, the **Federal Trade Commission Act** was passed, which set up the FTC as an agency watchdog to study industries, monitor behavior, establish ongoing rules, and engage in enforcement. The FTC's mission is to promote competition, protect consumers from anticompetitive mergers, and stop other unfair business practices. There are a number of publications and guides available on the FTC's website, which explain its role, its work, and the types of cases it investigates at the federal level (http://www.ftc.gov/bc/antitrust/).

Collusion businesses working together to set prices higher than they otherwise could by simply reacting to market forces.

Anticompetitive ways that businesses conspire to harm consumers via actions that distort competitive forces in the marketplace.

Antitrust laws the government's regulatory authority and police power to stop abuses by businesses and protect consumers.

Sherman anti-trust act law that prohibits companies from conspiring together to restrain trade, which would in effect raise prices for consumers because of lesser competition in the marketplace.

Monopoly when one company or entity is the sole provider of certain products or services, and thus is able to charge any price.

Clayton act law that prevents companies from joining forces in circumstances where doing so would limit competition or consumer choice.

Federal trade commission act law which set up the FTC as an agency watchdog to study industries, monitor behavior, establish ongoing rules, and engage in enforcement.

© ra2studio/Shutterstock, Inc.

The Uniform Commercial Code (UCC)

In order to make business transactions go smoothly, a set of guidelines and rules for businesses to follow has been established and is referred to collectively as the Uniform Commercial Code (UCC). These are not a set of federal regulations, but instead have been adopted by most states in one form or another to govern transactions across state lines. These laws cover things like the sale of goods and equipment leases, as well as **negotiable instruments**, which guarantee payment of a stated amount of money over time or on a specific date, such as promissory notes, checks, and so on. By having uniform regulations in place, businesses can transfer their interests to other people if there is appropriate language in the contract, such as wording you might find in a lease. The law goes one step further, stating that negotiable instruments can be transferred to any third party and that company or person will ultimately receive payment. So, if someone owes you money evidenced by a negotiable instrument, and you don't want to wait until a future promised date to receive payment, you can sell that "paper" to someone else. (You can see details of the UCC laws enacted for your state by visiting the Secretary of State's website.)

One benefit of having UCC regulations is that businesses can obtain cash now for money owed to them in the future. Of course, you should not expect to get the full **face value** written on the note, check, and so on, if you have to resort to obtaining money from a third party. There are several reasons that you may have to accept **discounting** and receive less than face value. First, of course, is the **time value of money**: A dollar promised to you next year is worth less than one you can have today. Another important reason may have to do with the credit worthiness or reputation of the payer. If that company (or person) is considered a credit risk for some reason, then a lesser amount will be paid out based on the possibility of default.

Purchase orders for future payment of goods delivered now *might* be considered negotiable instruments, depending on their language, but usually they are not because there are typically conditions stated as part of the transaction. For example, returns may be allowed. In this case, these conditions do not fulfill the requirements of a negotiable instrument, so the company wanting to receive money early must go to a **factor** who will discount the value of the money owed based on credit risk, industry, and any conditions in the purchase order since the factor typically assumes all risks of return and so on.

Now keep in mind that different arrangements or agreements have different rules, but a contract must usually be "**assigned**" (i.e., officially signed over) to

---

Negotiable instruments documents which guarantee payment of a stated amount of money over time or on a specific date, such as promissory notes, checks, etc.

Face value the amount written on the note, check, and so on.

Discounting receiving less than face value.

Time value of money concept which says that a dollar promised to you next year is worth less than one you can have today.

Purchase orders contractual agreement between buyer and seller stating quantities bought and conditions of sale.

Factor person or business who will discount the value of the money owed based on credit risk, industry, and any conditions in the purchase order since the factor typically assumes all risks of return, and so on.

Assign legally giving your rights and obligations in a contract to another party.

the new party. A purchase order is also a type of contract if it sets out duties that must be fulfilled by both parties. A negotiable instrument shares some features of a contract, but not all of them. Thus, because negotiable instruments are unconditional, they can then be transferred by "negotiation" under UCC rules. A lease is also a type of contract. Some of these differences will become clearer as we discuss contracts in the next section.

© lenetstan/Shutterstock, Inc.

CONTRACTS AND LIABILITY

Contracts and liability are tied closely together in the law. Contracts can create liability because there are certain promises that people exchange. A **contract** is a legally binding agreement or promise, which creates **liability** since each party is responsible for fulfilling his or her pledge(s) under the contract. Failure to fulfill a contract is just one more way that a company or person can be held liable under the law or in the court of public opinion.

Types of Contracts

You are probably familiar with what is typically referred to as a contract: a written legal document between two or more parties. Notice, though, that our definition of a contract ("a legally binding agreement or promise") didn't say anything about it being a "document" or even that it must be "written." Certainly, the best contracts for you to enforce against another party are those written down, which clearly spell out the terms and obligations of each person or entity. This is referred to as an **express contract**. Equally enforceable in many circumstances, though, is an **implied contract**, where the actions of the parties are interpreted by custom or by law to obligate them.

As a business owner, you can be on different sides of an implied contract from time to time. For example, when customers walk into your restaurant, there's an implied contract that people who sit down and eat the food you serve will pay for the meal. On the other hand, every time your company offers a product or service in the marketplace, the UCC laws that we discussed in the last section impose on you an **implied warranty** given to the buyer that the product (or service) can be used for its intended purpose. This is in addition to whatever **express warranty** that you may offer in writing to prospective buyers, spelling out any guarantees or policies you have with regard to repairing or replacing the product or parts for a specified period of time.

Contract a legally binding agreement or promise.

Liability when each party is responsible for fulfilling his or her pledge(s) under the contract. The obligations (debts) that the business owes to others (creditors) such as accounts payable, notes payable, unearned revenue.

Express contract contract that clearly spells out the terms and obligations of each person or entity.

Implied contract contract where the actions of the parties are interpreted by custom or aw to obligate them.

Implied warranty guarantee given by law from a seller to the buyer that the product (or service) can be used for its intended purpose.

Express warranty guarantee offered (usually in writing) from a seller to prospective buyers, spelling out any guarantees or policies you have with regard to repairing or replacing the product or parts for a specified period of time.

© newart-graphics/Shutterstock, Inc.

Valid   something that it is legal and enforceable.

Capacity   legal ability to enter a contract because a person is not a minor nor mentally ill.

"Age of majority"   when someone is no longer considered a minor (varies by state, but is usually 18 years of age).

Offers   when something of value is given by one party to entice another party to enter a contract. (This can even be just a "promise.")

Accept (or acceptance)   when the other party receives and agrees with what was offered by the other party and thus intends to enter a contract.

"Meeting of the minds"   when "offer" and "acceptance" has occurred, and thus, a legally binding contract was formed (as long as there was genuine mutual assent, with no fraud, deceit, duress, undue influence or mistake).

Consideration   something of value given by the parties for entering into the contract.

Lawful   legal purpose for a contract.

Void   when a contract is not valid or enforceable.

Voidable   when a minor may choose to cancel a contract.

Unenforceable   when a contract cannot be upheld because it is vaguely worded, can't be proven or is for something illegal.

Statute of frauds   law that requires certain contracts to be in writing and signed in order to be enforceable.

Power of attorney   where another person can legally sign for someone else.

Performing   when both sides fulfill and contract as promised and do what they agreed to do.

Breach of contract   if one side fails to perform as promised in a contract.

Contract Requirements

There are certain elements that must be present for a contract to be considered **valid**, meaning that it is legal and enforceable. The first requirement is that the parties to the contract must have legal **capacity** to enter the contract: they must not be a minor nor mentally ill. (Note that that the "**age of majority**" when someone is no longer considered a minor varies by state, but is usually 18 years of age.) Next, there must be an agreement where one party **offers** something and the other party **accepts**. (This is called a "**meeting of the minds**" in legal terms.) Note that this agreement must take place with genuine mutual assent, where there is no fraud, deceit, duress, undue influence, or mistake. There must also be **consideration** given by the parties for entering into the contract. Often the consideration is money—regardless of amount—but it could even just be a promise to do something. Finally, the purpose of the contract must be **lawful**.

If any of these elements are not present, then the contract is likely not enforceable because a true contract was not formed. For example, a contract is **void** if one of the parties signs it under threat of blackmail. Furthermore, a contract entered into by a minor is **voidable** by the minor (but not the other party). Or, if a contract is for something illegal, such as gambling debts, then it is **unenforceable**. A contract may also be unenforceable if it is vaguely worded (This is why lawyers are important!) or if the terms can't be proven. This last part is what makes verbal contracts difficult to enforce and the reason that many states have adopted the **statute of frauds,** which require certain contracts to be in writing and signed in order to be enforceable. In an effort to prevent fraud or forgetfulness, this statute applies to things like contracts for real estate, large sales above a certain dollar amount (varies by state), agreements stretched over long periods of time (perhaps leases for more than a year), and **powers of attorney** (where another person can legally sign for someone).

© Pressmaster/Shutterstock, Inc.

Liability for Breach of Contract

Most contracts are fulfilled as promised with both sides **performing** what they agreed to do. If one side fails to perform, then a **breach of contract** has occurred. Sometimes this is easy to determine; other times it is not. What if one party feels that he/she did what was required, but the other party thinks that it was not done well? Or, what if most things are done as promised, but not quite everything?

Is this a breach? In either of these cases, the parties could decide to negotiate a solution. If they still can't agree, though, this could result in legal action. Keep in mind that anyone can sue you for anything, so there's no need to be immediately alarmed if it happens. You need to determine the merits of the claims and see if, in fact, you might have some liability in the matter.

The first thing to consider is that generally if the other parties did not fulfill their part of the contract, then you are not obligated either. A court will look at whether or not there was actually a **material breach**—something important was not done as promised—before deciding who to side with. Even if a few minor things were not done but there was **substantial performance** by one party, then the other party is still required to perform. Sometimes a court will decide or a contract will clearly state that certain parts are **severable** from the rest of the contract and can be cut out without changing the rest of the contract. If the language of the contract is unclear, the court may look at intent or consider oral negotiations to fill in the blanks, but the written word almost always takes precedence.

Once the court decides who is **liable** (the responsible party at fault), then it must be determined how to remedy the breach. Sometimes the solution is **specific performance** where the court will order the breaching party to perform as promised, but there are times when this is not practical (e.g., the item was already sold to someone else) or not legal to do (e.g., forcing someone to follow through on a personal services contract). In these situations and many others, the court will simply order **damages** to be paid by the party responsible for the breach to the injured party. These can be a small **liquidated damages** amount agreed to beforehand and written into the contract, or a more substantial **compensatory damages** amount determined by the court to make up for any losses incurred by the injured party. Sometimes a very large **punitive damages** amount is imposed by the court as a penalty against the breaching party to discourage similar behavior in the future. Different circumstances call for different award types and amounts. Keep in mind that even if you **assign** the contract to another party, you may still have some liability for any breach (unless a **release** was signed by ALL parties).

© Pressmaster/Shutterstock, Inc.

LABOR LAWS

When large corporations hire people, this entails compliance with a fairly large number of rules and regulations. In fact, the U.S. Department of Labor administers and enforces more than 180 federal laws (http://www.dol.gov),

Material breach   when something important in a contract was not done as promised.

Substantial performance   when most of the promises in a contract are fulfilled and only a few minor things were not done.

Severable   when a court decides or a contract clearly states that certain parts can be cut out from a contract without changing the rest of the contract.

Liable   when it's determined that a responsible party is at fault for an injury, breach of contract, and so on.

Specific performance   one possible remedy for a breach of contract, where the court will order the breaching party to perform as promised.

Damages   money paid by the party responsible for the breach to the injured party.

Liquidated damages   an amount agreed to beforehand and written into the contract.

Compensatory damages   an amount determined by the court to make up for any losses incurred by the injured party.

Punitive damages   an amount is imposed by the court as a penalty against the breaching party to discourage similar behavior in the future.

Assign   legally giving your rights and obligations in a contract to another party.

Release   a signed waiver that absolves liability.

© Andrey_Popov/Shutterstock, Inc.

Independent contractors
A company that consists of a single person.

Civil Rights Act of 1964
law that prohibits discrimination on the basis of race, color, religion, sex or national origin for employment, education, and access to public facilities (including businesses).

Equal Employment Opportunity Act (EEOA)
law that applies to private employers, state and local governments, educational institutions, employment agencies, and labor organizations. (The provisions of EEOA added "disability" and "age" to the list of protected classes covered by original Civil Rights Act.)

Equal Employment Opportunity Commission (EEOC) agency established by EEOA to investigate and enforce alleged violations.

Affirmative action provisions in the law to encourage and promote equal opportunity for all protected classes.

Uniformed Services Employment and Reemployment Rights Act (USERRA) law that protects the jobs of anyone who voluntarily or involuntarily leaves an employment position for military service, meaning they get their job back upon return.

while numerous state laws must also be considered. Although you must comply even as a nonprofit corporation, the good news is that generally small businesses can focus on a smaller subset of these laws. This won't be a comprehensive list, but let's look at some of the major legal issues you need to consider.

The Decision Process

One of the first considerations you might have as a business owner is whether or not you want to actually hire people as employees or just enlist their services to help your company. Bringing someone onto your payroll does make you subject to a whole host of requirements compared with just paying them as an **independent contractor**, where the person works on his or her own and only as needed to produce a required result for the company. Independent contractors are responsible for their own taxes, benefits, insurance, and other things, so you can see the advantage of hiring someone that way. The downside is that you simply cannot run many businesses this way, especially if you have regular, consistent contact with the public. This is because under IRS rules you cannot control, direct, or require an independent contractor to do specific work or tasks. You are only allowed to direct the *result* of the work, not what will be done, or how it will be done, or even when it will be done (except for establishing deadlines).

So, if your business requires that you hire some full-time or part-time employees, there are some basic laws you must follow. Most important among these are antidiscrimination laws, beginning with the **Civil Rights Act of 1964**. This Act prohibits discrimination on the basis of race, color, religion, sex, or national origin for employment, education, and access to public facilities (including businesses). Various laws over the years have added to its breadth and enforcement, but none more so in the employment area than the **Equal Employment Opportunity Act of 1972 (EEOA)**.

The EEOA applies to private employers, state and local governments, educational institutions, employment agencies, and labor organizations. The provisions of EEOA added "disability" and "age" to the list of protected classes covered by the original Civil Rights Act and established the **Equal Employment Opportunity Commission (EEOC)** to investigate and enforce alleged violations. The EEOC looks for discrimination not only when people are hired, but also when they're fired or even passed over for promotions. Your best protection as an employer is to keep good documentation of all decisions you make so that others can see exactly how and why you arrived at your decisions.

There are also **affirmative action** provisions in the law to encourage and promote equal opportunity for all protected classes. Although often thought of as being used for women and minorities, affirmative action programs can also apply to people with disabilities, veterans, or any other group that is underrepresented in the workplace. Keep in mind also that the **Uniformed Services Employment and Reemployment Rights Act (USERRA)** protects the jobs of anyone who voluntarily or involuntarily leaves an employment position for military service, meaning they get their job back upon return.

Equal Employment Opportunity is
THE LAW

Private Employers, State and Local Governments, Educational Institutions, Employment Agencies and Labor Organizations

Applicants to and employees of most private employers, state and local governments, educational institutions, employment agencies and labor organizations are protected under Federal law from discrimination on the following bases:

RACE, COLOR, RELIGION, SEX, NATIONAL ORIGIN
Title VII of the Civil Rights Act of 1964, as amended, protects applicants and employees from discrimination in hiring, promotion, discharge, pay, fringe benefits, job training, classification, referral, and other aspects of employment, on the basis of race, color, religion, sex (including pregnancy), or national origin. Religious discrimination includes failing to reasonably accommodate an employee's religious practices where the accommodation does not impose undue hardship.

DISABILITY
Title I and Title V of the Americans with Disabilities Act of 1990, as amended, protect qualified individuals from discrimination on the basis of disability in hiring, promotion, discharge, pay, fringe benefits, job training, classification, referral, and other aspects of employment. Disability discrimination includes not making reasonable accommodation to the known physical or mental limitations of an otherwise qualified individual with a disability who is an applicant or employee, barring undue hardship.

AGE
The Age Discrimination in Employment Act of 1967, as amended, protects applicants and employees 40 years of age or older from discrimination based on age in hiring, promotion, discharge, pay, fringe benefits, job training, classification, referral, and other aspects of employment.

SEX (WAGES)
In addition to sex discrimination prohibited by Title VII of the Civil Rights Act, as amended, the Equal Pay Act of 1963, as amended, prohibits sex discrimination in the payment of wages to women and men performing substantially equal work, in jobs that require equal skill, effort, and responsibility, under similar working conditions, in the same establishment.

GENETICS
Title II of the Genetic Information Nondiscrimination Act of 2008 protects applicants and employees from discrimination based on genetic information in hiring, promotion, discharge, pay, fringe benefits, job training, classification, referral, and other aspects of employment. GINA also restricts employers' acquisition of genetic information and strictly limits disclosure of genetic information. Genetic information includes information about genetic tests of applicants, employees, or their family members; the manifestation of diseases or disorders in family members (family medical history); and requests for or receipt of genetic services by applicants, employees, or their family members.

RETALIATION
All of these Federal laws prohibit covered entities from retaliating against a person who files a charge of discrimination, participates in a discrimination proceeding, or otherwise opposes an unlawful employment practice.

WHAT TO DO IF YOU BELIEVE DISCRIMINATION HAS OCCURRED
There are strict time limits for filing charges of employment discrimination. To preserve the ability of EEOC to act on your behalf and to protect your right to file a private lawsuit, should you ultimately need to, you should contact EEOC promptly when discrimination is suspected:
The U.S. Equal Employment Opportunity Commission (EEOC), 1-800-669-4000 (toll-free) or 1-800-669-6820 (toll-free TTY number for individuals with hearing impairments). EEOC field office information is available at www.eeoc.gov or in most telephone directories in the U.S. Government or Federal Government section. Additional information about EEOC, including information about charge filing, is available at www.eeoc.gov.

The Law Requires that this EEO Poster Be Prominently Displayed in your Work Environment

Another area EEOC covers is prohibitions against **sexual harassment**, including unwanted sexual advances, obscene remarks, or anything of a sexual nature that can make others feel uncomfortable in the workplace. This can take the form of a *quid pro quo*, where someone feels compelled to consent to sexual conduct to protect her/his job or be awarded a promotion, or creation of a **hostile environment**, where lewd conduct or remarks are tolerated or encouraged. More information on the workings of the EEOC, including newly issued rulings and regulations, can be found at http://www.eeoc.gov.

Sexual harassment
unwanted sexual advances, obscene remarks, or anything of a sexual nature that can make others feel uncomfortable in the workplace.

quid pro quo sexual harassment situation where someone feels compelled to consent to sexual conduct to protect her/his job or be awarded a promotion.

Hostile environment
sexual harassment situation where lewd conduct or remarks are tolerated or encouraged.

© ostill/Shutterstock, Inc.

Hiring People

Form I-9 employment eligibility verification federal form to verify that each new employee is legally eligible to work in the United States.

Immigration and Nationality Act (INA) federal law that allows you to hire foreign workers on a temporary or permanent basis for certain types of work.

H-1B specialty visas U.S. entrance documents available for certain highly skilled occupations.

Work Opportunity Tax Credit (WOTC) tax incentive program for hiring certain groups of people, such as qualified military veterans or disabled people.

Americans with Disabilities Act (ADA) federal law that prohibits discrimination against people with disabilities and requires that you provide "reasonable accommodations" so that the applicant/employee can perform the duties of the job.

Once you've made the decision that you need to hire people to help in your business, you'll need to verify if they're eligible to work in the United States. You should NOT ask if someone is a U.S. citizen. This is discriminatory and can get you in trouble; besides, noncitizens are permitted to work in the United States provided that they have the required permits or documentation. Instead, federal law requires that you verify that each new employee is legally eligible to work in the United States by having the employee fill out **Form I-9, Employment Eligibility Verification** (available from http://www.uscis.gov/i-9-central). For frequent hiring, registering with e-Verify (http://www.uscis.gov/e-verify) can improve accuracy, ease tax reporting, and protect jobs for authorized workers to help maintain a legal workforce.

If the person you wish to hire does not have a Social Security card or is not immediately eligible to work in the United States, the **Immigration and Nationality Act (INA)** allows you to hire foreign workers on a temporary or permanent basis for certain types of work. You may have heard about **H-1B specialty visas** available for certain highly skilled occupations, but there are actually several other programs for guest workers. In addition to capping the number of visas in each category, the government also requires that you demonstrate that there are not enough qualified U.S. workers available who are willing and able to perform the work at prevailing wages. This means that you cannot use the guest worker program to obtain cheap labor, but rather for workers to fill a definite need.

As you think about your employment needs and who you might hire, keep in mind that from time to time there are tax incentives, like the **Work Opportunity Tax Credit (WOTC),** for hiring certain groups of people, such as qualified military veterans or disabled people. Not only is the building where you operate your business subject to the **Americans with Disabilities Act (ADA)**, but so too is your company in its hiring practices. If there is a disabled person capable of performing some work for you, the law requires that you provide "reasonable

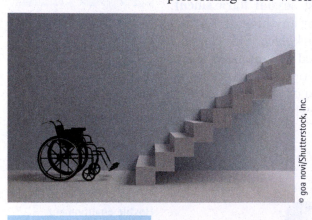

© goa novi/Shutterstock, Inc.

accommodations" so that the applicant/employee can perform the duties of the job. Although it seems subjective, common sense will often prevail. Obviously a blind person could not be a firefighter, but providing that person with a Braille keyboard and/or speaking software seems reasonable for many jobs. A wheelchair ramp would also fall into this category as would many other physical alterations to a building, unless doing so would cause significant hardship or expense for the employer. The EEOC or the courts are asked to weigh in on these determinations from time to time.

Fair Labor Standards Act of 1938 (FLSA) federal law that prohibits discrimination in pay and has been amended over the years to address additional topics such as minimum wage, overtime pay, child labor laws and other issues.

Compensation and Benefits

Just as it is illegal to discriminate when hiring, firing, or promoting, it is also illegal to discriminate in the wages you pay. For example, you cannot pay people of different races varying amounts on that basis alone. Furthermore, the law states that you must pay women equal wages for equal work. The **Fair Labor Standards Act of 1938 (FLSA)** has been amended over the years to address additional topics such as minimum wage, overtime pay, child labor laws, and other issues.

The current federal **minimum wage** that must be paid to most workers is $7.25 per hour, although legislation is introduced in Congress from time to time to raise that figure since it was last increased in 2009. Some workers are exempt, such as restaurant workers who receive tips as part of their compensation, and also keep in mind that some state and city governments have passed laws requiring higher pay than the federal minimum. FLSA also stipulates that hourly workers and nonsalaried employees who work in excess of a full-time week (generally 40 hrs) must be **paid overtime** equal to 1½ times their hourly wage rate.

In addition to wages, employers often offer additional benefits as compensation to entice workers to join the company and keep morale high while they work there. Businesses can deduct some of these costs as an added bonus to help their bottom line. Direct **employee benefits** can include things such as sick leave, vacation time, health insurance, retirement programs, and more. Additionally, there are other expenses that serve as indirect employee benefits, which employers must pay as pooled resources for other uses, such as unemployment insurance and worker's compensation (explained in the next section).

Some of the direct employee benefits offered by companies over the years have become required under the law so that employees can enjoy universal access to things such as unpaid leave to attend to family issues (Family and Medical Leave Act) or health insurance (Affordable Care Act, also known as Obamacare). The **Family and Medical Leave Act (FMLA)** was passed in 1993 to provide 12 weeks of unpaid leave for workers, during which time employers must keep an employee's job open. Monitoring varies by company, with some requiring documented proof of the reason for the leave, while others simply permit the time to be used piecemeal in any fashion the employee requests. The **Affordable Care Act (ACA)** was passed in 2010 and is being implemented in stages during 2014 and 2015. Some of the details may be subject to change, but the primary provision affecting employers is that companies with 50 or more full-time employees (defined as working 30+ hours per week) must provide a certain level of paid health-care coverage for their employees.

Minimum wage   the lowest hourly wage that must be paid to most workers (although some occupations are exempt, such as restaurant workers who receive tips).

Paid overtime   required payment equal to 1½ times the wage rate when hourly workers and non-salaried employees work in excess of a full-time week (generally 40 hrs).

Employee benefits   additional compensation to entice workers to join the company and keep morale high while they work there, including things such as sick leave, vacation time, health insurance, retirement programs, and more.

Family and Medical Leave Act (FMLA)   federal law which provides 12 weeks of unpaid leave for workers, during which time employers must keep an employee's job open.

Affordable Care Act (ACA)   federal law that says employers with 50 or more full-time employees (defined as working 30+ hr per week) must provide a certain level of paid health care coverage for their employees.

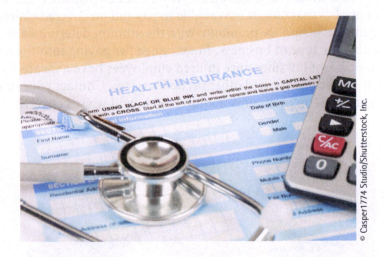

© Casper1774 Studio/Shutterstock, Inc.

Health and Safety

Over the years, health and safety of workers have become a more important topic. Initially, it was the push of labor unions that caused safety changes in companies. Today, most safety concerns are addressed by a combination of government regulations and industry self-regulation as businesses look to improve their image in the court of public opinion by being good corporate citizens.

Fair Labor Standards Act of 1938 (FLSA) federal law that prohibits discrimination in pay and has been amended over the years to address additional topics such as minimum wage overtime pay, child labor laws, and other issues.

Child labor worker defined under FLSA as anyone under the age of 14 and thus they may not work (except on farms or when self-employed, such as models or delivering papers).

Occupational Safety and Health Act (OSH Act) federal law that deals with unsafe working conditions by establishing safety rules and standards.

Occupational Safety and Health Administration (OSHA) federal agency under the Department of Labor that makes employers responsible for providing a safe workplace.

Standards OSHA's guidelines and rules to assure safe and healthful workplaces.

Bureau of Worker's Compensation (BWC) programs at the federal and state level to assist employees who may be injured on the job by offering compensation and care.

Much of the early labor concerns involved unsafe working conditions and the employ of children. The **Fair Labor Standards Act (FLSA)** referenced in the last section also had several provisions that dealt with **child labor**. FLSA states that children under the age of 14 may not work (except on farms or when self-employed, such as models or delivering papers) and further restricts the number of hours that children under the age of 16 may work. Anyone under the age of 18 may not work in any hazardous occupations as defined in the Act. These laws are in place to protect children and ensure that they have adequate time for schooling.

After passage of several smaller laws, unsafe working conditions were finally addressed in a big way in 1970 with the passage of the **Occupational Safety and Health Act (OSH Act)**. This Act established the **Occupational Safety and Health Administration (OSHA)** under the Department of Labor, making employers responsible for providing a safe workplace. OSHA's stated mission is "to assure safe and healthful workplaces by setting and enforcing standards, and by providing training, outreach, education and assistance." Businesses must comply with all OSHA **standards** and regulations applicable to their industry. More information can be obtained on their website: https://www.osha.gov/law-regs.html. Keep in mind that in addition to federal regulations issued by OSHA, which have the force of law, there are often more workplace safety regulations put in place by states with which your business must also comply.

As another way to promote worker's health and safety, there are several programs at the federal and state levels to assist employees who may be injured on the job. At the federal level, the Office of Worker's Compensation Bureau (OWCB) helps employees who become injured working on a federal project by providing wage replacement benefits, medical treatment, vocational rehab or retraining, and other benefits. At the state level, most states have a **Bureau of Worker's Compensation (BWC),** which offers similar type benefits to injured workers. This is significant to you as an employer because you are required to pay into this fund pool so that money is available to pay out on covered claims. Think of it as an additional insurance premium, with the amount determined by the risk associated with your type of business. In exchange for paying into the pool, you receive reduced risk of lawsuits since injured employees have a means to recover compensation, medical costs, and other needed services. Contact your state BWC for more information on premiums, requirements, and what's covered.

© Igor Sokolov (breezel)/Shutterstock, Inc.

TAX, ACCOUNTING, AND BANKRUPTCY LAWS

If you aren't already convinced that you need the help of a lawyer and an accountant for various parts of your business, this might be the section that finally does it. When filing taxes for a growing business, there are numerous areas of compliance that must be considered. Fortunately, there are tax services and payroll companies that can handle lots of these issues for you at a reasonable rate. Although the accounting requirements can become more burdensome the larger your company gets, again there are people you can hire for advice or assistance when you need them. Finally, bankruptcy is something no one likes to think about, but there are ways that it can be helpful if you receive good legal advice.

Tax Considerations

Your first encounter with tax decisions related to your business begins as soon as you decide what form your company will take. If you decide to open your business as a sole proprietorship, then you will simply add your business income earned onto your regular tax form (using Schedule C) and compute a **self-employment tax**. This tax is equal to about 15% of your earnings and essentially replaces the Social Security FICA taxes on a regular paycheck. If you work for someone else, that 15% is split between you and your employer. But as a sole proprietor, you are your own employer so you must pay both halves. This is in addition to any income tax you may owe on your profits also. Keep in mind that even though you still only file an annual return, as a self-employed person, you are supposed to make quarterly estimated payments of your tax liability using Form 1040-ES (or risk owing penalties).

If you decide that your business will take the form of a corporation, LLC, or other entity that is separate from you personally, then you will need to apply with the IRS to get a **Federal Tax Identification Number (TIN)** for that new, separate entity you are creating. (This is also sometimes called an Employer Identification Number, EIN.) You can get this number immediately by filing online at http://www.irs.gov. Sometimes customers will ask for this number from your business since they are required to file tax documents with the IRS if they pay you in excess of $600 per year.

© crotonoil/Shutterstock, Inc.

Additionally, you can use the IRS website to obtain a **W-4 Form, Employee's Withholding Allowance Certificate**, to determine how much income tax you should withhold from each of your employees' paychecks. The amount will be based on the number of exemptions they claim and other factors listed on the form. All new employees should fill out and sign this form when you first hire them, and you should keep it on file. Note that you may be required to withhold additional money from the wages of nonresident aliens working for you, based on their visa status.

It's important to know that all federal income tax, for businesses and individuals, is a **"pay-as-you-go tax,"** meaning you must pay the tax as income is earned. This is where the quarterly filings of estimated taxes come into play for your business. Likewise, you must also collect and submit the payroll taxes that you withhold from your employees' paychecks on a quarterly basis. Failure to

Self-employment tax a tax equal to about 15% of your earnings, paid by individuals who do not work for a company, to replace the Social Security FICA taxes on a regular paycheck. If you work for someone else, that 15% is split between you and your employer.

Federal Tax Identification Number (TIN) tax number assigned by the IRS to your business that is a corporation, LLC, or other entity that is separate from you personally. (This is also sometimes called an Employer Identification Number . . . EIN.)

W-4 Form, employee's withholding allowance certificate federal tax form used to determine how much income tax are withhold from each employee's paycheck.

"Pay-as-you-go-tax" tax concept that means you must pay the tax as income is earned using quarterly filings of estimated taxes.

© Monkey Business Images/Shutterstock, Inc.

submit these taxes is one of the biggest ways that businesses get into trouble with the IRS.

Other taxes that you may be required to collect include sales tax at the state and local levels. Consult your local taxing authority for these rules, regulations, and requirements. Note, too, that if you sell online, you may be required to collect taxes in certain jurisdictions and forward those monies to the proper authorities. Current rules say that you only have to collect taxes in locations where you have a **"substantial presence,"** but that is open to interpretation. Usually, it just means a physical presence, but even a warehouse used by a third-party logistics provider could subject you to tax collection rules. Furthermore, there is an effort in Congress to make all online businesses collect sales tax in all jurisdictions; so, keep on the alert for this.

"Substantial presence" jurisdictions where you are determined as doing business for tax purposes, meaning you must collect text and forward those monies to the proper authorities. (Usually it just means a physical presence, but even a warehouse used by a third party logistics provider could subject you to tax collection rules.)

Generally Accepted Accounting Principles (GAAP) the rules, guidelines and standards used by accountants in the preparation of any financial statements.

Sarbanes–Oxley Act (Sarbox) federal law passed to govern certain behaviors of public corporations in response to several accounting scandals. (For example, the CEO and CFO must now individually and personally certify all financial statements.)

Whistleblowers people who come forward with allegations of misconduct to the authorities, stakeholders, or the press.

Accounting Principles

Accounting issues will be discussed more thoroughly in its own chapter, but there are a couple of points we need to mention in this chapter on Law. First of all, there are numerous accounting rules and procedures you must follow to keep your books in compliance with what is expected by most taxing authorities, bank personnel, investors, and so on. Most of these accounting standards are contained in the **Generally Accepted Accounting Principles (GAAP)**, which are the rules, guidelines, and standards used by accountants in the preparation of any financial statements. There is not the force of law behind these guidelines for small businesses, but if you have big aspirations for your business to grow, then it is probably best to comply with these standards. It will serve you well with potential investors in the future or if you ever get audited by a taxing authority.

There are several laws that defer to GAAP standards when establishing financial requirements for businesses; some laws go farther and require more. One such law you need to be aware of is the **Sarbanes–Oxley Act (Sarbox)**. The Act was passed in 2002 in response to several accounting scandals at major public corporations, such as Enron, WorldCom, and others. Sarbox regulations mostly apply to public corporations with stock trading on one of the exchanges. For example, the CEO and CFO must now individually and personally certify all financial information and statements of the corporation as accurate, under the threat of increased criminal penalties for fraud.

Beyond that, there are a few provisions of note in the law, which can be related to owners of small businesses. One section of the bill gives increased protection for **whistleblowers** who come forward with allegations of misconduct. Another important part makes it a felony to destroy documents that are part of a criminal investigation and establishes severe criminal penalties for anyone who misleads or impedes any federal agency conducting an investigation. So, even if you are not a major public corporation, you can see where these last two points perhaps should influence your actions with your company, regardless of size. For example, you might put in place a program to retain records for a set period of time and then shred things beyond that date, as long as no investigations are pending.

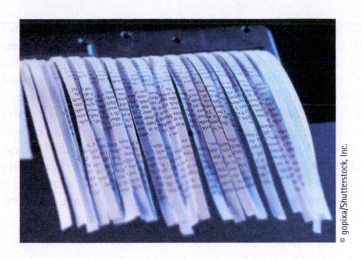

© gopixa/Shutterstock, Inc.

Bankruptcy Situations

If things do not go well for your business enterprise, you have several options. Simply closing the company is enough if you do not owe people money. File your final tax returns and notify the appropriate government entities that you are no longer "active." But if you do owe out more money than your company is worth, you should consider several **bankruptcy** options—some of which can give you more time to try and turn things around. The names of each type of bankruptcy come from the Chapter number of the federal law, which outlines all of the details, requirements, procedures, and so on. Keep in mind that state laws create some differences in how some portions of bankruptcy law are enforced. This final discussion on business law is probably the one that most requires the advice and assistance of an attorney since there are different types of bankruptcy options, both personally and for your company.

Chapters 7 and 13 are two types of personal bankruptcy to consider, especially useful if your company was a sole proprietorship. **Chapter 7** is a liquidation situation, where a trustee is appointed to sell off your assets and use that money to satisfy creditors to whatever extent possible. Some states will allow you to retain your home up to a stated value or a certain amount of personal property; other states do not. There are income limits in place for people to be eligible for Chapter 7, and some debts, such as student loans, cannot be **discharged** and thus will survive the bankruptcy and still be owed.

Chapter 13 is an adjustment of debts, where a person who still has a regular income might decide to enter a payment plan to get out debt after certain amounts have been reduced via the court's bankruptcy proceedings. This filing will allow a person more freedom in deciding which assets he or she may want to retain, but again some debts cannot be "adjusted" away or reorganized here, such as student loans and tax debts.

There are similar bankruptcy options for companies as well. A business can elect to liquidate itself voluntarily under Chapter 7, or three creditors can get together and try to force the company into bankruptcy. This could happen when a business is **insolvent** because it owes out more money than it has in assets or income. If the creditors do not trust that the business can eventually pay them, then they can petition a court to set up a bankruptcy situation. Chapter 7 would cause the business assets to be liquidated, creditors paid off portions of their debt from the sale proceeds, and the company would no longer exist.

Bankruptcy situation where companies or individuals owe more money than they are worth and cannot continue making payments on their debts.

Chapter 7 a liquidation bankruptcy, where a trustee is appointed to sell off your assets and use that money to satisfy creditors to whatever extent possible.

Chapter 13 a bankruptcy that allows for an adjustment of debts, where a person who still has a regular income might decide to enter a payment plan to get out debt after certain amounts have been reduced via the court's bankruptcy proceedings.

Discharged when a debt is cancelled and does not survive the bankruptcy. (Some debts, such as federal student loans, cannot be discharged and thus are still owed.)

Insolvent state of a company (or individual) when it owes out more money than it has in assets or income.

© Onypix/Shutterstock, Inc.

Chapter 11 a reorganization bankruptcy, which stops any creditor actions while the business submits a repayment plan to the court within 120 days. (This can be voluntary or as a response from an attempted forced bankruptcy.)

More common, though, is a company petitioning the court to enter **Chapter 11** reorganization bankruptcy voluntarily (or as a response from an attempted forced bankruptcy). This stops any creditor actions while the business submits a repayment plan to the court within 120 days. All assets and liabilities must be detailed to all parties so that creditors can evaluate the plan along with the court. (Keep in mind that failure to disclose all assets is considered fraud.) If the plan is approved, the business can continue operations while it repays a portion of some debts and discharges others. Typically, the company can also terminate leases, renegotiate labor contracts, and try to recover assets. By focusing its energy on profitability instead of servicing debt for a period of time, a company can often emerge from bankruptcy in a stronger financial position since it will have less debt, fewer obligations, and may have reorganized parts of its operations.

OPEN FOR BUSINESS IN THE REAL WORLD

After working on new build homes for the past six years, you finally decide it's time for you to start your own construction and remodeling business. You have some of the basic state licenses you need to perform some of the work yourself, but you also get a General Contractor's license so that you can oversee people to perform every possible thing that a home might need. Your LLC has an umbrella insurance policy to cover you in the event of liability from accidents, so the last thing you need to do to satisfy the state is become bonded. It's not as easy as you thought, but your background check comes back clean and you pay the necessary fees. Now you're ready to get other people on board with your new venture.

To start out small and see how things go, you've decided that for the first six months you will only actually hire one office person to sit at the front desk to answer the phone and greet walk-in customers. It's a good thing you found a payroll service that can take care of the details for you. As for the rest of the workers to actually do the jobs you get from customers, you've explored the IRS website and talked with your attorney so you feel okay with using your contractor friends and former coworkers as subcontractors until business is more steady and you're sure that you can sustain it.

You're ready to start advertising, and you figure the safest way is the basic approach: no fancy or outlandish claims, just touting your experience and your attention to detail at a very competitive price. As the orders start coming in, you realize this has a chance to work—if you don't mess it up. You call people back promptly and start setting up the jobs. You always make sure that everything done in your company's name is up to code and that you are in compliance with EPA and OSHA regulations. With your great quality and service, you expect to keep growing and growing, soon to hire on a few of those subcontractors as your full-time employees.

Chapter Summary

Business compliance with federal, state, and local regulations requires permits for some businesses. Federal permits are needed for farming, firearms, fishery, as well as aviation, mining, and broadcasting. States often require "experts" in a field to be licensed, bonded, and insured, especially if they will assist the public with repairs. Federal and state laws prohibit "deceptive" advertising likely to mislead a "reasonable consumer." Federal and state environmental laws are designed to protect the environment as well as the integrity of company claims for "going green." Finally, Truth-in-Lending laws ensure that businesses tell consumers the pertinent facts about any financing provided to them.

Company transactions among themselves are also subject to many laws and regulations. The Uniform Commercial Code (UCC) is a positive affirmation of what must be done to ensure that documents are negotiable. Other laws against kickbacks, bribes, and collusion detail unethical behavior that has the potential to harm consumers.

Contracts are legally binding promises, which can lead to liability if there's a breach of those duties. For a contract to be valid, the parties must: have legal capacity, reach a meeting of the minds, exchange consideration, and agree to a lawful purpose. The statute of frauds says that certain contracts must be in writing, such as those for real estate and powers of attorney. When there's a material breach of contract, courts can decide who is liable and impose remedies, which may include payment of liquid, compensatory, or punitive damages.

Labor laws include the Civil Rights Act of 1964, which prohibits discrimination against protected classes of people. The Equal Employment Opportunity Act established the EEOC to monitor compliance of fairness and promoting affirmative action policies. EEOC also investigates complaints of sexual harassment, including quid pro quo and hostile environment violations. The Americans with Disabilities Act says that employers must provide "reasonable accommodations" to those with disabilities so that they can perform their jobs. The Fair Labor Standards Act established the minimum wage and rules for payment of overtime. The Occupational Safety and Health Administration was established to implement rules and monitor compliance regarding workplace standards for health and safety.

Tax considerations for companies don't end once they choose a legal form for their business. Self-employment tax and withholding are ongoing compliance issues that must be dealt with. The GAAP rules must be followed for accounting documents, which will be presented to the public, and Sarbanes–Oxley regulations include requiring corporate officials to certify all financial documents. Bankruptcy options may be needed if a company (or individual) becomes insolvent and unable to pay its debts. Chapter 7 is a liquidation of all assets to pay debts. Chapter 13 is an adjustment of an individual's debts following a repayment schedule. Chapter 11 is a reorganization of a company's debts if courts receive an acceptable plan to discharge some debts and delay payment on others.

Review Questions

1. What are some businesses that you can think of which might require federal permits? State permits? No permits at all?

2. Explain the difference between "licensed", "bonded," and "insured", and state why each is important.

3. Under what conditions are you able to solicit business using the telephone? Via email?

4. If your company gives people more time to pay for an expensive remodeling job, are you subject to the Truth-in-Lending requirements? Why or why not?

5. Is it a violation of the Foreign Corrupt Practices Act to make a foreign official a part owner in your business? What if your intent is to get that person to help push through favorable projects or rulings that would help your business? What other laws apply?

6. Can you think of some possible ways to adjust your prices so that you remain competitive in your prices without running afoul of the laws against collusion? Does it matter if you are only doing this to make your prices cheaper; after all, the laws were designed to ensure that consumers and governments get the best possible prices.

7. Name two ways that the Uniform Commercial Code can help or hurt your business.

8. What are some things you can do to ensure that you always have a valid and enforceable contract with another party?

9. Consider remedies that are available for breach of contract; which ones are better? Do you think a court would consider whether or not you made any effort to "mitigate" (i.e., minimize) any damages caused from a breach by the other party? So, if you have a vacant apartment now because of a breach, do you need to advertise the apartment for rent again or can you just leave it vacant and make the other guy pay?

10. When deciding who you will hire, which labor law is most important?
11. How do you think companies get in trouble with the IRS, and how can you avoid it?
12. Explain the different types of bankruptcy and the pros and cons of each approach.

Discussion Questions

13. Which types of federal permits for businesses do you think are necessary, and which do you think could be done away with? Explain and defend your position.

14. How would you propose that companies doing business overseas deal with issues of bribery where local competitors are able to provide a bribe to get something done, but the U.S. company officials are not permitted to do so?

15. If a homeowner signs a contract with an installer for windows to be put in the house by the 15th of the month, but the installer does not receive the windows from the manufacturer until after that day so they cannot be installed on time, who is at fault? Has a breach occurred and what would the court likely decide with regard to liability, damages, and so on?

16. Your landscaping business is looking for help and you have several applicants who've applied. One person is handicapped and unable to ride a normal commercial mower unless you install special hand controls like they have in their car. You decide to pass over this person and hire someone else. Have you violated any labor laws?

17. An airline company has not been profitable for the past few years, but its situation has improved steadily and it's on track to be profitable next year. Management decides that they could speed up the process by declaring Chapter 11 bankruptcy to nullify their current union labor contract and renegotiate it. They file for bankruptcy next month. Has the airline company done anything illegal? Unethical?

Key Terms

- accepts
- affirmative action
- Affordable Care Act (ACA)
- age of majority
- Americans with Disabilities Act (ADA)
- anticompetitive
- antitrust laws
- assigned
- bankruptcy
- bait and switch
- biodegradable
- bonded
- breach of contract
- bribe
- Bureau of Worker's Compensation (BWC)
- Business law
- CAN-SPAM Rule
- Capacity
- Chapter 7

- Chapter 13
- Chapter 11
- child labor
- Civil Rights Act of 1964
- Clayton Act
- collusion
- compensatory damages
- consideration
- contract
- Copeland Anti-Kickback Act
- copyright
- damages
- discharged
- discounting
- Do Not Call Registry
- employee benefits
- Environmental Protection Agency (EPA)
- Equal Employment Opportunity Act of 1972 (EEOA)

- Equal Employment Opportunity Commission (EEOC)
- express contract
- express warranty
- face value
- factor
- Fair Labor Standards Act of 1938 (FLSA)
- Family and Medical Leave Act (FMLA)
- Federal Tax Identification Number (TIN)
- Federal Trade Commission (FTC)
- Federal Trade Commission Act
- Foreign Corrupt Practices Act
- Form I-9, Employment Eligibility Verification
- Generally Accepted Accounting Principles (GAAP)
- H-1B specialty visas
- hostile environment
- Immigration and Nationality Act (INA)
- implied contract
- implied warranty
- independent contractor
- insolvent
- insured
- intellectual property
- kickback
- lawful
- liability
- liable
- license
- liquidated damages
- material breach
- meeting of the minds
- minimum wage
- monopoly
- negotiable instruments
- paid overtime
- patents
- pay-as-you-go
- performing
- powers of attorney
- punitive damages
- purchase orders
- Occupational Safety and Health Act (OSH Act)
- Occupational Safety and Health Administration (OSHA)
- Offers
- *quid pro quo*
- recycled
- release
- Sarbanes–Oxley Act (Sarbox)
- self-employment tax
- severable
- sexual harassment
- Sherman Antitrust Act
- specific performance
- standards
- statute of frauds
- substantial performance
- substantial presence
- Telemarketing Sales Rule
- time value of money
- trademark
- Truth-in-Lending Act
- unenforceable
- Uniform Commercial Code (UCC)
- Uniformed Services Employment and Reemployment Rights Act (USERRA)
- valid
- void
- voidable
- W-4 Form, Employee's Withholding Allowance Certificate
- whistleblowers
- Work Opportunity Tax Credit (WOTC)

CHAPTER

4

Ethics

LEARNING OBJECTIVES

1. Define and identify how ethics are established over time and why they are important
2. Identify how ethical dilemmas occur and explain how to identify winners and losers
3. Identify different ways to improve ethical behavior
4. Explore Corporate Social Responsibility and its impact on business and society

© Ken Wolter/Shutterstock, Inc.

OPENING STORY

In 2014, the Veterans Health Administration (VHA) came under criticism for failing to properly treat military veterans. An investigation revealed that as many as 120,000 veterans either had not received any treatment or had to wait months or even years for that treatment, in spite of a rule that access to care must come within 14 days. This investigation also revealed that at least 35 veterans had died while waiting for an appointment at the Phoenix VA hospital, and as the investigation continued, it revealed that it was a common practice at many VA hospitals. In 1995, the VHA had established a waiting time limit of 30 days to receive care. In spite of difficulty in meeting that standard, it was lowered to 14 days in 2011 for access and within 7 days of the desired appointment date. Without significant increases in resources, this proved to be an impossible task.

However, rather than admit their inability to meet the standard, the administrators simply falsified records to indicate they had. When a person finally received an appointment, their records were changed to show that the appointment had been requested within the 14-day period. Some patients complained to the Veterans Administration about the wait, but when looked into, it appeared they had not waited long at all. As noted, some died while waiting and some wound up paying out of pocket for health care when they were entitled to it without charge at the VA hospital. Because of the scandal, the Secretary of Veterans Affairs, Eric Shinseki resigned and the top VHA health professional, Dr. Robert Petzel retired early. A criminal investigation was launched in June of 2014, by the Justice Department. Falsifying official government records is against the law. More than that, falsifying records to make it appear you were performing well when people were suffering is a huge violation of ethics. Some people were given bonuses because of their apparent excellent performance, while patients died without being able to see a physician.

How could anyone in good conscious perpetuate this practice? Well, they couldn't, but unfortunately, ethical breaches are not uncommon.

INTRODUCTION

Ethical behavior is acceptable behavior, based on a sense of fairness and based on societal norms. Over time, society changes what is and is not acceptable behavior. The elements that drive these changes are cultural norms, laws, and ethics. In the 1960s and earlier, it was not unusual to see Chambers of Commerce brochures touting smokestacks billowing out black smoke as signs of economic prosperity. Today, most people in our society find billowing smokestacks as an unethical sign of corporate misbehavior. Clean air laws have been written and enforced to prevent many of the worst polluters from operating. Other examples of ethics changing over time include issues like elimination of slavery, women being given the right to vote and inherit property, sexual harassment and child labor laws, and even mundane aspects of culture like our views on littering or people no longer accepting secondhand smoke as something to be ignored.

If one wants to have a simple way of defining **Ethics,** it might be "Doing the Right Thing." A way to describe **Ethical Behavior** is: How you act when no one is watching, or as noted earlier, acting within societal accepted behavior. The use of **ethical reasoning** is the process of assessing the facts and attempting to act with the best of intentions to achieve the best outcome within commonly accepted ethical limits. How a business or organization makes decisions on moral or social responsibility issues is at the heart of the ethical culture of that organization. An **ethical dilemma** occurs when an action needs to be taken and the options are not clear-cut from an ethical perspective. **For example:** U.S. law and American corporate ethics clearly make offering or taking a bribe for favorable business decisions unacceptable. However, bribes are a commonly accepted business practice and not altogether illegal in some countries. A business that is involved in international trade and competing with firms from around the world could be put at considerable disadvantage by refusing to offer or accept a bribe.

Ethics   doing the right thing.

Ethical behavior   how you act when no one is watching.

Ethical reasoning   the process of assessing facts and acting with the best intentions.

Ethical dilemma   when options are not clear-cut from an ethical perspective.

In such an instance, accepting a bribe might not be illegal or unethical in the setting, but both unethical and illegal according to U.S. law (Foreign Corrupt Practices Act, among other laws). By the same token, multinational corporations must follow the laws in the countries in which they operate. This is certainly a situation that is not clear-cut and one in which there may not be a correct answer. Actions taken to resolve an ethical dilemma often are complex and have winners and losers associated with the action taken. Arriving at the best way to resolve ethical dilemmas is a challenge for every organization and individual.

Many ethical dilemmas occur because of differences in culture. Spanking children was a common practice throughout the United States during most of our history and is still common in some places, but considered child abuse in others.

In 2014, NFL Player Adrian Peterson, of the Minnesota Vikings, admitted using a switch to spank his son. This was a fairly common practice by parents in the culture in which he grew up. However, in the twenty-first century, this is considered abusive behavior. Whereas some would call this acceptable and normal, others described it as hitting his child with a stick. People's view of ethics is frequently based on what is normal and acceptable for them and not what is normal and acceptable for the people about whom they speak.

Female circumcision is still practiced in parts of Africa, but considered mutilation in the Western world. Male circumcision is commonly practice in the Western world, but not in Africa.

Some actions are both illegal and unethical, but in many cases, they are unethical without being illegal. A former head football coach in Nebraska happened to also have a side job as a sales representative for Riddell, a sports equipment company. When his football program needed new equipment, he, acting as

© Jovan Nikolic/Shutterstock, Inc.

the football coach, bought it from himself, acting as a sales representative. This action was not illegal, nor was it in any way an abuse of funds, nor did the college fail to get their money's worth. However, it was a **conflict of interest**, that is, an action that benefits someone that might not have benefited had someone else made the decision. Conflicts of interest occur often and may be an indicator of wrongdoing, or may just have the appearance of it.

Many people would find that the best way to do the right thing with regard to others is to follow the **Golden Rule**, "Do onto others as you would have them do onto you." On the surface that sounds good and fairly easy, but requires that you project your values onto others. In other words, it assumes that others want to be treated exactly as you would want to be treated. In many cases, that is incorrect. Perhaps a better way to address how one treats others is, "Treat others as they would want you to treat them."

This requires that you communicate with others and find out how they would like to be treated. If that communication is possible, it should result in a much more effective relationship. If the situation does not allow communication prior to your taking actions, it would be important to check in after your actions to make sure your assumptions in following the "Golden Rule" were accurate with regard to the other person or group.

© Mr. Nikon/Shutterstock, Inc.

It is doubtful that someone can force another to think and always act ethically. However, "rehearsing" how to act in simulated or real-life situations can be an effective way in learning how to make ethical decisions, especially when there is not a policy or rule in place to provide guidance. **For example:** What if you are presented with a situation where the firm you work for has a policy of recycling all of their old electronics like computers, monitors, keyboards, and other circuit boards as a green initiative for the company? The company has posted that information proudly on its website boasting of its good record on the environment. Recycling has become very popular and a concept that you embrace personally. Due to your interest in the program and your desire to write a case study to encourage others in your industry to pursue a similar program, you investigate the process the company uses for sending off the electronics. To your dismay, you find that all of the recycling is done in a foreign country and the standards there are extremely low. There is much evidence that the workers are exposed to high levels of toxic chemicals and that waterways that provide all of the drinking water in the area are becoming polluted with the same kinds of chemicals. The dilemma you face is whether you should inform management about your findings. Management could very well take the information as a wakeup call to change policies or ignore the information to prevent the negative publicity.

Unfortunately, People that "tell on" their own organization, even internally, are sometimes treated poorly. These "**Whistleblowers**," people that report ethical issues to the authorities, stakeholders, or the press, are doing the right thing. However, whistleblowers have been fired for reporting problems outside of normal company channels, going public and going around the chain of command.

Conflict of interest action taken that benefits someone that might not have benefited had someone else taken the action.

Golden rule do onto others as you would have them do onto you or treat others as they would want you to treat them.

Whistleblowers people who come forward with allegations of misconduct to the authorities, stakeholders, or the press.

The **Whistleblower Protection Act of 1989** protects whistleblowers that work in government or for companies doing business with the government. Several states also have similar laws.

Understanding or rehearing your responses to a circumstance like that can be very eye-opening and give you insight as to how you might feel and/or react.

Gathering accurate and complete information about a situation is critical in being able to make the best and most ethical decision. When gathering information, it is important to assess the credibility of the information and where it came from. Think about the source and try to understand the perspective of that source and identify any conflicts of interest that source might have. For example, if a person presents you with information about the misconduct of another person in the organization, does that person have a personal bias against the person about whom they are presenting information or the person presenting the information? The same is true about the news media, professional journals, blogs, or other sources. In a situation where there are clear winners and losers, it is a good idea to "track the cash." Consider the situation with the former Vice President of the United States, Al Gore. Vice President Gore has been very vocal about global warming and has worked hard to influence legislation and public policy to change the way the country and world consume energy. Mr. Gore has invested millions of dollars in companies that participate in carbon trading markets and solar cells. These companies have benefited greatly from his public advocacy of these industries, and critics claim that Mr. Gore is unjustly enriching himself. Mr. Gore has countered these perceived conflicts of interest and ethical arguments by stating, "I absolutely believe in investing in ways that are consistent with my values and beliefs." When assessing the information from Mr. Gore and/or his critics, be sure to find out how the critics are paid and who benefits from their position. Even small situations can have similar conflicts of interests, which makes careful examination of the information presented an important practice.

Whistleblower protection act of 1989   Protects whistleblowers that work in government or for companies doing business with the government.

Making decisions when faced with ethical dilemmas is never perfect and effectively dealing with affected stakeholders (people who are affected by an organization's actions and decisions) after the decision is critical. Stakeholders who are negatively impacted by a decision are much more likely to accept the decision if the person or organization has built a trusting relationship with all stakeholders. However, a lack of trust can cause wasted energy, lack of commitment, despondency among impacted stakeholders, and unwillingness to accept future decisions. Trust is gained over time by a history of acting ethically and responsibly. However, it can be lost very quickly. Regaining trust is often harder to achieve than gaining it originally. A member of an organization that has not necessarily agreed with all the decisions of the organization, but trusted that they were made ethically, might view a decision negatively impacting him much differently than one who believes that the organization continuously had made unethical decisions.

BUSINESS ETHICS—MANAGING ETHICAL DILEMMAS AT WORK

© pichetw/Shutterstock, Inc.

Managing ethical behavior in an organization is a challenging task. **Compliance-based ethics** is the approach used by firms, government agencies, and regulators alike to prevent unlawful or unethical behavior. There are penalties for failing to comply with the rules or laws. Many industries have laws and regulations that require organizations and their employees to follow. For example, all organizations or individuals who sell financial products and securities to the public must follow rules issued, by one or more of SEC, FINRA, FDIC, state securities boards, and/or state insurance commissions. Failing to comply with these laws or regulations can lead to fines, suspension, loss of licenses, or even prison. Larger firms like Merrill Lynch, or JP Morgan Chase, have large compliance departments charged with protecting the firm from illegal or unethical behavior. Small firms are often challenged by keeping up with compliance issues due to the cost and difficulty in hiring quality compliance staff. One of the problems in relying solely on laws and regulations is that no set of rules or regulations can be complete enough to meet every situation. For example, it is unethical, and in many cases illegal, to peak in someone's window, but many organizations now operate photo drones that can fly above yards and businesses to spy on people. Many in the regulated industries and the public recognize that compliance-based ethics is sometimes ineffective in protecting the public. Because disclosure of illegal or unethical behavior can erode trust in an organization, most organizations have a **Code of Ethics** to provide guidelines for their staff to follow and help understand what are right and wrong behaviors. Most professional organizations like the American Bar Association (ABA), The American Institute of Certified Public Accountants (AICPA), and the American Medical Association (AMA) have professional codes of conduct that require standards of conduct without regard to organizational codes of conduct.

Compliance-based ethics approach by firms, government agencies, and regulators alike to prevent unlawful or unethical behavior.

© stevemart/Shutterstock, Inc.

Code of ethics guideline for an organization's staff to follow and help understand what are right and wrong behaviors.

Integrity-based ethics approach where an organization communicates its guiding principles and values and has a culture of supporting ethically responsible behavior.

Another way to manage ethical conduct is utilizing **Integrity-based ethics**. This approach is most effective when the organization communicates its guiding principles and values and has a culture of supporting ethically responsible behavior. Without support from the top management and shareholders, the organization cannot expect to be successful in maintaining the culture of ethical behavior. If a company's ethics policy specifies taking care of the customer first and management demands behaviors that are contrary to that policy, the customer will likely be subjected to unethical behavior. For example, given two identically priced products, if a product that fits all of the needs of a customer has a lower commission than a product that meets most of the needs of a customer, the sales person is incentivized to sell the inferior product.

Most organizations with effective integrity-based ethics practices provide effective ethics training programs. The best ethics training programs use role-playing and rehearsing situations where an ethical dilemma is involved. By rehearsing and learning those exercises, individuals can learn how to address those kinds of situations. Another key element in having an ethical organization is to provide discretion and guidelines for staff members to make a decision when confronted with a new situation. When the policy is, "Doing the Right Thing Is Never the Wrong Thing" and employees are encouraged to do the right thing, a culture of ethics and trust can flourish. How management reacts when their idea of doing the right thing is different than the employee will shape how proactive employees will be about doing the right thing. If a manager who was not present to address a customer complaint fires an employee who tried to do the right thing to address the situation, risk-taking by others may cease and cripple the way employees behave with respect to the code of ethics. The highest level of ethical behavior occurs when a person or organization does something costly but the right thing to do when nobody will ever know that it was done.

© docstockmedia/Shutterstock, Inc.

© iQoncept/Shutterstock, Inc.

Companies with ethical practices based on integrity and trust are often transparent as well. **Transparency** is having a policy of openness and availability. Inviting employees and sometimes the public to meetings is one source of openness. Another is publishing rules and policies, so everyone involved is aware of how things work. A transparent company may post all jobs and invite both internal and external applicants. Such a company would keep careful records and make them available for inspection upon request.

CORPORATE SOCIAL RESPONSIBILITY

Corporate Social Responsibility (CSR) can be defined as how ethically a company interacts with its stakeholders. Stakeholders for a company include stockholders, employees, vendors, customers, the communities it does business in, and society in general. Corporate social responsibility can also be seen as acts of generosity made with corporate assets. For example, many businesses will have someone with an additional duty to look for actions the company can take to express their generosity. Many companies sponsor youth ball teams or contribute to local school functions. In January 2015, the Burger Barn, in Manvel, Texas, prepared a free lunch for a large group of administrators that were ministering to a school that had lost three of their students in an automobile accident. Acts of corporate social responsibility are a way to demonstrate concern for the local community.

© Stuart Miles/Shutterstock, Inc.

Transparency having a policy of openness and availability.

Corporate responsibility acting in the best interest of society.

© mypokcik/Shutterstock, Inc.

© Dusit/Shutterstock, Inc.

The lowest standard that an organization must follow is to follow appropriate laws that govern its business and business practices. Being socially responsible is a higher standard, which includes acting ethically and in the best interest of the community in which it operates. Many corporate leaders feel pressure from stockholders to produce profits and increase the value of the company. Failure to meet those expectations can lead to removal of those leaders. However, meeting the expectations of stakeholders who expect an organization to be socially responsible is critical as well. A conflict can easily arise between short-term and long-term goals. Successful owners and managers can change their focus from short-term profits to long-term success. Long-term strategies can lead to bigger profits and greater sustainability even if short-term success is compromised. A study cited by James Epstein-Reeves (Covey, 2014) indicates that:

- More than 88% of consumers think companies should try to achieve their business goals while improving the society and the environment.

- 83% of consumers think companies should support charities and nonprofits with financial donations.

- 83% of employees would seriously consider leaving their job if their employer used child labor in sweatshop factories.

- 65% would seriously consider leaving their job if their company harmed the environment.

- 32% would seriously consider leaving their job if their company gave no/little money to charity.

These statistics indicate to company executives and board members that CSR is not only the right thing to do but it can be a profitable thing to do. There are challenges to organizations that desire to be socially responsible. Spending the money and time to be socially responsible can be difficult when competing with an organization that does not. For example, organizations that do not provide extensive benefits to their employees or produce products in overseas markets with lower wages have a cost advantage over an organization that tries to produce domestically and provides those benefits. How many of you would pay $50 more for a cell phone if it was produced domestically? Would you be willing to pay 20% more for your utilities if they were "greener?" Companies have combated these issues by including CSR in their marketing to encourage consumers to buy products from a socially responsible company. Target's history of community involvement, providing grants to educational, environmental,

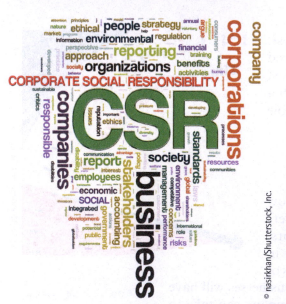

© nasirkhan/Shutterstock, Inc.

and diversity causes, and a corporate culture that rewards its staff for volunteering has served it well in the communities where it operates. That relationship has helped Target regain the trust of its customers after the data breach it suffered in 2013 by losing many of its clients' credit card information. Small companies and entrepreneurs can greatly benefit from community involvement. Volunteering in organizations like the local food bank, service clubs like Rotary International or Kiwanis, and youth sports organizations is an excellent way to increase one's local visibility and credibility. Most who are involved in this type of activity believe that the great feeling of providing service often times results in better results for their business as well.

OPEN FOR BUSINESS IN THE REAL WORLD

A marketing consultant sold a frequent diner program and system to a regional restaurant chain. The program consisted of the hardware, third-party software, and frequent diner cards required to gather data and provide benefits to the company' clients. The customers' frequent diner card was swiped every time they dined at any of the chain's restaurants. For each $250 the customer spent, they received a $25.00 gift certificate to spend at any of the company's restaurants. All of the data was captured in a database utilizing a software package that the consultant sold to the company for $250,000. Additionally, the consultant had a $75,000 per annum consulting contract to provide training, data evaluation, and program development to the company.

On a rainy Saturday afternoon, the marketing consultant was evaluating data from the first six months of the program. At one point, the consultant saw something that was very disturbing hidden deep in the data. It appeared that over 360,000 points were left in customers' accounts due to a software glitch. This amount was approximately 5% of the total points accumulated in the program. After checking things out with the third-party software developer, the consultants fear was confirmed. The software developer, who received $150,000 for the software and $15,000 yearly for support, also confirmed that if not fixed, this problem would continue to grow at least $800 a week. If all 360,000 points were redeemed, the value of the gift certificates would be $36,000. The software developer explained that he had no intention of paying any of the $36,000 or future cost **because nobody would ever be able to find out about the problem.** After all he said, "The Company makes money on those gift certificates." Also, because he was busy, he said he would have to shut down the company's software for at least a week.

So, the ethical dilemma was trying to decide what to do. After all, "nobody would ever find out about the problem." What if the company cancelled the $75,000 annual contract and $36,000 is a lot of money? The answer was difficult but clear. The consultant bought a plane ticket to the company's headquarters for the next day, arrived at 8:30 a.m. on Monday. He met with the Executive Vice President (EVP), who was the person in charge of purchasing and managing the program for the company. The consultant explained the situation to the EVP and handed him a check made out to the company for $36,000. The EVP was not willing to shut down the program and would not accept the check. His reasoning was that he had seven children and because he was responsible for buying the program, he could lose his job if the CEO found out about the problem. He also would not accept the check stating he had no way to deposit the money without the CEO finding out about

it. He then said he was finished discussing the issue and he would not support changing anything. When the consultant arrived home, he faced another ethical dilemma: what to do now?

After another sleepless night, he did the following:

1. He wrote a letter delivered by next-day-air to the EVP stating that the enclosed $36,000 was to cover the points earned erroneously up to the time the problem was discovered.

2. The consultant agreed to fund whatever points were earned between the discovery of the error and fixing the error if the company would allow the software developer to fix the problem.

3. He explained that he would no longer be responsible for point errors if the company did not allow him to fix the problem.

4. Finally, he said that if the company would not allow him to fix the problem, then he could no longer do business with them.

5. He gave the company 48 hr to respond after the arrival of the letter. If he received no response, he would assume that the contract between the consultant and the company would be cancelled immediately.

After waiting for a week, no response came from the company and the consultant wrote a letter confirming the cancellation of the annual contract. He found another software vendor. The consultant kept $36,000 in a bank account for nine years until the consultant closed the practice and the bank account and went on to another venture.

© donskarpo/Shutterstock, Inc.

Review Questions

1. How would you describe ethics?
2. How would you describe ethical behavior?
3. Why are ethical dilemmas so common at work?
4. What is a conflict of interest?
5. Can U.S. companies engage in bribery in a country where it is legal?
6. How can spanking your child with a switch be okay in 1960, but considered unethical and possibly illegal in 2015.

7. How is ethics different from corporate responsibility?
8. How would you define corporate social responsibility?
9. What is a code of ethics?
10. What is meant by the "Golden Rule?"
11. How do cultural differences make ethical behavior harder to evaluate?
12. If you owned 1,000 shares in a company that spent some of their revenue on social responsibility or charitable actions, would you approve or disapprove?
13. What U.S. law protects people from repercussions when informing on their own company?

Discussion Questions

14. What went wrong at the Veterans Health Administration hospitals? How was it so easy for them to fall into the trap of acting unethically?
15. Describe an ethical dilemma with which you are familiar: something you have read or may have happened where you work. What action occurred? What should have happened?
16. Describe a situation in which there was a conflict of interest. How might the participants have avoided the conflict? Was their actual wrongdoing, or did it just appear that way?
17. How can we do more to protect Whistleblowers?

Class Activity

Look into current events and find an example of corporate violation of ethics and/or law. Sadly, it should not be too hard to find one. As a class or in groups, discuss the issues surrounding this incident. What went wrong? Where was the ethical or legal breakdown? How could the people involved behave differently or better? Should they be punished by law or maybe by consumer reaction?

Key Terms

- Code of Ethics
- Compliance-based ethics
- conflict of interest
- corporate responsibility
- Ethical Behavior
- ethical dilemma
- ethical reasoning
- Ethics
- Golden Rule
- Integrity-based ethics
- Transparency
- Whistleblower Protection Act of 1989
- Whistleblowers

Works Cited

Stephen M. R. Covey's book, *The Speed of Trust*, introduces the concept of trust taxes—the price companies pay for low trust. It only takes a scratch along the surface to see how deeply trust can affect an organization. There is certainly a price paid for trust issues that go unresolved. It can be found in the wasted energy of working around a team member or the lack of commitment because of a fear to speak up. Low trust can even hinder innovation when ideas are not openly shared and tested. Retrieved January 27, 2014, from http://www.eksh.com/resources/articles/the-business-value-of-trust-by-kent-mcsparran

2

PEOPLE

2

PEOPLE

CHAPTER

5

Leadership and Performance Management

LEARNING OBJECTIVES

1. Identify the elements of leadership.
2. Explain the difference between leadership and management.
3. Detail the different styles of leadership.
4. Explain how to achieve top performance through people.

© arka38/Shutterstock, Inc.

© Rob Wilson/Shutterstock, Inc.

71

Nick Saban is the head football coach for the University of Alabama. Through his leadership, the football team has won three national titles and consistently been to top bowl games, as well as playing in the first Division One Championship Playoff. He is known as having a consistent and disciplined approach to leadership and is an outstanding leader, motivator, and organizer (Nick Saban, 2015). Saban shares many characteristics with successful leaders. Whether in business, sports, or the military, leadership involves careful planning and strategy, as well as the ability to motivate people to successful mission accomplishment.

What coach Saban understands is that he cannot win any football games; it is the players that win football games. His job is to create the environment in which they have the skills and desire to win. This is similar to the words of former GE CEO Jack Welch, who said "Before you are a leader, success is all about growing yourself. When you become a leader, success is all about growing others" (Kruse, 2015).

INTRODUCTION

Leadership motivating people, the human resources, to want to achieve those organizational goals.

Management the accomplishment of organizational goals, using the resources available.

There are many ways to define **leadership and management**—and to distinguish between the two. One way to define effective management is to simply say, it is the accomplishment of organizational goals, using the resources available. One way to define effective leadership is to say, it is to motivate people, the human resources, to want to achieve those organizational goals. Peter Drucker, often referred to as the man who invented modern management, said "Management is doing things right; leadership is doing the right thing" (Leadership, 2015).

All aspects of an organization need to be managed. Financial management controls the financial assets of a company to make sure the organization can conduct business. Facilities management ensures that the firm has a place in which to operate. Equipment and fleet management ensures that the company has the necessary tools to get the job done. Marketing management and sales management handles the business aspects of: producing, promoting, selling, and delivering the product or service. Human Resource management recruits, staffs, compensates, and retains the people. There are many other functions depending on the type of work done, and all need careful management.

Each manager is also a leader, because in every case, people are involved in working toward the goals. In addition, senior leadership does the strategic planning and organizational goal setting to determine the direction for the company. It is also true that many people use the terms interchangeably.

LEADERSHIP

Leadership is getting the job done through the efforts of others. The style of leadership may depend on the leader or on the industry or type of work being done, or on the people being led. Leadership of a group of trained professionals that do not need immediate supervision must be different from that of a group of unskilled workers.

Elements of Leadership

Leaders must make sense of a complex environment. Culture, technologies, politics, and laws are all rapidly changing. International trade and competition have put local businesses into situations in which they are competing with companies in China or India. Technologies that were the latest item just a few years ago are now obsolete. Leaders must be able to make sense of the rapidly changing environment and sort out how the company will operate now and in the future. Change is not optional. Firms can fight change or they can embrace it. Some organizations find the frequent technological changes too expensive and might want to continue using older methods to save money. However, older technologies may put them at a competitive disadvantage. Leaders must be able to evaluate the complexities and make logical decisions on how to proceed (Table 5.1 shows the elements of leadership, discussed below).

No organization gets it right every time and it is important to be able to learn from failure. History has many examples of companies that failed to learn the lesson. In 2015, RadioShack filed for bankruptcy protection and closed 1,700 stores in response to a steadily declining business. The company had seen declining business for years, but failed to learn from their mistakes. Time will tell if they can learn the lesson now. In business, sometimes success breeds failure because the organization may believe success is permanent and they fail to constantly monitor the environment. Sometimes, however, failure can breed success when a company learns from their mistakes and becomes stronger because of it. To paraphrase Harvey Mackay, No one plans to fail, but many fail to plan.

© sibgat/Shutterstock, Inc.

Another element of leadership is understanding people; this includes understanding one's self as well as others. People are complex creatures with competing goals. Everyone has strengths and weaknesses, and knowing our strengths allows us to focus on the things we do best. In the same way, understanding our weaknesses allows us to recognize growth potential. It is important for leaders to recognize the strengths of the people they hire so they can put them in the most effective positions: where there is the best fit between the person and the task. Understanding the weaknesses can avoid unrealistic expectations when people are improperly assigned. When the leader understands their own weaknesses, it

TABLE 5.1	Elements of Leadership
1	Making sense of a complex environment
2	Learn from failure
3	Understanding people, one's self and others
4	Transparency
5	Focus on the mission
6	Talk the talk and walk the walk

allows them the chance to find others to accomplish tasks they are not able to do themselves.

Transparency, in business, involves making decisions based on established rules and without hidden agendas. Many local governments have established "sunshine laws," which require meetings to be open to the public. Although this is not the case for private businesses, a company that has a policy of advertising contract opportunities and accepting multiple bids, and then selects a contractor without any competing bids, violates the concept of transparency. In the same way, a company may normally publish open positions but then promote someone within the company with posting the job. Transparency gives confidence to internal and external stakeholders of the company. Effective leaders should establish a goal for transparent decisions and a track record of doing it himself or herself.

Leaders must focus on the mission. That is, after all, why they were hired, to accomplish the goals of the organization. Companies must produce and sell the product, provide the service, win the contracts, or whatever it is that they do to make a profit. The leader must understand the needs of the workers and the local community and in doing so, establish internal and external relations that retain the employees and establish a good reputation for the firm. Through it all,

however, the leader must get the job done and earn a profit. No amount of good reputation will help a company that is losing money. Low turnover will not help a company that winds up laying off their workforce. Companies must spend the resources to establish a good image, but not so much that they lose money in pursuit of an image.

A final element of leadership is never asking the employees to do something the leader would not do. The leader must "walk the walk" and "talk the talk." That is, they must work hard, demonstrate integrity, and lead by example. Leaders must not just tell the workforce what is expected, but they must show them by their own actions. The right decision is not always the easy decision. When the employees see the senior management making the hard decision and acting ethically, the lesson is quickly learned throughout the organization.

Leadership Styles

Many leaders have particular styles of leadership. We can divide those styles into several categories, although it is important to remember that no particular style of leadership is necessarily right or wrong or the best for a particular situation.

Authoritative style of leadership; one in which the leader makes the decision, with or without checking with anyone.

Some leaders follow an **authoritative style** of leadership; that is, one in which the leader makes the decision, with or without checking with anyone. Many of the most successful and famous leaders use this style. Authoritarian leaders are very confident with both their leadership and with their decision-making. These leaders naturally assume that they know what to do and how to go about it.

This style is frequently associated with military leadership and athletic coaching. Authoritative leaders may check with others and gather information, but when it is time to make a decision, this style of leader does so by themselves. Authoritative leadership is particularly effective when there are time constraints or when subordinates are not trained to participate or do not have the necessary information to participate in the decision-making. One significant disadvantage to authoritative leadership is that it may fail to benefit from expertise by others.

© Rawpixel/Shutterstock, Inc.

Participative leadership, also known as democratic leadership, is a style that employs group input and sometimes group decision-making. In this style, a leader asks for input and debate. Decisions are made by a group or at least with substantial input from a group of knowledgeable people. Participative leadership is able to draw on the expertise of the group and frequently leads to not only better answers and decisions but also better buy-in by the employees. Participative leadership tends to be a better style when there is plenty of time and the answer is complex and needs to be made with careful consideration. Participative leadership, however, is much more time-consuming and can sometimes get off the track if strong but uninformed opinions lead the group astray.

© Rawpixel/Shutterstock, Inc.

Delegated leadership, also known as Laissez-Faire or free-rein leadership, is a style that moves the decision-making and leadership down the levels of management. This style is sometimes viewed as nonparticipating because the upper management is not participating in the decision-making. However, this style is very effective in an organization that is geographically spread out, communication is difficult, or people at all levels are well trained and able to make clear decisions. Delegated leadership is less effective if people making the decisions are not aware of all the factors that impact issue, but much more so if there are local issues of which the senior leadership is not aware. **For example:** Delegated leadership is often necessary for the branch offices of some multinational companies, allowing marketing decisions to be handled by local people who better understand the culture.

In one sense, authoritative leaders say, "I will decide"; participative leaders say, "We will decide"; and delegated managers say, "You will decide."

Another way to look at leadership styles is to consider transactional versus transformational leadership. **Transactional leadership** is said to be more mission-oriented. The transactional leader recognizes the task at hand and the skills of the people involved. This type of leader attempts to get the job done primarily by using the risk versus reward system. This leadership style focuses on the job and expects people to accomplish the job because they are supposed to and are paid to. Although not ignoring people's needs, they are secondary to the mission.

Transformational Leadership is more focused on the people and their motives and desires. This style of leadership tries to inspire people to go beyond

Participative leadership also known as democratic leadership is a style that employs group input and sometimes group decision making.

Delegated leadership also known as Laissez Faire or free-rein leadership, is a style that moves the decision making and leadership down the levels of management.

Transactional leadership is said to be more mission oriented, focusing on the job at hand with personal considerations secondary.

Transformational leadership is more focused on the people and their motives and desires.

just the job, but to be accountable for getting the job done with less need for supervision. Transformational leaders look beyond the immediate mission and to the bigger picture, trying to create a workforce that in a sense has less need for a leader. The transformational leader is more focused on the people and what they can do, than on the individual project.

Situational or Fluid Leadership, also sometimes known as adaptive leadership, is a style of leadership that depends on the situation at the time. Although most leaders adopt a style that best suits their personality, training, or environment, some are able to adjust their leadership style as the situation changes.

PLANNING

Planning is a necessary part of leadership. Guiding the organization toward the accomplishment of goals requires knowing the goals and the steps to get there. Planning can be categorized by the breadth and scope of the effort. Some planning is fairly short term and narrow in scope and some is very long range and encompasses the entire organization. Planning is generally divided into Operational, Tactical, Strategic, and Contingency plans.

"What if, and I know this sounds kooky, we communicated with the employees."

Operational Planning is usually short term and narrow in scope and designed to support and implement the tactical plan. Operational planning may be what needs to get done today, or this week, or this month. Operational planning may also be done entirely within a department or business section, without impacting the rest of the organization.

In doing operational planning, the leader must decide what specific objectives must be met and in which order and then what steps must be taken to reach the established targets. Finally, the leader must decide who will carry out those steps and the necessary resources to assign to the task. Operational planning might involve establishing daily or weekly sales goals and further breaking those down to individual sales goals.

Operational planning
planning that is usually short term and narrow in scope.

Tactical planning
mid-range planning done to cover the 3- to 6-month period that supports the strategic plan and is supported by the operational plan.

Tactical Planning is longer term and broader in scope than operational planning. Some tactical planning may take place at any level of an organization, but tends to be done more so at the departmental level and above by mid-level and senior managers. The focus is on the mid-term, for instance, three to six months out, and done to support the strategic plans. Tactical planning may include such things as bringing a new product online or opening a new sales region. Tactical planning may be looked at as a series of steps taken to move the organization to the strategic goals.

© Dusit/Shutterstock, Inc.

Strategic Planning is the longest term plan and biggest scope. It is normally done at the executive level of the organization, but may include input from mid-level managers. The strategic plans are developed directly from the overall goals of the organization and typically look out from 1 to 5 years, but may look out as far as 20 years into the future. Executives decide where the organization wants or needs to be in the future and then develops the strategic plan to get them there.

Contingency Planning, sometimes known as "what-if" planning, is done to anticipate disruptive problems before they happen. An organization may be ill-prepared to deal with emergencies if they have done no planning ahead of time. For instance, how would a manufacturing company deal with a strike by the employees of one of their suppliers or a natural disaster that destroyed an assembly plant? In 2011, Toyota manufacturing was shut down by first an earthquake, followed by a tsunami, which flooded much of the coastal part of the country, including the Fukushima Power plant, and then causing a nuclear disaster that is still not completely resolved four years later. This caused production interruptions in 5 European plants and 14 U.S. plants as well as throughout Japan. Although this kind of disruption is impossible to predict, Toyota does contingency planning that provided them with an initial set of responses and communications to minimize the problem and speed up the recovery.

Strategic planning the longest range and largest scope planning that looks out several years and is supported by the tactical plans. A disciplined process of decision making that sets in motion action plans and resource allocation to achieve company goals and objectives.

Contingency planning what planning is done to anticipate problems and the actions to take when they occur.

© Augusto Cabral/Shutterstock, Inc.

© meanep/Shutterstock, Inc.

© iQoncept/Shutterstock, Inc.

Some would say to plan for the best and prepare for the worst. Contingency planning is the way of preparing for the worst. Rather than predicting natural disasters, it sets out actions to take in the case of different kinds of disruptions. These steps are then adapted to the issue with which contingencies occur.

PERFORMANCE MANAGEMENT

Improving the employee performance and company results is the goal of **performance management**. This is done by using a variety of leadership tools, which include proper compensation, effective communications, timely training, empowerment, group dynamics, and effective performance appraisal.

Management Tools

Performance management
Improving employee performance and company results.

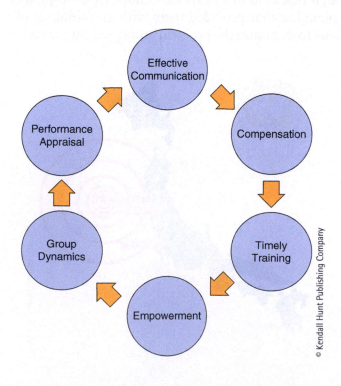

© Kendall Hunt Publishing Company

Effective Communication is a vital element in any organization. Communication takes place constantly; effective communication moves the right message through the right channels at the right speed to help the organization move forward.

To be successful, business managers and leaders need effective written and oral communication skills. This requires public speaking abilities and business writing skills. Being able to understand the message, the medium through which it is transmitted, and the audience is an important leadership skill.

Compensation is pay for work, although pay can take several forms and can be based on several different formulas. Usually, compensation is normally in the form of money, that is, a salary or wage. A wage is typically an amount paid by the hour, and in most cases, there is a minimum wage and overtime or one and a half of the normal wage for hours worked beyond 40 hr per week. A salary is normally a fixed amount paid for pay period such as per week, month, or year. Commission is pay for performance and is usually based on something like a percentage of sales. Many in the Jewelry business earn a combination of wage and commission like $12.50 per hour and 2.5% of gross sales. Some jobs, notably durable products sales, like auto sales, may be commission only. There is also piece work, which is also performance-based and includes agricultural pickers who might earn a fixed amount per bushel of crops. Many independent contractors work on a set fee or contract payment, which is a lump sum paid at the end of a particular job or task.

Other forms of compensation include benefits such as healthcare insurance, retirement benefits, uniforms, vacation, child care, and many other noncash types of pay. For many businesses, labor costs are among the largest business costs they face. Each company should have appropriate compensation, high enough to attract talented employees, but not too high to make them uncompetitive.

Timely Training is necessary to ensure that employees have the tools and skills to perform and compete in a rapidly changing competitive environment. As the tools of business change, the work force needs to keep up. Training must keep up as well. One technique is called Just-in-Time Training, which brings the training to the work place just as the employees need to start using new procedures or equipment. There can be "on-the-job" training, where

Effective communication moves the right message through the right channels at the right speed.

Compensation   pay for work.

Timely training   is necessary to ensure employees have the tools and skills to perform and compete in a rapidly changing competitive environment.

Empower
/em-pow-er/

def: Give someone the authority or power to do something. Most often used in a work or legal environment

employees learn as they work directly on equipment during their workday, or "off-the-job" training, where employees learn in a classroom or simulation before doing actual work.

Empowerment puts responsibility and authority in the hands of workers so they can use their own judgment to accomplish assigned tasks. A leader is often too busy with their duties to closely supervise all of the workers. Many workers are completely capable of operating on their own if given the chance to do so. Authority and responsibility rest with leadership as a function of positional power. That is, the authority comes with the position of leadership. To move this authority down to lower level management or to the worker level involves a deliberate and often formal decision to do so. Delegating is another word for this, giving the worker the authority to make decisions. Empowerment goes beyond delegation in allowing to decide for themselves what needs to be done and how to do it.

Empowerment allows workers to make decisions on their own, but also implies they know what to do and how to do it. One effective technique is for management to establish SMART goals. **SMART** goals are goals that are Specific, Measurable, Attainable, Relevant, and Time-Bound.

Goals are specific when they are clear to both the person establishing the goals and the person who must accomplishment it. Goals are measurable when there is some easily understood level that must be achieved. This could be numbers of sales, or time to finish a process, or a level of customer comments. Attainable goals are those that can be realistically achieved, given the necessary resources. When goals are attainable, but require significant effort, they are sometimes known as stretch goals. If they are not attainable, there is little motivation to try. Relevant goals apply directly to the goals of a company and are important. For example, a goal that establishes how many customers must be called during each shift might be as relevant as how many sales are made. A goal is time-bound when there is a time period during which, or by which, the goal must be accomplished.

Teamwork has always been important in business, but if anything it has become more significant in the highly competitive environment in which firms operate today. Having people in the same location or department does not make them a team. A team is a group of people who work together with a common purpose or goal. Teams may be permanently established. These standing teams may meet regularly for years and membership may change as people come and go from the organization. Ad Hoc teams are frequently formed to address a particular problem and will dissolve when that is done. Cross-functional teams are made up with members from different functional departments, bringing different skills and perspectives to an issue that effects the whole organization. In every case, the intent is to bring greater expertise and experience than one person would have and to use that combined effort to make better decisions.

Performance Appraisal is the action of evaluating the effectiveness with which employees meet stated goals and objectives. Performance appraisals may be used for promotion, pay raises, retention decisions, or

Empowerment responsibility and authority in the hands of workers so they can use their own judgment to accomplish assigned tasks.

SMART goals that are Specific, Measurable, Attainable, Relevant, and Time-bound.

© Keith Bell/Shutterstock, Inc.

Teamwork working together to achieve a common purpose of goal.

Performance appraisal evaluating the effectiveness with which employees meet stated goals and objectives.

© Rawpixel/Shutterstock, Inc.

© vinnstock/Shutterstock, Inc.

simply to regularly meet and discuss how the workers are doing. When done properly, they are an effective management and motivational tool. When done improperly, they are a source of conflict and a disincentive. Appraisals must be done regularly and be based on written criteria, which allow a person to understand the standards to which they are compared. If properly done, a performance appraisal should never come as a surprise to the employee. Evaluations are typically done each year, although more often frequently done for new employees. Appraisals can be entirely subjective with a written description of accomplishments or entirely objective with ratings or numerical scores. Many appraisals use a combination of scores and written comments. Documentation is very important though, so that you, as the manager, can show how and why you reached your conclusions in case there is an employee dispute at some point in the future.

"I'm a little concerned, Randolph. Six of our top competitors have written to thank us for hiring you."

© Cartoonresource/Shutterstock, Inc.

OPEN FOR BUSINESS IN THE REAL WORLD

Are leaders born or made? The jury is still out on that question. There is no doubt that some people have natural leadership abilities but even a natural leader may employ the wrong style depending on the situation. On the other hand, people can learn and develop leadership abilities even if they have no natural tendencies for it. Whether learned or natural, leadership abilities must be applied appropriately, to be effective.

Often, the best style is a function of who is being led more so than who is doing the leading. A college faculty is a group of highly educated people with considerable work experience, self-initiative, and good understanding of the mission. An authoritarian leader would probably not work well in that setting. A leader that believes in making the decision themselves and not checking with people would meet resistance when leading people that do not need to be told what to do or how to do it.

On the other hand, a delegated leadership style would not work well in an environment in which people are not used to making their own decisions or do not have the experience or knowledge to do so.

Different cultures, genders, or age groups may also need different leadership styles to be effective. The best leaders understand that it is the needs of those being led, the situation, or time constraints, not his or her own needs, that dictate the best style for any given situation. Effective leaders can adapt their style on the fly.

Chapter Summary

Leadership is getting the job done through others. Peter Drucker said "Management is doing things right; Leadership is doing the right thing."

Elements of leadership include:

1. Making sense of a complex environment
2. Learning from failure
3. Understanding people including one's self
4. Transparency
5. Focusing on the mission
6. Talking the talk and walking the walk.

Executives have different styles of leadership depending on their personality, the people being led, or the situation. These styles include the Authoritative style in which the leader makes the decisions alone; the Participative style in which the leader makes decisions in consultation with other people, the Delegated style in which the leaders lets others make the decisions themselves, and the Situational style in which the leader adapts his or her style to match what is best at the time. Another way to look at leadership styles is Transactional versus Transformational leadership. Transactional is strictly mission-oriented, whereas transformational is more concerned with people and their motives.

Operational planning is short term and with limited scope that is done to plan out on a day-to-day or week-to-week basis. This planning is done at the department level and must support the tactical plan. Tactical planning is done by mid-management and is longer term and broader in scope and is done to plan out for several months. Tactical plans must always support the strategic plan. Strategic planning is done at senior executive level and is long range and broad in scope to plan the future of the organization. Contingency planning is to plan how to react to unforeseen circumstances.

Performance management is done to improve employee performance and organizational results. Leadership tools involved in performance management include:

1. Effective communication
2. Compensation
3. Timely training
4. Empowerment
5. Teamwork
6. Performance appraisal.

Review Questions

1. How would you define leadership?
2. How would you distinguish leadership from management?
3. What is Operational planning, and which level of an organizational does it?
4. Which is the mid-level type of planning that is done at the department level?
5. Discuss strategic planning and who conducts it.
6. How is Authoritative leadership different from participative leadership?
7. Why might Situational leadership be considered the best style?
8. How can Contingency planning predict the unpredictable?
9. What are some of the forms of compensation?
10. How is empowerment a management tool?

11. Why is teamwork so important in business today?
12. What is meant by Walk the Walk?

Discussion Questions

13. Compare the characteristics of some well-known leaders.
14. How is strategic planning different than tactical planning?
15. Which style of leadership would be most appropriate in an organization of attorneys and which style more appropriate in a manufacturing plant? Why?
16. Discuss how compensation decision can influence performance management.
17. Discuss how SMART goals might improvement performance.

Key Terms

- authoritative style
- Contingency Planning
- Delegated leadership
- Effective Communication
- Empowerment
- leadership and management
- Operational Planning
- Participative leadership
- Performance Appraisal

- Performance Management
- SMART
- Strategic Planning
- Tactical Planning
- Teamwork
- Timely Training
- Transactional leadership
- Transformational Leadership

Works Cited

Kruse, K. (2015). Retrieved February 3, 2015, from http://www.forbes.com/sites/kevinkruse/2012/10/16/quotes-on-leadership/

(2011, April 13). Japan economy, Toyota feel effects of disaster. Retrieved February 9, 2015, from http://www.spacemart.com/reports/Japan_economy_Toyota_feel_effects_of_disaster_999.html

Leadership. (2015). Retrieved February 3, 2015, from https://www.psychologytoday.com/basics/leadership

Nick Saban. (2015). Retrieved January 27, 2015, from http://www.rolltide.com/sports/m-footbl/mtt/saban_nick00.html

Human Resource Management

LEARNING OBJECTIVES

1. Explain the Human Resource Management Functions
2. Explain how recruitment and selection put the right person, with the right skills, in the right job
3. Detail the functions of the Human Resource Management department of an organization
4. Identify potential advantages by considering diversity or sustainability in recruitment

© Rafal Olechowski/Shutterstock, Inc.

OPENING STORY

Igloo, the manufacturer of coolers, announced in October of 2013 that they were bringing jobs back from China and opening a huge production, warehouse, and distribution center in Katy, Texas, a suburb of Houston. The announcement said this facility will employ 280 new workers by the end of 2013 and 1100 once production and operations are at full strength. How could they possibly know how many people will work at this facility years in the future? Human Resource (HR) Managers had already been involved in forecasting the employee needs and will continue through the opening and operation of the company for years to come. Human Resource forecasting involves studying the market, the area in which the facility will be built, evaluating the regulatory environment, looking at transportation availability, studying the demographics to determine skill sets, income levels, and available workers, and studying the competition to determine probable success. All of this is done before the first shovel of dirt is turned.

INTRODUCTION

We tend to think of organizations as though they are entities, but any organization is a group of people there for some common purpose. The success or failure of a business is often tied directly to the people that work there. From the president of the company to the line employees, staffing the company with the best possible people is vital to the future of the organization. Organizations must have many resources to be successful. The company will need capital assets such as equipment, buildings, and raw materials. The firm will need financial assets as well. During the operation, the company will need to manage these assets along with the work flow, decision-making, marketing, contracts, dealing with competition and customers, the legal and regulatory environment, and many other business aspects. The human resources will do this work, but also represents another vital business asset to manage.

HUMAN RESOURCE FUNCTIONS

The size of a business will often dictate the size and complexity of its organizational structure. However, even small businesses must do all the things involved in running a business. In some very small companies, the owner is the president, the middle manager, the Human Resource director, the budget officer, and one of the workers. In large firms, there will probably be a separate HR department that itself may have a large number of people. Human Resources may be a permanent part of the organizational structure or it can be outsourced. Staffing companies like G. B. Tech, in League City, Texas, specialize in performing some of the **Human Resource functions**, especially recruiting and selection, for other organizations that would rather contract that out than do it themselves. In the case of G. B. Tech, they had the contract with NASA to recruit and hire the aerospace engineers that worked on the International Space Station.

Many companies proudly boast that their employees are their best or most important asset. In fact, many large companies use employees in their advertisements. Southwest Airlines has been doing this for years. HEB, a Texas grocery store chain, uses the company president discussing products and services with the workers, in many of their television ads.

If the employees come to work satisfied with their jobs, feeling like the work is important, believing that the company appreciates their efforts, properly trained, motivated, and compensated, then the company will probably be successful. After all, it is the employees, not management, that produce the products or offer the services that consumers touch.

Human resource functions
Forecasting, recruiting, selection, training and developing, retain and motivate, appraise, and corrective action.

© Dusit/Shutterstock, Inc.

Figure 6.1   Human Resource Functions.

Regardless of whether a company conducts the human resource functions with their own HR department, a single person, or an outsourced company, it will be up to HR, to recruit or attract, select and hire, train and motivate, retain, compensate, appraise and evaluate, take corrective action and separation, and running through all of this is the constant function of forecasting needs both before an organization is created and throughout its operation (Figure 6.1).

HUMAN RESOURCE FORECASTING

The purpose of HR, just like the purpose of the rest of the company's departments, is to accomplish the organizational goals. Careful study of the firm's strategy and goals will allow HR to forecast the needs, that is, how many people with what skills, hired in what order, placed in which positions, at what pay rate, are needed to allow the company to compete in the marketplace. This forecasting function must be done when a company opens or expands, but is also an ongoing function to make sure the evolving marketplace does not surprise the organization and put them into a noncompetitive situation.

Forecasting is not done in a vacuum, but instead is a function performed in close coordination with the leaders in different departments working together with senior management to endure the size and make-up of the workforce, contributing directly to the organization's strategic goals. Failing to keep Human Resources in the planning loop can prove disastrous for a company that can wind up with a staff that does not meet its needs. Forecasting includes reviewing the budget, future sales or operational projections, strategic operational forecasts, market and industry trends, and senior leadership directives. Trying to determine future HR needs also involves studying the past decisions to see how they worked out. Determining the future direction of the firm also involves evaluating the current workforce to see if the right skills are already present or if not what additional training and development are necessary.

Forecasting includes the people, but also includes the human resource budget. How will the total compensation for the people affect the company's budget? What is the **salary** or wage range necessary to attract and keep the best people? How is the location of the company unit likely to affect how much pay is necessary since the local cost of living has a great to deal to do with how much compensation it takes?

In addition to internal review, HR forecasting also requires an outward view to look at things like the customer base, the potential employee base, and the legal/regulatory environment in which the company operates. The local unemployment rate has an impact as well. A very low unemployment rate will make it very difficult to find employees or it may drive up wages to get people to leave their current position.

Forecasting is frequently done in determining what the company needs in the way of expansion, that is, what additional human resources are needed and with what skills. Almost as often, however, forecasting is done to plan drawdowns or reductions in force. This is sometimes referred to as downsizing or rightsizing. Reducing the size of the company workforce must be carefully done to avoid too much loss of productivity. Great care must be taken to avoid losing important talent—not only with the people that are laid off, but also in creating an environment of uncertainty that might lead others to leave the company.

Salary   A set pay, typically annually or perhaps monthly for a particular job, with little association with the number of hours worked.

RECRUITMENT

© Santiago Cornejo/Shutterstock, Inc.

Recruitment is the process of locating a body of potential employees, reviewing their qualifications, and selecting and hiring the best possible candidate for the job. Sometimes the recruitment process is as simple as hanging a sign in the window that says, now hiring or help wanted. Sometimes it is as complicated as conducting a worldwide job search through professional channels to find a highly skilled applicant. Some jobs require little or no prior knowledge and all necessary training can be done once the person is hired, and some jobs require a highly trained and skilled person that is ready to step in and begin immediately.

What skill sets are needed for what positions? Before a person can be hired, the recruiter needs to understand what the job is and what the organization expects from the successful candidate. A **Job Specification** and a **Job Description** should be prepared by the department. The Job Specification shows the critical and preferred skills necessary to succeed and therefore necessary for the search for candidates. The Job Description describes the key duties of the role the new hire will perform. Both of these documents form the basis for a job posting that alerts potential job seekers that a position is available, what type of skills the company is seeking, and what the job entails.

Companies do still hang signs in the windows. They also put up billboards, post notices in the jobs sections of local and sometimes national newspapers. Companies recruit through employment agencies, attend job fairs, work with college placement offices, connect with and search through Internet sites like Monster.com, and more and more companies recruit through their own website. Most company websites will have a section called working with us, openings, or employment opportunities, or maybe it will just be part of the human resources link. A very common way of recruiting is simply to ask the existing

Job specifications   shows the critical and preferred skills necessary to succeed and therefore necessary for the search for candidates.

Job description   describes the key duties of the role the new hire will perform.

employees to talk to people they know and try to get the best to apply. **For example**: West Telemarketing, in Omaha, has been known to offer a $100 bonus or a television to employees that bring in a friend.

Locating the right person for the right job is not always an easy task. Even when unemployment is high or the position is very desirable, and there are lots of applicants, finding the right fit can be difficult. What do companies want? They want the level of education that demonstrates basic knowledge and skills as well as the ability to learn new skills as the job evolves. They want the right type and level of experience that demonstrates the applicant's ability to perform on the job. Just as importantly, they want the right attitude, personality, or values, which indicate whether the person will be successful in the atmosphere or culture present in any organization. Organizations take on a sort of personality, known as **Organizational Culture**, which establishes the way things work in that company. Even two similar organizations in the same area and industry may have very different environments. One may be loud and hectic, whereas another might be quiet and paced. One may be formal and have reserved dress code, while another might be informal and casual. Fitting in is important for both the employee and the company.

Organizational culture   a sort of personality that establishes the way things work in that company.

There is considerable debate about whether to recruit internally or externally; in other words, do you promote from within or look outside the company? Each has its advantages and disadvantages. Promoting from within opens up opportunities to reward the best employees as well as give the motivational opportunity for advancement within the company. Promoting from within allows the company to have a much better understanding of the true ability of the person being promoted. The person is much more likely to be productive right from the beginning and obviously, it is much less expensive. However, promoting from within just takes the vacancy and pushes it down the organizational chart. A new person is still needed, although, usually the lower on the chart, the less expensive it is to locate applicants. Internal recruiting also limits new ideas since the person can be influenced by the way things have always been done. Sometimes, internal recruiting can breed resentment from the person's old peers that were overlooked for the new position.

External recruiting has the distinct advantage of opening up the search to the whole world potentially; therefore, many more qualified candidates may be considered. Bringing in people from the outside can introduce new ideas and get experience from the industry that may not be available internally. However, it is much more expensive and time-consuming and there is the inherent risk of making a poor choice among the candidates. Many companies now post openings both internally and externally to try to find the best candidate regardless of the source.

Recruitment and Selection follow a standard process of steps that leads to a new employee. These steps do not, however, have to always take place in the same order. For instance, sometimes checking references or fact checking resumes may take place after secondary interviews and even sometimes after a person is hired (Figure 6.2).

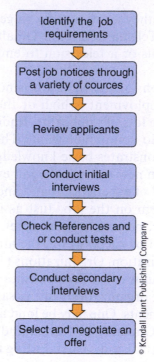

Identify the job requirements

⬇

Post job notices through a variety of cources

⬇

Review applicants

⬇

Conduct initial interviews

⬇

Check References and or conduct tests

⬇

Conduct secondary interviews

⬇

Select and negotiate an offer

© Kendall Hunt Publishing Company

Figure 6.2   Selection Process.

Key Considerations

Diversity   Most companies now realize that serving a diverse customer base is best done with a diverse staff. Diversity in the workplace is creating a staff

© wavebreakmedia/Shutterstock, Inc.

that has representatives from many groups of people. Diversity exists in race, gender, culture, age, national origin, and many other groupings. The population of the United States has a vast number of different cultures, each with a different set of values and mores. The more diverse a firm's staff, the more they are able to related to these different groups.

Although diversity is almost universally seen as a benefit, there are also obstacles to a diverse workplace. People from different cultures or different ages can have significantly different view on what is proper. Dealing with religious beliefs or languages can present challenges to organizations. In spite of these challenges, businesses have benefited from a more diverse group of employees.

Labor Unions   Labor laws have sought to even the power between companies and their workers to prevent the abuse by either side toward the other. Unions were created to allow workers to act as a group in negotiating things like compensation, workplace safety, hours, benefits, and worker rights. Unions are organized labor groups that work to protect the rights of workers. Workers began organizing in the late nineteenth century. The American Federation of Labor (AFL) was formed in 1886 and the Industrial Workers of the World in 1905. The actual legislation that recognized unions came much later. The National Labor Relations Act of 1935, also known as the **Wagner Act**, is the national legislation

Wagner Act   the national legislations that for the first time, officially recognized the right of workers to organize a union and use it to bargain collectively.

that, for the first time, officially recognized the right of workers to organize a union and use it to bargain collectively. This law was further amended by the National Labor Relations Act of 1947, also known as the **Taft-Hartley Act**.

Unions can negotiate on behalf of the workers, and once an agreement is made, the contract is binding for both workers and the company. If negotiations break down, the union can call a strike or management can enforce a lockout. A **strike**, a work stoppage or walkout, is a tool used by unions to force their point home to management by trying to stop the organization from conducting business. On the other hand, a **lockout**, baring the employees from working, is a similar tool used to deny employees the right to work and therefore get paid, used by management.

As you can see in Figure 6.3, union membership has been declining over the years. This is generally thought to be because many workplace laws passed in the last half century have address for all workers what the unions used to negotiate only for members. Actually, the decline in union membership in the private sector is greater than the chart indicates. The decline there has been partially offset by an increase in public sector unions representing city and state employees.

© Nic Neufeld/Shutterstock, Inc.

Sustainability   Going Green or sustainability have become both buzz words and key considerations for companies. National interest in reducing pollution, minimizing carbon emissions, and recycling or limiting resource consumption has caused businesses to consider the impact they are having on the environment. This has an impact on recruiting because experience and interest in sustainable methods are becoming more important for companies. Firms that can forecast the need and recruit the workforce that is prepared to go Green can gain a competitive advantage or keep up with growing trends in an ever-evolving marketplace.

Taft–Hartley Act   Further amended the Wagner Act.

Strike   a work stoppage or walkout by the employees.

Lockout   baring the employees from working is a similar tool, used to deny employees the right to work.

Year	Annual
2002	13.3
2003	12.9
2004	12.5
2005	12.5
2006	12.0
2007	12.1
2008	12.4
2009	12.3
2010	11.9
2011	11.8
2012	11.3

Figure 6.3   Union membership as a percentage of employed workers.
Source: http://data.bls.gov/pdq/SurveyOutputServlet, accessed 10/31/13

Not only do sustainability considerations help keep the company with current national interests, it also may position them to take advantage of government contracts or tax credits or deductions that also give them advantages.

SELECTION

It is the Human Resources Department job to recruit applicants through a variety of sources and, in some cases, to conduct initial screening of those applicants. However, it is usually the operational manager or hiring manager that does the final selection. In essence, the person to whom the new worker will report generally makes the final hiring decision. Human Resources, however, must validate the process. Every company must adhere to state and federal employment laws as well as internal policies. Following is a partial list of applicable federal statutes that govern hiring practices

- Title VII of the Civil Rights Act of 1964, as amended, prohibits discrimination based on Race, Color, Religion, Sex, or National Origin. Some states have added Ethnic Groups and Sexual Orientation to the list.
- The Americans with Disabilities Act prohibits discrimination against disabled applicants.
- The Equal Employment Opportunities Commission (EEOC), Established by the Civil Rights Act, is the enforcement organization that investigates complaints of employment violations.
- State and local laws may further restrict hiring practices.

Companies are free to hire the man or woman who they consider the best possible applicant. However, in doing so, the firm may not establish hiring practices or trends that violate compliance with Equal Employment or Discrimination laws.

© Brian A Jackson/Shutterstock, Inc.

Companies may use a standard paper or online employment application form, or they may prefer applicants submit a resume or in the case of academic organization a curriculum vitae (CV). Some organizations use both an application form and a resume or CV. Some organizations will have HR and hiring managers scan those applicants, while other organizations will use automated scanners that search for certain facts or key words and flag the resume for further review. It is commonplace for organizations to spend very little time during an initial resume review, often less than a minute per applicant.

Once the applicant pool is narrowed down to a small number, perhaps four to eight people are selected for an interview. These lucky few are then scheduled to interview for the position. Normally, interviews are done in a face-to-face meeting although they may occasionally be done over phone or through technological methods like FaceTime or Skype. Although many interviews are done with a single decision-maker, some are also done in small groups. A recent trend is to use working interviews, in which the person is actually placed on the job for a predetermined period of time before a final decision is made. Candidates

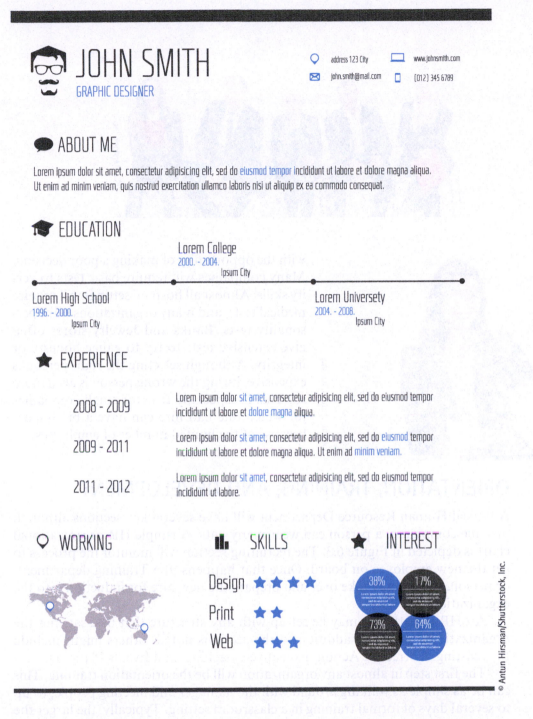

should carefully, for an interview, do research on the company and the position. Learn the interviewer's name and how to pronounce it, dress appropriately, and practice looking directly at people, shaking hands, and answering predictable questions.

Recruiting and selecting employees can be time-consuming and expensive. Searches can take weeks or months, often while a position sits vacant. The workload of the vacant position may need to be shouldered by others or it may not get done at all. Advertising, in some case transporting applicants, training, perhaps medical examinations, all can be very expensive. The entire process is fraught

with the opportunity of making a poor decision. Many companies will require basic tests to verify skills. Almost all hospital settings will require medical tests, and many organizations want personality tests. Banks and Jewelry stores often give extensive tests to try to gauge honesty or integrity. Although selecting the right person is expensive, hiring the wrong person is even more so. This is especially true for small companies for which one bad hire can have a big impact because of the limited number of employees.

ORIENTATION, TRAINING, AND DEVELOPMENT

A typical Human Resource Department will have several key sections although in some companies, a person can wear many hats. A simple HR organizational chart is depicted in Figure 6.3. The recruiting section will monitor the process to get the new employee on board. Once that happens, the Training department, or person, will usually take over and prepare the new hire for induction into the organization.

An HR department may be set up with any structure that best satisfies the organizational goals. In addition to the sections noted, others might include Forecasting, Corrective Action, Executive Coaching, and Events Planning.

The first step in almost any organization will be the orientation training. This can be as simple as walking around with the manager and meeting people, to up to several days of formal training in a classroom setting. Typically, the larger the

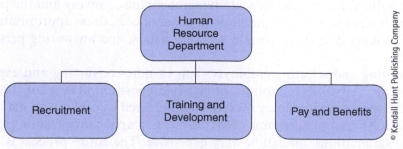

Figure 6.3 Typical simple Human Resource Department Structure.

organization, the more complex the orientation. A well-done orientation can set the stage for successful employment. Especially, organizations with a lot of compliance regulations will wish to provide extensive and detailed training for all new staff. Companies that have 401k/403b or other retirement plans will want to explain them. Sexual Harassment training is required in most companies as well as any number of local laws or corporate policies. Companies with large staffs that hire regularly will often have their own classrooms and regularly schedule new hire orientation classes.

Most companies will not stop their training at orientation. Depending on the complexity of the job itself, training may continue for a long time, in some cases even throughout a person's employment. A lot of this training may occur in the workplace itself. On-the-Job Training (OJT) is frequently done in the actually work setting and often by a manager or coworkers. It may be informal, or it may be very formal including recording and verifying skill check and perhaps rechecks over time.

Many large organizations will include in their training department an emphasis on management or staff development. Although training and development may seem like the same thing, training typically focuses on either compliance training, like sexual harassment training, or specific workplace skill sets required on the job, such as computer skills as a new computer or software system is installed. By contrast, development frequently deals with management skills that are required by newly promoted managers or to constantly improve the management skills of even senior managers.

In the American workplace, it is fairly common for people to move from new hire, to skilled technician, to manager, without having the benefit of a formal education in the new skills necessary to manage others. A variety of contractors, consultants, and internal training and development departments have developed courses and guidance to address the need to provide that new skill set. A skilled and experience nurse might get promoted to nurse supervisor and find herself dealing with a whole new set of problems without having any formal education on how to do so. In many management positions, the person in fact may rarely use the skills they worked so hard to develop, but now find themselves supervising others who do.

A fairly new focus on training for senior management is professional or **executive coaching**. This is management training, but is typically done in an individual or one-on-one style that requires frequent, or even fairly constant, meetings to discuss issues, responses, lessons learned, and introduction of new management techniques. Executive coaching is conducted with senior executives where there is a belief that fine-tuned management skills are necessary, the executive is already skilled enough in the typical management training focus, and the resources are sufficient to devote a one-on-one approach.

Executive coaching conducted with senior executives where there is a belief that fine-tuned management skills are necessary.

Another area of training and development focus is on **Succession Planning**. This is the process of identifying people who have demonstrated value to the company and the potential for promotion to higher levels. These people are then singled out for careful skill assessments and the development of detailed individual training and development plans to ensure their preparation for future promotion to senior levels.

Succession planning The process of identifying people who have demonstrated value to the company and the potential for promotion to higher levels.

Retention and Motivation

As noted earlier, companies spend a lot of time and money to attract the right employees; therefore, low turnover is important. Every lost employee means lost productivity and increased cost to find and train a replacement. Retaining and motivating employees is a vital function of Human Resources, working in conjunction with operational departments.

Compensation   Employees must be paid for their work and that pay is an important part of retention. Workers must feel their pay is appropriate. Some companies will pay a premium, that is, pay at the top of the industry scale. Employees at such a company earn more than their contemporaries at competing companies. However, this means a higher labor cost for the firm and the people hired must be able to perform well enough to justify that higher pay. Other companies will try to offer lower than industry standard pay to hold down their labor costs. Although the lower cost can be an advantage, these companies will have trouble attracting a well-qualified staff and may suffer lower productivity because of it. In fact, companies offering lower than industry standard compensation also lose their best people to better paying companies, thus, in essence, training their competition. Many companies carefully study the industry and local area pay levels and carefully locate themselves in the middle to avoid the problems associated with higher or lower pay.

Compensation can take on many forms. **Salaries** are using a set pay, typically annually or perhaps monthly for a particular job, with little association with the number of hours worked. **Wages** are compensation based on an hourly pay. Someone earning a wage will earn more by working more hours and less by working fewer hours. Most wage earning jobs also pay extra, typically 1.5 times the wage, if the employee works more than 40 hr in a week. Some jobs pay a commission instead of any set amount of pay. A **commission** is based on a percentage of sales. For instance, car sales people may receive 25% of net profit on any car they sell. Some jobs like jewelry sales may combine a wage and small commission. This pays them for their time, but also rewards them for being more productive. **Piece work** pay is compensation based on production. This is common in construction in which a sheetrock installer will be paid by the sheetrock pieces that are hung, in agriculture where a picker is paid by the bushel, and in sports officiating, in which a baseball umpire is paid by the game. Outside of regular compensation, some people earn **bonuses**, which are special pay for special circumstances. This might be based on the overall success of the company or a person's department or for achieving certain personal production goals.

Wages Compensation based on an hourly pay.

Commission pay based on a percentage of sales.

Piece work compensation based on production.

Bonuses special pay for certain circumstances.

© zimmytws/Shutterstock, Inc.

Benefits Other types of compensation can be nonmonetary. Workers have come to expect some benefits and they can take many forms. They include paid time off in the form of vacation or sick pay, uniforms, discounts on company products, tuition reimbursement, retirement plans, and health care. Historically, benefits developed as a noncash form of labor costs to give companies a competitive advantage in attracting the best employees. Sometimes there are limits on the wages available, so noncash compensation can be used to make the position more attractive. Over the years, some benefits have become required by law. These include Workmen's Compensation contributions by the company, Unemployment taxes charged by states, and health-care coverage. All of these depend on the size of the company and the employment status of the individual worker. Some companies institute what are referred to as cafeteria plans. This allots a set amount of money for each employee's benefits and lets the worker select from a menu of benefits. For instance, some companies might offer on-site child care, but that would not motivate a childless worker, so they can use their benefit dollars to best suit their individual needs.

Benefits can have a positive financial impact on both the employees and the company. Since they are nonmonetary, they are not taxed. If a company gives an employee benefits worth $10,000 instead of $10,000 in cash, the employee gets the same financial reward, but saves the taxes that would be paid on that income. The company also saves the matching payroll taxes they would pay on the income as well.

Flexible Scheduling Many companies have experimented with giving employees the option of working different schedules or in different locations. Where possible technologically and where close supervision is not necessary, flexible schedules are very attractive and motivational. The increasing ability of mobile computing has allowed more Telecommuting, that is, working from out of state or even out of country, wherever one can get on line. Some companies even offer to pay to set up a home office for workers. This saves office space in the company building for different uses. Other companies allow great flexibility in letting the worker come in to the office some days, but, for instance, if child care issues cropped up, the worker could stay at home and do their work from their home office. **For example:** Medical Coders take doctors notes and bills and code them into systems to match medical insurance requirements. Many such companies offer the option for the coder to work at home or come into the company and use a workstation there.

Flexible scheduling can take on many forms. **Flextime** is a system of required hours with flexible hours around them. **For example:** A company may require everyone to work from 9 until 3, but allow the worker to complete their 8-hr work day by coming in earlier, working later, or some of both. Job Sharing allows two equally qualified people to share a job. Married couple sometimes do this to also share child-rearing duties. Adjusting hours: if a job requires 40 hr a week but there is no particular number of days, a company may allow a worker to work their schedule to whatever suits them. **For example:** Many colleges allow professors to select the classes they wish to teach and then build their work week around those classes in any way they wish.

Flextime a system of required hours with flexible hours around them.

Employee Stock Option Plans (ESOP) these plans give employees of the company the opportunity to buy stock in the company, often at a discount.

Another benefit many publically traded corporations offer is **Employee Stock Option Plans (ESOP)**. These plans give employees of the company the opportunity to buy stock in the company, often at a discount. **For example:** Kay Jewelers establishes a stock price at 75% of the market price on a chosen day and allows employees to set aside a portion of their pay for two years and then use that money to buy stock at the original agreed upon price and with no stock broker fee. If the stock price has gone up, the employee can enjoy considerable savings. If it has gone down, the employee can simply get their money back.

© Kzenon/Shutterstock, Inc.

© Jerry Sliwowski/Shutterstock, Inc.

Retirement Plans   Organizations may offer a variety of retirement plans for their staff. These may include defined benefits plans, which are more traditional pension plans, or defined contribution plans such as 401k or 403b plans. Defined benefit plans typically define a set pension as a percentage of annual earnings, based on the number of years of service. **For example:** A teacher my earn 75% of the average of their highest 3 years of salary, after reaching 60 and having 30 years of teaching. Defined contribution plans allow an employee to contribute pretax income into a retirement plan of their choosing, based on what the company offers. These plans also frequently have matching contributions from the company. **For example**: Sterling Jewelers, the parent company of both Kay Jewelers and

Jared Jewelers, will match 50% of employee's contributions up to 3%. So, an employee contributing 6% of their salary to the 401.k plan will have the company match 3% as well.

Other Motivational Techniques   Companies may employee a wide variety of other techniques to maintain morale or motivate the staff. These might include annual picnics or holiday parties, lavish retirement events or award ceremonies, special department recognition, employee of the month awards, or decorating contests. The more the company can establish the sense that they genuinely appreciate and value their staff, the more retention and morale they will get.

Appraise

Performance appraisals or evaluations are a means to formally evaluate how well employees are performing their job. This is done to give feedback both to the employee and to the company. They can be used in deciding about promotions or new assignments as well as decision about additional training or corrective action. Performance appraisals are often seen in a negative light by workers, but if used properly, can be motivational and rewarding.

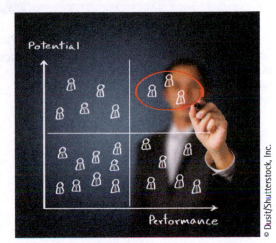

© Dusit/Shutterstock, Inc.

Many organizations establish a formal performance appraisal system that calls for periodic evaluations, typically done annually, but sometimes more often for new employees. Companies can use a structured form that includes ratings with numbers or phrases, by checking a block, or they may use a less structured form that requires a narrative written by a supervisor. Some companies also give the employee some input in evaluating their boss. One technique used in management levels in many firms is a 360° evaluation in which managers are evaluated by their boss, their subordinates, and their peers.

© adirekjob/Shutterstock, Inc.

Many companies have difficulty with performance evaluations. Since they can be viewed as career damaging, there is a tendency to inflate the appraisals so that everyone seems like the perfect employee. This is especially true if promotions are competitive and the appraisals are a substantial percentage of the decision. Getting a true picture of a person's ability and potential is a valuable tool for the company. Therefore, companies should work hard to remove fear from the process. They can do this by using the appraisal as a session intended to evaluate past successes and to set goals and develop plans for the future. Having objective measures is also helpful. For instance, telling someone the quality of their work is poor is not nearly as helpful as saying their work standard expectation is 75% sales and their performance is 65%. By using objective and measurable standards, the worker is given a much clearer idea of where they stand and how they can improve. This also removes perceptions of favoritism from the process.

Corrective Action and Separation

Although companies apply a lot or resources to find the best fit for their organization, things do not always work out. Individuals may need to be released from the company because they are not performing to standards. Sometimes people need to

© Alexander Raths/Shutterstock, Inc.

Corrective action   a series of actions taken to improve substandard performance.

© AirOne/Shutterstock, Inc.

© R. Gino Santa Maria/Shutterstock, Inc.

be fired for illegal or unethical actions. Sometimes a larger force of people may need to be laid off because of declining business or a poor economy.

In addition to releasing people from the company, sometimes an organization needs to take corrective action to retrain or remotivate an employee whose actions or performance is substandard, but not to the extent the company wants to fire them. In those instances, a formal program of corrective action may be warranted.

Corrective action is a general term for a series of actions taken to improve substandard performance regardless of what kind. To avoid lawsuits or complaints of discrimination, it is in the interest of the company to establish a formal process of identifying substandard performance and a written and fairly applied process of addressing it.

Businesses may use terms like admonishment, counseling, or reprimand to describe the actions. Most of the time, the specific substandard performance should be spelled out, although there can be a catch-all phrase such as actions that are unbecoming or not in accordance with accepted practice. When corrective action is taken, Human Resources generally gets involved to ensure that all regulations and policies are carefully followed. Identified individuals are notified of the action, the reason for the action, and the steps that will be taken. **For example**: Someone that has shown up late for work three times in the last month might receive a letter of admonishment and be told that any further incidents of tardiness in the next six months will result in an unpaid week of suspension. Continued tardiness after that would result in separation from the company.

Layoffs can occur for a variety of reasons. **A layoff** is generally a large-scale termination of employees for causes other than their individual performance. If a major contract expires, the industry declines, or the economy is in recession, a company may no longer have the business to support the number of employees it currently has. Sometimes additional regulations or costs drive up the cost of doing business and the company may have to operate with fewer employees. For example: The Affordable Care Act increased costs substantially in the medical industry, forcing a number of health-care organizations to lay off employees.

OPEN FOR BUSINESS IN THE REAL WORLD

One of the most important, but least appreciated, departments in Human Resources is the Training and Development department. It seems that almost every organization recognizes the need for up-to-date training, but training is often the first function to go when the business declines and the budget gets tight. There is also a perception, as noted earlier in this chapter, that sometimes you are spending money on training your competition. If a company spends $5,000 on training someone, they may rightly feel that person owes them some loyalty for the company investing in them. The person, however, may rightly feel since they are now worth more, the company should give them a raise or promotion, to acknowledge their greater skills. If a company feels they cannot afford the raise because they already spent money on the person, they may, in fact, drive them to their competition.

© Zurijeta/Shutterstock, Inc.

Training is specific job skill related, and although it may be done at all levels, especially for regulatory training like sexual harassment training, it is generally more focused on lower level employees who can benefit from specific skill enhancements. **Development** is broader, overall skills that help make a person more valuable in general. A person learning the latest level of Microsoft Word, because their job requires it, is receiving training. A manager taking a class on better communications techniques, because any job in management requires it, is receiving development.

Both training and development are vital for success in many companies. Changing technologies and evolving markets require organizations to change as well or face becoming obsolete. It is often difficult to determine the **Return on Investment (ROI)** for the training and development dollar, but it is easy to see the impact of failing to make that investment.

Training   specific job skill related to education.

Development   broader, overall skills that help make a person more valuable in general.

Return on Investment (ROI)   the profit that is ultimately received from creating a new product.

Chapter Summary

Human Resources is responsible for recruiting or attracting, hiring, training and motivating, retaining, compensating, appraising and evaluating, taking corrective action and separating, and running through all of this is the constant function of forecasting needs. Each of these functions has its challenges.

Review Questions

1. What are the primary functions of a company Human Resource Department?
2. What are the purposes of Human Resource Forecasting?
3. What are the advantages and disadvantages of internal and external recruiting? Which is more expensive?
4. What are some key laws with which Human Resources must comply?
5. How would you distinguish between training and development?
6. Describe several different types of pay or compensation.

7. How do benefits provide a financial reward for both employees and companies?
8. Describe some of the motivational techniques companies use to help with employee retention? Why is retention so important?
9. What is the purpose of Performance Appraisal?
10. What are some of the difficulties companies have with Performance Appraisal?
11. What are some of the important considerations when a company downsizes?
12. How do employee benefits help attract and retain the best employees?

Discussion Questions

13. If you were setting up a business with 75 employees, would you prefer to pay them a salary, a wage, piece work, or commission? Does the type of work you are going to do make a difference? Does their total compensation make a difference? Does everyone in the organization need to have the same pay type?
14. If the company budget grew tight because of declining business and there was discussion of eliminating the training department to save money, what argument would you make to keep it?
15. What arguments would you make to the CEO to include Human Resources on a planning committee doing strategic planning for the next 10 years of operations?

Key Terms

- Benefits
- bonuses
- commission
- Compensation
- Corrective action
- Development
- Diversity
- Employee Stock Option Plans (ESOP)
- executive coaching
- Flextime
- Human Resource functions
- Job Description
- Job Specification
- Labor Unions
- layoff
- lockout
- Organizational Culture
- Piece work
- Retirement Plans
- Return on Investment (ROI)
- salary
- strike
- Succession Planning
- Sustainability
- Taft-Hartley Act
- Training
- Wages
- Wagner Act

CHAPTER

7

Organizational Structure

LEANING OBJECTIVES

1. Explain the different types of organizational structure.
2. Detail the purpose of the organizational chart.
3. Differentiate between line and staff authority.
4. Explain business situations, which cause a business to consider reorganizing.

© alexmillos/Shutterstock, Inc.

OPENING STORY

Transocean is a deepwater gas and oil drilling company that is headquartered in Geneva, Switzerland, which builds its rigs in Singapore and operates worldwide. They build and then lease the rigs to companies that have located energy in sites up to two plus miles below the surface of the ocean and then down miles from there. The company is famous, or infamous, for owning and operating the rig that blew up in the Gulf of Mexico on April 20, 2010. Transocean was launched in 1919 in Louisiana and began offshore drilling in 1954. With all their experience, one of the things they do most is reorganizing.

The stress of the oil rig explosion, which killed 11 employees and put them at risk for lawsuits, plus a change in strategy to concentrate on deepwater drilling and give up shallow water rigs, has caused the company to rethink how they are structured. Organizations must have some form of structure, but there are many different forms and no one form is necessarily the best. Even within a given form of structure, responsibilities and working relationships can and do change often as leaders change and as external relationships change.

Although no one has specifically mentioned organizational structure as part of the issue that led to the disaster, they have mentioned communication, which is part of organizational structure. British Petroleum owns the oil well and contracted with Transocean to lease and operate the drilling and pumping apparatus. Halliburton, another energy company, built and installed the Blowout Preventer that failed and caused the explosion. The organizational structure did not take into account the interorganizational communications necessary for three companies to work closely together.

As Transocean has encountered a constantly changing business environment, they have altered their structure to try to find one that fits best in any situation. They have not found it and continue to reorganize frequently.

INTRODUCTION

Every organization of any type must take some form. That form, or organizational structure, creates a framework that supports the organization. It is not unlike the human skeleton supports the human frame or body. The organizational structure helps us understand the flow of work, the movement of communications, and the hierarchy of authority within the business. There are a number of different ways to organize a company and no single method is necessarily correct or superior to another. The structure must meet the needs of the business and facilitate the process in which the firm engages.

This chapter discusses several approaches to organizational structure and the advantages and disadvantages to each.

ORGANIZATIONAL STRUCTURE

Chain of command the flow of authority within the organizations.

Organizational structure determines the **chain of command** and authority, the flow of information, the working relationships, and the division of effort. Organizational structure gives a framework to the organization in the same way the skeleton gives a framework to a person. Not only does the structure give the members of the company information about how they operate, but it also lets people outside the organization understand the working relationships. Organizational structure is one of many components that define how a business operates and whether or not they will be successful. The structure defines how the work moves and gives some insight into what work is done.

Organizations can adopt a very formal structure that remains the same over years, or they can take on a more fluid structure, which changes as the business environment changes. Some businesses have clearly defined lines of

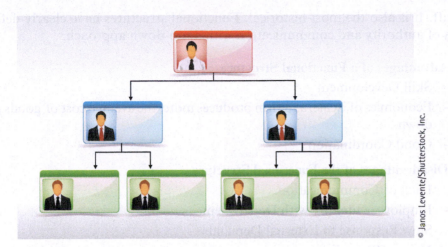

© Janos Levente/Shutterstock, Inc.

communication and authority in which everyone understands exactly where they fall in the company hierarchy and other businesses may have a loose structure that sometimes leaves in doubt who works for whom.

© auremar/Shutterstock, Inc.

The only real purpose of organization structure is to facilitate accomplishing organizational goals by defining how the organization operates. There are considerable differences in how organizations set up their structure to achieve those goals. In some cases, the way structure is set up is simply defined by what the members are used to. In other cases, there is considerable study by the company to see what will work best. Once established, the organization may change the structure if needed.

Types of Organizational Structure

A common form of organizing is to use a **functional structure**, which is one that is set up, so people doing the same type of job are in divisions working together. For example: a company using a functional structure would have the marketing people working together, the sales people working together, accounting, human resources, product development, shipping and receiving, training and development, and many other groupings of people with similar skills working together. This type of structure is the most common structure and is somewhat of a naturally logical way to set up

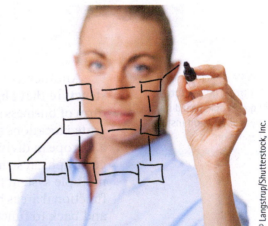

© Langstrup/Shutterstock, Inc.

Functional structure is one that is set up so people doing the same type of job are in divisions working together.

a staff. It is also the most historical. Functional structures have clearly defined lines of authority and communication with a top-down approach.

Advantages of a Functional Structure
- Skill Development
- Economies of Scale; as a firm produces more, the average cost of goods goes down.
- Good Coordination

Disadvantages of the Functional Structure
- Lack of Communication
- Employees Identify with Department
- Slow Response to External Demands
- Narrow Specialists
- Groupthink

Geographic structure aligns people based on physical location instead of function.

Another company in the same line of work might set up a **geographic structure** that aligns people based on physical location instead of function. This form of business structure is common in large organizations that have widely separated locations around the country or around the world. For example: Ford has a European division to handle sales of their cars in that region of the world. The geographical structure can be combined with the functional structure to create a multiple system that first breaks the company into regional areas and then into functional areas below that. Sometimes it can go from functional to geographical and back to functional. A national company might have overall accounting and finance, pay and compensation, and legal, but then break down into East coast, Midwest, West coast, and then into sales, marketing, human resources, and so on. One common problem with a geographical structure is that many functions may be duplicated, thus increasing the number of people and therefore the labor cost of a company. Although this may be most effective, the extra cost is one thing that is a definite concern for any company.

Regional Corporate Hierarchy & International Support Systems

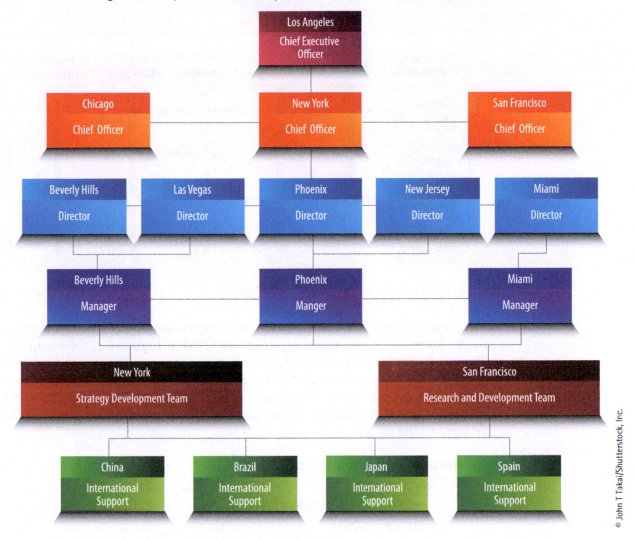

© John T Takai/Shutterstock, Inc.

Advantages of a Geographic Structure:
- Management Close to Customers
- Cultural Differences (North vs. South)
- Time Zone Differences
- Salaries/Commissions Can Be Altered due to Cost of Living or Competition.
- More Opportunity for Advancement

Disadvantages of a Geographic Structure:
- Difficulties in Maintaining Company Standards across Regions
- Communication Challenges with Management
- Greater expense

Some organizations use what is known as a **matrix structure**, which has more of a grid-like pattern and lines of authority leading from and to different directions. In a matrix structure, a person may have more than one boss, depending on the issue. **For example:** At Metropolitan Community College in Nebraska, a business faculty member would go to the business academic dean to resolve an

Matrix structure   has more of a grid-like pattern and lines of authority leading from and to different directions.

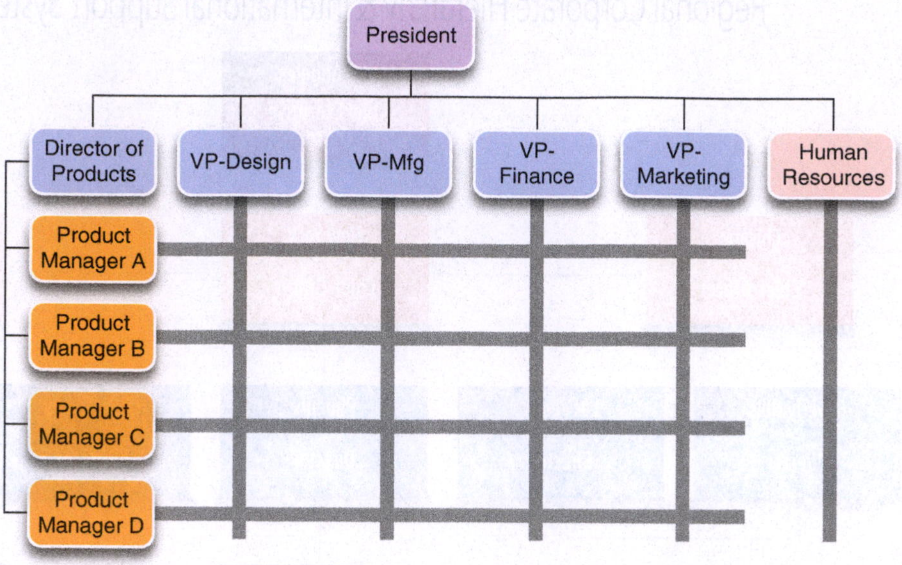

Figure 7.1   Matrix organizational structure.

© Kendall Hunt Publishing Company.

issue regarding academic work, but to the campus dean to resolve an issue related to the location. In the matrix structure depicted in Figure 7.1, the members of Project B would work for the Project B manager for all issues related to the project, but still work for their functional manager for other issues. **For example:** A person who is a finance specialist would still work in finance and under the vice president of finance, but would report to the project manager for anything relating to the project.

Advantages of a Matrix Structure:
- Flexibility
- Cooperation and Teamwork
- Creativity
- More Efficient Use of Resources

Disadvantages of a Matrix Structure:
- Costly/Complex
- Confusion in Loyalty
- Requires Good Interpersonal Skills and Cooperation
- Not Permanent

Some organizations do not like to have a fixed structure at all. Organizations that have fluid types of businesses that operate on contracts to support various projects may constantly change where and for whom people work. These organizations may adopt a **teamwork structure** that creates teams with multidisciplinary members that work together, for a team leader for the length of a project or contract. This is sometimes referred to as a **Cross-Functional Team**, where members from different departments come together for a period of time. After the work is done, the members would return to a previous position or move on to the next team. These fluid organizations may never establish a formal organizational chart since it would be constantly changing. Or, they may have a chart that depicts only the top echelons of the organizations and leave the lower, constantly changing, levels out. One might think of a fluid structure as one that is

Teamwork structure creates teams with multi-disciplinary members that work together.

Cross-functional team where members from different departments come together for a period of time.

constantly suffering organizational change. The attitude in these organizations, however, is not one of constant reorganization, but one of shifting job responsibilities. A person is assigned to a team for the length of the project to which they are assigned and then the individual gets assigned to another team. Sometimes these organizations have an underlying structure, sort of a shadow structure to which people return between team assignments.

Advantages of the Cross-Functional Team Structure:
- Flexibility
- Facilitates Interdepartmental Cooperation, Teamwork, and Buy-In.
- Institutional Knowledge Is Enhanced.
- Efficient Use of Internal and External Resources

Disadvantages of the Cross-Functional Team Structure:
- Confusion in Loyalty
- Potential Pushback on Who Pays Costs
- Potential for Group Think

A final type of organizational structure is a virtual structure. The **virtual structure** uses technology to link people, who may not be physically together, in a work group. The virtual structure may not be drawn any differently in the organizational chart than any of the others, but recognizes that people do not have to be in the same room, building, or even country to work together if technologies allow. The use of email, Internet, Intranets, and teleconferencing technologies allows members of a department to easily communicate and develop working relationships in a virtual structure that might not have been possible until these technologies were developed.

Virtual structures can be used in many ways. This is especially important for new entrepreneurs that may need expertise from many sources. A business can have a functioning core staff and use a virtual staff of many experts in various fields to assist. A small company can have outside, virtual attorneys, CPAs, staffing specialist, pay specialists, and even CFOs or CEOs to help out with the business either on a permanent basis or until the business is established.

> **Virtual structure** usses technology to link people, who may not be physically together in a work group.

Organizational Chart

The visual representation of the organizational structure is the **organizational chart**, which depicts the levels of management, the lines of communication, line and staff authority, and the division of effort. **Line authority** is operational or functional authority: that is, authority that is directly in line with the operation or function of the organization. Someone that has line authority makes decisions and directs the efforts of others in conduct of the business at hand. The sales manager, for instance, has line authority over the sales people in his or her division. **Staff authority,** on the other hand, is advisory authority. For instance, a company attorney may give guidance or advice on the legality of actions planned by the company. It is important to note that people in staff positions are not without authority. A corporate lawyer may not have anyone in the organization that directly works for them, but they still have considerable influence over company actions. Staff functions are normally established for individuals with professional expertise who might be considered subject matter experts. Even within staff functions, there may be line authority such as in the case of the attorney,

> **Organizational chart** depicts the levels of management, the lines of communication, line and staff authority, and the division of effort.

> **Line authority** is operational or functional authority; that is, authority that is directly in line with the operation or function of the organization.

> **Staff authority** advisory authority.

there may be a legal assistant, over which the lawyer has line authority. Staff functions are normally depicted off to the side of the primary chart with a line the level of the organization they represent. The lines drawn to a staff function may also be a dashed line instead of a solid line.

Organizational charts will usually appear as a traditional hierarchy type structure with the president or CEO at the top and the various levels of management below that. Sometimes, a company will reverse the appearance of the chart and put the bosses at the bottom. This is a symbolic way of showing that management is there to serve the workers and help them accomplish the work. In others, the chart may be drawn sideways. None of these different appearances are intended to disguise who is the boss and who is the worker, but more to demonstrate that no one is more important than anyone else in the firm.

Note in Figure 7.2, the lines of authority or command run from the CEO down to various staff functions below. Boxes depicted at the same level are normally at the same level of management and authority and generally and

Corporate Hierarchy Structure

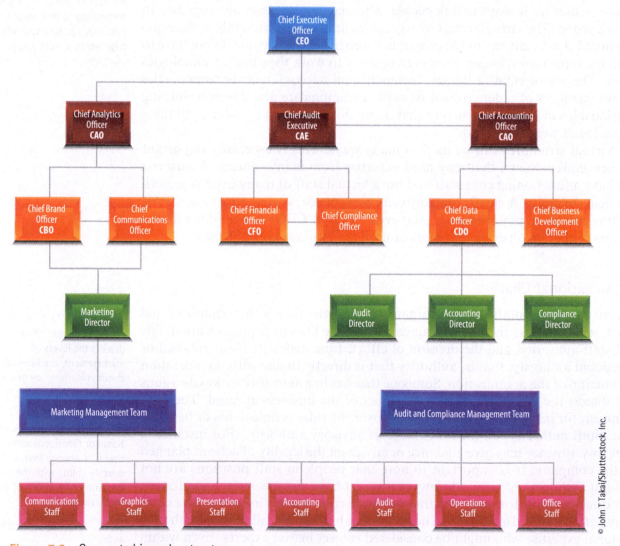

Figure 7.2   Corporate hierarchy structure.

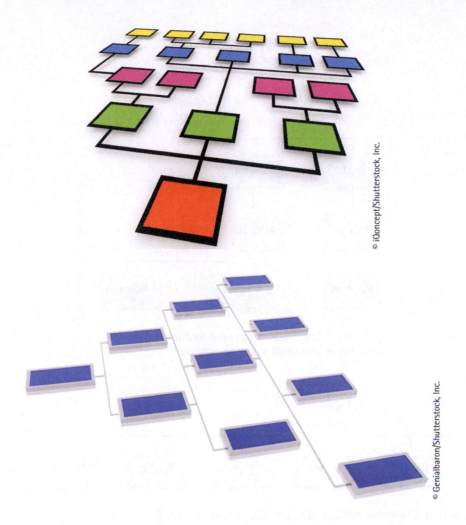

© iQoncept/Shutterstock, Inc.

© Genialbaron/Shutterstock, Inc.

approximately the same level of compensation. Each level of the chart depicts a level of management, so the more the levels of management in the organizations, the more the levels of boxes in the organizational chart.

Organizations with many levels of management are sometimes referred to as **tall organizations** based on the appearance of the organizational chart. This tall type of organization has relative small spans of control or authority. The **span of control** refers to how many people work for a particular manager. With small spans of control, the company needs more managers, who then need managers, and this builds in layers of management. Other organizations may use wide spans of control with managers having more people working for them. This uses fewer levels of management and results in a **flat organization** and a relatively short and wide organizational chart. There is considerable disagreement about the optimum number of people a supervisor can control. Some would say from 8 to 12 is about right. Others would say, that creates too much control and stifles creativity and individualism. A tall organization may have the owner and top management far removed from individual workers, whereas a flat organization may have an owner or managers with direct contact to the workers or with few levels between them. **For example:** Midwest Umpires, a sports officiating organization in Nebraska, had a single owner directly supervising 157 sports officials. Figure 7.3 depicts a tall organization, and Figure 7.4 depicts a flat organization.

Advantages of a tall organization include: more control by the Top Management, more chances for advancement, greater specialization, and closer

Tall organization   many layers of management and small spans of control.

Span of control   how many people work for a particular manager.

Flat organization   a relatively short and wide organizational chart.

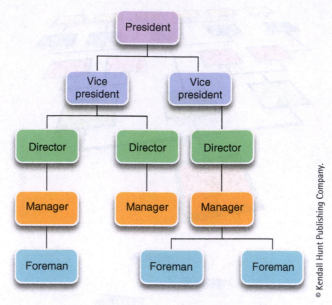

Figure 7.3   Tall organization with multiple layers of management and small spans of control.

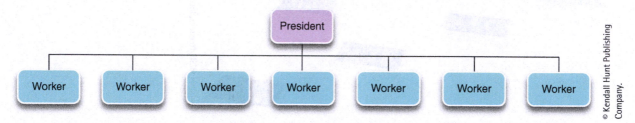

Figure 7.4   Flat organization with few layers of management and wide spans of control.

supervision. Disadvantages include: less empowerment, higher costs, delayed decision-making, and less responsiveness to customers.

Although workers are depicted in Figure 7.4, it is customary for the organizational chart to show offices and depict the head of that office, such as vice president, director, manager, supervisor, and not depict the individual worker anywhere on the chart.

Advantages to a flat organization include: reduced costs, more responsiveness to customers, faster decision-making, and more empowerment. Disadvantages include fewer chances for advancement, overworked managers, loss of control, and less management expertise.

Drivers of Organizational Structure and Change

Organizations come in many forms, but all have a common purpose: that is, to satisfy their goals. It is the desire to satisfy the goals that drive the establishment of an organizational structure and also to drive changes to that structure when either the satisfaction of goals is in doubt or new goals are created.

Things that would cause an organization to consider changing structure include the following shown in Figure 7.5.

New Competition That Has Surfaced   Companies tend to begin their structures based on what they think will work while looking internally. That is, they

New Competion	Business Failure	New Laws or Regulations
Business Expansion	New Leadership	Technological Change

© Kendall Hunt Publishing Company.

Figure 7.5   Business situations that cause a company to reorganize.

set up the company without much regard to the outside. Companies start with a boss, have middle management, have workers, and generally have at least fairly defined lines of communication and authority. They say to themselves, "I think it will work this way." Competition brings new considerations. Other companies enter the marketplace and are either successful or not. Even if they are not, they may cause a company to look at themselves again and consider if they are structured appropriately. If the competition is successful, this is especially so. Competitors will probably be structured differently if for no other reason than different people created them. This will cause companies to wonder if they are set up to operate in a more competitive environment.

© MicroWorks/Shutterstock, Inc.

Business Failure or Contraction   Business failure does not have to mean the company has gone bankrupt. The marketplace is constantly evolving and companies must evolve with them or problems will quickly develop. If a firm begins to see declining sales, they must quickly recognize a trend from an anomaly, determine a cause, and take steps to address and correct the problem. Often, this leads to organizational restructuring as they try to better confront the marketplace and competition. Are the right people, in the right positions, working through the right channels to get the job done? Unfortunately, business declines often lead to layoffs, which also necessitate reorganization

© Christophe BOISSON/Shutterstock, Inc.

as layers of management are consolidated or eliminated. Should Organizational Training and Development be a separate department or come under Human Resources. Although much training is actually operations related, the function is normally led by at most someone at director level and typically comes under Human Resources for leadership. This can and often does change and, in some cases, changes several times.

Changes in the Economy or the Legal Regulatory Environment
Changes in the environment in which a company operates can force them to reorganize as well. A declining economy can cause restructuring even in a well-run company. Even if they are strong competitively, sales may falter because consumers have fewer

© Stuart Miles/Shutterstock, Inc.

resources available. A declining economy may not necessarily be bad for business. Some companies, usually discount sales, can thrive in a down economy. Even more traditional companies may see competitors fail. For Example: Kay Jewelers did very well during the recession of 2007 through 2009. The industry as a whole suffered dramatically lowered sales and several companies went out of business. This left Kay Jewelers with a larger piece of a smaller pie.

In addition to economic changes, the legal regulatory environment evolves as well. Such changes as the Affordable Care Act, state and local licensing, zoning restrictions, redevelopment efforts, and a myriad of other changes in the environment may change how they operate and therefore the structure they use.

Business Expansion   Although business contraction is a stress for any company, so is business expansion. As the company expands, new layers of management are added and the lines of communication may change as well as the responsibilities (Figure 7.6). Tasks previously under one vice president may shift to another as the first department has to take on more tasks and must also give up some. The lines of communication and authority may all change within the firm.

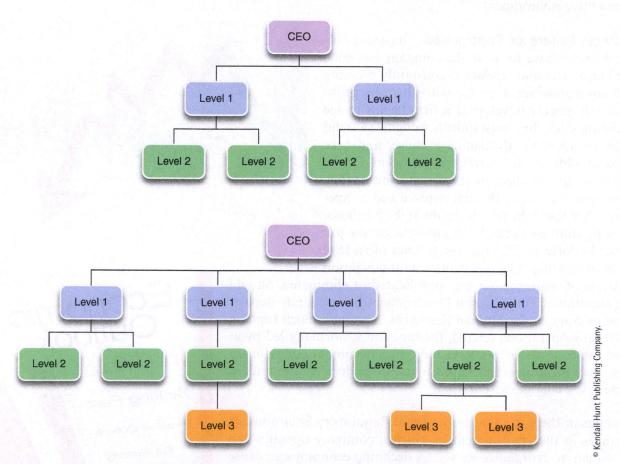

Figure 7.6   Organizational structure with expansion, adding layers of management and changing responsibilities.

New Leadership   The simple fact is, new leaders may want to do things differently. Whether bringing in leaders from outside the organization, or promoting from within, people will frequently want to operate things differently than their predecessor. Senior leaders coming in from the outside will frequently bring ideas gleamed from throughout the industry, or they may have original ideas and want to try them out. Certainly, if leadership changes were caused by declining sales or business failure, a structural change may be looked at as necessary.

Related to new leadership is internal conflict, also known as turf battles. Leaders at all levels of management sometimes look at the size of their responsibility as a reflection of their importance to the company. Sizing another department, thus expanding one's turf or organizational reach, is seen as increasing one's value and perhaps influencing future promotions.

Technological Change   Changing technologies change how we work, what we do, and, sometimes, where we work. Companies have dreamed of a paperless operation since the introduction of computers to businesses beginning in the 1970s. Only in the last couple of years, however, has this begun to take hold as tablets and smartphones and the acceptance of electronic signatures have become commonplace. The Internet has also given growth to Intranets, which allow rapid data sharing across a business regardless of where people are. Data storage has replaced file cabinets. Another significant change allowed by technology is the idea of virtual offices or telecommuting. People can do much of their work from a distance. Many colleges now offer online classes, and some colleges offer nothing else. The majority of graduate programs now occur online, and the trend will continue into the future as technologies we cannot even imagine now will change how work and education are conducted in the future.

OPEN FOR BUSINESS IN THE REAL WORLD

Rapidly changing technologies, especially communications and robotics, have already begun to change the nature and structure of organizations, and the pace of that change will continue to increase. Customers can order merchandise for pickup or delivery. Some grocery stores now allow a customer to place an order and pick it up at a drive-through location. People order pizza via the Internet. Voice recognition software has eliminated the need for telephone receptionists; in Colorado, many fast food restaurants use a common drive-up order center that relays the order to the applicable restaurant. Call centers can be located anywhere, including other countries. Furniture delivery drivers carry a tablet instead of forms for customers to sign.

These rapidly changing technologies will influence how organizations are structured in the future. As the environment in which they operate changes, businesses must also change. Less permanent and more fluid structures are becoming more common. The business world and the customers are changing and the company needs to change with it. Does a business ever have to see its customers? Does the manager even have to see the employees? Can payment collection be made by every company representative on the spot instead of sending out bills?

Someone starting a business needs to ask themselves these questions and many more about how they will organize to best meet their organizational goals.

Review Questions

1. Which is the most traditional form of organizational structure?
2. What does the organizational structure do for a firm?
3. How might combining different forms of organizational structure cause an increase in a company's expenses?
4. How have recent technological advances changed how some companies structure their organization?
5. Why might it be said that a person working in a company with a matrix organization has more than one boss?
6. What information can a person learn by studying the organizational chart?
7. What is the difference between a tall organization and a flat organization? How will the organizational chart reflect this difference?
8. Why does having a change of leadership often cause a company to reorganize?
9. Why would both business contraction and business expansion cause a company to consider reorganization?
10. What is meant by reorganization caused by changes in the legal/regulatory environment in which a business operates?
11. What are some of the benefits and consequences of reorganizing?
12. Why does a business really need to organize; can't the boss just tell everyone what to do?

Discussion Questions

13. If you were starting a business, what type of organizational structure would you choose? Does the answer change depending on the type of business? What about the size of the business?
14. What type of structure would you use for a business that will have several children's clothing stores located in a large city? Would it be different if it was just a single store?
15. How might changing technologies lead to a complete organizational change?

Key Terms

- chain of command
- Cross-Functional Team
- flat organization
- functional structure
- geographic structure
- Line authority
- matrix structure
- organizational chart
- span of control
- Staff authority
- tall organizations
- teamwork structure
- virtual structure

CHAPTER

8

Economics

LEARNING OBJECTIVES

1. Explain basic economic theory and economic systems.
2. Discuss supply and demand and how they impact business.
3. Detail different competitive environments in the marketplace.
4. Discuss reasons for government involvement in the economy.
5. Explain government goals and tools for managing growth and inflation.

OPENING STORY: THE FED

The U.S. Federal Reserve embarked on a program of buying bonds in 2009 in an effort to help the struggling U.S. economy weather a significant downturn in economic activity. The scope of the government's plan was controversial, especially given the capitalist free markets that are at the heart of the U.S. economic system. The Fed bought bonds (referred to by the moniker "Quantitative Easing" or QE) as a means of putting money into the economy, hoping that it would be spent and thus spur economic activity. The official end of the program was October 2014, after the announcement of a gradual slow down in buying in 2013. From 2009 until October 2014, more than "$3.5 trillion (was added) to the Fed's balance sheet—an amount roughly equal to the size of the German economy."

© Dgrilla/Shutterstock, Inc.

As we explore in this chapter, too much money can cause inflation, yet the government was more concerned with trying to generate growth and increase jobs. "Whether the Fed tapered too soon, given global economic weakness, or too late, given signs of bubbles in some markets, was hotly debated. But even after the taper's end the Fed has continued to pump support into the economy the old-fashioned way, by holding its interest rates near zero." We won't know if there are inflation effects on the horizon for some time yet.

(Source: http://www.bloombergview.com/quicktake/federal-reserve-quantitative-easing-tape)

INTRODUCTION

You hear on the news that interest rates are going up and consumer confidence is going down, but what does it all mean? How will this impact you, your management decisions, your business? To make sense of the business and economic news around you, it's important that you have an understanding of basic economics. But economics can be scary because you've heard that it involves lots of graphs. Well, this chapter gives you lots of information with just two simple graphs—and in the first section, we start with the most basic economics graph of all that only has one line to it!

BASIC ECONOMIC THEORY

Economics the study of the allocation of resources.

Tradeoff having more of one thing and less of another (e.g., working more means less time for leisure).

Opportunity cost the lost chance of not having something because you decided to choose or do something else, such as deciding between using resources for different activities.

Economics is the study of the allocation of resources. Some texts will call these resources "scarce," but it is probably more accurate to say "finite." We care about those resources that are plentiful as well because there is still *always* a limit as to how much we can produce or consume. This is because we must make a **tradeoff** between having more of one thing and less of another. For example, we can look at a tradeoff of work and leisure. If someone chooses to work more, then he or she will have less time for leisure. We can thus say that there is a "cost" to working more, and that is the **opportunity cost** of not having as much leisure time. In traditional economics textbooks, this concept is introduced to students as the tradeoff when countries must decide between using resources for "guns and butter."

© CookKengzz/Shutterstock, Inc.

Production Possibilities Curve

To better understand these tradeoffs, economists will draw a very simple graph called the **production possibilities curve** representing the maximum output that can be generated from all of the inputs available. We can see this "maximum output" as the red line in the following figure. Ignoring the political ramifications for the moment, the figure shows us that if a country uses more of its resources on the military (represented by "Guns" on the left vertical axis), then it will have fewer resources to allocate for food (represented by "Butter" on the bottom horizontal axis), and vice versa—spending more on food will leave less available for the military. Changing the level of one causes a change in the other since the total output possible is limited by the red line showing total output that can be produced. This curve will work for any two goods or services or activities where a tradeoff is involved and the opportunity cost must be considered.

Economic Systems

In our example, it sounds like "the country" is deciding where to allocate the resources. If that is literally the case, then that would be a **communist economic system** where the government owns the resources and decides how to allocate them, with a central authority making all production decisions for the entire economy. This economic system was most famously advocated by Karl Marx, whose Marxist ideology saw communism as a way to make everyone equal in society. Some extreme examples where you can see the communist economic system in place today are Cuba and North Korea where the government owns the means of production and decides what will be produced and in what quantities.

At the other end of the spectrum is the **capitalist economic system** where private people own and control the resources and other means of production, making individual decisions about what to make and how much to produce. The first advocate of this classical theory economic system was Adam Smith, who said that the government should be "hands off" (referred to as "*laissez-faire*") and instead let the "invisible hand" of the marketplace work. The **"invisible hand"** refers to constant adjustments of quantity and price balancing supply and demand as hoards of individual people and companies act in their own self-interest as they compete in the marketplace. This leads to economic prosperity as the greatest number of people have their needs and wants met. This system is followed to varying degrees in the United States, Germany, and Japan.

In between these two economic systems is the **socialist economic system** where the government controls the resources and means of production. In one variation, the government actually owns those large industries that it deems important (such as military manufacturing) while directing smaller enterprises owned by individuals (such as the corner bakery). In this way, the government can ensure that it has the means to sustain itself, while still moving toward its stated goals (one of which is income equality) by taxing away any excess profits of the smaller businesses that become successful beyond what the government deems necessary or acceptable. Several northern European economies have strong socialist elements, such as Norway where the government has a major stake or outright ownership in companies that provide transportation, communications, and natural resources.

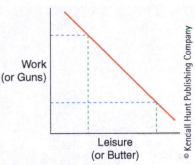

Simple Production Possibilities Curve

© Kendall Hunt Publishing Company

Production possibilities curve economics graph representing the maximum output that can be generated from all of the inputs available.

Communist economic system when the government owns the resources and decides how to allocate them, with a central authority making all production decisions for the entire economy.

Capitalist economic system when private people own and control the resources and other means of production, making individual decisions about what to make and how much to produce.

Invisible hand the constant, automatic adjustments of quantity and price balancing supply and demand as hoards of individual people and companies act in their own self-interest as they compete in the marketplace.

Socialist economic system when the government controls the resources and means of production (taxing away excess business profits, and sometimes owning the larger or important businesses).

Factors of Production

When we talk about "allocating resources" and "controlling the means of production," we are referring to the **factors of production,** which are all of the inputs necessary to make a good or provide a service. There are four basic categories used: land, labor, capital, and knowledge/entrepreneurship. Let's think about which of these might be most important to have a thriving economic system. Land (which also includes natural resources) is necessary for making goods as well as having facilities to manufacture and store products, but if that were the most important factor of production, then we would expect Russia to have the largest economy in the world. Labor is certainly important, but we don't see India at the top of the economic list, so there must be more needed. Capital is more than just money; it is the machines, equipment, buildings, and any other assets we can buy with that money. But capital is not the determining factor either, so that leaves just one.

© Jackchen/Shutterstock, Inc.

The most important factor of production is knowledge/entrepreneurship, since the other factors alone cannot lead to improved efficiency to the same degree. Because of **factor mobility**, labor-intensive production moves to countries with large pools of low cost labor and capital-intensive production moves to countries with more capital, but each of these can still be improved with knowledge or entrepreneurship because increases in **productivity** result in greater amounts of output generated from given inputs. This ingenuity comes into play in any number of ways: when land is in short supply, a building can be designed to maximize the space available; as labor costs increase, new production methods can create better workflows for accomplishing tasks more efficiently; and as capital becomes scarce, different technologies can be introduced to improve outcomes. Thus, the engine for economic advancement is skill-based technological changes brought about by the successful application of knowledge and entrepreneurship to meet the challenges of the marketplace.

Economic Prosperity

The best system for economic growth of a country is the free market capitalist system where market forces create incentives for individuals to take risks, and who are then rewarded if they are successful. Even communist countries such as China see the benefit in allowing people to keep more of what they earn as an incentive for **entrepreneurs** to risk their time and money to start a business. Thus, the Chinese government many years back introduced market reforms that have some capitalist elements to them so that people would contribute to economic growth.

By contrast, the largest free market economy in the world present in the United States actually has introduced several programs over the years that go against the "*laissez faire,*" hands-off approach of pure capitalism espoused by Adam Smith. Our prosperity has allowed us to introduce a "safety net" (such as welfare and food stamps) for people who are struggling or are not able to fully participate in our economic prosperity. While taxes are necessary to pay for these benefits, it would not rise to the level of socialism until the tax burden is much higher and more punitive. Instead, we look at the United States as a **mixed economy** where there is mostly private ownership, but some level of government involvement in certain aspects of the economy for various reasons.

In addition to a safety net, the U.S. government also maintains tax incentives to promote certain activities seen as worthwhile (such as the mortgage interest deduction to encourage home ownership), supports specific industries through its actions (via farm subsidies or laws that mandate ethanol in gasoline), and funds basic research for the common good (like the funding of the Defense Advanced Research Projects Agency [DARPA], which created the foundations of what became the Internet). This level of government involvement would not happen in a pure capitalist economy. Although many people today would agree that the government spends too much money that it doesn't have, it is hard to get people to agree on which programs should be cut—so we'll leave that for a class on politics.

> **Mixed economy** when there is mostly private ownership of businesses and resources, but some level of government involvement in certain aspects of the economy for various reasons.

Macroeconomics versus Microeconomics

As we discuss economics throughout this chapter, keep in mind that there is an important distinction that we must make between **macroeconomics** (the aggregate economic activity of all people and businesses in the entire country as a whole) and **microeconomics** (the individual economic activity of people and businesses in particular markets). We can see from the "macro" prefix that macroeconomics deals with big picture things affecting the entire country: growth, output, unemployment, inflation, overall price levels, and international trade as well as money and banking. Conversely, the "micro" in microeconomics tells us that it's concerned with smaller issues for individuals and companies: spending, consumption, pricing, investment, and tradeoffs. Often, people making microeconomic decisions are reacting to events that occur at the macroeconomic level, but we'll initially limit our discussion to microeconomic issues.

> **Macroeconomics** the aggregate economic activity of all people and businesses in the entire country as a whole.
>
> **Microeconomics** the individual economic activity of people and businesses in particular markets.

© ravl/Shutterstock, Inc.

SUPPLY AND DEMAND

When we talk about "free markets" in an economy, it's important to understand that a **market** is any place where goods are bought and sold. Thus, we can define a market as broadly as an entire industry or as narrowly as a particular product or service. Even with our mixed economy, most decisions are made by individual

> **Market** any place where goods are bought and sold (thus, a market can be as broad as an entire industry or as narrow as that for a particular product or service).

© 3D character/Shutterstock, Inc.

people and businesses. They may be influenced by what the government does, but ultimately they have the freedom to choose how and when they will engage in economic activity. We assume that everyone is trying to maximize their position—business profit, personal cash, surplus, enjoyment, and so on—and all of these interactions act as the "invisible hand" that balances out quantities and prices, supply and demand.

Supply and demand law of economics that says for all products, goods, and services when supply exceeds demand, prices will fall and when demand exceeds supply, prices will rise.

The law of **supply and demand** says that for all products, goods, and services, when supply exceeds demand, prices will fall and when demand exceeds supply, prices will rise. This is an inverse relationship and makes intuitive sense: If you have a lot of something and want to make sure that you can sell all of it, then you would have to put a lower price on it. Conversely, if you have only a small amount of something that many people want, then you can put a higher price on those items. The best way to visualize this relationship is with a simple graph made up of just two curves. In fact, we'll see that there are several economic concepts we can understand based on this supply and demand graph (which we draw in the next few sections of this chapter).

Drawing the Demand Curve

Demand curve economics graph showing the amount of a particular good or service people would desire to buy at various prices.

Demand the willingness and *ability* to buy something at a given price.

Demand schedule a chart listing the survey results of asking lots of people how much they would be willing (and able) to buy at various prices, used to construct a demand curve line.

Since we are all more familiar with buying things than we are with making or selling them, let's start with a **demand curve** showing what amount of a particular good or service people would desire to buy at various prices. **Demand** is the willingness *and ability* to buy something at a given price. "Ability" is a very important component of this definition. You may want a Ferrari, but if you don't have the ability to actually buy one, then your "demand" doesn't count in the marketplace. In reality, we would construct this demand curve line by creating a **demand schedule**, which is simply a chart listing the survey results of asking lots of people how much they would be willing (and able) to buy at various prices. Without that specific data, however, we can still draw the general shape of the curve by thinking about human behavior.

What we find for most goods and services is that if the price is high, people will want to buy less of it, so we need to put this as a point on our graph. You can see in Part D of the following figure that we have drawn a typical economics graph with monetary units on the left vertical axis (*PRICE* in this case) and quantity or time units on the bottom horizontal axis (*QUANTITY* in this case). So, on this graph, the fact that people will buy less quantity at high prices is represented as Point "C."

Furthermore, we know that if the price of something is low, then most people will want to buy more of it, so that gives us Point "D." Connecting the two points gives us our typical downward sloping demand curve. Always remember the "D's": Demand curve goes *Down*. So, now we have a curve that represents **market demand**, which is the total of all individual demands in the marketplace for this good or service. Each person may be at a different point on the curve, but we put it all together to create just one demand curve for this market. This is shown in *Part "D"* of the following figure.

Market demand   curve on a graph that shows the total of all individual demands in the marketplace for this good or service.

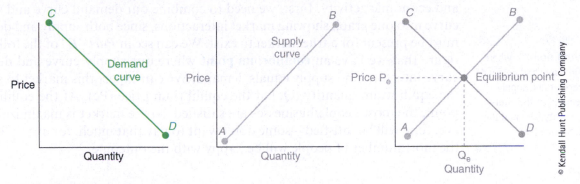

Part D: The Demand Curve

Drawing the Supply Curve

Next, we have to think about businesses, so a **supply curve** shows the amount of a particular good or service that companies or individuals would produce and sell at various prices. **Supply** is the willingness *and ability* to sell something at a given price. Again, "ability" is a very important part of this definition. If you are not in a position to produce something, then your desire to "supply" something doesn't count in the marketplace. Just like the demand curve, we would ideally construct the supply curve line by creating a **supply schedule**, which is a chart listing the survey results of asking lots of businesses how much they would be willing (and able) to make and sell at various prices. Here again, though, without specific data, we will draw the general shape of the curve by thinking about business behavior.

If businesses can only get a low price for their goods and services, then we can assume that most businesses would typically want to sell less. So, on our graph, the fact that businesses will sell less quantity at low prices is represented as Point "A." On the other hand, when businesses can get a high price for something, then most would want to make and sell more of it, so that gives us Point "B." Connecting the two points gives us our typical upward sloping supply curve. Remember that it's *Up* for the *S*upply curve: "U.S." So, now we have a curve that represents **market supply**, the sum of all supplier intentions at various price points. Again, each business may be at a different point on the curve, but we put it all together to create just one supply curve for this market. This is shown in *Part "S"* of the following figure.

Supply curve   economics graph showing the amount of a particular good or service that companies or individuals would produce and sell at various prices.

Supply   the willingness and *ability* to sell something at a given price.

Supply schedule   a chart listing the survey results of asking lots of businesses how much they would be willing (and able) to make and sell at various prices, used to construct a supply curve line.

Market supply   the sum of all supplier intentions at various price points.

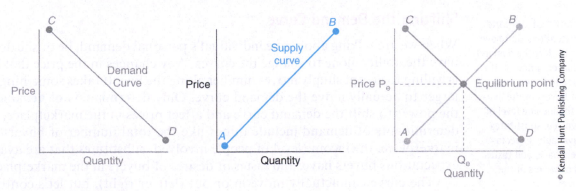

Part S: The Supply Curve

Supply and Demand in Balance

So, the question becomes: how does the market mechanism work so that needs and wants are produced in sufficient quantities such that supply meets demand? Economic theory of the "invisible hand" says that supply and demand always seek to balance each other, and thus, the free market responds with price changes and economic activity. First, we need to combine our demand curve and supply curve into one graph showing market interactions, since both supply and demand must be present for a true market to exist. We can see in *Part "E"* of the following figure that we have an **equilibrium point** where our supply curve and demand curve intersect, and supply equals demand. We can expect this market to supply the equilibrium quantity (Qe) at the equilibrium price (Pe). At the equilibrium point, the most people/businesses are satisfied, so the market is maximized. Not everyone will be satisfied—some don't want to pay that much, for example—but the most number of people will be happy with the outcome.

Equilibrium point where supply and curve and demand curve intersect and supply equals demand at the equilibrium quantity (Qe) and the equilibrium price (Pe).

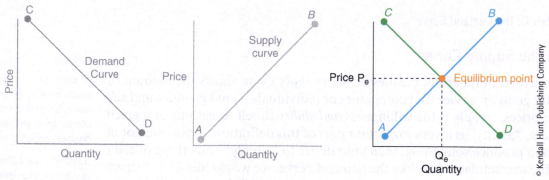

Part E: Equilibrium Point

© Kendall Hunt Publishing Company

It's easiest to think about this market example being in balance when we are talking about a product or service that is nearly identical. Commodities are a great example of this: my hunk of copper is essentially the same as your hunk of copper. Here people would make buying decisions strictly based on price. In order to entice businesses to supply more than the equilibrium quantity in the marketplace, we have to see a rise in prices. This is what happens when demand exceeds supply; prices go up, thereby stimulating more production from businesses (current producers or new entrants) eager to get those higher prices. All of this occurs whenever there are significant numbers of new buyers coming into the marketplace demanding a good or service, because this causes the demand curve to shift out to the right. Let's look at how this works.

Shifting the Demand Curve

Determinants of demand events or situations that have the power to shift the demand curve and affect prices in the marketplace (e.g., the total number of buyers in the marketplace, the income level of people involved, substitutes that are available, expectations buyers have, and tastes or desires of buyers in the marketplace).

When we are talking about one individual's personal demand, he or she does not have the ability alone to change the curves. Any changes in the price that he/she is willing to accept simply moves him/her along the line. It takes something much larger to actually move the demand curve. Only **determinants of demand** have the power to shift the demand curve and affect prices in the marketplace. These determinants of demand include things like the total number of buyers in the marketplace, the income level of people involved, substitutes that are available, expectations buyers have, and tastes or desires of buyers in the marketplace.

The curve can actually move in or out (left or right), but let's continue in the following figure with the example we started in the last section. If we see a significant number of new buyers come into the marketplace, then we can see the demand curve shift out to the right. This means that the new equilibrium in this market is now at Q*d* (Quantity from new *d*emand) and P*d* (Price from the new *d*emand). Buyers are forced to pay the higher prices, and businesses are supplying products at these new, higher output levels.

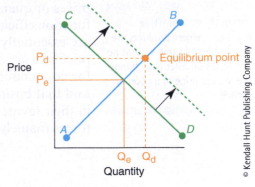

Demand Curve Shifted Out

Perhaps, we can expand our customer base by increasing demand for our products or services. In fact, that's exactly why companies spend so much money on marketing—trying to influence the determinants of demand. Certainly, sometimes companies hope to get new people to buy and use their products (i.e., increase the total number of buyers), but it is often easier to influence people already in the market for a product or service to want *your* product (i.e., sway the tastes or desires of buyers).

There are two reasons people will buy products from your business: your products are cheaper or your products are better. If you don't want to constantly cut prices to get business from customers only shopping based on price (which is usually a losing strategy in the long run), then you can try to get a loyal following of customers who think your products are superior in quality, style, and so on. If your marketing is successful, you will have effectively shifted the demand curve out for your business and you will sell more products at a higher price point.

Shifting the Supply Curve

Just as the demand curve can shift from certain events, **determinants of supply** have the power to shift the supply curve and affect prices or quantities in the marketplace. These determinants of supply include things like the total number of sellers in the marketplace, the cost of inputs or factors of production, technological advances, substitutes that are available, expectations in the marketplace, and taxes or subsidies for businesses.

Again, the curve can actually move in or out (left or right), but let's look at an example that moves the curve out in the next figure. As technology improves, products can be made more efficiently, shifting the supply curve out to the right and allowing businesses to sell more product Q*s* (Quantity from new *s*upply) at lower P*s* (Price from the new *s*upply). Buyers are now able to enjoy increased savings while the market expands, either for a particular company that has a unique advantage to make its products excel in the marketplace or for an entire product category. This is a typical scenario for consumer electronics that get cheaper over their life span.

Notice that supply influences price and is influenced by price. Demand also influences price and is influenced by price. It's important to understand, though, that demand and supply do not influence each other; both are reactions to pricing in the marketplace. Only changes in the determinants of supply or the determinants of demand in the marketplace have the power to actually move the curves in or out.

Determinants of supply events or situations that have the power to shift the supply curve and affect prices or quantities in the marketplace (e.g., the total number of sellers in the marketplace, the cost of inputs or factors of production, technological advances, substitutes that are available, expectations in the marketplace, and taxes or subsidies for businesses).

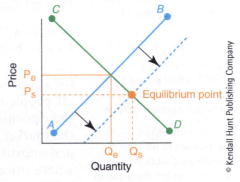

Supply Curve Shifted Out

COMPETITION

In the last section on Supply and Demand, we said that one person alone does not have the ability to change the curves. Most of our theory about equilibrium points also assumes that businesses do not have the **market power** ability to set

Market power   the ability to set prices or quantities on their own either.

prices or quantities on their own either. In fact, in order for the marketplace to function efficiently, we must have a **perfectly competitive market** where products are essentially the same so that no one buyer or seller can change the market price of a good or service. The best example of a perfectly competitive market is for commodities, like our copper example earlier. For most other products, we said that businesses can try to use marketing to perhaps shift the demand curve in their favor, but they are still not dictating the price and must rely on market forces (namely attracting more buyers) to actually enjoy higher prices.

Perfectly competitive market where products are essentially the same so that no one buyer or seller can change the market price of a good or service.

© 3D character/Shutterstock, Inc.

Competitive firm company without market power because it has output that is small compared to the entire marketplace, and as such, its output decisions do not have a significant impact on market prices.

Price taker a firm that must accept the equilibrium price dictated by market forces.

Perfect competition situation that exists in a marketplace where no one buyer or seller can control prices or output for a good or service.

Market mechanism situation where prices and quantities signal desired output and resource allocation to producers, with all people and businesses acting in their own best interests to maximize their position and that acts as the "invisible hand" that keeps the market at equilibrium.

A **competitive firm** without market power has output that is small compared to the entire marketplace, and as such its output decisions do not have a significant impact on market prices. The firm is a **price taker,** which must accept the equilibrium price dictated by market forces. Now we have enough background to understand how the "invisible hand" creates market forces that cause resources to be allocated efficiently, and more or less output to be produced as dictated by competition in the marketplace.

Perfect Competition

We know that classical economic theory says that supply and demand always seek to balance each other in a competitive free market. **Perfect competition** exists in a marketplace where no one buyer or seller can control prices or output for a good or service. We also said at the beginning of this chapter that we assume all people and businesses are acting in their own best interests to maximize their position and that they are free to decide if/when they will participate in the market. Thus, if buyers and sellers are armed with information on prices and substitutes available in this market, we have a great **market mechanism** where prices and quantities signal desired output and resource allocation to producers.

When demand for a product exceeds supply, the demand curve will shift out and the price for that product will rise, thereby encouraging more production by existing producers—or maybe even enticing new producers to enter the market and contribute even more of that product or service. In theory, new producers will keep entering a market as long as profits exist. These profits signal to producers that consumers in the market want more quantity, and thus, it is an efficient allocation of resources for producers to supply this need or want.

If these production increases are the result of new firms entering the market, then the supply curve also shifts out and with this we may see prices settle back down to the original price point—but at a greater output level. You can see this in the following figure: more buyers shifted the demand curve out; more suppliers shifted the supply curve out; the result is more quantity in the market, but at the same price level as before.

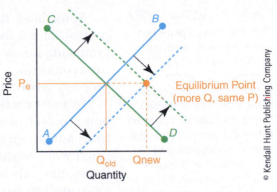

Both Supply and Demand Curve Shifted Out
(New Equilibrium: more Q, same P)

Initially, this is a good thing as the demand is satisfied, but eventually there could be a situation where the supply exceeds demand. This could be because of overproduction by current firms or by too many new firms entering the marketplace. Falling prices lead to falling profits. As the "**economic profit**" moves toward zero (that minimum amount needed to stay in business), this signals to producers that consumers want or need less production here. Some larger firms may now decide to exit the market and reallocate their resources to other areas. (Of course, this may present an opportunity for a smaller company to now offer that product or service, such as support for obsolete computer equipment or programs.)

Economic profit   the minimum amount of money needed to stay in business.

Monopolies

In some markets, there is a **monopoly** where one firm produces the entire market supply of a good or service. A monopoly firm actually gets higher prices and makes a larger profit by decreasing output, since there are no competitors who can bring in extra supply to drive down prices. Although monopolies appear to be bad for consumers, there are times when they are necessary and thus tolerated by the government—or even encouraged. The most obvious example are utilities. Here **natural monopolies** exist where it is impractical for competing firms to supply a good or service because of high fixed costs for infrastructure or other structural reasons. These **barriers to entry** are obstacles that can keep firms out of any market, but they are more obvious and pronounced in the case of monopolies. For example, utilities not only require a large initial cash outlay for transmission lines, it is not practical for you to have multiple lines running into your house so that you can switch back and forth between providers based on cost or service. Recognizing this, the government allows these monopolies to exist in exchange for regulatory authority over rates and other consumer protections.

Monopoly   when one company or entity is the sole provider of certain products or services, and thus is able to charge any price.

Natural monopolies situation that exists where it is impractical for competing firms to supply a good or service because of high fixed costs for infrastructure or other structural reasons.

Barriers to entry   obstacles that can keep firms out of any market, such as government regulations or patents.

Sometimes, though, the government grants monopolies without any type of control. This is the case for **patents**, where companies are granted a monopoly on producing a new product that is deemed sufficiently innovative to be protected from competition. The exclusive period of use for this and other types of intellectual property gives companies an incentive to create new technologies and products.

In most cases, however, the government uses its regulatory authority and police power to make sure that markets are free and consumers are protected from anticompetitive behavior. If no one was watching businesses, then they could work together to set prices at a level higher than that dictated by market forces. Since these actions violate the spirit of free markets and hurt consumers, **antitrust laws** have the government intervene to prevent abuses of market power. For example, the Sherman Antitrust Act prohibits companies from conspiring together to restrain trade, the Clayton Act outlaws price gouging and limits monopolies, and the Federal Trade Commission Act set up the FTC as an agency watchdog to study industries.

Monopolistic Competition

© You can more/Shutterstock, Inc.

Sometimes there is a unique situation where a few companies dominate a market, but for reasons that have nothing to do with collusion. As companies do things to set themselves apart from the rest of the industry, they may attract a loyal following that gives the company a unique position in the marketplace. They are not subject to the whims of customers who are solely basing a purchase decision on price, but at the same time, they cannot raise their prices beyond reason for most people because there are substitutes that people *could* turn to instead. We call this **monopolistic competition** when there are a number of providers who produce similar goods, but enjoy tremendous brand loyalty that allows them some market power.

We can see this with most Apple products, where loyal customers are more than willing to pay a little more for the brand's style, quality, and reputation. For example, an Android phone *could* provide a substitute if the iPhone became ridiculously expensive. But as long as Apple continues to innovate and price the phone "within reason," then Apple is in a position to command a small premium for its phones because of the goodwill and brand loyalty it has cultivated from its users. Another good example of monopolistic competition are McDonald's and Burger King, among other fast food hamburger chains. They all offer essentially the same beef patties served on buns with toppings, but customers are drawn by the companies' marketing of differences in features or quality. Some people prefer the taste of one over the other, while others are swayed by the marketing messages. In the end, though, the brands need to continue to advertise to attract new, loyal users and must also remain price competitive or risk losing market share.

Oligopolies

Another competitive situation is an **oligopoly** when there are several large firms that dominate a market. The firms are able to have some market power by virtue of their size and their control of a large percentage of the market share in a particular industry. Typically, these firms produce goods that are not easily replaced by outside firms, since the barriers to entry are so high for a new company to get started, nor are the items easy for consumers to create for themselves. Some good examples of oligopoly markets would be oil companies, airline travel, and automobiles. By contrast, even though there are only a few large soap producers in the country, this does not fit the traditional definition of oligopolies, since you *could* make your own soap if you had to.

In the United States, government regulations prohibit firms from getting together and setting prices. Collusion of this sort to fix prices is illegal—and can even result in jail time—however, there are other ways that prices change, which do not break the law. For example, you often see gas stations on opposite corners with virtually the same prices. If they sit in a room to discuss pricing, they would be in trouble; but nothing is stopping them from observing the prices posted by their competitors across the street. Of course, market forces still ultimately drive the price, but this ensures that they are competitive when raising or lowering prices. A similar situation occurs when auto manufacturers start offering low finance rates to move cars: once one company or brand starts offering these, others may feel that they need similar incentives to stay competitive.

© Tupungato/Shutterstock, Inc.

Usually, what happens in an oligopoly market is that the largest player in that market is a **price leader** and attempts to raise prices and see if other firms in the market will follow. Thus, without any formal discussion, new price levels might take hold, but if others don't follow, then the market leader will likely lower prices back to the old level again and wait for another opportunity to attempt a price hike. The $25 baggage handling fee that is now fairly standard among all major airline carriers (except Southwest) began this way. One or two of the large carriers tried to impose this charge several times, but early efforts did not see the smaller companies go along with the extra fees and so the large carrier retreated. But once the smaller carriers followed the lead of the large carriers, this new fee was here to stay.

Price leader when the largest player in an oligopoly market attempts to raise prices to see if other firms in the market will follow.

GOVERNMENT INVOLVEMENT

Even with the virtues of a free market capitalist economy, there are times when the government decides to get involved to avert or correct "market failures." We mentioned, for example, that laws have been created to prevent collusion or other abuses of market power. But what about those instances where the traditional supply and demand mechanism cannot or does not produce an optimum outcome? This can often become the basis for government intervention. We'll look at three specific areas: public goods, externalities, and business cycles.

Public Goods

Public goods are items that benefit more than one person, and consumption by one person does not exclude others from using that item. The best examples of these are roads and the military. The marketplace cannot be used to allocate resources

Public goods items that benefit more than one person, and consumption by one person does not exclude others from using that item (e.g., the roads or the military).

© Hung Chung Chih/Shutterstock, Inc.

for these types of goods or services because there is not an effective means of collecting payment from those who use the good or service. When you have a situation where there might be freeloaders who choose not to pay, then the government can step in to collect tax money to pay for those items. The only other solution is entirely impractical: a series of toll gates at almost every intersection so that those using a particular road would also pay for it. Similarly, with the military, it is not feasible to have people in the marketplace buying national defense equipment or services. Although it's on a smaller scale, you would run into similar problems with police and fire, so this is another area where the government chooses to get involved.

Externalities

Externalities items that have costs (or benefits) to third parties, and not to the people who produce or consume them, and thus we cannot rely on the market because people will overproduce goods where they retain the benefit but the cost is shifted to other people (e.g., pollution).

Externalities have costs (or benefits) to third parties and not to the people who produce or consume them. In this type of situation, we cannot rely on the market because people will overproduce goods where they retain the benefit, but the cost is shifted to other people. The best example of this is pollution: if a person or business is not concerned about the social cost, then they have no incentive to reduce pollution. This means that there has to be an outside force at work in order to avoid an undesired outcome. Presently, the government uses agencies, such as the Environmental Protection Agency (EPA), to monitor, regulate, and punish those who violate standards that have been put in place.

Business Cycles

Business cycles general swings in business activity, moving from Expansion to Peak to Contraction and Tough during different phases of the cycle, then repeating.

Although the marketplace is the most efficient allocation of resources in supplying wants and needs, the changes that occur are not instantaneous. It takes time for markets to respond, and during that time, growth can slow down, prices might not adjust quickly enough, and people might lose their jobs as businesses retool. These all contribute to **business cycles** with general swings in business activity, moving from **E**xpansion to **P**eak to **C**ontraction and **T**rough during different phases of the cycle, then repeating. (EPCoT can help you remember the business cycle in order.) Cycles last for varying lengths of time. The good part about this model is that it does not try to predict how high the peaks will be, nor how low the troughs will be. Eventually both will lead to turnarounds, but no one knows when.

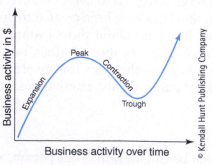

© Kendall Hunt Publishing Company

Business Cycle: Expansion, Peak, Contraction, Trough (EPCoT)

Macroeconomics

As we said near the beginning of this chapter, **macroeconomics** is the aggregate economic activity of all people and businesses in the entire country as a whole. The U.S. government does take an interest in the health and well-being of the economy since that is what generates the tax money, which allows the government to function. Because of the uncertainty in the business cycles, economist John Maynard Keynes said that the private economy was inherently unstable, and he proposed a number of government intervention methods, which are still used today to try and promote three macroeconomics goals for the country: **economic growth**, **price stability**, and **full employment**.

Economic Growth

Economic growth is important for a country to grow and prosper, increase the wealth of citizens and businesses, and create jobs for a growing population. Growth is measured using **gross domestic product (GDP),** which is the total market value of all goods and services produced in the country. This measure of output is called **real GDP** if it is adjusted for inflation. That is, a much better basis for comparison than **nominal GDP**, which only tells you the raw number. Although there is not always a specific target for growth, the government definitely wants to avoid negative quarters of GDP, since a **recession** is defined as two consecutive quarters of declining GDP. The formula for calculating GDP is:

**GDP = Consumer Spending "C" + Business Investment Spending "I"
+ Government Spending "G" ± Net Exports "N"**

Here is a breakdown: GDP = 70% C + 17% I + 19% G − 6% N

Note that the figure for Government Spending at 19% only counts actual purchases, such as roads and military spending. The figure does NOT include transfer payments, such as welfare or food stamps.

We can see in the figure below that the "ideal" Quantity of output for the economy (Q_{GDP}) is at a GDP level where Aggregate Supply and Aggregate Demand for the entire economy intersect at the Equilibrium Point for the entire economy. This also gives us an indication of the "ideal" Price level for the economy as a whole (P_{GDP}) at that GDP level.

Price Stability

Price stability is important because prices rising or falling too quickly or unpredictably make it difficult for individuals and businesses to plan or grow. The target for the country as a whole is an increase in prices of about 3% per year. This allows businesses to comfortably pass along increases, maintain profit levels, and show growth. For individuals, it allows some savings growth without seeing prices rise too quickly ahead of incomes.

Prices are measured using **inflation**, which is defined as a general increase in the overall level of prices for goods or services. Along with this "definition," it's helpful to also understand two causes/types of inflation. The first is simply

Macroeconomics   the aggregate economic activity of all people and businesses in the entire country as a whole.

Economic growth   expansion or increase in business activity, important for a country to grow and prosper, increase the wealth of citizens and businesses, and create jobs for a growing population.

Price stability   economic goal of having modest inflation to prevent prices from rising (or falling) too quickly or unpredictably, with about 3% inflation considered an acceptable rate so that individuals and businesses can plan and grow.

Full employment   economic goal of having most citizens who want a job able to find one, with about 5% unemployment as an acceptable rate for those job seekers in a state of flux in their circumstances.

Gross Domestic Product (GDP)   measurement of growth which is the total market value of all goods and services produced in the country.

Real GDP   measure of economic growth or output that is adjusted for inflation.

Nominal GDP   measure of economic growth or output that only states the raw number.

Recession   two consecutive quarters of declining GDP.

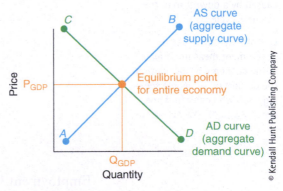

Aggregate Supply and Demand Curve at Equilibrium

© Kendall Hunt Publishing Company

Inflation   measurement of prices which shows the general increase in the overall level of prices for goods or services.

Cost inflation   increases in prices are passed along to consumers (e.g., businesses raising prices to customers to recoup the money spent on rising gas prices).

Demand inflation   too much money chasing too few goods (e.g., businesses charging more for an item that is very popular but in short supply).

Consumer Price Index (CPI)   government index that measures the fixed cost of a market basket of goods and services used by consumers (such as food, transportation, energy, andhousing).

Producer Price Index (PPI)   government index that measures the price level of typical inputs used by a variety of businesses.

Frictional unemployment   when someone is out of work if they have leave one job and are looking for another.

Structural unemployment   when someone is out of work if they have stopped working while they go back to school or get training for a new career.

Cyclical unemployment   when people are out of work caused by a downturn in the business cycle.

Unemployment rate   government measure of jobs in the economy by calculating the proportion of people seeking a job who can't find one.

cost inflation: increases in prices are passed along to consumers, thus a business that sees an increase in the delivery charges for goods because of rising gas prices will charge higher prices to its customers because of these rising costs. The second is **demand inflation**: too much money chasing too few goods, where something is very popular and lots of people want to buy it, but a business doesn't have very many of that item so the company can charge customers more for the item because of this increased demand.

In order to help measure and analyze inflationary trends, the government developed the **consumer price index (CPI),** which measures the fixed cost of a market basket of goods and services used by consumers. CPI includes components from the food, transportation, energy, housing, and clothing sectors, as well as other items, but it excludes taxes. The CPI figure is published monthly and is used as an inflation adjuster for things like Social Security benefits, union wage contracts, and other cost of living adjustments. (There's also a **producer price index (PPI),** which measures the price level of typical inputs used by a variety of businesses, published to help managers plan.)

Full Employment

Full employment is an important goal in the economy so that citizens can find jobs and be productive members of society. Oddly enough, "full employment" does not mean that everyone has a job. Instead, the country's goal expects that some people's employment situation will be in a state of flux as their circumstances change. For example, people are said to be experiencing **frictional unemployment** if they have leave one job and are looking for another or **structural unemployment** if they have stopped working while they go back to school or get training for a new career, so this is not always a bad thing. But when too many people aren't working, then the economy can suffer—especially if it is **cyclical unemployment** caused by a downturn in the business cycle. Remember that one of our determinants of demand was the number of buyers. So, if unemployment causes a significant amount of people to stop spending money, then the "aggregate" demand curve for the economy as a whole shifts to the left and results in less quantity of total output—that is, lower GDP for the entire country than the ideal GDP expected.

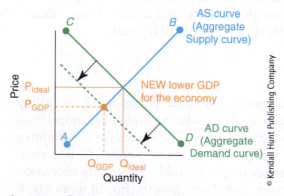

Aggregate Supply and Demand Curve shifted left, lower Q$_{GDP}$

Employment levels are measured using the **unemployment rate**, which is the proportion of people seeking a job who can't find one. These numbers are determined based on a survey over the phone and are extrapolated to the entire population. The U.S. Bureau of Labor Statistics actually publishes six different unemployment numbers. The one typically quoted on the news is the U3 number, which does not count those people who have given up looking for work. Not only can this be a way to massage the numbers, it does not give a true picture of all those people who could be working but are not for one reason or another. Thus, a better indication of the true unemployment picture is to look at the U6 number, which basically counts all people who are able-bodied and of working age. Just to illustrate a comparison, the published numbers by U.S. Bureau of Labor Statistics for July 2013 for the U3 was 7.4%, while for the U6 was 14%.

Fiscal Policy

Fiscal policy is the government's plan for spending, taxation, and debt management. This is done by the Congress passing laws directing the U.S. Treasury Department to collect money so that the government can spend it. John Maynard Keynes believed that government spending is one way to counteract business cycles and make up for any decrease in GDP, but of course, this goes against the principle of *laissez-faire*, which is the cornerstone of classical economic theory. Noted modern-day classical economist Milton Friedman, on the other hand, argued against government intervention saying that freedom is the best tool of capitalism and that government doing things in the private sector leads to inefficiencies and can also be inflationary.

The goods and services purchased by the government are a large part of economic activity and thus have a "stimulus" effect on the economy talked about by politicians. Furthermore, money spent by government and individuals or businesses all has a **multiplier effect**, meaning that $1 of spending contributes more than $1 of economic activity because the person receiving the dollar will often go out and spend it as well. The problem with government spending the money is that people see this as potential future tax increases at some point in the future and may curtail their current spending even more in anticipation of having to pay a higher tax bill later on. Higher taxes mean that individuals and businesses have less money to spend or invest. Thus, another way to stimulate the economy is to cut taxes and let individuals and businesses have more money to spend.

The ultimate goals of fiscal policy are supposed to be economic growth, price stability, and full employment. There's much debate over which policies actually promote those results, however, and the government's fiscal policy is always subject to political pressure, meaning that other agendas or priorities may be at work. Furthermore, lack of fiscal discipline can lead to inflation if government spends money too freely without regard to cost (e.g., defense items purchased for more than the same item costs at a hardware store) or without forcing suppliers to feel competitive pressures (e.g., increases in health-care costs). When government borrows money to cover budget deficits or because of excessive debt, then less money is available for private borrowers—which could push up interest rates.

Fiscal policy the government's plan for spending, taxation, and debt management.

Multiplier effect when spending by individuals, businesses or government is larger than the initial expenditure, since the person receiving the dollar will often go out and spend it as well, thus $1 of spending contributes more than $1 of economic activity.

© kentoh/Shutterstock, Inc.

Monetary Policy

Monetary policy the government's means of controlling the supply and cost of money. Can influence the inflation or deflation of prices because it affects the flow and availability of money.

Federal Reserve Board ("The Fed") agency responsible for implementing U.S. monetary policy and regulating commercial banks, among other things.

Open market operations when The Fed acts as an agent of the U.S. Treasury, selling and buying Treasury securities (bonds).

Monetary policy is the government's means of controlling the supply and cost of money. This is done via actions of the **Federal Reserve Board ("The Fed")**, which is responsible for implementing U.S. monetary policy and regulating commercial banks, among other things. For example, The Fed sets limits for how much money banks must keep on reserve and ready for customers who have deposited money in the bank and may want to withdraw funds. Monetary policy also has the goals of economic growth and full employment, plus monetary policy tries to maintain stability in prices, interest rates, and financial markets.

The Federal Reserve is directly involved with the physical money supply of the United States in two ways. First, the Federal Reserve oversees the printing of more currency performed by the U.S. Treasury. Second, through its **open market operations**, The Fed acts as an agent of the U.S. Treasury, selling and buying Treasury securities (bonds). When the Fed *sells* securities, it increases its stockpile of cash and takes money out of circulation. When banks buy the securities that The Fed is selling, the banks then have less money available to lend out, and this raises interest rates. Conversely, if the Fed *buys* securities, it decreases its stockpile of cash and puts more money into circulation. When banks sell securities that they own or hold back to The Fed, the banks have more money available to lend, and this lowers interest rates. This happens because "money" responds to the laws of supply and demand just like any other good or service—and "interest rates" are the "price" of that money.

© larry1235/Shutterstock, Inc.

The Fed can actively try to manage the economy through the use of monetary policy, since interest rates have a large effect on economic activity. When inflation is a concern, then The Fed can make credit tighter to discourage additional spending. But if growth has slowed, The Fed can make credit easier to encourage borrowing in an effort to boost GDP. When interest rates are very low and there is still not enough borrowing activity, The

Quantitative easing The Fed policy that puts additional money into circulation to try and stimulate economic activity.

Fed can implement a policy of **quantitative easing,** which puts additional money into circulation to try and stimulate economic activity. This is an effort to shift the aggregate demand curve back to the right, with the goal of getting back to original equilibrium output at ideal GDP levels—but without overshooting that target, which could cause inflation.

OPEN FOR BUSINESS IN THE REAL WORLD

You've finally decided to take the plunge and be an entrepreneur, and so you think about what type of business you might start. You've heard people warn you about the high failure rate of restaurants, but you feel that's what you know best and so you will try to use what you've learned to increase your chances of success. You really want to start a hamburger joint, but you realize that you might not be able to compete well in that market. The stakes are pretty high there because of the monopolistic competition, where entrenched players like McDonald's and Burger King have done what they can to erect as many barriers to entry as possible: constant marketing, exclusive product variations, and trademarks. (A customer who wants a "Whopper" can only get it at Burger King; kids who want a "Happy Meal" will insist that their parents take them only to McDonald's.)

You finally decide to open a sub shop. You are aware of Subway's vast presence, but you see them as your only primary competitor. You won't be in monopolistic competition with them from Day 1 because you have to earn your loyal following of customers over time, but you have a few ideas of how you can improve your chances. You decide to match Subway's loyalty program, but go a step further and offer exclusive sales and promotions via social media. Marketing meets economics as you start on the path of making your sub shop more than just a regular competitor. You keep searching for things that will make you different and better so that you can establish yourself as a monopolistic competitor.

You know that you don't want to only be competing on price, so you decide that in addition to "cheap" food, you will also offer more unique options, such as specialty premium meats and organic vegetables. This can help you move the demand curve in your favor by attracting a unique group of customers with different tastes who may be willing to pay just a bit more for your products. Once these people see you as the only place for those options, then you are on your way to being a viable competitor. You couple this with imaginative promotions and incentives for kids that Subway can't match, and you are starting to feel like you might have a chance of creating a niche for your sub shop and survive in monopolistic competition with Subway and the rest.

Chapter Summary

Economics is the study of the allocation of resources. Governments, companies, and individuals must do this since everything involves tradeoffs. Government economic systems can be capitalist, socialist, or communist, depending on who owns, directs, or controls the means of production. The factors of production are land, labor, capital, and knowledge/entrepreneurship, with this last one being the most important for increased productivity and wealth. Macroeconomics considers the aggregate activity of all people and businesses in the entire country, dealing with big picture things like growth, output, unemployment, inflation, overall price levels, banking, and international trade. Microeconomics considers the individual economic activity of people and businesses in particular markets, dealing with smaller issues like spending, consumption, pricing, investment, and tradeoffs.

A market is any place where goods are bought and sold. The law of supply and demand says that in markets for all products, goods, and services, when supply exceeds demand, then prices will fall, and when demand exceeds supply, then prices will rise. We can graph this with a downward sloping demand curve showing how many goods consumers are willing and able to buy at various prices and an upward sloping supply curve showing how many goods producers are willing and able to sell at various prices. Businesses want to find ways to sell more products by moving the demand curve out to the right via marketing to attract more buyers. Businesses can also lower prices by moving the supply curve out to the right via economies of scale to cut their costs.

Businesses compete in a variety of market structures, from perfect competition where no one has market power and all are price takers, all the way to monopolies where there is only one producer with the power to set prices. Monopolistic competition has a number of firms trying to differentiate themselves to gain limited pricing power by marketing to move the demand curve, and oligopolies have a few large firms who are able to move prices in unison by following the market leader. When companies have too much power to affect prices, the government typically moves in to restrict this behavior. Government also gets involved to provide for public goods that all enjoy (e.g., roads) by collecting taxes to pay for things and regulating externalities that are deemed bad but have no direct costs (e.g., pollution). The ultimate government intervention comes in trying to promote economic growth, stabilize prices, and bring about full employment via fiscal policy (taxes, spending) and monetary policy (actions of the Federal Reserve).

Review Questions

1. What countries do you think rank the highest in having free market economies? (View some comparison data here: http://www.heritage.org/index/ranking .)

2. Can you think of some goods or services that you would buy, even if the price continued to rise? What about products or services that you would never buy, no matter how cheap they are?

3. How can you use the knowledge about shifting the demand curve to your advantage and help your business make money?

4. If your company can use more efficient technology to make products cheaper, what would you do with the cost savings: Lower prices to sell more? Increase your marketing budget to sell more? Invest in new products or features? Something else?

5. The true test of whether or not a market is perfectly competitive comes down to a single question: Can a firm raise its prices without losing all of its customers? If a firm *can* do this, then the market is not perfectly competitive. Consider whether or not these firms compete in a perfectly competitive market: McDonald's? Delta Airlines? Ivy League colleges? Other universities?

6. Can you think of some possible ways to introduce market incentives to reduce pollution or other undesired externalities? Markets could emerge as problems appear and dissolve once a problem has been solved. What happens in the government when a problem is "solved?"

7. What do you think about Consumer Spending being 70% of GDP?

8. What do you think about Government Spending being 19% of GDP?

9. Which country do you think has the highest per capita GDP? (Surprise! It's not the United States: https://www.cia.gov/library/publications/the-world-factbook/rankorder/2004rank.html .)

10. Which number do you think gives a more accurate picture of unemployment in the United States: U3? U6? Another figure? (You can view current # here: http://www.bls.gov/news.release/empsit.t15.htm .)

11. Can you think of other reasons that government spending may not produce the same economic activity that business or consumer spending might produce?

12. Is quantitative easing always inflationary? What will happen when The Fed decides to stop quantitative easing?

Discussion Questions

13. Give some examples of how knowledge/entrepreneurship interacts with the other factors of production to help an economy. What do you think is the second most important factor of production? Explain and defend your position.

14. Do you think that macroeconomic factors influence microeconomic factors, or do you think that microeconomic factors have more influence over macroeconomic factors? Explain your reasoning.

15. Although the government tries to stop businesses from exerting monopoly power in some instances (e.g., regulating prices of utilities), it encourages monopoly activities in other instances (e.g., granting patents). Argue whether you think government should support all monopolies or permit no monopolies. Could there be beneficial outcomes to either of these policies?

15. The government often gets involved when there are "failures" of the free market system, such as paying for public goods like roadways or preventing undesirable externalities like pollution. Are there other solutions to these types of issues?

16. The Fed's policy of quantitative easing has often been cited as one of the factors contributing to the rising stock market, even when other factors may have not been favorable. Do you think this has led to inflation of stock prices, and what might happen when the quantitative easing stops?

Key Terms

- antitrust laws
- barriers to entry
- business cycles
- capitalist economic system
- communist economic system
- competitive firm
- consumer price index (CPI)
- cost inflation
- cyclical unemployment
- demand
- demand curve
- demand inflation
- demand schedule
- determinants of demand
- determinants of supply
- economic growth
- economic profit
- economics
- entrepreneurs
- equilibrium point
- externalities
- factor mobility
- factors of production
- Federal Reserve Board (The Fed)
- fiscal policy
- frictional unemployment
- full employment
- gross domestic product (GDP)
- inflation
- "invisible hand"
- macroeconomics
- market
- market demand
- market mechanism
- market power
- market supply
- microeconomics
- mixed economy
- monetary policy
- monopolistic competition
- monopoly
- multiplier effect
- natural monopolies
- nominal GDP
- oligopoly
- open market operations
- opportunity cost
- patents
- perfect competition
- perfectly competitive market
- price leader
- price stability
- price taker
- producer price index (PPI)
- production possibilities curve
- productivity
- public goods
- quantitative easing
- real GDP
- recession
- socialist economic system
- structural unemployment
- supply
- supply and demand
- supply curve
- supply schedule
- tradeoff
- unemployment rate

SECTION

3

BUSINESS PROCESSES

CHAPTER

9

Marketing

LEARNING OBJECTIVES

1. Explain how marketing is about communicating value and benefits to customers.
2. Discuss how consumers view the Total Product Offer before deciding to buy.
3. Detail the four P's of Marketing: Product, Price, Place, Promotion.
4. Discuss the differences between selling to businesses and selling to consumers.
5. Explain the marketing utilities companies must use to add value and make profits.

OPENING STORY: GEICO INSURANCE

How do you sell something that nobody wants to pay for but everybody needs? Worse yet, you have a large number of competitors all vying for the attention of consumers. Answer: You make sure people remember you because you are funny, in many different ways and often! GEICO was founded in 1936 as a privately held corporation, but is now owned by Berkshire Hathaway (Warren Buffet's company). That gave one of the top automobile insurers in the nation the impetus needed to gain market share by gaining mind share among consumers.

© Miro Vrlik Photography/Shutterstock, Inc.

141

A variety of advertising campaigns have gotten them noticed, from the animated gecko to the various celebrities touting the 15% savings that can be had in 15 min. If you want people to remember you when it's time to need a service, marketing can be key. The message has to be communicated and remembered, and it seems that GEICO has found a way to rise above the clutter of competitors, then have their message heard, remembered, and acted upon. "As of 2007, GEICO boasted over 13 million insured vehicles with over 11 million policyholders."

(Source: http://www.carinsuranceguidebook.com/geico-customer-reviews/)

INTRODUCTION

Marketing is about communicating features and value so that you can get your products and services into the hands of your customers. Marketing is giving people reasons to choose your business over your competitors. With so many competitors in the marketplace, you might be wondering how to get noticed. If you simply rely on regular advertising, you will be at a competitive disadvantage compared to a business that uses several marketing angles to deliver a message of value to customers. When you finish this chapter, you will know how to coordinate various strategies to deliver a unified message informing customers about your products, your benefits, and why they should buy products or services from you.

Marketing   any activity that informs or promotes your products and services in a way that helps you sell to your customers and end users.

Market research   collecting and analyzing information for good decision making before you develop and introduce products (and also collecting and analyzing feedback afterwards as well).

MARKETING YOUR PRODUCTS AND SERVICES

There are many ways to define "marketing" because such a wide range of activities are involved when businesses communicate with end users of products and services. **Marketing** is any activity that informs or promotes your products and services in a way that helps you sell to your customers and end users. Marketing is more than just advertising, as we explore in this chapter. Marketing is about making a connection with your buying public. Sometimes that can be done through mass media advertising; other times it must be done via personal relationships. In fact, most marketers consider the present time to be the "customer relationship" era of marketing. While there's no exact date for when this began, it can likely be traced to the advent of widespread use of computers by businesses and the Internet by consumers in the early 1990s. That's because computer databases and the Internet make it easy for marketers to track consumer buying patterns and use those to try and foster customer loyalty.

Now more than ever, customers want to feel that you understand what they want and need. So, not only do you need to perform **market research** to collect and analyze information for good decision-making before you develop and introduce products, but you also need to constantly collect and analyze feedback afterward. This will help you evaluate, adjust, and react to changing consumer

© violetkaipa/Shutterstock, Inc.

needs, wants/desires, and expectations before your competitors do. Sometimes you can customize your product to fit certain consumers' wants; other times you can tailor your marketing message to show how your service fits with consumers' desired lifestyle. Market research can also help you anticipate future needs of customers (which will be useful in the Product Development chapter).

From this focus on customers, a new business discipline has emerged: **Customer Relationship Management (CRM).** CRM says that businesses should learn as much as possible about their customers, then direct all of the companies' efforts and resources toward satisfying what the customers want. Figuring out how to do this profitably is what makes marketing successful. Marketing needs to have a customer focus (to figure out what customers want or need), a service focus (to ensure that customers are satisfied), *and* a profit focus (to make money for the company so that it can continue in business).

© violetkaipa/Shutterstock, Inc.

Customer Relationship Management (CRM) business discipline that says businesses should learn as much as possible about their customers, then direct all of the companies' efforts and resources toward satisfying what the customers want.

Competitive Advantage

We said in the Economics chapter that there are two reasons why people will buy products from your business: your products are cheaper or your products are better. Your business has a **competitive advantage** if you are able to deliver products or services that have better features or at a lower cost than other companies, so you can charge a lower price. For a competitive advantage to be valuable to your company, though, it must be **sustainable**. This means that you can deliver your unique value proposition to your customers consistently and ideally in a way that can't be copied by competitors. Any good idea that you introduce will likely be copied unless it can be protected with a patent or © or ®.

Whether you can protect yourself or not, you must still be constantly innovating to stay one step ahead of your competitors—and then ensure through your marketing efforts that customers recognize your unique position in the market. Consumers might like going to a certain fast food chain to try the newest menu offerings. It's all "food," but patrons of that particular chain come to have certain expectations for variety and quality. Or, customers might enjoy flying one airline over another because of friendly staff who make trips smooth with planes that arrive on time. When you know your company is better and other companies can't do things as well as you can, or if you have better people who will make the end user's experience with your business exceptional, then that's where it's up to your marketing to tell potential consumers why you should get their business.

Keep in mind that this competitive advantage can be real or sometimes just perceived in the minds of consumers. This is why marketing is such an important tool for businesses. If you have the lowest prices, that should be an easy message to convey, but you still have to get the word out to people who may or may not know about your company's prices. If you are promoting your products or services as having better features or value than others, however, that can be more challenging. You need to be able to convince the end users that your products or services are worth the price you are charging, or that you will deliver a better experience than other companies and thus you should be their preferred choice over your competitors. So, to be a successful marketer, you have to understand how your customers think.

Competitive advantage being able to deliver products or services that have better features or at a lower cost than other companies so you can charge a lower price.

Sustainable delivering your unique value proposition to your customers consistently and ideally in a way that can't be copied by competitors.

© VLADGRIN/Shutterstock, Inc.

Total Product Offer

There might be just one reason why consumers choose to buy a product, but often it's a combination of reasons. The **Total Product Offer (TPO)** is everything a customer evaluates when deciding to buy something. Keep in mind that only some of these things are objective and quantifiable. For example, when a customer is deciding whether or not to buy a product online versus in store, any shipping charges would be added to the online price before a comparison is made. Other points of comparison are subjective and not easily determined in dollars and cents. When considering an online versus store purchase, two different consumers might have completely different perceptions on the benefit of getting a product right away compared with waiting for it to be shipped.

Total Product Offer (TPO) everything a customer evaluates when deciding to buy something.

© maimu/Shutterstock, Inc.

Certainly, many customers shop based on price, but most customers also consider **value**. Value can be defined any number of ways. The basic definition of **value** is the worth or usefulness of something. Later we'll see that your business customers may have different perceptions of value, but continuing our early focus on consumers, we can also say that they see **value** as good quality at a fair price. So, putting this all together, when customers look at your TPO, they are looking at your price, your quality, and the benefits of your product or service, among other things.

Value the work or usefulness of something. Also, good quality at a fair price.

Product line a group of related products offered by the same company.

Product mix a combination of all the product lines offered by a single source.

Product Line, Product Mix

It's hard, though, for businesses to be all things to all people, especially with a single product. That's why companies try to offer a complete **product line** and a **product mix** to capture as many customers as possible. A **product line** is a group of related products offered by the same company. Think of this as a group of similar products all lined up beside each other on the store shelf, trying to appeal to different consumer needs, wants, and desires. So, for example, the Coca-Cola product line includes Coke, Diet Coke, Caffeine-Free Coke, Cherry Coke, and so many more. Even the offering of Diet Coke and Coke Zero nearly side by side is intended to give consumers maximum choice for taste or ingredients and keep them from buying a competitor's product.

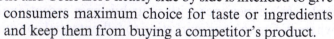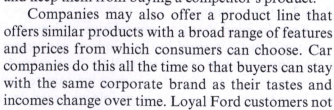

© Chones/Shutterstock, Inc.

Companies may also offer a product line that offers similar products with a broad range of features and prices from which consumers can choose. Car companies do this all the time so that buyers can stay with the same corporate brand as their tastes and incomes change over time. Loyal Ford customers not only have a wide range of options and features that can be added to customize a low-end Fiesta, they can also move up in the Ford product line by choosing the benefits and value of a Focus or Fusion or Taurus.

A **product mix** is a combination of all the product lines offered by a single source. Think of this as an assortment of products offered by a manufacturer to provide consumers with additional items they typically buy together and thus get more sales from their current customers. So, for example, the product mix offered by PepsiCo includes not only the Pepsi-Cola product line of soft drinks, but also the Frito-Lay product line of snack chips. The consumer might have to visit another aisle in the store, but this related product mix makes sense since many people buy soft drinks and snacks at the same time. Not only does this give consumers more choices, but it also helps the company capture more sales from customers with whom they might have built a loyal following.

Back to our Ford example, customers in the market for a truck can choose an F-150 since that is part of Ford's product mix and stay loyal when they're ready for a luxury car by considering a Lincoln (which is also owned by Ford). In fact, as we'll see by the end of this chapter, it's often easier and less expensive for you to sell more to your existing customers than it is to get the attention of new customers and convert them into buyers.

FOUR P'S OF MARKETING

You might think that it's easy for customers to figure out which product they want to buy, which one suits their needs. That is not always the case, of course, and so that's why you need to "help" customers with your marketing efforts. You need to be clear about the benefits of the different products you offer, as well as how you are better than your competitors. Marketing is about helping buyers buy your products. You do this through your **marketing mix**: a combination of strategies and messages designed to influence consumer behavior. You have several chances to do that during the decision buying process, thus you should focus your efforts on four distinct areas often referred to as the **Four "P's" of Marketing**: **Product**, **Price**, **Place**, **Promotion**.

Product

Your **product** is simply the good or service you sell, along with whatever enhancements you include with it. Your product should be very **customer-focused**, finding out and then fulfilling customers' needs, wants/desires, and expectations. You can do this effectively if you consider all three levels of your product that contribute to the **Total Product Concept**. Basically, the Total Product Concept starts by looking at the **core product** that fulfills a customer's needs. So, a Snapple

Marketing mix   a combination of strategies and messages designed to influence consumer behavior.

Four "P's" of Marketing   Product, Price, Place, Promotion.

Product   the good or service you sell, along with whatever enhancements you include with it.

Price   what you charge customers for your good or service.

Place   where and how you make your products and services available for purchase.

Promotion   how you make your product or service attractive to potential buyers to generate sales (now or in the future).

Customer-focused   finding out and then fulfilling customers' needs, wants/desires, and expectations.

Total product concept   all three levels of your product that contribute to its essence; core product, actual/expected product, and augmented product.

Core product   basic product function that fulfills a customer's needs. (The first level of Total Product Concept.)

ice tea is, at its core, just a drink to satisfy thirst; a Jeep is, at its core, just a vehicle that provides transportation. You must identify the core need consumers have so as to ensure that your product meets this at a minimum, but if your product stops there, then you can't really command any premium above your competition.

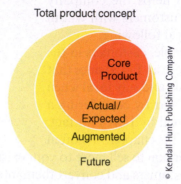

Total product concept

Core Product

Actual/ Expected

Augmented

Future

© Kendall Hunt Publishing Company

You want to get to the second level of the Total Product Concept where your **actual product** (or **expected product**) is able to fulfill a customer's wants/desires, and thus your product is seen as different from your competitors. This **product differentiation** is what makes your product (or service) unique from others (and hopefully better) in the eyes of your customers. This can be because of features, quality, or even a comfort level because the product carries a certain **brand** name on it. So, Jeep® is seen as a rugged vehicle for people who like to venture off road; Snapple is "made from the best stuff on earth®." Each product adds just enough features (Jeep's off-road capabilities) or benefits (Snapple's all natural ingredients) to get people in the target market group to want that product. If done right, then you will be successful in persuading those people to buy from you because they want/desire those features and benefits.

Finally, to seal the deal, you can go one step further to meet or exceed customers' expectations with the third level of the Total Product Concept by offering an **augmented product**. Here you can provide things like a quality guarantee, an extended warranty, free installation, or easy financing to help make your product irresistible to those unsure of which product to finally select. Although these benefits may appear intangible, they serve to reinforce with customers the company's belief and commitment to quality and service. Keep in mind, though, that over time these augmented product features may become expected as actual product features by consumers in the future. Think about how the length of car warranties has increased over the years or how many consumers wait to purchase vehicles until special low rate financing is offered.

Price

The **price** is what you charge customers for your good or service. We try to make a careful distinction between this and the **cost** or expense you incur to make something. They are related, and some people talk about the cost *to* consumers, but it's important that you don't confuse the two. It's best if you consider "cost" as what you need to pay and "price" as what you sell something for—and then always try to consider both "cost" and "price" together as you make business decisions. If you only focus on price, then you will be tempted to cut your price to try and boost sales (even if your costs don't justify the reduction). This is

© iceink/Shutterstock, Inc.

short-sighted and is generally a long-term losing strategy for your business. Unless you are also able to cut your costs to preserve enough of a profit margin, you might not be able to stay in business. Instead of focusing exclusively on price to compete, you should instead focus on creating value. Remember that one definition of value is good quality at a fair price. If your marketing convinces customers that you offer a better-quality product, then they will be more likely to pay you more. Same goes if you add usefulness to your product with extra features or benefits, as long as you can charge more than your costs.

© Robert Kneschke/Shutterstock, Inc.

Sometimes you can even *raise* prices on products and remain profitable. Your first instinct might be that you will lose customers. That's possible, but you need to look at the overall picture of how much product you can sell and at what price point. Not everyone is buying solely on price, and your marketing can convince some that your product is worth the price you charge. If you don't lose all of your sales, then it's quite possible that you will make more off of the customers who remain. If you increase your quality, for example, or add value in other ways, then you should expect to command a higher price in the marketplace. As long as enough customers agree, then you will not hurt your business in the long run.

Some of the flexibility you have in setting prices is locked in by decisions you make during the product development process. For example, using higher quality materials might prevent you from being the low-cost (and hence the low-price) leader in your market space. On the other hand, if you are able to sell more and take advantage of economies of scale, then you have found a way to cut costs, so you have another decision to make: Will you cut your prices to new lower levels or instead take the newfound "extra" profits to add more features to your products while maintaining your "old" price? Think about this: decades ago, most cars were sold with manual crank windows and power windows were available for

© GooGag/Shutterstock, Inc.

an extra charge. Today, with the high volume of power windows the automakers have sold through the years, economies of scale have brought the price down to a point where manufacturers usually install power windows at no extra charge in the vehicles they sell. (We'll revisit this in the Product Development chapter.)

Don't think, though, that you should include everything to get the highest possible price because that does not always work. Customers have different perceptions of value when they consider the Total Product Offering. Not everything adds "value" in the eyes of the consumer, so don't include things that you can't recoup in your pricing structure. Furthermore, you might provide some things "free" and include other things as "extras" for an additional charge. This gives consumers maximum options and lets you offer a variety of prices points so that you can capture as many consumers as possible.

Place

Convenience having your products and services available where (and when) your customers need them.

Convenience good product consumers can readily buy on impulse (such as candy).

Place is where and how you make your products and services available for purchase. You need to provide **convenience** so your products and services are available where (and when) your customers need them. Of course, not every product is a "**convenience good**" that consumers can readily buy on impulse, but you want your products to be widely distributed and easy to find. If you are providing a service, you also need to be concerned with how accessible is your business. These are important considerations in marketing. Above all, make it easy to buy things from you!

© 3dmask/Shutterstock, Inc.

For services, "place" is mostly about location. That's why you see pharmacies like Walgreens and CVS on many different street corners all around the city and fast food places like Wendy's and McDonald's on every major route. If you are a small business with just one location, you want to pick the best spot, not just with lots of traffic, but the "right" traffic. A high-end spa would do best in an affluent neighborhood, whereas a family restaurant would do best where demographics show middle-income patrons with kids are located.

Distribution channels using various marketing intermediaries to get products from the manufacturer or producer to the consumer or end user.

With products, you may be able to use marketing that sells your products directly via your website or through other electronic means. You can also use telemarketing, vending machines, kiosks, or independent sales representatives, but these types of direct sales are often a small part of the total sales for larger companies. Instead, they broaden their reach by setting up **distribution channels** that use various marketing intermediaries to get products from the manufacturer or producer to the consumer or end user. These **intermediaries** act as middlemen who assist in the movement of goods and add value by providing transportation, storage, and other services.

The typical distribution channel for consumer goods involves two stages between producer and end user. Manufacturers sell large quantities of goods in bulk to a **wholesaler** who takes delivery of goods, stores them, and breaks them into smaller lots. These smaller lots are purchased by **retailers** who place goods on store shelves so that they are available for consumers to examine, compare, and purchase individual units. Companies that intend their products for consumers can have a retail distribution strategy that is **intensive** where they will sell to anyone and try to be everywhere (e.g., candy or beverages), or **selective** where they will choose a preferred group of stores (e.g., appliances or brand-name clothing), or **exclusive** where they will decide on only one location per area (e.g., vehicles or luxury watches). Larger retailers willing to provide their own distribution and storage often buy directly from manufacturers.

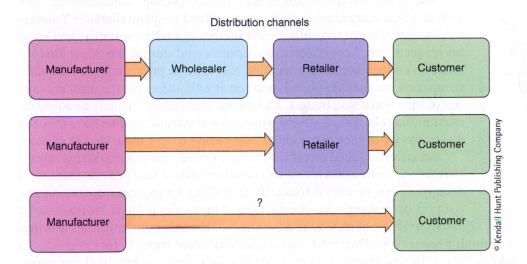

Distribution channels

© Kendall Hunt Publishing Company

Intermediaries middlemen who assist in the movement of goods and add value by providing transportation, storage, and other services.

Wholesaler marketing intermediary that takes delivery of goods, stores them, and breaks them into smaller lots.

Retailer marketing intermediary that places goods on store shelves so that they are available for consumers to examine, compare, and purchase individual units.

Intensive retail distribution strategy where companies will sell to anyone and try to be everywhere (e.g., candy or beverages).

Selective a retail distribution strategy where companies will choose a preferred group of stores (e.g., appliances or brand-name clothing).

Exclusive a retail distribution strategy where companies will decide on only one location per area (e.g., vehicles or luxury watches).

Some wholesalers specialize in selling only to business customers and do not deal with the public. This can mean fewer frills at the point of sale—sometimes the sales floor is just a warehouse—but there are other ways these transactions can be different. Whereas consumers often purchase individual units, business customers usually purchase greater quantities. So, even though there may be fewer business customers in an area, they are typically larger customers. Business customers care more about rational facts of the products' benefits rather than responding to emotional messages or marketing ploys. Finally, consider that personal relationships are often important for business customers who feel more comfortable buying from salespeople they know and trust.

Promotion

Promotion is how you make your product or service attractive to potential buyers to generate sales (now or in the future). This is all about **communication** to inform and motivate customers, raising their awareness of your products or services and the reasons that yours are better. Information is one thing—it can increase brand

Communication informing and motivating customers, raising their awareness of your products or services and the reasons that yours are better.

© hamidisc/Shutterstock, Inc.

© Black Jack/Shutterstock, Inc.

awareness, provide good word-of-mouth, and lead to future sales—but motivation is the key to make those extra sales occur now.

The most effective promotions typically prompt consumers to take action. Large companies can sometimes afford to spend marketing dollars to associate their brand with certain images to make consumers feel good about them, but how effective is a commercial during the Super Bowl if you don't remember the product that had the cute puppy in the ad? Smaller companies, on the other hand, must ensure that they get the most mileage out of their marketing budget. This means that rather than relying solely on mass media (like TV ads), these companies must find creative ways to reach customers when they are ready to buy—and prompt them to take action.

An effective social media campaign or other guerilla marketing efforts that inform consumers about a product or service and provide them with a coupon can be useful tools. By including an expiration date on the coupon or making sure the recipient knows the offer is "for a limited time," this can spur someone to take advantage of the sale now instead of waiting. Although people typically need to see something three times before deciding to take action, effective marketing can push that sense of urgency in clever ways. A free sample not only lets consumers see how much they enjoy your product, but if done in person, it might compel someone to purchase more on the spot. Or, if you make people think that they might miss out, then they are more likely to act.

Of course, large companies do all of these things—and you should, too. The **promotion mix** provides the right combination of traditional advertising, promotions, and publicity. A successful mix will also include personal selling, word-of-mouth, and various other "official" and "unofficial" marketing and promotion activities. It used to be enough just to have a strategy of **publicity** to inform the media about your new product or service, but with so much noise and many sources of information, companies large and small have had to get creative to get noticed. You have probably seen **viral marketing** that gets people to share a message (perhaps in the form of a video) that doesn't seem like a commercial. The idea is for it to feel like something personal shared between friends, and the company's product or service just happens to be there as a side benefit. Small companies started these, but now companies of all sizes see this as a way to get attention.

Promotion mix   the right combination of traditional advertising, promotions, and publicity. (A successful mix will also include personal selling, word-of-mouth, and various other "official" and "un-official" marketing and promotion activities.)

Publicity   strategy to inform the media about your new product or service.

Viral marketing   getting people to share a message (perhaps in the form of a video) that doesn't seem like a commercial.

A FEW MORE P'S

There are a few more ways that you can market to consumers, trying to persuade them to choose your product over the competition. These final opportunities can cause people to purchase your product at the point of sale. Here we are referring to **Packaging, Positioning, and People**.

Packaging

Although **packaging** protects your product during shipping, it also can help you sell the benefits of buying from you. This may be your last chance to inform people and influence the customer's choice, especially if you are selling an ordinary product in a large retail environment. There may be no one around to answer questions about the benefits of your product, so the packaging is often your final link to the customer before purchase. With colorful or clever packaging, you can grab the attention of buyers, then once they hopefully pick up your product, you have one last opportunity to explain the features and convey the value of what you are selling.

In addition to explaining your "normal" product features, you could also use the packaging to highlight added benefits, point out the product guarantee, or detail your extended warranty provisions. A company might **bundle** a small free sample of toothpaste when you buy a toothbrush, package together extra software inside your video game system to give customers more perceived value, or announce that this package includes more bonus product free in an effort to convince consumers to choose a particular product at the point of sale.

Companies may also change packaging once in awhile in the hope that customers will give them a second look. Often, the product will tell consumers in big letters that the product is "new and improved" or "new look, same great taste. " A new formulation might actually have improved the taste or usability of a product. Upon closer inspection, a clever consumer might also notice that sometimes the manufacturer has changed the size of the product. The "new look" of the peanut butter label might be hoping to distract you from the fact that the jar that used to be 20 ounces is now only 18 ounces or the 16 ounce cake mix is now 15.25 ounces—a small change perhaps, but a clever way to hold retail prices steady in the face of rising material costs so that profit margins can be maintained.

© Sheila_Fitzgerald/Shutterstock, Inc.

Less nefarious packaging changes might contribute to marketing by actually helping the producer sell more. The invention of juice boxes extended the shelf life of those products and made them more accessible for kids at various outings, for example. But, sometimes, you can figure out ways to sell more with just words! How much more snack foods do you think manufacturers sell by announcing that their products are "Low Fat" or "Gluten Free?" Certainly, some foods are specially formulated that way, but other foods already fit into those categories and the food companies' marketing departments realized that they could increase sales by announcing those "features" to consumers without having to change a thing—except the packaging.

Packaging   something that protects your product during shipping and can also help you sell the benefits of buying from you.

Positioning   deciding which target market you want to reach with your products and then pursuing that market segment based on demographics, geography, benefits; dividing the market into groups to reach the ideal prospective customers for your product or service.

People   anyone who works for your company, ultimately sales people for your product or service.

Bundle   including something extra in a package, usually an additional item or sample to increase value.

Positioning

With **positioning,** you decide which target market you want to reach with your products and then pursue that market segment based on demographics, geography,

benefits, or some other way that you think is best to divide the market into groups to reach the ideal prospective customers for your product or service. As we said earlier, your marketing efforts should be focused on helping those targeted customers recognize your unique position in the market. You then design a marketing strategy whereby you occupy a market niche based on being "best" at one or more of the four P's: product, price, place, or promotion. Let your product features define your position and vice versa; use tiered pricing based on the income of your buyers and the prestige you offer; be where customers are and make sure your products are easy to buy; advertise to help customers understand and give people a reason to make that purchase, now.

Your goal is to inform consumers and influence them to buy. Tell customers why your products are better or cheaper. Remember that your marketing message can convey facts as they are, or try to change perceptions of consumers perhaps by turning a potential disadvantage into an advantage. Companies might brag that they aren't the cheapest because they are the best; or tell consumers that it's worth the effort to find a certain product. Sometimes you might point out the weaknesses in your competitors' product or services, but usually a positive message is best. Consider that a great brand image cultivated over time can convey a certain prestige to customers who will seek you out.

People

People are important in any business endeavor, but they can be a critical component in the success of your marketing efforts. The first thing to understand is that in every company, all people are potential ambassadors of your products and services, your image, and your brand. For example, if your advertising gives the impression that you are a fun place to shop, those marketing dollars are wasted if a customer comes in and encounters an unfriendly employee. The experience should match the message for maximum effect. All people who work for your company are ultimately sales people for your product or service. They need to be knowledgeable about your marketing as well.

The person selected to be the official spokesperson for a company is also an important marketing choice. Will the President of the company appear on TV or be quoted in your marketing materials? If you are selling a health product, would employing a Doctor give more credence to your health claims? Can ordinary people giving a testimonial be beneficial, or should you hire a famous person to endorse your product? Don't think that a celebrity can make up for having a bad product or service that people don't want. A celebrity may command attention if chosen correctly and make sure that people in the target market will listen, but ultimately the marketing message has to be clear and accurate. Usually, it's not enough that kids want to "Be Like Mike," which was a famous tagline when Michael Jordan was endorsing products beyond the basketball realm. The product must deliver what you promise.

Whatever avenue you choose, ultimately, the customer must be satisfied with your product once they purchase it if you want your marketing efforts to succeed. A marketing message that exaggerates is just as bad as a salesperson who makes promises that can't be kept. That's why it's so important for all of the people in your organization to know and understand the marketing message that your company is trying to convey. People are just as important as the four P's of marketing when making sales and keeping customers. In fact, people can be your competitive advantage if you consistently hire workers who deliver the best customer service experience to the buying public.

SELLING TO BUSINESSES VERSUS SELLING TO CONSUMERS

When we talk about the value of people to marketing your business successfully, keep in mind that your employees do play a slightly different role depending on whether you are selling to businesses or selling to consumers. Let's examine some of the differences between the **Business-to-Consumer (B2C)** and **Business-to-Business (B2B)** markets. As we compare both of these, know that what ultimately determines which market you are selling in comes down to the buyer's reason for buying your products and the end use of what is purchased.

Business-to-Consumer (B2C) the consumer market and all individuals and households that buy products for personal use.

Business-to-Business (B2B) the industrial market and all the businesses (and individuals) that buy products to re-sell, as components for making goods, or for other business uses.

You might think that consumer goods are those things that ordinary people buy in stores, whereas business goods are industrial-type products purchased as components for making other goods. While that distinction might seem clear-cut, think about other things with dual uses. That's when you need to keep the buyer's reason and end use in mind. Thus, the small cans of tomato paste on the grocery store shelf are a B2C product, whereas the large cans of tomato paste sold to a local pizzeria are a B2B product.

Business to Consumer (B2C)

Business to Consumer (B2C) refers to the consumer market and all individuals and households that buy products for personal use. Much of what we've discussed in this chapter applies directly to the selling of goods in the B2C market. That's because it is the largest market of potential purchasers, and individual consumers are the easiest to reach through large-scale marketing campaigns. It's getting harder to reach specific consumers, however, as the audience for media has become more fragmented.

© Monkey Business Images/Shutterstock, Inc.

That's one reason why the price of sports advertising has continued to rise significantly even as the costs of other forms of media advertising have not grown as much. Sporting events are one of the last ways to reach a mass audience with people tuning in live to be part of the shared experience. Most other forms of entertainment can be recorded and watched on demand by consumers (which also means that commercials can potentially be skipped). So, while mass media advertising has become more challenging, other forms of electronic media provide unique ways to track the effectiveness of a marketing campaign. Social media provides a unique frontier of reaching a large audience while maintaining the appeal of a personal campaign. Expect more exciting marketing opportunities to emerge as this continues to evolve.

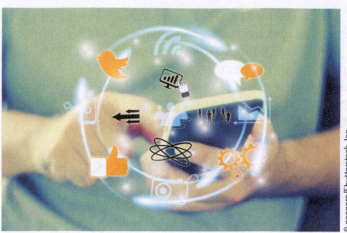

© nopporn/Shutterstock, Inc.

Business to Business (B2B)

© wavebreakmedia/Shutterstock, Inc.

Business to Business (B2B) refers to the industrial market and all the businesses (and individuals) that buy products to resell, as components for making goods or for other business uses. Although much of what we've been talking about seems to be tilted toward consumers and consumer products, many of those concepts do apply to business customers as well. We've already pointed out that there are typically fewer business customers for most products, but they do tend to order more. There's typically more direct, personal selling since business buyers are generally more rational and need facts rather than hyperbole to make a purchase decision. Relationships and trust can be an important factor in B2B sales.

We also said earlier that business customers have different perceptions of value than consumers. Take financing, for example. Making something affordable by offering payment terms is an effective marketing strategy to get customers to make a purchase. But, whereas a consumer who sees a cool car ad on TV and wants to buy one will likely just focus on whether or not he/she can afford the monthly payment, a business customer will be very concerned about interest rate, repayment date, and other specific details of the transaction. Furthermore, business customers are usually much better at negotiating and realize they have some bargaining power in the process, compared with most consumers who buy many items in a store with no haggling.

Push versus Pull Marketing

Although it may seem that the consumer market and the business market are very distinct, you often need to deal with both—sometimes simultaneously. Keep in mind that there might be several people you need to convince to buy your product along the way. If you are selling a consumer product that will appear on retail shelves, how can a person buy it in the store if you don't first convince a business customer (a wholesaler or a retailer) to buy the product? When we first discussed the four P's of Marketing we said that you need to "help buyers buy," but now we're saying that you also need to "help sellers sell. " This is where Push and Pull Marketing comes in.

Push marketing marketing directed toward businesses, convincing wholesalers, and retailers to stock and sell your product.

Push Marketing is marketing directed toward businesses, convincing wholesalers and retailers to stock and sell your product. They will be interested in the benefits of your product and the value proposition you are presenting to customers, but they will also want to know what advertising and marketing you are doing so that customers will know about your products and ultimately purchase them.

Pull Marketing is marketing directed toward consumers, getting them to go into stores and buy your product off of retail shelves—or request it if they don't see it. You need to create this demand by using the four P's of marketing to convince consumers that they want or need your products. This is where brand loyalty can be a huge benefit.

Both of these ideally need to work together. You need to "push" the product onto the shelves at retail and also get consumers to "pull" the product off of the shelves. If you only do Push Marketing, you have lots of unhappy retail customers who have shelves filled with product they can't sell and ultimately have to discount or clearance out. If you only do Pull Marketing, you have scores of frustrated consumers who can't find a product they're interested in and may buy something else from a competitor instead of continuing to hunt for your product.

Pull marketing   marketing directed toward consumers, getting them to go into stores and buy your product off of retail shelves—or request it if they don't see it.

© Lisa S./Shutterstock, Inc.

THE MARKETING UTILITIES

In order for us to transform these marketing concepts into ways to make money, it helps if we understand the marketing utilities and how they apply at various stages of the distribution channel. **Utility** is the usefulness of something, the ability to satisfy a want or need. These are additional marketing considerations that companies integrate with the four P's of marketing. By increasing the usefulness of a product or service, companies add value for which they charge money and attempt to make a profit. If buyers agree, then they will pay more and companies will continue to provide more. If a company does not add value, then it should expect to go out of business.

These **marketing utilities** are ways that products (or services) are made more "useful" to customers or end users. Manufacturers, distributors, retailers, and marketing intermediaries at all stages of production, distribution, or selling need to add value so that these companies can make money from the process. Sometimes steps that create

Utility   the usefulness of something; the ability to satisfy a want or need.

Marketing utilities   ways that products (or services) are made more "useful" to customers or end users.

© marinini/Shutterstock, Inc.

value occur when goods and services change hands between companies; sometimes value is added in ways that get products into the hands of consumers. Although businesses and consumers may have different perceptions of value, in the end, only functions that add value can result in sales and profits.

- **Form Utility.** This is when you change the form of materials into something consumers or businesses can use. Obviously, the manufacturing process can turn components into final products, but even a butcher cutting a side of beef into steaks is creating value through form utility. (Sometimes services use the term **task utility**.)
- **Time Utility.** This is making products available when consumers or businesses need them. Businesses that use just-in-time inventory processes find this utility valuable; stocking products in a store that's open 24 hours is a time utility consumers enjoy.
- **Place Utility.** This is making products available where consumers or businesses need them. Delivery is one kind of place utility enjoyed by businesses and consumers; so is the convenience of having multiple locations where products and services are available.
- **Possession Utility.** This makes it easier for services to be purchased and goods to transfer ownership. Allowing customers to pay on credit is an obvious benefit. When a large item (e.g., a furnace) needs to be installed, this is another possession utility that customers expect to pair for separately or accept that it's built into the price.

Some other utilities we can consider include:

- **Information Utility.** This gives point-of-sale marketing materials to businesses or consumers to help close the sale. Everything, from brochures to displays to samples, provides a value that is often not directly added to the final price, but is incorporated during the process of selling the goods and services.
- **Service Utility.** This provides additional value to keep customers happy with their purchase. Service utility can be anything from training to service after the sale. Sometimes there's a specified level of service included in the price; other times it's an extra charge that customers pay.

As we said, companies must add value if they expect to make a profit. If a company buys a raw hunk of copper, the company cannot turn around and resell the metal for more money unless value is added, perhaps by making it into something (form utility) or delivering it to the end user when needed (time utility).

Form utility when you change the form of materials into something, consumers or businesses can use. (Sometimes services use the term **task utility**.)

Task utility when your labor produces something consumers or businesses can use. (For manufacturers use the term **form utility**.)

Time utility making products available when consumers or businesses need them.

Place utility making products available where consumers or businesses need them.

Possession utility makes it easier for services to be purchased and goods to transfer ownership.

Information utility gives point-of-sale marketing materials to businesses or consumers to help close the sale (e.g., brochures, displays, and samples).

Service utility provides additional value to keep customers happy with their purchase (e.g., training, service after the sale).

© testing/Shutterstock, Inc.

Also, keep in mind that customers may or may not know the amount of markup they are paying for a given utility, since not all of these utilities are charged directly to the buyer. While sometimes costs of the utilities are built into the price, other times additions are obvious.

When a consumer buys a pound of coffee from a display at the grocery store, the information utility for the displays is simply a marketing cost added to the final price of the coffee at some point in the distribution chain, but it's hard to pinpoint the exact extra amount. On the other hand, a consumer can fairly accurately calculate the additional charge made for the place utility of buying a cup of coffee that is sold next to the departure gate at the airport. The consumer's decision to buy or not buy each of these products ultimately determines whether or not the price point can be sustained in the future and the various utilities will continue to be offered.

PUTTING IT ALL TOGETHER TO INCREASE SALES

We finish up this chapter summarizing how marketing can increase sales and make profits for you. Marketing is not about getting people to buy stuff they don't need; marketing is moving the demand curve. You want to increase the number of people buying your products or services. Sometimes that is getting the word to completely new customers and growing the market; other times that is persuading people who are already in the market for something that they should buy from you and not your competitors. You do this by communicating your value proposition via your marketing.

Sometimes your product already has the features people want because you are very customer-focused. Other times you have the best price because you were able to control costs; or maybe you aren't the cheapest but your price is still a good value for what you have to offer. You have your product available in as many places as possible, making it convenient for people to buy from you when they're ready. Finally, you use effective promotions to communicate with—and motivate—customers to buy from you.

Once you are good at the four P's of marketing (Product, Price, Place, Promotion) and the corresponding four C's (customer focus, cost, convenience, communication), you have to decide how to get the word out. Money is always an issue, so you have to make sure that you reach the most potential customers with your marketing dollars. That's why mass media advertising is not always as good as a focused, personal campaign (perhaps using social media). Once you have some satisfied customers who have bought from you in the past, it is often much cheaper and easier to target the existing customers and keep them coming back than it is to get the attention of new customers and convert them into buyers.

We mentioned service as one of the marketing utilities. Good service can definitely keep people coming back—even if you cost a little bit more. Another way to get customers to consider more than simply price is offering some type of loyalty program. This can be another good marketing tool that rewards repeat business and might sway customers to keep buying from you even if your competitors drop their price a little bit or you need to raise your price. To create an opportunity for new customers to hear your message and consider buying from you, you might resort to a celebrity endorsement, event sponsorship, or a contest.

Finally, there are numerous other ways that you can use marketing to capture consumer attention and hopefully make you appear "better" than your competitors. As much as we like to think companies pursue community projects for philanthropic

© PILart/Shutterstock, Inc.

© Michelangelus/Shutterstock, Inc.

reasons, part of the thought behind Corporate Social Responsibility (CSR) in the Boardroom is the recognition that there is good publicity and customer loyalty that can be gained by spending some marketing dollars on "giving back. " Maybe you can't afford to make donations from Day 1, but once you're established as a viable business, then there is synergy to be realized in finding ways to support the community. Even "going green" is often a marketing strategy: if a company can't make a profit from recycling, then the hope is that goodwill can increase sales to offset any added costs from environmental efforts.

So, remember that marketing is communication: telling people why you are better at meeting their needs. Whether you discuss value or demonstrate philanthropy, your goal is always getting the word out about your company and its products or services. Use everything at your disposal, from advertising to positioning to labeling. All of your marketing should have the same unified message and goal, always giving customers reasons to buy from you.

OPEN FOR BUSINESS IN THE REAL WORLD

At first, you thought that just putting up a website and advertising were enough, but now you are ready to rethink your entire marketing plan. You were going to have some flyers printed up to hand out at the local rec center, but now you realize you have to include more than just your name and phone number. You know that your personal trainer business is better than people only going to the gym alone; now you just have to convince people why that is the case. The four P's of Marketing are a good starting place to get your business on the right track for success.

Looking at the product portion of your business, you feel that your service is already very customer-focused. In fact, you tailor the workout to each client's individual needs. The problem was that you weren't saying that before until you met up with new people for the first time. Instead, now you added some language on your site and to the brochure that explains exactly what you do, how you customize your personal training workout to match the goals of each client. Done.

As far as price goes, you really only have the cost of renting the facilities. Since you're a member at the gym and can bring a guest any time, you have that figured out. It helps that your costs are fixed, even if you can't do anything to cut them right now. You've decided that you aren't going to cut your price, though. You're already cheaper than some other personal trainers you know, but that's not your focus. (Why tell potential clients what others charge anyway if they don't already know that?) Instead, you decide to point out on your site and in your flyer that you are saving clients' money since they don't have to buy their own gym membership! That fact alone can save people some significant money; plus you point out that personal attention 1-on-1 makes you worth what you're asking.

Place is another really good aspect of this business. With your gym membership, you can visit any of the gym's locations to work out and so you make sure clients know that you can come to them. Since your schedule is very flexible, you'll meet them any time as long as you don't have another appointment. You note this fact also in another bullet point on your site and this advertising flyer you're revising.

Finally, promotion: this is what has you the most excited. Let's see, buy six lessons and get one free. That seems like a good idea. You also plan to give a $15 gift card to say "Thank you" for any new referrals you get from current clients. Finally, you settle on a 10% discount for the first lesson if people "hire" you before the end of the month. You've got it all covered: loyalty program, referral bonus, and a discount that prompts them to take action right away. You also point out in your marketing that there are no up-front fees and people can pay for each lesson one at a time.

The final piece of the marketing puzzle is the fact that you have a pretty well-known local sports figure who is a good friend of yours. You and he used to work out together, and he's the one who inspired you to start the personal trainer business since you helped him so much—and he's willing to say that in your marketing materials! Now in addition to handing out those flyers you give the local newspaper a call. Have you got a story for them! Your business wasn't "interesting" until you got this endorsement from your friend/spokesman, but now you think you'll get mentioned on the "Local" section of the newspaper's website. This marketing has turned exciting and you're ready to go.

Chapter Summary

There are a wide range of activities involved when businesses communicate with end users of products and services. Marketing is any activity that informs or promotes products and services to help buyers buy. Companies use marketing to help differentiate their products so that a customer will think that their products are cheaper or better. This can help give businesses a competitive advantage over other companies. Customers look at the total product offer to compare price, quality, value, and other things. Companies have a product line to offer choices to consumers and a product mix to capture more sales from loyal customers.

The Four P's of Marketing give companies several opportunities to influence customer buying patterns. Product tries to be customer-focused so that there are expected and augmented benefits offered to entice a purchase. Here product differentiation can include real or perceived benefits or maybe comfort with a brand. Price tries to charge consumers based on preference and quality. Companies must control their costs in order to be a price leader, or provide more value to justify a higher price, or offer a range of options. Place tries to make it as convenient as possible for customers to purchase. This is about how products are distributed, where they are made available, and may even include delivery. Promotion tries to communicate with customers to inform and motivate them to take action. In addition to traditional advertising, a company's promotion mix may include social media, viral marketing, or sampling with limited time offers.

Additional ways to sway customers toward your products include: packaging, where you can grab attention or explain additional advantages; positioning, which allows for targeting a certain market segment to promote unique advantages; and people, who can help cut through the noise to ensure that your message is heard.

Selling to businesses via B2B marketing involves more fact-based and relationship selling, compared to consumers via B2C marketing where finding ways to reach them is important. You also need to engage in push and pull marketing: push marketing to wholesale and retail customers to get your products on the shelves, and pull marketing to consumers to generate demand and get your products sold off of the shelves.

The marketing utilities are ways that products are made more useful to customers or end users: form, making materials into something usable; time, making products available when needed; place, making products available where needed; possession, making credit or installation for easier purchasing; information, providing displays or samples; service, to keep customers happy after the sale.

Review Questions

1. When you think about Customer Relationship Management (CRM), what do you think is the most important aspect to cultivate with your customers?

2. List some of the larger companies in any industry and try to determine some of their sustainable competitive advantages? What is the best marketing communication vehicle for each?

3. If customers look at the Total Product Offering (TPO) and start to expect Augmented Product features as part of the Actual/Expected product, is there anything you can do?

4. Are companies better off expanding their Product Line or their Product Mix? Explain.

5. Which of the four P's of Marketing do you think is most important? Least important? Should companies try to adjust them all at the same time or focus their efforts?

6. Come up with a new way that a promotion can prompt customers to "act now. "

7. What are some other packaging changes you can think of which might help manufacturers sell more of a product?

8. Do you think advertising is more effective when it uses testimonials from actual users or a celebrity endorser?

9. Can you think of products that are exclusively B2C or B2B, or is every product a potential candidate for both the B2C and B2B markets?

10. Which is the "easier" marketing effort: Push Marketing or Pull Marketing? Why?

11. If we look at the Marketing Utilities, there is a definite correlation between those and one or more of the four P's of Marketing. Detail what you think are the primary and secondary "P's" for each utility.

12. Discuss how you would go about getting customers to view your company as better than your competitors through CSR or other similar means. Are you persuaded by that type of marketing message? Will it make you shop at a certain place or buy something?

Discussion Questions

13. What are some things you can do so that your competitive advantage is more sustainable? Is there ever such a thing as a permanent sustainable advantage? Why or why not?

14. If you could only spend your time and money on one of the four P's of Marketing, which would you say is most important to work on? Explain and defend your position.

15. While it's useful to hire someone famous to help gain attention and ensure that your marketing message is heard, do you think this is a good use of marketing money? Are you persuaded by celebrity endorsements? Are there better alternatives?

16. Which do you think is more important: push marketing or pull marketing? Is there a way to try and do both with one message? Come up with some creative options.

17. The marketing utilities are all about making it easier for customers to buy from you. Which ones do you think create the most value in the minds of customers? Which ones do you think you can charge extra for?

Key Terms

- actual product
- augmented product
- brand
- bundle
- Business to Business (B2B)
- Business to Consumer (B2C)
- Communication
- competitive advantage
- convenience
- convenience good

- core product
- Cost
- customer-focused
- Customer Relationship Management (CRM)
- distribution channels
- exclusive
- expected product
- Form Utility
- Four "P's" of Marketing
- Information Utility

- intensive
- intermediaries
- market research
- Marketing
- marketing mix
- marketing utilities
- packaging
- People
- Place
- Place Utility
- positioning
- Possession Utility
- price
- product
- product differentiation
- product line
- product mix
- Promotion
- promotion mix
- publicity
- Pull Marketing
- Push Marketing
- retailers
- selective
- Service Utility
- sustainable
- task utility
- Time Utility
- Total Product Concept
- Total Product Offer (TPO)
- Utility
- value
- viral marketing
- wholesaler

CHAPTER

10

Production and Operations Management

LEARNING OBJECTIVES

1. Explain the difference between mass production, custom production, and flexible production.
2. Identify the steps in the production process.
3. Explain the primary functions a production manager must perform.
4. Explain the process of ensuring quality production.

© RedTC/Shutterstock, Inc.

OPENING STORY

Some markets are very efficient, that is, there are no or almost no transactions that fail to take place. Other markets are very inefficient and many transactions do not occur. From the productions and operations management perspective, one may work in an industry where everything you build is sold and every sales order is met; that is an efficient market. In another inefficient market, you might build a product that never gets sold, or have a customer that is unable to find the product they want, because no one builds it.

The magazine industry is very inefficient for its nonsubscription sales. They place them in grocery stores, drug stores, and gas stations, and hope you buy one. They have no idea where you might buy or even if you will in any given month so they must overprint and place them all over the place. If there are magazines left over at the end of the publishing period, they must buy them back from the grocery stores. Subscription prices are much lower, because the sales are predictable; therefore, production levels are known and the market is efficient. Nonsubscription sales are difficult to predict and inefficient, with huge inventory returns, so the cost is much higher, driving higher prices.

Another inefficient market is the auto industry. They produce automobiles to park at dealerships all over the country, hoping they get the colors and option packages right to attract buyers. At the end of each model year, they are putting on huge sales to try and get rid of the overproduction.

They must also guess when to stop production for a given model year so they do not over- or underproduce. If they underproduce, the dealerships run out of vehicles for their customers, and if the factory overproduces, the old cars are competing with the new cars.

Aircraft and some house production are efficient. Boeing does not have lots where you can wander looking at the aircraft and pick out the model, color, and options you want. They only build it when you have ordered it. Many home builders are the same way. In a new neighborhood, they let you look at model homes and then contract to build. Once the contract is signed, then they build the home. Market efficiency saves huge costs for producers and allows the firm to keep prices down. This does not stifle competition, however, as other companies in the same industry will also be efficient.

INTRODUCTION

Production and operations management varies considerably with the type of market, the processes used, and the efficiency of the market. When we discuss production, we are not just discussing products. Production and Operations Management also applies to services. Massage Envy offers massages, facials, aroma therapy, and other therapeutic services. They have facilities around the country, management, budgets, human resources, equipment, and inventory, as well as the standard problems of personnel turnover, competition, economy, and changes in consumer preferences and tastes. The process of producing and marketing a service is not much different than producing and marketing a good, except for the transportation of the good and the location of the service.

Whether producing a good or a service, the steps must be carefully laid out, the resources applied, and the production quality controlled.

An earlier chapter discussed all the various parts of a business that need to be managed. The various assets like cash and capital assets, vehicle fleets, the facility itself, the human resources, finance, and the list goes on. Every business must realize that every asset it owns or uses must be protected and used in the most efficient manner to get the most out of the asset. In a similar way, the work itself must also be carefully managed so the production is done at the most effective pace, at the best cost, in compliance with the existing regulations, and meeting the customer's needs.

Economics discusses the need to create utility or satisfaction with each product or service. From the individual perspective, we discuss how much utility or satisfaction, compared to cost, that is derived from consumption of a product. Utility, from the businesses standpoint, comes in four different types, time, place, ownership, and form. Marketing provides utility in three of these different types, time utility, place utility, and ownership utility. In other words, get the product at the right time, at the right place, and at the right price.

Production and Operations Management provides the fourth utility, that is, form utility. Although a tree has form utility as it is, to provide shade, attractive landscaping, oxygen production, and others, the tree's form can also be changed to provide paper, fuel, lumber for houses, or furniture, fencing, toys, and countless other products. Iron ore has no utility sitting in the \ground, but through production and operations management, can become a toaster, building, automobile, or the machinery used to print this textbook.

© V.J. Matthew/Shutterstock, Inc.

THE PRODUCTION PROCESS

How a company goes about producing its product or service depends on many factors and even two companies within same industry may do things differently. Production processes generally fall into several different categories; mass production, custom production, and flexible production.

Mass production is the method by which companies produce large quantities of identical or very similar products, typically using an assembly line process. Mass production is used for products that have wide appeal, which drives the need to produce many items and to keep the cost as low as possible so as not to be undersold by a competitor. **Assembly line** processes aid in this by using interchangeable parts, automation or robotics, and rapid production. In an assembly line, a product typically moves along a conveyer and workers or robots add parts until the product is finished. An alternate method is not to move the product, but move the workers. In large aircraft production, for instance, workers move from station to station as they assemble the aircraft, each worker or team of workers completing their specialty and moving to the next. A similar process is used in building several co-located apartment buildings, with one group doing a foundation and moving to the next site while the framers begin on the first site.

Mass production the method by which companies produce large quantities of identical or very similar products.

Assembly line using interchangeable parts, automation or robotics, and rapid production.

© bibiphoto/Shutterstock, Inc.

Mass production, while very productive, may be inflexible in what it produces. As long as every product is identical or very similar, mass production is fast and efficient. Automobile manufacturers have been able to develop variations in the cars they produce with the use of Just-in-Time parts delivery. **Just-in-Time systems** deliver the needed part to the assembly position, precisely as it is needed. **For example**: One car coming along the line might need a standard driver's side mirror and the next one might need a lighted mirror. In an older system, a worker would have to check to see which would go on the car and get the correct one from a bin of parts. Just-in-Time delivers the correct part through a separate conveyer, just as the matching car arrives.

Henry Ford is generally credited with the first efficient use of mass production, used to produce automobiles in an era when they were handcrafted and quite expensive. Prior to that, muskets were mass-produced for the Continental Army, by building standard parts and assembling the guns when before, they had each been handcrafted. If a part broke, a new one would need to also be handcrafted. The standard parts allowed muskets to be fixed using a replacement part and greatly speeded up production and cut cost.

Custom Production is the method by which companies produce similar products, but which are specifically designed and produced to meet customer-driven needs. **For example**: A swimming pool installation company can provide a standard rectangular pool, or they can design and install a pool that is built for a given homeowner's yard, with waterfalls, fountains, slides, sunning shelf, spas, diving boards, and many other features. Several organizations specialize in training service animals to provide a wide variety of services for impaired people. Service animals also can be trained to alert on conditions such as blood sugar changes for diabetics. Service animal training is custom production, in that the product is similar, but each person has special needs that must be addressed in the training process.

Just-in-time systems inventory method used so that components, materials, and even finished goods are received just as needed for production and distribution.

Custom production the method by which companies produce similar products but which are specifically designed and produced to meet customer-driven needs.

© Andrey Armyagov/Shutterstock, Inc.

© Jeroen van den Broek/Shutterstock, Inc.

Custom production does not mean a company cannot or does not use assembly line, or at least assembly line like processes, in its operations. Installing swimming pools is an example; the group that digs the hole can move from site to site, continuing to dig the holes as their specialty. As they leave each site, the experts that lay the water pipes and drains arrive, do their work, and follow the diggers to the next site. Soon thereafter, another group is blowing the concrete material into the frame and other groups follow the same pattern. Although construction follows a similar pattern and the product is similar, custom production allows a company to produce exactly what the customer wants. Although production cost is always

© Randy Miramontez/Shutterstock, Inc.

a consideration, custom production allows a wide variation in production cost and therefore price. Since the product is created to satisfy customer specifications, the cost and therefore the price will be dictated by the customer.

Flexible Production is a method by which companies use advanced robotics and computer software to build different products on the same assembly line. Flexible production has elements of both mass production and custom production. The products are normally produced on an assembly line, using machinery and robotics and produced in mass quantities at the lowest cost possible while maintaining quality. However, products may be substantially different from one production run to another. **For example**: An automobile company may use the same assembly line to produce two different model cars.

Flexible production
method by which companies use advanced robotics and computer software to build different products on the same assembly line.

LOCATION – LOCATION – LOCATION

Deciding where to locate a production facility can be a critical factor in the success or failure of a business. Looking for the right location will involve a number of considerations (Figure 10.1).

Labor   One significant factor is the cost and availability of labor. Different parts of the country and the world have widely different labor costs and widely different availability of skill sets. A trained work force is critical to operations. Too few workers with the right skills or, in some cases, too few workers period may drive the location decision. **For example**: In 1999, BMW decided against locating an automobile

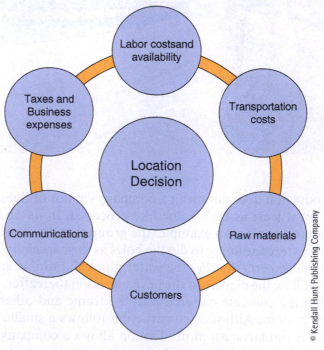

© Kendall Hunt Publishing Company

Figure 10.1   Factors influencing the location decision

© mast3r/Shutterstock, Inc.

assembly plant in Omaha, Nebraska, because of an extremely low unemployment rate, indicating a shortage of labor and therefore difficulty in staffing a large production plant. A production company must consider what the normal industry labor costs are for their type of company. Offering pay that is too low will not attract the quality of employee they might need, but offering pay that is too high may make them uncompetitive. Sometimes the decision is to outsource or offshore, that is, use the lower labor costs frequently found in other countries, such as Mexico or China. Although this can save considerable labor costs, it generally increases the next item to be considered: transportation. Products produced in a central location must be distributed to the customer.

Transportation   Costs and methods can have an impact on the cost of operations. Labor cost savings from producing in another country may be overcome by higher transportation costs. Even within the United States, transportation cost must be considered. The most common forms of transportation include trucking, railroads, waterways, and air cargo. Each type of transportation has its advantages and disadvantages. Trucks can get almost anywhere, but are the most expensive of the large-scale transportation methods. Shipping by ship or barge is the cheapest, but obviously requires not just a river, but one large enough to have navigable channels and docking facilities in the right locations. Railroads are relatively low cost, but do not go everywhere and are inefficient unless shipping large amounts. Air transport is the most expensive and is generally only used for relatively small, high-value shipments that have prices large enough to make transportation a minor part of the price, or important enough that it does not matter.

© Andrey Tirakhov/Shutterstock, Inc.

© Aleksey Stemmer/Shutterstock, Inc.

Raw Materials   Not only is transporting the final product important, but so is shipping the raw materials. Although many production processes may use common items, others may require specialized ingredients such as the rare earths necessary for high-tech instruments. Location near the sources of component parts or materials can ease supply chain worries as well as costs. Just as the final product incurs transportation costs, so do raw materials or components.

Customers   In addition to the location of the raw materials, the location and needs of a company's customers are a vital component of the production process. Some products have mass appeal and the potential customers are everywhere. When Proctor & Gamble produces toothpaste, they ship it around the country to be available for everyone. Many companies will also produce in different places. Many of the vegetables we purchase from grocery stores are actually produced by independent canning companies who have a contract from the name brand company. This shortens the supply chain and reduces transportation costs. The Kellogg's cereal plant in Omaha, Nebraska, produces the name brand products and then also produces store brands under contract.

Communications   New technologies are rapidly changing the nature of internal and external business communications. Not many years ago, facsimiles or faxes were an emerging technology that got around the need for mailing documents. Now email, remotely accessed databases, document sharing, and worldwide wireless telephones have brought almost instant communications and access to documentation. Although businesses can and do still travel for face-to-face meetings, the use of phone and video teleconferencing has reduced the need for that and virtual meetings can take place so that everyone in the meeting can see and hear the other participants without leaving their office. Communication is still a consideration within the company. The cost and availability of communication technologies will continue to make an impact on businesses.

Taxes, Regulations, and Business Expenses

Different states and cities are perceived as either more or less friendly toward businesses. Businesses bring jobs, which are good for localities, but local governments also tax businesses for revenue purposes. Companies making a location decision must consider state and local taxes along with business regulations and licensing requirements when making those decisions. The Keystone XL pipeline company spent years trying to get approval to route their pipeline through Nebraska to connect the oil production facilities in Canada and the Dakotas, to the oil refineries in the Texas Gulf Coast region. Taxes and licenses are a drain on business gross profits. In a competitive market, lowering business costs, including taxes, just a few percent can make a big difference in the competitive position of a company.

THE TECHNOLOGY DECISION

Some processes are naturally labor-intensive, that is, they are done by hand with people doing most or all of the work. Other processes may be capital-intensive, which is using machines or robots to do the bulk of the work. Even within a single industry, a company may choose one over the other. The rapid improvements of robotics have made heavy production much easier and less expensive by using robots to do much of the repetitive, heavy, or dangerous work.

Although much more expensive to purchase, robots give companies considerable savings over the long run.

FUNCTIONS OF A PRODUCTION MANAGERS' JOB

In simple terms, every manager's job is the same, that is, to satisfy organizational goals through the management of organizational resources. Production managers must use the people, capital, machinery, raw materials, and processes to create the form utility or go from inputs to outputs. This involves four critical steps:

1. Planning the Production Process from start to finish
2. Creating the Best Layout that creates efficiency of operations with the flow of materials and work
3. Implementing the Production Plan that has been planned
4. Controlling the Production Process to ensure quality outputs.

| Planning the Production Process | ⇨ | Creating the Best Layout | ⇨ | Implementing the Production Process | ⇨ | Controlling the Production Process |

Figure 10.2   Functions in the production manager's job

Planning the Production Process

Planning the Process includes everything from research on what products are needed and at what price to determining what will be produced, how it will be produced, at what pricing point, at what quality level, and the target market for the product or service. In the planning process, the production manager must recognize not just what the customers want, but also what they are willing to pay. Most products and services can be produced in different ways, each of which will have a cost associated with it as well as a quality standard (Figure 10.2).

Creating the Best Layout

The physical layout of the plant or production process is critical to efficient operations. There are several types of layouts depending on the product or service being produced and the physical size and shape of the facility in use. In every case, the purpose of creating the best layout is to create efficiencies in operations. If a worker has to interrupt their operations to go and get a part, or the part is not available when needed, the process becomes inefficient and unnecessarily expensive.

Types of layouts include:

Product Layout

This type of layout is most associated with assembling a product in an assembly line process such as building an automobile. The goal is to standardize the time spent at each station so the good being built can flow smoothly through the process.

Fixed Position Layout

This type of design is used for operations in a building or facility in which there is no movement of the product. Ship building uses this type of layout as do staffing and locating workers in a large building. The purpose in layout design is to create efficiencies and avoid people and equipment getting in each other's way.

Process Layout   The process layout designs the movement of people and materials through a process that may or may not all take place in the same location. A process layout is what is done by package shipping companies. They must receive the packages, sort them, prepare them for movement, move them, resort for delivery, and finally, deliver the packages. The entire process may take several facilities and potentially thousands of miles of separation.

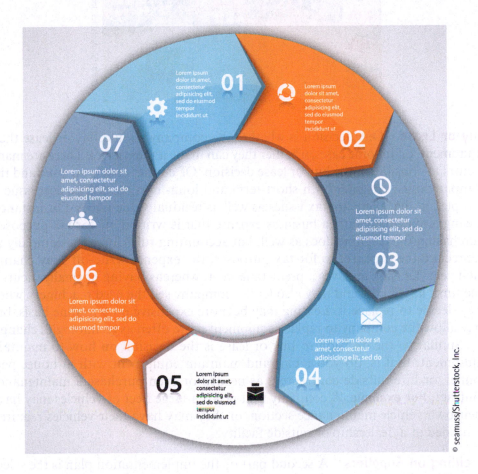

Retail Layout   In a retail layout, the purpose is to provide ease of flow of the customer in a logical way that allows the customer to find the products they want, while also displaying the highest value products (Figure 10.3).

Implementing the Production Plan; after planning and layout design, comes putting the plan into action. Implementing the plan seems like a natural step, but it also frequently includes dealing with unexpected obstacles and making numerous business decisions.

Figure 10.3   Layout design types

© wizdata1/Shutterstock, Inc.

Buy or Lease   One decision is whether the company should buy or lease their equipment, or, in some cases, whether they can make it themselves. There are many factors to consider in the buy or lease decision. Of course, cost is an issue and the company must consider both short-term and long-term costs. The cost issue is complex in that there are tax issues as well as residual value issues. For instance, leasing a machine incurs a business expense that is written off for tax purposes. Purchasing the machine does as well, but accounting rules force the company to depreciate the expense, so for tax purposes, the expense write-off may change each year. Leasing involves a predictable cost, whereas buying normally incurs a one time, larger cost and may also let the company sell the used machinery when they decide to replace it. Leasing may be more expensive on a routine basis, but may allow the company to replace equipment more often as technologies change.

Similar to the decision to buy or lease is the decision on how to maintain equipment, that is, do you repair and maintain equipment with in-house personnel, or hire outside contractors as needed or even purchase a maintenance contract. **For example**: A company that needs a large fleet of vehicles may have their own vehicle maintenance section, or they may have their vehicles repaired as needed at a dealership or outside facility.

Deciding on Suppliers   A second part of the implementation plan is the selection of suppliers. Most companies have close associations with other companies. Selecting suppliers include such considerations as their price, reliability, quality, speed, and the working relationship itself. Just as the company's own customers want value from the products, so does the company want value from the supplier.

Making the supplier decision involves comparing all of those factors. The Internet has made the process much easier and provides a great deal of information to that used to require extensive research and phone calls. Many suppliers allow orders to be placed without human involvement. **For example**: Grocery store cash registers are also inventory control links that place orders for new merchandise when they reach a certain point of sales, which are tracked by the registers.

Inventory Control   Another step in implementation is controlling the inventory. This includes the preproduction supplies, the in-process inventory, and the postproduction inventory that is awaiting sale or shipment. Warehousing materials, whether supplies or postproduction inventory, is expensive in direct costs and expensive in tying up capital. What every company wants is the right material available at the right time to produce their product and then to move the finished product to the customer as quickly as possible. To make sure they never run out of supplies, some companies will build or lease a warehouse to stock the parts or raw materials they will need. They can then purchase in bulk and store it ahead. Again, however, this is expensive. Using Just-in-Time inventory systems has allowed companies to build systems to deliver the supplies and materials just as they are needed. Doing this involves a close working relationship with suppliers as well as a lot of faith in their ability to deliver. Just-in-Time can save a company a great deal of money by not having to purchase early and store materials, but lose them a great deal of money if the system breaks down and delivery is interrupted.

Controlling the Production Process   Once the process is set up and ongoing, controlling becomes the Production Manager's focus. Controlling requires ensuring everything works, the costs are controlled, the quality is maintained, and the company operates at maximum efficiency. Each step of the production process has standards and ensuring those standards are met is the primary task. When customers drive up to the order position at a Berger King restaurant, the company tracks the time it takes from placing the order to handing the customer his or order. Telephone sales companies track how many telephone calls per hour are made or received by their personnel. Jewelry Sales companies track individual and store sales against goals. Assembly lines production tracks the number of products finished as well as the flow-through time. In each of these control processes, the standard is a target and deviation away from the target, more or less, may be an indicator of problems. The quicker problems can be discovered and analyzed, the quicker the company can correct deviations.

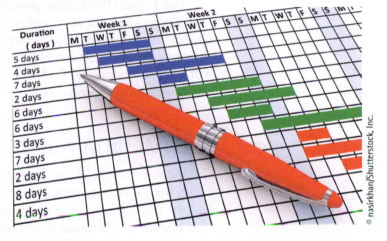

Designing the process in the first place requires careful analysis of each step, in which order, and how each step depends on and influences other steps. One tool often used is a Gantt Chart. This tool shows various work steps or processes and how they relate to each other. The Gantt chart helps show what steps must occur and in what order to arrive at the finished product or service at the right time. It provides a focus on lead time to ensure, for instance, that supplies are ordered exactly six weeks before a product is supposed to be finished for a customer.

Another planning tool is the **PERT** diagram. A PERT (Program Evaluation and Review Technique) uses a similar process breakdown to that of a Gantt chart, but does so more like a flow chart, which shows the work moving from step to step.

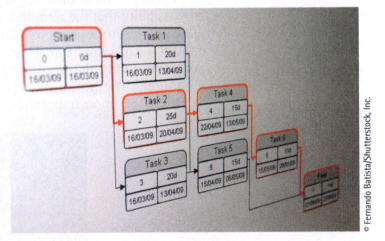

THE QUESTION OF QUALITY

Producing quality products and services has become a major goal for companies around the world. Customers want high-quality products, and they want low-price products. Traditionally, these two goals were at opposite ends of what is possible. If you can have good or you can have cheap, but cannot have both, which do you choose. Over the last 60 years, there has been more of a movement toward good quality instead of low price. Also, greater technology and carefully developed production techniques have allowed many companies to produce both good and cheap and allow their customers to have both.

The quality movement began after World War II as countries, notably Japan, rebuilt their production capacity and entered the worldwide marketplace. The principles behind the quality movement are most associated with W. Edwards Deming and Joseph Juran. These two American production experts took the quality management concepts they developed in the United States to Japan. There they developed the movement toward building high-quality products, which allowed Japan to quickly move from a country known for mass production of cheap, low-quality products to a country that was emulated and envied for its high-quality, competitively priced goods. Many companies will have a quality control section that periodically tests their products to ensure that they are meeting standards. The quality movement ideas include building in the quality to the extent that quality control is not necessary.

The Toyota Production process has so fully implemented the quality concepts that it represents the standard by which other production processes are designed. Customers still want high-quality and low-priced goods and services. Where both are not possible, customers have demonstrated a preference for quality. There will always be a market for low-priced alternatives, but most companies and most customers have chosen quality.

THE IMPORTANCE OF SUSTAINABILITY

Companies must produce their goods and services with the customer and costs in mind, but more and more, they must also consider the impact on the environment and the use and misuse of resources. The widespread consumption of nonrenewable resources has raised pollution and global climate change concerns. In addition, the depletion of these resources raises costs as supply diminishes and raises the possibility that the resources may run out altogether. Developing and using renewable resources and production methods allows a company to get involved in the "Green" movement. There are public relations dividends to be earned, but more importantly, the long-term goal is to sustain production in spite of depletion of resources. The investment in pollution abatement can result in cost savings and tax credits, but more importantly is the right thing to do in the long term.

© Dusit/Shutterstock, Inc.

© Dandesign86/Shutterstock, Inc.

OPEN FOR BUSINESS IN THE REAL WORLD

Whenever the U.S. Military wants a new major weapons system, they will ask competing companies for bids. Since there are frequently many considerations of capability and price, it is not just a simple matter of selecting the lowest bid. Companies are sometimes asked to design and build a prototype that will have a competitive operational test before the final selection. This is a high-cost and high-risk opportunity for a military defense company.

One such competition was recently between Boeing, which wants to improve and modernize the FA-18 Fighter aircraft, and Lockheed/Martin, which wants to produce the F-35 Joint Strike Fighter. The contract is worth billions and a huge benefit to whichever company gets it. Not only will the companies need to produce a high-quality product, but they will also need to use every aspect of production and operations management to improve quality while holding down costs to give them the most profit potential.

Lockheed/Martin won the competition and the F-35 will be produced and will replace the F-18, F-16, A-10, and AV-8 aircraft. Employing innovation, advanced technologies, and every aspect of sound management allowed this company to win a valuable, multiyear contract.

© Keith Tarrier/Shutterstock, Inc.

Chapter Summary

Production and Operations Management is the big business operation, especially in manufacturing. Organizing and managing large production companies brings special challenges.

The production process may be mass production in which large numbers of essentially identical goods are produced. Just-in-Time part delivery systems can be used to speed up the process and reduce costs. Custom production is used in developing products that meet specific customer design requirements, such as a custom house. Flexible production is used to produce nonidentical goods on the same assembly line or using the same tools.

Locating a production facility involves carefully considering six factors: labor cost and availability, transportation costs, raw material availability, customers, communications, and taxes and expenses. Another decision that needs to be made is the extent of technology that will be employed when there is a tradeoff between labor and capital.

The functions of a production manager's job include: planning the production, creating the best physical layout of the process, implementing and then controlling the production process. The question of quality arises when deciding the competition and price point at which the business wants to establish itself. Higher quality and price products may bring greater value to the customer, but may also eliminate some customers.

Review Questions

1. Describe how Production and Operations Management ensures that form utility is created.
2. Differentiate between Mass Production, Custom Production, and Flexible Production.
3. Why do custom production costs vary much more widely than either mass production or flexible production?
4. Explain the factors to be considered in the location decision.
5. Discuss the transportation considerations necessary in a production company.
6. What location considerations must a company make in regard to its customers' needs and wants? How does this impact the decision to select mass, custom, or flexible production methods?
7. What is the impact do taxes and business expenses have on the location decision?
8. What are the primary functions a production manager must perform?
9. What are the different layout designs a Production Manager might consider?
10. What are some of the factors that a Production Manager must consider when deciding on suppliers?
11. Identify some of the inventory control issues that face a Production Manager
12. How has the movement toward quality production changed over the years, and who are the key people associated with that movement?
13. How has sustainability become an important consideration for production companies?

Discussion Questions

14. Discuss how you might design a Just-In-Time system to produce and ship shirts to Kohl's, so they arrive just as stock inventory reaches the point where an order for more is necessary.
15. Select several common items you normally purchase. Are they more likely to need custom production or mass production? Why? Could either apply?
16. If you were tasked with building a casino in a Midwestern city, what are some of the locations factors you would need to consider? Discuss.
17. What type of layout design would be most efficient for a community college? Why?
18. How did the quality movement develop, and who is credited with starting it?

Key Terms

- Assembly line
- Custom Production
- Fixed Position Layout
- Flexible Production
- Just-in-Time

- Mass production
- Process Layout
- Product Layout
- Retail Layout

CHAPTER

11

Global Supply Chain

LEARNING OBJECTIVES

1. Explain how Supply Chain Management is integral for procurement, outsourcing.
2. Discuss how choice of partners can influence operations decisions.
3. Detail basic and advanced logistics concepts for the movement of goods.
4. Discuss strategies for global markets, from low-risk exporting to high-risk FDI.
5. Explain the business of international trade, including the role of free trade.

OPENING STORY: ODW LOGISTICS

ODW Logistics, Inc. has been an industry leader in providing supply chain logistics solutions for medium and large businesses since 1971. They started as specialists in warehousing and transportation, but have evolved into a full- service third-party logistics (3PL) provider. ODW has their own asset-based fleet carrier (Dist-Trans Co.) offering regional trucking services, and operates warehouses throughout the country in both shared and dedicated sites. As times changed, ODW's services evolved to include a full-service transportation solution (LTS) that includes management, brokerage, consulting, intermodal, and international freight. Their newest addition to the plethora of services they offer is Manufacturing Support and Services (Demand-Driven Logistics™ (DDL)), offering the full value chain from the supplier to customer, door to door.

© DmitryKalinovsky/Shutterstock, Inc.

The supply chain has grown and evolved from simply transportation and storage to sophisticated information tracking. We'll see how information is the most important commodity, and how companies handle this determines the value added of any 3PL provider. Small and medium businesses want cost-effective, turnkey solutions for their distribution needs; medium and larger companies demand state-of-the-art inventory management systems to ensure proper tracking of goods. Today, ODW has more than 1,000 employees and over four million square feet of warehouse space, offering solutions and services that make the global supply chain easier for businesses of all sizes. Let's look at why this is becoming crucial as supply chain management evolves.

(Source: http://www.odwlogistics.com/about/index.htm)

INTRODUCTION

Global supply chain
movement of raw materials, parts & components, and finished goods throughout all stages or production, distribution, and sale of products (or services) around the world.

Supply chain movement that begins with raw materials (from suppliers) and ends with the final end-users (your customers) for the product or service.

Supply Chain Management (SCM) efficiently planning and coordinating the movement of your goods through all stages of manufacture, from raw materials to finished product in the hands of your buyer.

As you look for ways to make your business more profitable, you should at some point consider if your business is a good candidate for going global. There are actually two sides of "going global" that you need to consider by asking yourself some questions: Can I make more money by marketing and selling my products or services to more customers internationally? Can I make more money by manufacturing or sourcing my products from suppliers internationally? Keep in mind that the first question will cost you some money; the second question is about cutting costs to save you some money. In this chapter, we look at how managing your supply chain—and possibly turning it into a *global* supply chain—can assist you with both of these potential ways to boost profits.

GLOBAL SUPPLY CHAIN

Global supply chain involves movement of raw materials, parts and components, and finished goods throughout all stages of production, distribution, and sale of products (or services) around the world. Note here that "supply chain" starts from raw materials and thus begins at an earlier stage of management than the "distribution channels" that are important for marketing and moving of finished products. The **supply chain** begins with raw materials (from suppliers) and ends with the final end-users (your customers) for the product or service. This means that all companies and organizations—suppliers, manufacturers, distributors, sellers—must work together during all phases in this process of **supply chain management (SCM)**.

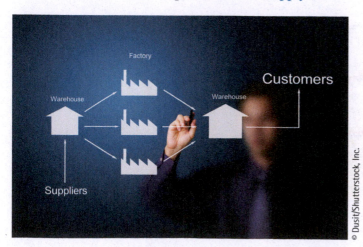

Supply Chain Management (SCM)

Whether or not your business "goes global" initially, you would be wise to consider your ultimate goals early on. Critical to your long-term success is effective domestic or international **supply chain management (SCM)**, efficiently planning and coordinating the movement of your goods through all stages of manufacture, from raw materials to finished product in the hands of your buyer. SCM can also be applied to all stages and steps required for your company to provide a service. Every business or entity that comes into contact with your good or service and contributes value to it is considered part of your supply chain, so sometimes this is also referred to as the **value chain**.

As we saw in the Marketing chapter, value can be added in any number of ways—assembling, packaging, transporting, storing, distributing, delivering—so we need to consider every aspect of the product beyond just sourcing materials or parts (often referred to as **procurement**). The more outside companies that you involve in the process of producing your good or service, the more important it is to have good coordination and communication between these partners. You must also consider whether you strategically want these to be long-term partners with whom you plan to build a relationship, or if instead you will use these as third-party vendors who simply win your business with a bid for each transaction you need completed.

While there are pros and cons to managing your supply chain in each fashion, you may also come to realize that for your particular good or service, some functions lend themselves to one style (e.g., parts are bid out for each production run based on your specs), while other functions are best handled in other ways (e.g., final assembly is done by one trusted partner with whom you can share intimate details about future sales projections so that you can plan to grow together). All of these decisions will ultimately be based on your business model, what functions you want to keep in-house versus which functions you will have performed by others in your supply chain, and the level of involvement you want to have in managing the overall process.

Value chain every business or entity that comes into contact with your good or service and is considered part of your supply chain (because they add "value" at various stages).

Procurement sourcing materials or parts.

Outsourcing

Just as we've talked about hiring subcontractors as a possible strategy to reduce up-front costs for people you need, you can also consider **outsourcing** such that other businesses are utilized or contracted to perform various functions for your business. When most people hear the word "outsourcing," they immediately think about companies moving production to China to take advantage of cheaper labor. But outsourcing doesn't have to be international and could be as simple as closing your in-house IT department and hiring an expert computer company down the street to handle those functions for you. It's safe to say, though, that the further away your "partners" are, the more careful you need to be about choosing the right one(s).

With the wealth of resources available via the Internet, it becomes relatively easy to find companies that produce the parts

Outsourcing when other businesses are utilized or contracted to perform various functions for your business.

or perform the functions your business may need. Whether you find them this way or through old-fashioned introductions from business associates, keep in mind that you should still perform some type of background research and check references to follow up on any recommendations you may receive. Such sleuthing cannot uncover everything, but the more you research, the greater comfort level you can have with these potential partners. Firms often have a reputation, and you may be able to find out positive or negative things about a person or company even if you aren't able to conduct an in-person "meet and greet" right away.

Keep in mind, though, that you cannot skimp on these travel costs forever, and a large contract or investment with a business—particularly one overseas—

© Jirsak/Shutterstock, Inc.

will require that you spend time and money to nurture that relationship. Just as some tenants will eventually take advantage of an absentee property owner, so too will you have a higher risk of something going wrong if you are not ready, willing, and able to travel when necessary. You may also want to hire someone in your company who has experience and expertise dealing with foreign companies, if that's the route you choose. Language barriers are less of a problem initially, but can become an issue for specific details that were not brought up at the outset or in dealing with problems that may arise due to cultural differences. Furthermore, you may not get the same level of diligence and productivity from offshore outsourcing partners, so, for example, hiring programmers overseas at half the hourly rate of U.S. workers does not necessarily translate into a 50% cost savings.

While there are cost savings and strategic advantages we will discuss shortly, let's continue to briefly address other possible downsides and risks of outsourcing. Whether you choose domestic or international partners to whom you outsource all or some of your business functions, keep in mind that there's always a risk that intellectual property, specialized knowledge, business secrets, and other competitive advantages you have may need to be shared with those partners in intimate detail. There is a degree of trust necessary, and you may not have the luxury of building it over time as with a normal relationship. Even if you trust the

© Stuart Jenner/Shutterstock, Inc.

supplier or manufacturer, be aware that there are additional eyes on your products and processes that you cannot control. Contracts and agreements can help, but they may be difficult and costly to enforce in foreign countries or against international companies.

Other potential downsides to consider with outsourcing are negative employee reaction if jobs are eliminated, difficulties with coordinating efforts if different time zones are involved, miscommunication possibilities if you enlist the services of foreign companies, and potential public backlash if your products are no longer "Made in America." We'll see, though, that some of the advantages in operations planning, cost savings, and potential business partnerships often outweigh these concerns.

Operations Planning

There are two important aspects of Operations Planning, which specifically apply to outsourcing considerations in the global supply chain. Recall that **Operations Planning** is the process of creating an effective strategy to convert or transform resources into goods or services. One of your goals here should be to "reduce time to market," and this involves locating your facility and operations close to your customers and transportation. Thus, any outsourcing partners you enlist should also help you with that goal. Of course, we know that suppliers will try to cater to your needs to earn your business. Just make sure that they are able to provide you with timely deliveries of parts or products so that your relationship with your customers does not suffer.

Another major consideration for Operations Planning is the procurement and purchasing process itself. Here a relationship with a provider can prove valuable in more ways than just obtaining parts at a low price. The best supplier is one that provides you with a good balance of quality, price, and logistics assistance. We'll discuss logistics more in a future section, but suffice it to say that a top supplier will work with you to ensure that your order is filled in a timely manner and delivered on time to the place you designate.

When you have fewer reliable suppliers who you have come to trust, it becomes easier to see them more like a partner. They will be an important ally in your quality control program so that inferior parts or products do not get through, and they should also work with you to provide **just-in-time** inventory so that your components, materials, and even additional finished goods are received just as needed. This way you are not burdened with additional costs associated with maintaining excess stockpiles of parts or products. Paying for storage and tying up funds for financing can prove costly!

Operations planning the process of creating an effective strategy to convert or transform resources into goods or services (often to "reduce time to market").

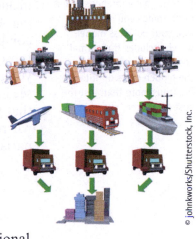
© johnkworks/Shutterstock, Inc.

Just-in-time systems inventory method used so that components, materials, and even finished goods are received just as needed for production and distribution.

Cost Considerations

Working closely with suppliers in your supply chain is just one way that you can attempt to lower costs for your business. Be sure, though, that you are considering all costs when making decisions about procurement, which suppliers to use, and whether or not you will outsource some or all of your functions to domestic or international partners. We mentioned in the last section that skillful cultivation of a just-in-time relationship with suppliers can save you money. Not only do you have less warehousing space that you must use for storage, you also free up more of your capital so that you can redeploy your funds for other cash flow needs.

Again, choosing a supply chain partner is not just about the price of the items you are buying. For example, if you are able to source materials or parts locally, you can reduce the need for long and costly delivery. Delivery charges must get added to your calculations for component prices, as well as financing charges (if you can't get the supplier to extend you credit). On top of shipping, you may also incur costs for duties, tariffs, and customs brokerage fees on international shipments.

Keep in mind that the more outside partners you enlist for parts and outsourcing of other functions, the more you may have to set aside time, money, and personnel hours to monitor and evaluate these supplier relationships. Most businesses have a formal **RFP (Request for Proposal)** process that all potential suppliers must enter to be considered for potential business relationships. There

© tkemot/Shutterstock, Inc.

RFP (Request for Proposal) formal process to monitor and evaluate supplier relationships.

are additional costs associated with checking out potential partners and then maintaining those relationships. Even legal fees can be incurred with drawing up contracts and agreements for anything more complicated than simple parts sourcing, not to mention enforcement if something goes wrong.

You may see some of all of these costs we've discussed whether you use domestic or international outsourcers, but every function in the supply chain has the potential to incur costs beyond just the part or service itself. **B**y no means is this a comprehensive list of all things you must price into your business model. A sound business strategy will have a portion of funds set aside for these contingencies and consider them a cost of doing business along with everything else.

Just be sure that you consider the **total cost of outsourcing (TCO)**, which includes the normal costs businesses see as well as the hidden costs of outsourcing. Understand that you cannot simply do a part price comparison or a wage comparison between your workers and outsourced workers, then use either of those alone as a basis for calculating cost savings to your company—especially if you plan to have a global supply chain using international suppliers. What we'll see in the next section is that outsourcing is best used strategically for functions that you or your company are not capable of doing well on your own. That is where business partnerships can contribute more than just lower costs for some parts, people, or services.

Total Cost of Outsourcing (TCO)   a comprehensive list of all things you must price into your business model, which includes the normal costs businesses see as well as the hidden costs of outsourcing (thus more than just the cost of workers' wages).

© KPG_Payless/Shutterstock, Inc.

Business Partnerships

Business partnerships can do more for your company than simply provide cost savings. In fact, you will often spend lots of time and money trying to move your business functions to partners and outsourcers, particularly if they're overseas. Remember, it takes effort and energy (not to mention capital) to transfer know-how and train others to do what your company already does well. Generally, it makes sense to begin outsourcing for functions your business does *not* currently do well, and that way you can bring in partners that can further your business in other ways also. Certainly, **vertical integration** (combining business functions at various stages of production, such as buying from a parts supplier) can save you money, but **horizontal integration** (several firms working together to share resources at the same stage of production, such as partnering with a foreign trading company) can actually help you open new markets.

In addition to looking for cost savings, you should seek out business relationships with potential partners who can help you manage your supply chain *and*

Vertical integration   combining business functions at various stages of production, such as buying from a parts supplier.

Horizontal integration   several firms working together to share resources at the same stage of production, such as partnering with a foreign trading company.

provide additional value. Sometimes this value will come in the way of potential marketing arrangements that benefit all companies involved. Such cooperative marketing can actually open up new markets for your products in the foreign country where your outsource partners are based. If you have a good working relationship with them and they believe in your company and its products, then that can provide a way for you to sell into those foreign markets.

© Goodluz/Shutterstock, Inc.

With a global supply chain, you'll see that if partners are chosen wisely, then perhaps there will be some opportunities to sell to these businesses. If your partners like your products and see value in what you have to offer, then they may want to offer your products or services to customers in their home country where they have selling expertise. This represents the new way of looking at supply chain management as a partnership. You will want to integrate as many functions as possible, coordinating within your company and across all of these partners, creating a high performing business that takes competitive advantage of all potential synergies. This new cross-functional approach with an emphasis on horizontal integration across your organization and all of these partners in an outsourcing alliance is referred to as **business process outsourcing (BPO)**.

BPO moves beyond simply cutting costs and instead leads to efficiency, competitive advantage, and strategic market opportunities not available alone. You can be more responsive to changes in the marketplace and even develop new products or services demanded by your customers. Global supply chain is about planning and managing all activities for sourcing and procurement, as well as collaboration with partners. These partners can be suppliers, manufacturers, distributors, sellers, and even your customers. Coordination and collaboration in the supply chain open up new opportunities. These links all begin with information, which is at the heart of logistics.

LOGISTICS

In business, **logistics** is planning, coordinating, managing, and controlling the movement of all aspects of goods (or services), including all related information flows during the entire process. This is an integral part of the marketing function for a business and actually goes one step further than supply chain management with information being the key component here. Logistics is what links all parts of the chain and helps organize the coordination of these processes allowing for

Business Process Outsourcing (BPO)   new cross-functional approach for outsourcing alliances, with an emphasis on horizontal integration across your organization and all of these partners, which leads to efficiency, competitive advantage, and strategic market opportunities not available alone.

Logistics   planning, coordinating, managing, and controlling the movement of all aspects of goods (or services), including all related information flows during the entire process.

successful procurement, production, storage, and delivery to the ultimate buyer. Logistics management is what makes an order into a sale. If the information is used well, it can form the basis of repeated sales to keep the channels full and even reveal future sales opportunities.

Basic Logistics Concepts: Warehousing and Flows

When most people hear the word "logistics," their thoughts go to storing and moving goods. There are actually two main types of warehouses used for most logistics purposes. A **storage warehouse** is a large building where finished goods, components, parts, raw materials, and so on are kept for the long term until they are needed. A **distribution warehouse** is a facility designed for short-term storage such that finished goods, components, parts, raw materials, and so on can be redirected easily to their final destination. There is no set amount of time used to distinguish "long term" from "short term." It can vary by industry and depends on the intent of the companies involved.

Storage warehouse large building where finished goods, components, parts, raw materials, and so on are kept for long term until they are needed.

Distribution warehouse a facility designed for short-term storage such that finished goods, components, parts, raw materials, and so on, can be redirected easily to their final destination.

Inbound logistics any raw materials, parts, goods, and so on, that you receive into your facility for the purpose of using, modifying, storing, or distributing those items.

Outbound logistics any raw materials, parts, goods, and so on, that you send out of your facility, primarily for distributing those items to your customers.

The movement of goods, parts, and so on also has its own terminology and depends on the perspective of where the company sits in the supply chain. From your perspective, **inbound logistics** has to do with any raw materials, parts, goods, and so on that you receive into your facility for the purpose of using, modifying, storing, or distributing those items. **Outbound logistics** has to do with any raw materials, parts, goods, and so on that you send out of your facility, primarily for distributing those items to your customers. So, typically you receive materials or parts or components inbound, process them to add value, and then send your finished products outbound.

While items are in your possession and need to be moved around your warehouse, factory, and so on, that logistics process is **materials handling**. Every partner in your supply chain will likely do some type of materials handling within their own facilities as well. A final type of logistics you should be familiar with is **reverse logistics**, whereby items are sent from customers back to you or other partners in your supply chain for various reasons. Defective returns are likely the first thing you might think of here, but reverse logistics is also necessary for recycling efforts (e.g., used oil or dead rechargeable battery disposal), core recapturing (e.g., old car parts are returned to be remanufactured into new items), or formal recalls (e.g., when repairs or replacements are done by companies voluntarily or ordered by the government).

Think of inbound logistics as bringing parts and materials into your operations for processing; then you send the finished products on their way using outbound logistics. As part of the chain, you must also be sure to do effective sales and marketing to sell the products with follow-up service to take care of satisfied customers. When you can't do all the steps yourself, then you need some help from outside third parties.

Materials handling   items that are moved around inside a warehouse, factory, and so on.

Reverse logistics   when items are sent from customers back to you or other partners in your supply chain for various reasons.

Inbound Logistics → Operations → Outbound Logistics → Marketing & Sales → Service

© Kheng Guan Toh/Shutterstock, Inc.

Third-Party Logistics (3PL)

Although you may be able to do some of these logistics functions on your own, it's likely that you will need to utilize outside companies to help with some or all of your logistics needs. **3PL (Third-Party Logistics)** firms provide various services to customers in support of supply chain management functions. This is one type of outsourcing that can perform all or some of the functions you need to effectively and efficiently manage your flow of items and information. 3PL functions usually include transportation, warehousing, storage, and materials handling. Early in the supply chain, some 3PL companies can also help with parts procurement and vendor management. Late in the supply chain, additional 3PL services can include inventory management, order fulfillment, and customer service.

3PL (Third Party Logistics) outside firms that provide various services to customers in support of supply chain management functions. 3PL functions usually include transportation, warehousing, storage, and materials handling, and can also include inventory management, order fulfillment, and customer service.

"Pick and pack"   when individual customer orders are received into a warehouse and personnel "pick" the listed items from inventory and "pack" them together for shipment to the buyer.

One common arrangement is for a small manufacturing company to focus its energy on designing, creating, and making innovative products, while that small company enlists the services of a 3PL company to **"pick and pack."** Here the 3PL company has a section of its warehouse devoted to a variety of finished goods from the manufacturer. As individual customer orders are received, 3PL personnel will "pick" the listed items from inventory and "pack" them together for shipment to the buyer. In this way, the 3PL adds significant value beyond mere transportation and warehousing while the manufacturer does not have to maintain extra personnel, storage, or capital for facilities.

© Monkey Business Images/Shutterstock, Inc.

Effective SCM uses your resources in coordination with various partners in your value chain. Some of these will be in-house, others will be outside companies. These partners may provide incidental services to secure their place in your value chain; other times you will need to enlist the services of a separate 3PL company that can provide specific services you need. SCM integrates these functions with logistics information to coordinate and manage all of these various roles and processes within your company, as well as across all of your partner companies to create an integrated and cohesive business operation that benefits your customers.

Information Flows and ERP

Effective information management is what makes logistics an important component of supply chain management. Coordination of these various processes (procurement, manufacturing, distribution, etc.) can drive sales and help all partners in the value chain. Information can help you be more profitable: inventories can be kept lean and customer needs can be met. Collaboration begins with suppliers at each stage of production, and information flows can help everyone match their supply to actual demand in the market. The earlier this information is known, the better planning and forecasting can be put in place.

One innovation that has helped everyone share in the information flow is the continued expansion of ERP software. **Enterprise Resource Planning (ERP)** software allows companies to integrate business functions using shared data at every stage of production. The key to ERP is its use of one database, which all departments, personnel and even outside companies can access for up to the minute information for planning purposes. Let's look at how ERP can show the flow of useful information, not only for the manufacturing process, but also other departments in your company, such as human resources, accounting, finance, even sales and marketing.

Whenever a new order from one of your large customers comes in, all pertinent data are entered into the system's ERP software. Instantly, your parts department knows that more components must be ordered, human resources knows that more overtime will need to be scheduled, and your finance people can decide what lines of credit or other financial avenues must be tapped to pay for everything. ERP can help coordinate business activities for procurement, manufacturing, sales, marketing, finance, and more. Even the ideas for new products can be gleaned from data flows showing which designs and features are the most popular with your customers.

ERP uses information technology to help managers plan, organize, lead, and control the entire process. Information helps companies make more money since resources are used more efficiently and effectively. By monitoring all business resources—raw materials, components, production capacity, personnel—and allocating those as needed—for procurement, inventory, current orders, payroll—capital is only used to produce output as needed. Reducing **cycle time** needed to complete production of an item from the time the order is received until the item can be shipped to the customer increases productivity and profits. Better cash flow may also result from knowing exactly when items have shipped so that money can be collected as soon as it's due.

From raw materials to final shipment of the finished product, ERP can make collaboration easier and aid your supply chain efforts, using logistics coupled

© iQoncept/Shutterstock, Inc.

Enterprise Resource Planning (ERP)   software that allows companies to integrate business functions using shared data at every stage of production, helping everyone share in the information flow.

Cycle time   the time needed to complete production of an item or produce output from the time the order is received until the item can be shipped to the customer.

with information to create a value chain. Logistics makes sure that things get to where they need to go; ERP ensures that nothing goes where it isn't needed and everything gets to where it is needed on time. Planning ahead means that money is saved by avoiding rush shipments that are more costly.

© Macrovector/Shutterstock, Inc.

Advanced Logistics Concepts: Transportation Terminology

In the first part of this section, we discussed logistics terms for the flow of goods (inbound, outbound, etc.). Here we go a little deeper and get you familiar with terms you may hear from the transportation and logistics companies handling your freight. Both domestically and internationally, there are a number of modes of transportation you can use to have your parts or products shipped as cheaply as possible. Truck and train may be the most familiar to you, but you can also use water and air. Going from cheapest to most expensive, generally it is water/ocean, train/rail, truck/over-the-road, air. Using a combination of these shipping methods is referred to as **intermodal**, and this is often needed both because of where your goods are located or need to go and also to obtain the best total shipping price.

If you procure any components or manufacturing overseas, you will likely use water or ocean shipping of your cargo quite a bit. Although it can take three weeks or more for goods to reach North America from Asia, there is tremendous cost savings—especially when compared to the alternative of air shipments. Certainly for special customers or in time-sensitive situations, you may choose air even with the extreme cost, but you will need to be familiar with ocean cargo voyages for long-term profitability.

Intermodal using a combination of shipping methods (water/ocean, train/rail, truck/over-the-road, and air) both because of where goods are located or need to go and also to obtain the best total shipping price.

© Egorov Artem/Shutterstock, Inc.

For all but the biggest companies, most will use a **freight forwarder**, who combines many small shipments into one larger shipment that can fill a standard ocean container. Generally, these containers are just under 8' tall and 8' wide, and come in standard lengths of 20' or 40'. That's a lot of cargo space! If your goods are the first ones in, you may wait a few extra days for the freight forwarder to fill up the container. The party responsible for shipping and insurance will depend on terms agreed to when the purchase contract was negotiated. In addition to any **purchase order** agreement between you and the seller stating quantities bought

Freight forwarder transportation specialist that combines many small shipments into one larger shipment that can fill a standard ocean container.

Purchase orders contractual agreement between buyer and seller stating quantities bought and conditions of sale.

Bill of lading   an additional document given from the seller to the shipper of the goods showing details of the shipment, such as description, quantity, destination, and conditions of transport.

Free On Board (FOB) shipping designation meaning that the seller will only deliver the goods to a terminal from which the goods can be shipped out of the seller's home country (e.g., FOB and Taiwan).

Letter of credit   document whereby an international bank releases money from buyer's account to the seller once it has been confirmed that all conditions of the sale have been fulfilled.

and conditions of the sale, an additional document called a **bill of lading** is given from the seller to the shipper of the goods showing details of the shipment, such as description, quantity, destination, and conditions of transport.

Typically, the cheapest price quote for you to buy stuff will be negotiated as "FOB, <u>city.</u>" This designation of **Free on Board (FOB)** means that the seller will only deliver the goods to a terminal from which the goods can be shipped out of the seller's home country. This would be an ocean port in a foreign country, for example, and once delivered to the port and put onto the boat, then you as the buyer become responsible for all shipping charges, insurance, and so on during the journey to get the goods where you need them. So, for example, you negotiate to buy some components "FOB, Taiwan," then the maker/seller of those parts will deliver them to a boat dock in Keelung, Taiwan, and once the goods are put onto the boat of your designated freight forwarder, then you are responsible for them (shipping charges, insurance, etc.) to your home country. At that point, the seller will typically expect to get paid as well. This usually happens via a **Letter of Credit**, whereby an international bank releases money from your account to the seller once it has been confirmed that all conditions of the sale have been fulfilled.

© Luis Abrantes/Shutterstock, Inc.

Cost, Insurance, Freight (CIF)   shipping designation meaning that the seller will be responsible for the cost of insurance and freight charges to deliver the goods to a port city the buyer designates, usually on the coast of the home country or where buyer need the goods to be sent (e.g., CIF and L.A.).

"Piggyback" transportation technology that allows special intermodal containers to be lifted from a boat and placed directly onto flatbed train cars or onto special truck frames so that the goods can be hauled via rail or roads without having to be unloaded until the reach their final destination.

Another arrangement that is less hassle for you, but more expensive, is to negotiate to buy goods "CIF, <u>city.</u>" This designation of **Cost, Insurance, Freight (CIF)** means that the seller will be responsible for the cost of insurance and freight charges to deliver the goods to a port city you designate, usually on the coast of your home country or where you need the goods to be sent. You as the buyer only become responsible for the goods once they reach that port, but then are responsible for shipping charges, insurance, and so on for distribution within your country. So, for example, you negotiate to buy some goods "CIF, Los Angeles," then the maker/seller of those products will deliver them to an ocean freight port on the west coast and once there will get paid not only for the goods, but also for the shipping charges and other fees you have agreed to up to that point. You then take possession of the goods and continue their journey to a final destination.

Your goods will continue their intermodal journey to your factory, warehouse, or distribution center. Here there are some advances in transportation that have made the process much easier. Decades ago, the cargo would have to be unloaded from the ocean shipping container and then reloaded onto train cars or into trucks to continue the trip to your facilities. Today, new transportation technology allows special intermodal containers to be lifted from the boat and placed **"piggyback"** directly onto flatbed train cars or onto special truck frames so that the goods can be hauled via rail or roads without having to be unloaded until they reach their final destination. (Sometimes the cargo containers loaded onto ocean vessels are called **"fishy back,"** and cargo containers loaded onto airplane transports are called **"birdy back."**)

This multimodal system makes transportation and distribution much more efficient and greatly enhances the logistics part of the supply chain process. Other advances, such as **barcode scanning** technology, provide more information on where the goods are in the flow from raw materials to finished products. The system can be set up to track components, work-in-progress, and/or goods at various stages. Movement in and around warehouses, factories, or other facilities can also be monitored. New technologies are being perfected, which would track products continuously, without needing to be scanned. The so-called **RFID tags (Radio Frequency Identification tags)** actually send out a constant radio signal to computers, which can provide precise, up-to-the-minute location status reports to all parties via ERP or other software.

© SasinT/Shutterstock, Inc.

"Fishy back" transportation technology that allows cargo containers to be loaded onto ocean vessels.

"Birdy back" transportation technology that allows cargo containers to be loaded onto airplane transports.

Bar-code scanning technology that provides information on where goods are in the flow from raw materials to finished products if items are scanned by electronic readers.

RFID tags (Radio Frequency Identification tags) technology that sends out a constant radio signal to computers that can provide precise, up-to-the-minute location status reports to all parties via ERP or other software.

STRATEGIES FOR GLOBAL MARKETS

In the previous sections, we discussed finding, evaluating, and using partners to enhance your global supply chain. If you've done a good job of selecting these partners, they may be a resource to help you begin selling your products into global markets. If you look at demographic data, there are over 310 million people in the United States, but 7.1 billion people worldwide, so any product or service that you can sell into a global market opens up a much larger potential customer base. Just be sure that you've explored as many domestic markets as you can before you start thinking about going global. If your resources are spread too thinly, then your success in other markets can suffer. Still, there are ways that you can enter global markets for less of an investment than you might think. Let's examine some ways to make international markets work as part of your overall business strategy.

Preparing to Go Global

One of the first things you should do as you consider selling your products into a particular foreign country is to educate yourself about that country. It's especially helpful to know what other similar products are already being sold. Can you learn something from these about how to approach the market successfully? How about some ideas for new ways that your products might fit in with the local culture? It's important to know the legal and financial aspects of a particular foreign market, but a crucial element to market success is understanding the culture.

The more serious you are about being successful in a country, the more important it is for you to

© minifilm/Shutterstock, Inc.

consult with local people who can tell you if your products and marketing will appeal to consumers there. If you do not have the financial resources to hire native people, this is where you may be able to tap knowledge and experience from your supply chain partners who are in a great position to offer advice on the consumers in their market.

You can never assume that you know what's best in a country with which you are not familiar. Trying to replicate things in a foreign country the same way you do them domestically because you think that you know what's best or that your culture is superior (**ethnocentricity**) is setting yourself up for failure. There are numerous stories of marketing disasters that came about because of this faulty logic. (Imagine GM selling a U.S. car called the "Nova" in Spanish speaking countries without changing the name. No one thought to ask the locals, who laughed at the "No-va" car—which means "Won't Go" in Spanish—and so sales were abysmal.)

Whether you will have a large or small presence in a foreign market, there are a few basic things you should do: learn the culture, find out what local people want and need, ask people who know (better yet, hire someone), and investigate any laws you may have to comply with (such as packaging changes). In the end, nothing replaces getting good help or advice from people who are a part of that culture. This is why we come back to your business partners as a resource. You may or may not want to turn everything over to them, but their input can be invaluable. After all, if you sell more product in their country (or anywhere for that matter), you and your supplier(s) all benefit.

Low-Risk Market Entry

One of the cheapest ways to enter an international market is by **licensing** your product to foreign manufacturers who will make and distribute your product in their local market in exchange for paying you a royalty. It is not always the easiest relationship to find—and you have to have something pretty special to get foreign companies interested—but the right partner here can mean easy profits with virtually no investment on your part. The profits will be smaller than if you do more of the work yourself, but that's the key here: you have to do little or no work with a licensing arrangement.

You should have an attorney construct an agreement that protects your interests, but that is the case with any sales arrangement involving partners—foreign or domestic. Always set some sort of performance goals for keeping the agreement alive or renewing it, and establish an acceptable royalty rate so that you are fairly compensated but the local company can still make a profit. Initially, it may be hard to demand an advance payment up-front against future royalty income unless you have something well-known or with a proven track record of sales. You can put penalties in your agreement, but honestly, they are hard to monitor and enforce so far away. Trust is always an important component because you want maximum sales efforts, and you don't want your product to get knocked off and copies sold cheaply. This is why any supply chain partner who also has a vested interest in your success—and will gain from it as well—is a good candidate for collaboration in international markets where they have expertise.

You can also research **trading companies** who may sign on to represent your product and include your sales information materials in presentations to their customers. You might even get them to do the translations of these things for you. They may or may

Ethnocentricity trying to replicate things in a foreign country the same way you do them domestically because you think that you know what's best or that your culture is superior.

Licensing contractually allowing foreign manufacturers to make and distribute your products in their local market in exchange for paying a royalty.

Trading companies companies who sign on to represent a product in a foreign market and include sales information materials in presentation to their customers.

© Maksim Shmeljov/Shutterstock, Inc.

not actually purchase your product (depending on size, price, and a number of other factors), but they might buy some after they've made a sale. Or, perhaps they will just make an introduction if their customers show an interest in what you have to offer. You also have to consider if you will have an exclusive representation agreement with the trading company or if they will continue to sell similar products as yours at the same time. **Foreign distributors** will act in a similar capacity as the trading companies, but are more likely to actually purchase a small amount of your product to have it readily available to ship to customers.

If you are looking for a cheap way to go it alone, you can consider setting up a **website** that would allow customers to find your products, inquire about them, and place orders. Of course, you will have some expense in translating the site, and you also have to figure out how to take foreign currency for your sales (www. PayPal.com converts many currencies from online transactions.), but overall, this is a way for you to get more of the profits from your sales if you are willing to put forth a little more effort and investment. You may even be able to **drop ship** your products such that they are sent directly to your customers from the manufacturer, instead of bringing items all the way to the United States for processing, repackaging, and sending the goods off again to a foreign land.

Similarly, you can simply **export** products out of the United States and sell directly to customers, trading companies, or other entities overseas. Of course, finding the customers is what's time-consuming about this approach. Definitely not as expensive as some other methods we'll discuss in future sections, but you will still have additional costs in translating product information, brochures, and other marketing materials. This is not really much more work than what you'd have to do for a website, and in fact, many customers may find you via the Internet. Generally, we make the distinction that generating sales from the website is a method of direct sales to individuals, whereas exporting is a method of direct sales geared toward larger sales in bulk, often to business customers.

Committing Some Resources to International Markets

Sometimes you are in a unique position with a popular product or service that has a well-known brand you want to sell into foreign markets without giving up complete control over sales and marketing as you would under a license agreement. Instead, you could negotiate a **franchise agreement** where you license the name, the product or service, your business know-how, and so on to a foreign company who will sell your product or service in another market in exchange for a percentage of the profits, but you maintain control over final say for the marketing and other aspects of the business. Of course, you can do franchises domestically as well, but there are times when you may feel that your sales and marketing team can handle the U.S. part of your business, but you need help with international markets with which you are not as familiar.

You have to make some commitment, though, to the international partner(s) you are signing the franchise agreement with because you are agreeing to provide them with help and materials. You expect the local owners to have insight into the country they will share, but you retain final approval. You may also provide other services, depending on your business. Think of a McDonald's franchise. The royalties that franchise owners pay also mean that in return they expect the main company to provide everything from marketing dollars for advertising to

Foreign distributors companies who sign on to represent a product in a foreign market and may actually purchase a small amount of product to have it readily available to ship to customers.

Website   internet presence that allows customers to find your products, inquire about them, and place orders.

Drop ship   selling products in other markets, such that they are sent directly to your customers from the manufacturer, instead of bringing items all the way to the United States for processing, repackaging, and sending the goods off again to a foreign land.

Export   selling goods to a foreign country.

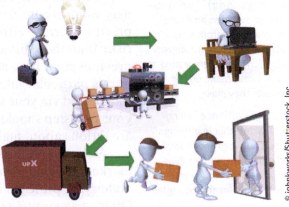

© johnkworks/Shutterstock, Inc.

Franchise agreement   a special arrangement with a popular service or product where you license the name, your business know-how, and so on, to a foreign company who will sell your product or service in another market in exchange for a percentage of the profits, but you maintain control over final say for the marketing and other aspects of the business.

© TonyV3112/Shutterstock, Inc.

Contract manufacturing when additional facilities are hired to produce goods for you and put your name or brand on them.

OEM (Original Equipment Manufacturing) when you agree to purchase an entire production run from a contract manufacturing company as the "cost" of them letting you put your name on the products they make.

Strategic alliance long-term partnership in a foreign market between your company and one of the partnerships you've established via your supply chain (or through other means).

designing wrapper papers for the sandwiches. They agree to buy everything from you so that you can ensure uniformity of your business and your brand no matter what market location they serve.

Although franchises work best for services, you have more options with products. If you have sales or distribution channels in a foreign country where you want to distribute and sell you products to see how they do, you could add some additional **contract manufacturing** facilities to produce goods for you and put your name or brand on them. This is similar to expanding production capacity temporarily to meet a sudden increase in demand from your domestic customers, but this also works well to meet international market demand. You have a little larger commitment of cash since you must agree to purchase an entire production run from this **OEM (Original Equipment Manufacturing)** company as the "cost" of them letting you put your name on the products they make. This is still a lot less expensive than if you had to pay for extra people or equipment to make the products you need to meet this (temporary?) surge in demand from a new market before you're sure you can grow sales there. The other big benefit is that you can have this OEM company modify the product to meet local tastes so that you are not changing the setup of your regular goods as desired at home or in other markets.

High-Risk, High-Reward Market Entry

If you are committed to expanding sales in a particular global market, then you may want to consider an approach that gives you the most control and the most profit from your efforts. All of the strategies we discuss in this section are more risky than those listed earlier, so this may not be your first step until some of the previous steps have acted as a test market to prove the viability of your products in this particular international market. Still, because of the partnerships you've established via your supply chain (or through other means), you may decide that your first step should show your partners, stakeholders, and customers that you are serious about making this new market a success.

A **strategic alliance** can form the basis of a long-term partnership in a foreign market. There are many forms this can take and directions that it can go, but the underlying principle is one of a continuing relationship where both parties gain. Often, a synergy is created as the alliance grows over time. The framework and responsibilities are set out in a separate agreement, but new areas of cooperation are allowed to form as long as everything continues to be in the mutual best interest of both parties. This can be a logical progression and maturation of a partnership formed initially as a supply chain relationship.

© snapgalleria/Shutterstock, Inc.

A more formal arrangement is a **joint venture (JV)** where two or more companies work together for a common purpose, with each performing a defined role. A JV may be formed to share technology, to spread risk for research and development (R&D), or to focus on specializations. This divided focus works especially well in foreign markets where one JV company may be experienced at marketing in that country while the other JV company has management know-how to share. A JV arrangement may also be necessary to comply with local government laws. Often in developing countries, foreign companies are not allowed to come in and set up operations without sharing knowledge and skills at a high level to benefit the host country and its people. By requiring 51% local ownership, for example, the government can preserve its goals and thus a JV is formed as a means to allow your outside company access into the marketplace.

The last arrangement we'll discuss is the most costly. **Foreign Direct Investment (FDI)** is when your company has a physical presence in another country. This can be anything from a simple branch office on foreign soil from which your sales force operates to a large manufacturing facility where you make your products for the locals to buy. Keep in mind that this branch office must operate like a foreign subsidiary that you own and control. If you have a commission-only sales force that does not have an office or support staff, then this does not count as FDI. But FDI can be any business function—even a marketing office, research and development (R&D) facility, or other management area.

There are additional advantages to using FDI to make products in a foreign market. Not only do you reduce time to market so that you can get your products in consumers' hands quickly, but you can also get closer to your customers so that you know what they want. From a business standpoint, you do not have to worry as much about punitive quotas and tariffs, and you may also get preferential treatment from local governments for tax purposes. Plus you benefit from goodwill in the community because you are providing jobs while putting money into the local economy. Finally, from a financial standpoint, your transactions all take place in the local currency so that you are not subject to variations in the exchange rate except for when you are sending profits home. You sell in the local currency and then pay wages and spend marketing money without having to convert back and forth. This provides added stability to your forecasting.

Joint ventures   A combining of separate businesses is a Joint Venture, which combines the activities of two or more businesses acting as a single company for a specific project or period of time. A formal arrangement where two or more companies work together for a common purpose, with each performing a defined role, such as to share technology, spread risk for research and development (R&D), or focus on specializations.

Foreign Direct Investment (FDI)   when a company has a physical presence in another country, from a simple branch office on foreign soil from which a sales force operates, to a large manufacturing facility making product for the locals to buy.

© Lisa S./Shutterstock, Inc.

BUSINESS OF INTERNATIONAL TRADE

If think you might go global with your supply chain, outsource parts of your business, or want to sell your products into new international markets, it's important that you understand some of the underlying principles of economics and trade laws that create the foundation for the business of international trade. It's important to understand what might give countries or companies an advantage on the world stage, all the while complying with the rules that all countries agree to abide by. Being part of free trade means that countries and companies, as well as customers, suppliers, and partners, will all benefit.

Comparative Advantage

Comparative advantage says that each country should make and sell goods that it produces more efficiently and then buy the other goods and services it needs from other countries. Focusing efforts in industries where a country excels means that resources will be allocated efficiently. Even if countries could produce a wide variety of items, some would be better at producing certain goods than others. Remember the tradeoffs we discussed in the Economics chapter? The angle of the red total output line in the production possibilities curve is different for each country. This means that although the country can produce both items, total world consumption would be greater if each country spent more of its resources producing items it is better at making. So, France should make more wine, and the United States should make more cheese.

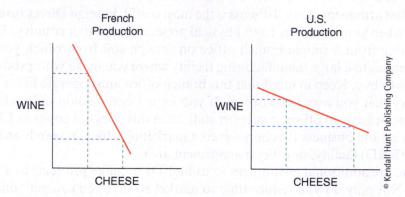

We can examine the same situation for industries within countries to see why some places specialize in different types of products or services. If you've ever wondered why companies move their shoe manufacturing to China, it's because that country has a comparative advantage of cheap labor for production; but at the same time, designing shoes is the forte of U.S. companies, so much of that work is done with U.S. talent.

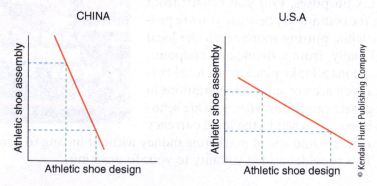

In some situations, one country or just a few countries enjoy an **absolute advantage** with a virtual monopoly on production of a specific product, ingredient, or resource. Some examples are: diamonds (Russia, Botswana, Angola, South Africa), cocoa beans (Ivory Coast, Indonesia, Ghana), uranium (Australia, Kazakhstan, Canada).

Free Trade

Free trade is the movement of goods and services across international borders without economic or political barriers. This goes for **imports** (buying goods from a foreign country) as well as **exports** (selling goods to a foreign country).

When foreign firms are forced to compete on a level playing field, we can see the same benefits from global free markets that competition usually provides: lower prices, better quality, and more innovation. In an effort to ensure this free flow of goods, some countries enter into arrangements as a **trading bloc**, forming a **common market** among a regional group of countries that agree to coordinate laws and trading rules, have no internal tariffs, and have common external tariffs, if necessary. Although it has run into some trouble recently, this was part of the grand design that formed the **European Union (EU)**. On a less formal level, **ASEAN** (Association of Southeast Asian Nations) was formed to ease the movement of goods and labor across borders. Closer to home, we have **NAFTA** (North American Free Trade Agreement) whereby Canada, the United States, and Mexico agreed to reduce and eliminate barriers for everything from transportation to food.

For more information, visit www.Europa.eu, www.ASEAN.org, www.NAFTAnow.org.

Trading bloc   when a country's enter into arrangements to ensure the free flow of goods.

Common market   when a regional group of countries agree to coordinate laws and trading rules, have no internal tariffs, and have common external tariffs, if necessary.

European Union (EU) common market formed by various European countries.

ASEAN (Association of Southeast Asian Nations) trading bloc formed to ease the movement of goods and labor across borders.

NAFTA (North American Fee Trade Agreement) treaty whereby Canada, the United States, and Mexico agreed to reduce and eliminate barriers for everything from transportation to food.

© Pressmaster/Shutterstock, Inc.

Trade Protectionism

Trade protectionism is the use of government regulations to alter market prices, either by limiting imports or by some other means. This still exists among some countries, particularly where agriculture is concerned. A government may offer **subsidy** payments to farmers so that their agricultural products can be sold more cheaply than comparable foreign food. Other times, foreign governments may

Trade protectionism   the use of government regulations to alter market prices, either by limiting imports or some other means.

Subsidy   government payments to producers (especially farmers) so that their goods (agricultural products) can be sold more cheaply than comparable foreign products (food).

Import Tariffs
(higher prices from the tariff at P_t leads to less quantity demanded at Q_t)

Import Quotas
(restricted quantity at Q_q leads to higher prices at P_q)

© Kendall Hunt Publishing Company

Tariff   import tax levied by governments on products coming into their country.

Quotas   limits imposed by governments on the quantity of goods that can be brought into the country.

Noneconomic trade barriers   more subtle, indirect trade barriers that can effectively restrain trade without direct costs imposed by governments (such as requiring redesigned packaging for imports).

GATT, the General Agreement on Tariffs and Trade   agreement that serves as a framework to promote free trade among member countries. All signatories agree to reduce trade restrictions and work to eliminate tariffs or quotas for most goods.

World Trade Organization (WTO)   international body established by GATT to provide rules and procedures for mediating disputes between those member countries.

Dumping   when products are sold in a foreign country for a lower price than they are sold in the domestic market.

charge a **tariff** (import tax) on products coming into their country or impose **quotas** limiting the quantity of goods that can be brought into the country. Both tariffs and quotas can have the same net effect on the supply and demand model, raising prices and making those targeted goods more expensive in the market, thus giving an advantage to the cheaper domestic alternatives.

Although these limitations and restrictions on trade are obvious, there are other more subtle trade barriers, which can effectively restrain trade as well, without direct costs imposed by governments. These are often called **noneconomic trade barriers**. For example, selling goods into Japan often requires use of its very complex distribution system. This serves to keep some foreign competition out and also adds extra layers of costs to make foreign goods more expensive. Another way that countries can set limits on foreign goods is by passing regulations, such as requiring special packaging for food as is done in some cases by Brazil.

© Lightspring/Shutterstock, Inc.

Trade Disputes

Most countries who engage in international trade are signatories of **GATT, the General Agreement on Tariffs and Trade**, which provided a framework to promote free trade among member countries. All agree that they will reduce trade restrictions and work to eliminate tariffs or quotas for most goods. GATT paved the way for establishing the **World Trade Organization (WTO)** to provide rules and procedures for mediating disputes between member countries. The main principles WTO adheres to include the pledge that dispute resolution will be equitable, fast, effective, and mutually acceptable. The unique multilateral system has members judge cases and provide self-enforcement.

A dispute can take many forms, but usually a complaint is brought when one country adopts a trade policy or takes an action that other WTO members consider a violation. For example, if there is an allegation of **dumping** whereby products are being sold in a foreign country for a lower price than they are sold in the domestic market, then the case is brought before a panel of peer countries for a consultation hearing. The panel eventually issues a report, which becomes a ruling within a year of the initial action. This is a great improvement over previous cooperative attempts to solve problems because WTO emphasizes that prompt settlement is essential for its rulings to be an effective deterrent or allow for remedies. Cases are accelerated whenever possible.

For more info on rules, procedures, and member countries, visit www.WTO.org.

© Joinmepic/Shutterstock, Inc.

Foreign Exchange

Foreign exchange of currencies is important for international commerce to occur. The **exchange rate** is the price of one country's currency relative to another country's currency. Although a few countries have their currency artificially controlled or "pegged" to the U.S. Dollar, most countries allow their currencies to float on the open market. This means that the price of the currencies fluctuates based on supply and demand, just like for any other product or commodity.

The strength or weakness of a currency is all relative and depends on whether the country is talking about their own currency or that of another country. If a country has a **weak currency**, then it can be exchanged for *less* of a foreign currency. This makes foreign imports expensive, but it makes exports cheap. This is a policy pursued by China and thus partially explains its large **trade surplus** whereby its exports exceed its imports. If a country has a **strong currency**, then it can be exchanged for *more* of a foreign currency. This makes foreign imports cheaper, but makes its exports expensive. A strong currency, though, may attract foreign investment into a stable country since foreign investors want their investment to enjoy capital appreciation (income or interest) in the safe environment and accumulate wealth in that stronger currency.

From a U.S. perspective, understand that a weak dollar would make foreign imports expensive and make U.S. exports cheaper for other countries and would also make U.S. investments less attractive to foreigners. On the other hand, a strong dollar makes foreign imports cheaper and makes U.S. exports more expensive for other countries and would also attract foreign investment money into the United States.

When considering the flow of goods and other money between countries, we also need to know that **balance of trade** is the total value of all exports of a country compared to its imports. More exports leads to a **trade surplus**; more imports leads to a **trade deficit**. If we consider not only goods but also all other money—tourism, aid, military spending, investment money, and so on—then that is referred to as the **balance of payments**: the difference between all money coming into a country and out of a country. More money coming in is a **favorable balance of payments**; more money going out is an **unfavorable balance of payments**.

Other International Economic Considerations

The first "rule" of international business is to make sure that you get local advice and input from people in the country or who are very familiar with the cultural norms of the target country. Not only do you need to understand the markets, you need to understand the people. Things that are acceptable at home may be awkward abroad. There are multiple ways to insult people, look foolish with a marketing campaign, or even break laws that you may not be aware of.

Even though you have a presence in a local country, hire people there, maybe even live and work overseas yourself, as a U.S. citizen and working for a foreign subsidiary of a U.S. company you are still subject to the laws of the United States. This goes for everything from tax reporting requirements to prohibitions against bribing local officials. Although in some countries it is normal to pay

Exchange rate   the price of one country's currency relative to another country's currency.

Weak currency   when a country's currency can be exchanged for less of a foreign currency, thus making foreign imports expensive and making exports cheap.

Trade surplus   when a country's exports exceed its imports.

Strong currency   when a country's currency can be exchanged for more of a foreign currency, thus making foreign imports cheaper and making exports expensive.

© Nagy-Bagoly Arpad/Shutterstock, Inc.

Balance of trade   the total value of all exports of a country compared to its imports.

Trade deficit   when a country's imports exceed its exports.

Balance of payment   the difference between all money coming into a country and out of a country.

Favorable balance of payments   when more money is coming in to a country.

Unfavorable balance of payments   when more money is going out of a country.

© Augusto Cabral/Shutterstock, Inc.

"Four tigers" the economies of Hong Kohn, Taiwan, South Korea, and Singapore.

BRIC the emerging economies of Brazil, Russia, India, and China.

bribes to get routine things accomplished, the Foreign Corrupt Practices Act prevents U.S. citizens or other people working for subsidiaries of U.S. companies to engage in this type of behavior. You risk fines and jail time if you do so.

Finally, as we look outside of the United States for economic expansion opportunities, keep in mind that today's struggling countries may be tomorrow's engines for growth. Back in the late 1980s and early 1990s, talk was of the **"Four Tigers"**, emerging economies in Hong Kong, Taiwan, South Korea, and Singapore. Today, those countries have thriving economies that have exhibited steady growth over the decades. Commerce or investment in any of those really helped companies and those countries grow. The talk currently is of the next up-and-coming group that is **BRIC**, emerging economies in Brazil, Russia, India, and China. We see how economic policies in each of those countries have the potential to lead them to growth and prosperity as well.

OPEN FOR BUSINESS: GLOBAL SUPPLY CHAIN IN THE REAL WORLD

As you ponder how to improve your bottom line, you consider that you really have two problems: your costs are too high and your sales are too low. You decide to try and address both issues at the same time by contacting some parts suppliers in Mexico. You don't really want to disrupt your business by moving production south of the border and you also know that having your products "Made in the U.S.A." has been a great help to your marketing efforts as a point of differentiation. But while you can still do the final assembly of your computer desks in the United States from specially crafted Amish wood, you think that you can buy the knobs for the drawers and other metal parts from Mexico a lot cheaper to help cut costs.

The other benefit is that you've read on trade websites about the expanding upscale business market in Mexico, and shipping your desks there seems doable with the increased trucking competition due to NAFTA. China can probably supply the knobs a little bit cheaper, but shipping desks to China would be cost prohibitive and so you would lose that opportunity to grow your sales. You decide to research some companies in Mexico, and look for ones who can supply the parts you want but also have the distribution connections to possibly help you sell some desks into Mexico as well.

The first supplier has decent prices, but no desire to help with your sales efforts in Mexico. The second one likes the thought of selling your desks, but only if you send them desks on consignment so that you have money tied up in inventory plus pay the shipping. Finally, the third place seems like a good fit. They can supply you with the parts you need at a better price than you were paying before, and they have connections with a fairly good sized distribution network in Mexico. They'll only buy a half a dozen desks or so at the beginning, but there's some real potential here—and they pay cash.

Chapter Summary

Global supply chain involves movement of raw materials, parts and components, and finished goods throughout all stages of production, distribution, and sale of products (or services) around the world. Supply chain management (SCM) is efficiently planning and coordinating the movement of goods through all stages into the hands of your buyer. Sourcing is procuring parts or raw materials, whereas outsourcing is using outside companies to perform various functions for your business. Operations planning is the process of creating an effective strategy to convert or transform resources into goods or services. Cost considerations are just as important as business relationships here.

Logistics is planning, coordinating, managing, and controlling the movement of all aspects of goods (or services), plus all related information—especially important with ERP software. Logistics involves the flow of goods, warehousing, and materials handling. 3PL (Third- Party Logistics) firms may provide additional services, such as inventory management, order fulfillment, and customer service. Goods often travel via various intermodal shipping methods to save on costs, beginning with the cheapest ocean voyages. A freight forwarder will consolidate smaller shipments, relinquishing control FOB their home port or providing more complete CIF shipping to customers' home port.

Strategies for entering global markets range from low- risk licensing or exporting via foreign distributors, to high- risk strategic alliances or foreign direct investment. Most products are sold in markets where a country has a comparative advantage. Free trade means that all consumers worldwide are better off when governments do not restrict or tax goods crossing international borders. Most countries are signatories to GATT, and agree to bring trade disputes before the WTO. The next up- and- coming economies appear to be in Brazil, Russia, India, and China (BRIC).

Review Questions

1. What are some other ways that Supply Chain partners can add to the Value Chain?
2. Can you think of some other important considerations when deciding whether to outsource certain aspects of a business?
3. How does Just-in-Time inventory save company resources?
4. When might you want to use a storage warehouse? A distribution warehouse?
5. Name some advantages of a small company using a 3PL provider to handle most or all of its order fulfillment. Are there any downsides to this?
6. How can ERP software make the intermodal transportation links more smooth during the movement of materials, parts, or finished goods?
7. Which strategy for entering a global market do you think makes the most sense? Does the potential country you want to enter change the considerations?
8. What are some other noneconomic trade barriers you can think of?
9. Can you think of other countries that have an absolute advantage in something?

10. What would you do if the official who can approve a road leading to your factory wants a bribe in exchange for approving the project?
11. Can you think of reasons why a country might want a strong currency? Weak currency?
12. What economic regions or countries do you think might emerge in the next decade?

Discussion Questions

13. Do you agree or disagree that there are always winners and losers when companies outsource? Explain. What are some alternatives that would alter these outcomes positively for companies, . . . for workers . . . , and for consumers?
14. Discuss whether you think cost considerations or business relationships are more important? What can you do when these two ideals are in conflict?
15. 3PL's have become very important to the logistics operations of companies both large and small. Are there any downsides to this expanded role? Does your position depend on whether or not the company hiring the 3PL is large or small?
16. Explain how a company's global strategy would likely differ depending on the products being sold. Choose two examples to illustrate your point. It's also safe to assume that the size of the company also matters. How does this alter the risk?
17. If countries can clearly see the benefits of free trade given the charts we've discussed, why are there persistent disputes brought before the WTO? Is there a better way for countries to respond when they perceive unfairness in how their products are sold or not sold into a particular country?

Key Terms

- 3PL (Third-Party Logistics)
- absolute advantage
- ASEAN
- balance of payments
- balance of trade
- barcode scanning
- bill of lading
- "birdy back"
- BRIC
- business process outsourcing (BPO)
- common market
- Comparative advantage
- contract manufacturing
- Cost, Insurance, Freight (CIF)
- cycle time
- distribution warehouse
- drop ship
- dumping
- Enterprise Resource Planning (ERP)
- ethnocentricity
- European Union (EU)

- exchange rate
- export
- exporting
- favorable balance of payments
- "fishy back"
- Foreign Direct Investment (FDI)
- Foreign distributors
- "Four Tigers"
- franchise agreement
- Free on Board (FOB)
- Free trade
- freight forwarder
- GATT, the General Agreement on Tariffs and Trade
- Global supply chain
- horizontal integration
- Imports
- inbound logistics
- intermodal
- joint venture (JV)
- just-in-time

- Letter of Credit
- licensing
- logistics
- materials handling
- NAFTA
- noneconomic trade barriers
- OEM (Original Equipment Manufacturing)
- Operations Planning
- Outbound logistics
- outsourcing
- "pick and pack"
- "piggyback"
- procurement
- purchase order
- quotas
- reverse logistics
- RFID tags (Radio Frequency Identification tags)
- RFP (Request for Proposal)
- storage warehouse
- strategic alliance
- strong currency
- subsidy
- supply chain
- supply chain management (SCM)
- tariff
- Third-Party Logistics (3PL)
- total cost of outsourcing (TCO)
- trade deficit
- Trade protectionism
- trade surplus
- trading bloc
- trading companies
- unfavorable balance of payments
- value chain
- vertical integration
- weak currency
- website
- World Trade Organization (WTO)

4

BUSINESS DEVELOPMENT

SECTION

4

BUSINESS DEVELOPMENT

Product Development and Design

LEARNING OBJECTIVES

1. Explain strategies for deciding what products your customers want developed.
2. Discuss market research techniques, including focus groups and test markets.
3. Detail product development and design considerations, as well as adaptation.
4. Discuss pricing strategies and how they're related to the development process.
5. Explain the role of Product Life Cycle and BCG Matrix in product decisions.

© lucadp/Shutterstock, Inc.

OPENING STORY: 3-D PRINTING TECHNOLOGY

Product development has always started in the lab. Years and years ago, it was skilled artisans making prototype samples by hand. Gradually, computers became more and more involved in the process, with CAD (Computer- Aided Design) programs giving a big boost to productivity. Today, several companies are giving us yet another revolution in product development: 3-D printing.

3-D printing was invented in 1983, but it's only recently that these products have been put within reach of small- to medium- sized companies. DDD, Stratasys, and ExOne all make printers of various sizes, some that fit on desktops and can be had for under $1000. "3-D printing is an '"additive"' manufacturing process that creates an object using a repetitive layer-by-layer building process." This allows for rapid prototyping that does not require any tooling. There are limitations to what can be made with traditional methods, but now designers can quickly and easily create complicated designs to see how they work, and how they are received by consumers. This significantly reduces product development times, and allows for more changes to be made quickly. "3-D printing speed and capabilities . . . (are) giving designers even more time to *improve* their designs." This will continue to make product development and design better and more efficient.

(Source: http://www.fool.com/investing/general/2014/02/14/how-3-d-printing-is-changing-the-world-of-manufact.aspx)

INTRODUCTION

Product design and development might seem like something that is only done at the beginning of a new business venture. What we see in this chapter, though, is that you need to start thinking about product development as an ongoing process. Successful companies not only start with developing innovative products (and services), but they stay at the forefront of their industry through constant innovation. Whether it's developing new features or designing completely new products, there are definite things you can do to have the best chance of creating products people will buy.

FIGURING OUT WHAT PEOPLE WANT AND NEED

The hardest part of product development and design is figuring out what people want, not just one person, but enough people so that you can make money from your efforts. There are lots of neat gadgets that circulate among engineers that never make it out of the lab. Even some of those that do make it into the hands of the buying public have a short life span because they are too expensive or too complicated. Any number of problems can surface that make a company decide to scrap a new product idea and change direction or start over, such as what happened with Google Glass.

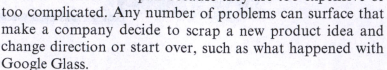

© Hattanas Kumchai/Shutterstock, Inc.

But product failures should not stop any company or individual from trying new things. Sometimes you learn from a failure and can reintroduce a better product later that is well-received by the buying public. Perhaps before, the technology needed was not quite ready or was too expensive. Or, maybe the success of your product ultimately depends on other complementary products or technologies. Apple's Newton handheld computing device in the early 1990s ultimately failed due to a combination of these factors. Bulky technology that was slow didn't help, but ultimately, the Newton couldn't succeed as well as its spiritual successor, the iPad, because there was no cellular infrastructure to deliver high-speed Internet access to the device. Think about everyone using their iPads to access social media, check email, watch streaming movies, and surf the web. Without Internet connections over WiFi or cell technology, the iPad would likely not enjoy such widespread success.

© karnoff/Shutterstock, Inc.

Even if you have a great product that fills consumer needs or desires, you still have to overcome **path dependency**. People are reluctant to change the way they've always done things even if a new product is better. They're comfortable and change requires effort, or they have time or money (or ego) invested in the status quo. There's an old saying among salespeople for computer competitors that had trouble closing a deal: "No one ever got fired for buying IBM." What that means is that you have to work even harder as the newcomer to convince people that your products are better and worth taking a chance on. We just spent a whole chapter giving you ideas how you can do that via your marketing, but you can help those efforts tremendously the earlier you start figuring out what people actually want from your products and services.

Market Research

Recall that **market research** is collecting and analyzing information for good decision-making before you develop and introduce products or new features. Of course, first you must come up with some concepts for new products to make or new features to add to existing products. Sometimes you're hit with an inspiration; other times you and your team sit in a room and **brainstorm**, throwing out ideas at others in the group until you refine something silly into something that seems worthwhile. Once you or your team are convinced that you have a great idea, that's when the real "research" often begins.

Your product idea should help you with the first step in the market research process. You must determine the question to be asked: **What problem are we trying to solve?** Once you think you have a new product (or feature) that's a winner, you need to ask if it's something that people want, need, and will pay for. So, next you develop a hypothesis: **Will people see our product or feature as making things easier or better for them?** You need to figure out if they'll leave behind the old and make the switch. The best way to do that is by collecting data: **Is Primary Data or Secondary Data best?** We'll discuss that shortly. Ultimately, though, your analysis of the data you do collect is your most important step. It will help you answer: **Do we need to refine our product or feature so that we give ourselves the best chance of success in the marketplace?** Finally, your conclusion: **Should we proceed with introducing this new product or feature?**

Path dependency   when people are reluctant to change the way they've always done things even if a new product or other alternative is better.

Market research   collecting and analyzing information for good decision making before you develop and introduce products (and also collecting and analyzing feedback afterwards as well).

Brainstorm   throwing out ideas at others in the group until something silly is refined into something that seems worthwhile.

© Stella Levi/Shutterstock, Inc.

Primary data any information or responses you collect yourself. (This can be done in any number of ways, from surveys to focus groups to test markets.)

Secondary data any information that is examined which was already compiled by other people.

Business intelligence information obtained by looking on the internet, scouring industry publications, attending trade shows, reading corporate annual reports, and pursuing other avenues of data collection.

Focus group when a group of potential customers are brought into a room where they are shown product concepts or perhaps a finished prototype.

Prototype a finished sample of a product that is not in production yet.

Collecting Data

There are two types of data that can be collected for any market research project: **primary data** and **secondary data**. **Primary data** are any information or responses you collect yourself. This can be done in any number of ways, from surveys to focus groups to test markets--all of which we'll discuss momentarily. **Secondary data** are any information you examine that were already compiled by other people. Even though the name implies "second," it's actually the one you should do first! Although the info is secondhand (hence the name), it's much cheaper to simply review the findings of others before you decide to spend money on gathering info yourself. You can see if anything similar has been done by looking on the Internet, scouring industry publications, attending trade shows, reading corporate annual reports, and pursuing other avenues of **business intelligence** as you collect secondary data.

If secondary data do not reveal something that makes you think your idea has already been done or might not work like you thought, then it's time to invest in primary data collection. "Invest" is the correct word choice because this will cost you some money. The easiest and least expensive primary data collection are **surveys** where you ask people questions about their wants or needs. You are trying to find out if they see your potential new product or feature as valuable and get an idea of how much they might be willing to pay for it.

If you get favorable replies here, then you might spend more money and conduct a **focus group** where a group of potential customers are brought into

a room where they are shown product concepts or perhaps a finished **prototype**. Their reactions and responses are recorded by a professional marketing research person, even as you may be sitting behind a one-way mirror watching events unfold. While it's helpful to see actual people interacting with and discussing your product, this is not a perfect environment. First of all, people will often know that they are part of a market research focus group. Second, it might be the case that one or two participants with strong personalities are able to sway the group into liking or disliking something.

But the third and perhaps most important potential flaw is that a focus group does not actually simulate real consumer behavior. Sometimes consumers do not know that they want and need something that is radically new—especially if it's just discussed and not given to them to try out. How many people would be open to the idea of eating food that had been bombarded with radiation to cook it until they had a chance to actually use a microwave oven to know how convenient it is to have one?

Just because people liked the sweeter taste of "New Coke" in blind focus group testing, that did not translate into actual sales once people were confronted in stores on April 23, 1985, with choices that did not include the "Coca-Cola Classic" formula. "The fabled secret formula for Coca-Cola was changed, adopting a formula preferred in taste tests of nearly 200,000 consumers. What these tests didn't show, of course, was the bond consumers felt with their Coca-Cola—something they didn't want anyone, including The Coca-Cola Company, tampering with." (Source: http://www.coca-colacompany.com/history/the-real-story-of-new-coke) Just 79 days later, "Coca-Cola Classic" was returned to the shelves.

To avoid similar pitfalls, after a successful focus group, many large companies often go to the expense of a **test market**. This is a rollout for new products in a few locations, perhaps supplying a medium-sized city or two, in order to see consumer reaction and sales data in real time under real market conditions. While it can be expensive to incur the costs for small production runs of product, prepare advertising and marketing campaigns and roll out distribution to the test locations; this gives the best indication of whether or not a product can be successful. Real people making real choices to spend real money and in actual market conditions where they are confronted with their regular options as well as the new products. Fast food restaurants do this all the time trying out new menu items. While test market costs are relatively high, it's still cheaper to do this before going into large-scale production to supply the entire country with a product that might flop.

> **Test market** a rollout for new products in a few locations, perhaps supplying a medium-sized city or two, in order to see consumer reaction and sales data in real time under real market conditions.

© Tanjala Gica/Shutterstock, Inc.

Market Segmentation

The data that you collect while doing your market research might suggest that there are some changes you should make to your product before introducing it to the market. You have to find a profitable market to target. You can try to do this by producing something with **mass market** appeal and attempt to sell to everyone, assuming that you have the resources and production capacity to do this. Alternatively, you can try to find a **niche market**, which is small and profitable, but currently underserved. Larger companies might not be able to make enough profit on small product runs or they are not able to provide enough personalized service demanded by certain customers, so this could open up an opportunity for a smaller company.

> **Mass market** an attempt to sell to everyone.
>
> **Niche market** a small and profitable, but currently under-served, place or method to sell something.

As you refine your product offering, it helps to focus on who you envision as your customers. If you weren't sure before the initial market research, hopefully now you have a better idea of who are the best candidates to buy from you. By positioning your product correctly, you can decide which target market you want to reach with your products to give them the best chance for success. You should divide your potential customers into groups with the same characteristics and

© Dusit/Shutterstock, Inc.

Market segment dividing potential customers into groups with the same characteristics.

Demography dividing people by gender, age, race, income levels, household size, and many other personal characteristics.

Geography dividing potential customers by physical location, such as region of the country, or maybe group potential markets by city population size.

Occasions dividing the target market by life stage, life events, or other celebrations.

Benefits non-monetary compensation. Dividing people by what they want most from the product, such as convenience, quality, thrift, or luxury.

Behavior dividing potential customers by their buying habits, spending patterns, and other similar factors.

Psychographics dividing the target market by what psychological criteria are important to them; their values, attitudes, or even a quest for the "cool" factor. **Commercialization** final product phase such that it's ready to be sold.

Research and Development (R&D) spending time and resources to learn about customers and the market and then using the info to create new products, features, processes, and so on.

then modify your product or your marketing message so that you can go after the most profitable **market segment**:

- **Demography.** This divides people by gender, age, race, income levels, household size, and many other personal characteristics.
- **Geography.** This divides potential customers by physical location, such as region of the country, or might group potential markets by city population size.
- **Occasions.** This divides your target market by life stage, life events, or other celebrations. You can even use this for reasons why someone might buy from you.
- **Benefits.** This divides people by what they want most from the product, such as convenience, quality, thrift, or luxury.
- **Behavior.** This divides potential customers by their buying habits, spending patterns, and other similar factors.
- **Psychographics.** This divides your target market by what psychological criteria are important to them; their values, attitudes, or even a quest for the "cool" factor.

As you think about each of these potential market segments for your product, review the marketing principles discussed in that chapter. Can you make your product appeal to one or more of these segments? Will people easily recognize your benefits and thus a mass market approach is best, or is your product specialized and better-suited for a one-on-one marketing appeal? Make sure that you pay attention to all of the things going on in the environment around you as well.

You are not selling products in a vacuum and must be aware of shifting sociocultural norms taking place. It's obvious that things like competition, technology, and the economy can affect your product positioning, but so can the changing lifestyles of your consumers. If the majority of your customers want certain features or decide they prefer things made from a particular material, then you must try to satisfy those desires. You need to constantly collect and analyze feedback while you're developing products, as well as after your products have been introduced in the market, so you can adjust and react to changing consumer expectations.

PRODUCT DEVELOPMENT AND DESIGN

Whether you are creating a brand new product from scratch or modifying a current product to adapt it to different market segments, you can increase the odds of success by being systematic in your approach. There's a reason why companies spend so much money on R&D, **Research and Development**, in that order. We saw some of the market research methods that companies use early in the process, but research and development are ongoing back and forth until the product is final in the **commercialization** phase and ready to be sold.

Along the way, each phase of the product development process has most companies do continued **concept testing**, where consumers are shown products at various stages of completion so that companies can get feedback to hone their approach. The advent of 3-D printers like those in the opening vignette has made the prototyping and concept testing phases much faster and cheaper for companies of all sizes. This emphasis on hands-on evaluation of products gives the final version released and sold the maximum chance of success in the marketplace.

Product Design

When you're designing a new product or a new feature for an existing product, one of your priorities should be **utilization**: imagine all the ways that customers might use your product so that you can maximize function and form with a purpose in mind. This will help you satisfy your target market. Keep in mind, though, that people often find new ways to use products—ways maybe you never envisioned. When you discover that, see if you can feed off of these customer innovations to further expand the product with your marketing. Baking soda is just one example of new uses extending the life and growing sales of an established product. In addition to baking, people use baking soda for cleaning surfaces, brushing their teeth, absorbing odors in the fridge, and any number of creative applications. Clever marketing shows how the packaging now touts these "Hundreds of uses."

Product **type** helps you group products that are similar. If the new product design can steer the current project into a grouping with the existing products, then this can help with marketing. It's especially useful for new features, which can be targeted at the existing users who may be looking to upgrade. Product **size** may give you an opportunity to pursue a new demographic or segment that is looking for "bigger and tougher" or "smaller and sleeker." Your research can drive these decisions.

Packaging has become a key element of product design. As we said in the Marketing chapter, you can use the box or other container for your product in numerous ways beyond just basic protection for shipping: announce product benefits, explain advantages, promote guarantees, or create other ways to inspire customers' confidence that they are making the right choice. You might introduce your new product initially as part of a bundle with a successful product, or find some other way to increase the perceived value of the purchase. If your product is designed with minimal packaging that is environmentally friendly, perhaps highlighting its recycled content right on the label, you may reap intangible benefits in the minds of some consumers.

This gets us to the **distinctiveness** of your product. Any of these product design elements can contribute to making your product unique. You often have to do something to set you apart from the competition, and product design or features can be one path to differentiation. Finally, make sure that your **brand** fits into the product design on some level. Elevate the status of the name or symbols that identify your company. The more unique your product, the more you may have to rely on "brand" to get attention from consumers so you have a chance to sell them on your product.

Product Adaptation

We saw how market segmentation can lead a product to become highly specialized. What often happens, though, is that companies may create different variations of an existing product to better meet the needs of one or more market segments so that the company can have products in as many

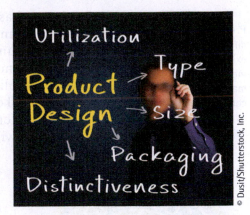

Commercialization final product phase such that it's ready to be sold.

Concept testing where consumers are shown products at various stages of completion so that companies can get feedback to hone their approach.

Utilization all the ways that customers might use a product.

Type one way to group products that are similar by same kind.

Packaging something that protects your product during shipping and can also help you sell the benefits of buying from you.

Distinctiveness any product design element that contributes to making a product unique to set it apart from the competition and then using that product design or feature as a path to differentiation.

Brand distinctive name or other characteristic of a product.

niches as feasible. This is referred to as **Product Adaptation**. One of the easiest ways for companies to do this is to sell a basic product to capture the price-sensitive consumer and also a more expensive version to appeal to the higher income demographic shopper. As many variations as can be done without major retooling may fill the shelves, if stores can be convinced that consumer demand will create the sell-through necessary to stock so many items. Companies will offer different sizes and styles and colors if their evidence shows that customers will buy them—research from their R&D.

© antishock/Shutterstock, Inc.

Before producing so many variations, companies will conduct much of the same research and testing that's done for a new product offering. In some ways, that's what these variations are—new products. Any time the company wants to go beyond a simple variation and sell a related product, there are usually some additional steps to ensure that the product will be well-received. One of the first tests that is likely to be done is called **product screening**, where products are rigorously evaluated for market sales potential AND how well they fit with the current product line or product mix being offered by the company. The reasons for this are two-fold. First, the company does not want to create confusion in the minds of consumers. A complementary product is beneficial, but an unrelated product might change the perception of the company's other products in the minds of consumers. That may also lead to the company having to spend additional marketing dollars chasing a new market. That's the second potential problem; without synergy, marketing money will have to be used in ways that will not benefit the core product line.

Sometimes companies will also do **distributed product development**, where regional managers are permitted to sell authorized variations of established products. These variations would be based on local preferences. One example might be sports and tourist memorabilia designs that change based on the area of the country. Menu items are another realm where this distributed product development approach can be seen. Regional food tastes—think of barbeque, for example—are becoming more important in the domestic restaurant business. If you go overseas to Asia, you can have official Pizza Hut pies with shrimp, squid, teriyaki sauce, and any number of other local cuisine preferences.

© Kei Shooting/Shutterstock, Inc.

PRICING STRATEGIES

One of the decisions that will drive your product development is **pricing**: How much can you charge customers for your products or services? You actually need to try and get an idea of this from your earliest research

efforts. With a completely new product that the public has never seen before, this can be somewhat problematic. But you need to have some idea of the price you can charge customers as well as projections of your costs of manufacturing so that you can know if an acceptable profit is possible. Remember, you are not only covering your costs of manufacturing and marketing, but you should also expect to get a **Return on Investment (ROI)** for initial development money you have spent creating your new product.

Break Even Analysis

When a company is looking at launching a new product, it's often useful to determine what level of sales must occur for the company to "**break even**." This means that prior to reaching that sales volume, the company is still losing money on its initial investment, and only after achieving that sales volume can any profits be realized. There are a number of ways to calculate this, but one very simply formula is useful for this purpose:

$$BEP = \frac{FC}{(P - VC)}$$

Return on Investment (ROI) the profit that is ultimately received from creating a new product.

Break even the level of sales that must occur for the company to realize any profits.

In this formula, we are solving for the **Break Even Point or BEP**. This BEP will be expressed in "units," as in units of product sold, even though all of the figures we plug in on the other side of the equation are represented as dollar amounts! **Fixed Costs (FC)** are those costs that *DO NOT* change no matter how many units are sold. The easiest item to think about in this category is rent; we have to pay this cost even if we don't sell anything and do not pay extra just because we sell a lot in any particular month. Other fixed costs include things like equipment, executive salaries, and for a new product, we can include here any R&D money that we might have invested and need to recoup.

We divide those fixed costs by the lower part of the equation, where we have **Price (P)** minus **Variable Costs (VC)**. Note that this lower part of the equation is in parentheses, so the order of operations in math says that we must do that first! We take what we project as our likely selling price and subtract all of our **Variable Costs**, which are those costs that *DO* change depending on how many units are sold. The easiest item to think about in this category are parts or materials or ingredients; the more we make, the more we will have to buy and use to make those finished units. Other variable costs include things like labor for hourly workers who will do the actual assembly.

As an example, if we have rent of $2,000 per month, our salary of $3,000 per month, and R&D money we spent of $5,000, we see that if we add these up, our total fixed costs are $10,000 (entered in the following formula). We project that we can sell our product for $10, and the materials and labor total $5 per unit. So:

$$BEP = \frac{\$10,000}{(\$10 - \$5)}$$

Break Even Point (BEP) the number of units of product that must be sold to realize any profits.

Fixed Costs (FC) those costs that DO NOT change no matter how many units are sold. (Fixed costs include things such as rent, equipment, executive salaries, and any R&D money.)

Price what you charge customers for your good or service.

Varied Costs (VC) those costs which DO change depending on how many units are sold. (Variable costs include things such as parts or materials or ingredients and labor for hourly workers.)

Thus, our calculation of $10,000 divided by $5 gives us 2,000 UNITS, not Dollars. We would need to sell 2,000 units of our product before we can start making a profit. So, our 2,001st unit is actually profitable for us, since 2,000 units is our BEP or Break Even Point.

Determining Pricing

First and foremost, understand that pricing must be cost-driven. Decisions you make during the product R&D stage will greatly influence your pricing, but these decisions must also be made with an idea of your marketing strategy. For example, if your market research determines that people are most interested in high quality for the new product you are contemplating, then you must strongly consider using high-quality materials. You must be convinced

© mushan/Shutterstock, Inc.

Cost plus pricing method that takes the actual total costs incurred to make the product and then adds a profit margin.

Targeted return pricing method where its first decided what total ROI is expected on the investment, then divide that number of units expected to sell. (This gives the per unit "profit" that must be added to the cost of making the goods.)

Value based pricing method where the price charged is equal to the perceived value of the customers. (Typically what competitors are charging is considered as well.)

Psychological pricing pricing method that considers consumer reaction most of all. (A high price might be chosen for image or prestige, but more likely a company is trying to make products appear less expensive, for example, by going just below a price threshold such as charging a price of $29.99.)

Dynamic pricing using info from databases and cookies to offer different prices to people based on preferences and past buying habits.

Pricing objectives strategies that help businesses reach their goals, either by setting their prices to maximize profits or by setting their prices to maximize units sold.

that you can deliver a marketing message that will explain to consumers the quality and value that set your product apart from competitors, and you must also be confident that you will be successful enough to command the higher price necessary to use those higher quality materials. A higher cost basis for your product generally means that you must charge a higher price to customers.

There are four main **Pricing Methods**:

- **Cost Plus**. This pricing method has you take the actual total costs incurred to make the product, and then add your profit margin. When calculating "total costs," you definitely need to include all Variable Costs (such as materials and labor) as well as a portion of Fixed Costs (such as facility and equipment). To this, add a profit margin you need to make, usually consistent with what's standard for your particular industry.

- **Targeted Return**. This pricing method has you decide what total ROI you expect on your investment, then divide that by the number of units you expect to sell. This gives you the per unit "profit" that you must add to your costs of making the goods. You have to determine if there's enough demand to support the price you'll have to charge to get the desired ROI.

- **Value Based**. This pricing method says that you should charge a price equal to the perceived value of your customers. Of course, that price must be above your costs to make it worthwhile. Typically, you will consider what your competitors are charging as well. You don't necessarily want to be the cheapest, but you need to know where they are so you know where you fit into the marketplace. With a few large competitors in an oligopoly situation (airlines, for example), generally you would follow the up and down pricing movements of the largest price leader in your industry.

- **Psychological Pricing**. This pricing method considers consumer reaction most of all. Certainly, you must always charge something "fair" in the minds of your typical customers, but you can do other things to influence buying behavior. You might choose a high price for image or prestige, but more likely you are trying to make your products appear less expensive. You might establish whole dollar increments ($1 Value Menu, $5 Lunch Deal), but one effective strategy is to go just below a price threshold. Even though customers see a price of $29.99 and realize the item costs $30, research has shown that when consumers do comparisons in their minds, they group the $29.99 item with others that have prices ranging from $20 to $29.

Of course, in addition to those specific factors considered for each method, other things can influence how price is determined. Marketing is a big part of this. Consumers are willing to pay more for convenience, like when they buy individual soft drinks or single-serving size snacks; but consumers have also come to expect discounts for volume purchases when they buy the larger package. We can also let our marketing promote our nonprice advantages, such as service, so that we might be able to add a bit more to our price. We could adjust our price based on demand, so that discounts can be offered at certain times to increase sales during that period. (This is actually an important part of the business model for movie theaters.)

With technology, we can take this one step further where database information and cookies can allow us to do **dynamic pricing** for website sales. Amazon is a master at doing this, offering different prices to people based on preferences and past buying habits. Prices can also change in real time when excess product is available instead of having to plan sales in advance, which is typical for a traditional retail store environment. But in the end, the price and method we choose are determined by our **pricing objectives**.

© Carolyn Franks/Shutterstock, Inc.

Pricing Objectives

Pricing objectives can help businesses reach their goals and are influenced by everything, from marketing considerations to customer expectations. A company that is looking to utilize excess capacity might price products lower than another company, which is not in a strong financial position and thus can't have money tied up in inventory. There are companies who price their products to maximize profits, while others set their prices to maximize units sold. Sometimes prices are changed over time, evolving along with marketing plans or reflecting other considerations. We can break these down into two primary objectives (**skimming**, **penetration**) and then discuss changes that occur.

© Odua Images/Shutterstock, Inc.

Skimming is an objective where prices are kept high in an effort to maximize profits. This works best when a product is new and has few direct competitive substitutes. Customers are typically less price sensitive when either or both of these conditions are met. In this situation, companies are able to "skim" profits off the top from eager customers who want to buy products as **early adopters**. This is common with new consumer electronics, where customers are willing to pay more to be the first to have the latest gadget with little regard to price. The company may or may not be able to increase production to achieve economies of scale and typically does not worry about doing so at this stage of the product's life. Demand is high so prices can be kept high.

Penetration is an objective where prices are kept low in an effort to maximize units sold. This works best when a company can produce high volumes to sell and wants to attract customers to establish a large installed user base, gain market share, or discourage competitors from entering the space. Customers may be perceived as price-sensitive here as well. Producing large quantities can help the company achieve economies of scale more quickly, so the company makes the consumer buying decision easy by keeping the price lower. Typically, this also increases quantities demanded, so the product can gain mass appeal quickly, and the company may also benefit from selling additional complementary products to those same consumers.

A perfect example of both of these strategies and how they change over time is when a company introduces a new video game console. Initially, early adopters of the system are willing to pay higher prices to be first to play the new games. A skimming strategy is the best way to profit from this behavior. In a subsequent year that the system is out, however, the company is enjoying economies of scale

Skimming   a pricing objective where prices are kept high in an effort to maximize profits. (This works best when a product is new and has few direct competitive substitutes since these customers are typically less price sensitive when either or both of these conditions are met.)

Early adopters   people who want to be first to buy new products to get the latest technology and will often help spread the word.

Penetration   a pricing objective where prices are kept low in an effort to maximize units sold. (This works best when a company can produce high volumes and wants to attract customers to establish a large installed user base, gain market share, or discourage competitors from entering the space.)

© Barone Firenze/Shutterstock, Inc.

and is able to offer a price cut. The idea is that the lower price will make the system more attractive to additional buyers, so now with a penetration strategy, the company wants to get the system into as many households as possible. This usually also has the added benefit of selling more software with all of these users. Marketing comes into play as the company is finding ways to increase perceived value of the system, perhaps bundling it with some games in addition to a price drop.

It is common for a product to be sold with a skimming strategy at first, and then a penetration strategy after early adopters have bought in and the company has reached some economies of scale. But this is not always the chosen path because companies also consider what competitors might do and how they will react. When one company is skimming, the market looks attractive to competitors because they see the higher profits. So, even if a company does not currently have direct competitors, it may still choose a penetration strategy to try and keep the market to itself for a longer period of time. Typically, though, pricing is continually reevaluated over the life cycle of the product so that a company can be responsive to customers in the marketplace.

PRODUCT LIFE CYCLE

All *successful* products go through a complete life cycle eventually, but not all products make it as we'll discuss shortly. When you have a winner, though, being able to manage the product through the cycle really helps improve the bottom line for a company. Product development is an important part of that process at various stages. What you'll discover is that different types of products go through their life cycle at much different speeds, with consumer electronics and other tech products going through the fastest.

You can see that our **Product Life Cycle** graph is like most business graphs: some sort of monetary figure up the left side on y-axis (profit or revenue; in this case, "Sales"), and some sort of units across the bottom on x-axis (quantity or time; in this case, "Time").

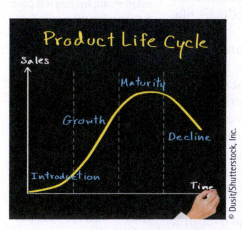

© Dusit/Shutterstock, Inc.

Introduction

Introduction is the first stage of the Product Life Cycle when products are made available to the public. Companies try their best to market these new products, but it takes a special kind of attention to nurture these—and often more direct contact with potential users. Early adopters are important because they will help spread the word. Later when we equate this to the BCG Matrix, the Introduction stage is the equivalent of a "**Question Mark**." At this stage, companies are spending lots of money trying to realize the product's full potential. Sometimes the investment pays off and sometimes it doesn't, so companies must monitor these closely.

© Quka/Shutterstock, Inc.

Growth

Growth is the second stage of the Product Life Cycle when products have made the leap into general acceptance by the public and are now enjoying tremendous sales. Market share is high and profits are good if the product is in a fast-growing industry. Marketing is still important because companies want to maintain the momentum and retain any leadership position they may have being viewed as an innovator. Later when we equate this to the BCG Matrix, the Growth stage is the equivalent of a "**Star**." Not every product is able to "cross the chasm" from Introduction to Growth, however. It looks simple on the chart, but it is often very difficult and many products die trying to make the leap. Everyone knows about the success of Twitter, but there were several other companies doing the same thing with very similar technology. Twitter was able to cross the chasm into high growth via mainstream public acceptance, while the others were not.

Maturity

Maturity is the third stage of the Product Life Cycle when products have maintained their leadership and high market share from the Growth stage, but growth has slowed. Still there is money to be made here, and companies should switch from a marketing focus to a manufacturing focus. Sustained high sales volumes mean that economies of scale can be reached, and the focus on developing new processes at this point will drive costs down so that profits can continue to increase. Later when we equate this to the BCG Matrix, the Maturity stage is the equivalent of a "**Cash Cow**."

As that name implies, the original model said that products in this stage should be "milked," and money redirected to the next Question Mark so that it can become a Star. The problem with this old approach is that the transition does not always happen. Yes, you must invest some money in potential Question Marks. But that does not necessarily mean that you neglect nurturing a Cash Cow. Good marketing that keeps you relevant in the minds of consumers can sometimes help you prolong the Maturity stage of a product. Look at the tremendous job that Gatorade has done over the years extending their flagship product.

Question mark BCG Matrix quadrant that is equivalent to product life cycle "Introduction."

Growth the second stage of the Product Life Cycle when products have made the leap into general acceptance by the public and are now enjoying tremendous sales. Market share is high and profits are good if the product is in a fast-growing industry. Not every product is able to "cross the chasm" from Introduction to Growth. (BCG Matrix equivalent is "Star.")

Star BCG Matrix quadrant equivalent to product life cycle "Growth."

Maturity the third stage of the Product Life Cycle when products have maintained their leadership and high market share from the Growth stage, but growth has slowed. Sustained high sales volumes mean that economies of scale can be reached. (BCG Matrix equivalent is "Cash Cow.")

Cash cow BCG matrix quadrant that is equivalent to product life cycle "Maturity."

© Sheila_Fitzgerald/Shutterstock, Inc.

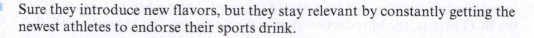

Sure they introduce new flavors, but they stay relevant by constantly getting the newest athletes to endorse their sports drink.

Decline

Decline is the fourth stage of the Product Life Cycle when products no longer enjoy high market share or growth potential, and profits are now hard to come by. A focus on manufacturing still might be able to eke out a little money here, but the transition from Maturity to Decline has occurred partly because of new entrants trying to chase some profits at the end of the Maturity stage. More players in the market have driven down profits such that the economic profit is at or near zero at this point. Later when we equate this to the BCG Matrix, the Decline stage is the equivalent of a "**Dog**."

The original approach to the model said that products that are Dogs should be sold off or phased out since they aren't profitable. But a new way of thinking says that managers need to evaluate if Dogs may be still contributing to the company in other ways. For example, video game companies keep around last-generation game consoles at price points with little or no profit late in their life so as to sell more profitable software. Shaving companies need to hang onto the cheap handle business that isn't profitable because that's needed for the razor blade business, which is very profitable. Sometimes you sell off a Dog product when you can't figure out a way for it to contribute to your bottom line (like when IBM sold its laptop division to Lenovo). Other times, you hang onto a Dog product because it's a cheap gateway product for lower end or younger consumers to acquire your products with the potential of being a future loyal customer (likely a reason that Apple keeps around the iPod even after its high profit days are over).

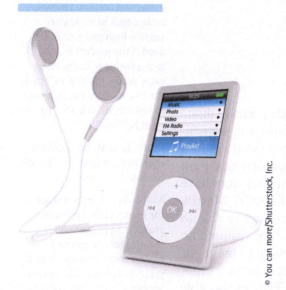

© You can more/Shutterstock, Inc.

Life Cycle Examples

One of the things that companies can do to manage the life cycle of a product is to try and revive the product by introducing new features or an updated version of the product when it's near the end of the Maturity stage. This is one way to try and reset the cycle somewhat. That's why there's an iPhone 4, iPhone 5, iPhone 6. Companies also have a chance at this point to re-engineer the product to try and cut costs and make it more profitable its next time through one or more stages of the Product Life Cycle. Product development is needed at various points for adding features to the next version of the product and also to create new processes that can reduce costs and boost profits.

It used to be that companies waited much longer to introduce the next version, but with the competitive environment we're in now there's a need to bring things out quickly. Not so many years ago. Black-and-white TVs were out for a long time before color TVs were introduced; then it was awhile before those TVs were in decline and replaced with flat screens. So, where are we now with HDTV? If you look at a company's action, that will tell you where *they* think HDTV is in the product life cycle.

As one of the early pioneers of HDTV, Sony now thinks that HDTV is in decline. How do we know? Because they tried to reset the cycle with 3-D TV. That did not seem to "cross the chasm" into mainstream acceptance, so now Sony is touting 4-D TV. Other companies, though, are looking at the same market and seeing different things. Some off-brand TV companies must think HDTV is still in the late Growth stage because they're just jumping in now. A lower cost basis helps, but they would invest their money in other industries if they didn't think they could make profits in HDTV. Companies can look at the same market data and come to different conclusions based on their marketing ability, their cost basis allowing different prices or acceptable profit margins, and their ability to differentiate their products via development of new features. This is why competition is great for consumers!

© nexus7/Shutterstock, Inc.

BCG MATRIX (OR GROWTH–SHARE MATRIX)

A final tool that you should be familiar with in order to find product development opportunities and synergies is the **BCG Matrix (Boston Consulting Group Matrix)**. We talked about "high market share" and "high market growth" during our Product Life Cycle discussion; the BCG Matrix is a way to visually represent those positions—and a whole lot more.

The first thing to notice about the BCG Matrix is that it does line up pretty well with the Product Life Cycle stages. But with the BCG Matrix, you can actually look at all of your products at the same time. Each product in your product line or product mix is assigned an appropriate quadrant on the chart. Then a circle is drawn bigger or smaller, representing the relative size of each product compared to overall sales at the company. By glancing at a completed chart, managers can see where the biggest circles are—which represent where most of your product sales actually come from at present.

Ideally, companies should have some products in all quadrants, but since it's best to have high market growth and high market share, then you'd want the biggest circles in the Star quadrant. You would probably need to revisit the chart periodically to see if your biggest circles are ending up where you want them to be. If you wanted to take the chart a step further, you could also include circles for your chief competitors so that you can see exactly what your position is in the marketplace compared to the competition for each product category. This way managers at your company can see what products are doing well—and what your rivals are doing, too. Also, this type of information can help you focus on developing products and features that fill gaps in your strategy, as well as identify potentially neglected areas by your competitors, which you may decide to pursue.

BCG Matrix (Boston Consulting Group Matrix) chart that visually represents products which are "high market share" and "high market growth" during the Product Life Cycle in a way so that people can actually compare all of the products at the same time.

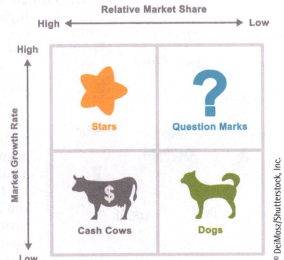

© DeiMosz/Shutterstock, Inc.

DEVELOPMENT OPPORTUNITIES

It's fun to create something new—that's where the big bucks are, too! But that's also where the big gamble is. Products you develop that cross the chasm from Introduction to Growth offer tremendous opportunities for your company, but sometimes the safer route is developing a new feature for one of your existing products, which can give you a nice boost in sales. If you're looking for the more profitable route, you may want to consider developing a new process instead.

If you're wondering why developing a process can end up being more profitable than developing a new product or feature, take a look at the graph in the left margin.

The potential profits from a new product or feature start out very high. That's because assuming that you are the only one with something desirable at the start, people will more readily buy those products or features from you as the only source. But over time, competitors see your new "innovation" and rush in to bring out something similar. In a short period of time, your extra profits will likely erode. Now consider the potential profits from a new process. Your returns from a new process innovation are small at first since it takes time to spread the new process and realize economies of scale from it. But over time, this increases gradually, then dramatically. Since your process innovation is likely hidden away where competitors can't discover and replicate it so easily, then you can realize those gains over a longer life span.

Planning Possibilities and Potential Problems

Project slippage   when deadlines are missed and can delay product (hurting "new-ness" factor).

Scope creep   when the parameters of the product keep expanding, often making the final product that is created to expensive.

As with any good plan, for any type of development plan (product or feature or process), you need to set goals and set deadlines. Without deadlines, product development has the potential to fall prey to **project slippage**, where deadlines are missed, or **scope creep**, where the parameters of the product keep expanding. Both of these have the potential to derail an effort at creating "newness" by delaying product introductions or making the final product you create too expensive. You have to cut off adding features at some point, and once you hit that date, then you can take the "late" ideas and file them away for the next version.

For the Product Development process to work—whether it's for a whole new product, a different feature, or a new process—it's best to follow a plan. You begin with an idea, however you are able to generate it, and then you start your market research. The research part never really ends. Once you know the product or features you'll be working on, put down a plan in writing so that you can distribute the details to everyone involved: goals, scope, deadlines. The implementation step is always the most challenging. Work with what and who you have available. Once you have your product out on the market, it's time to start measuring outcomes. Did you get the results you intended or anticipated? Make corrections or improvements if needed, and go through the planning loop again.

Just remember to be open to all of the possibilities around you as far as creating new products or features. Examine your environment and your industry. You should always ask yourself what opportunity do you see. Is that one you want to take advantage of? What need can you fill for customers? What market is currently underserved? What's missing in our industry? What gaps do we have in the products we offer? Once you have some of those answers, then it's back to the R&D. You want to determine if your product will be well-received. You need to test and refine so that your product has the best chance of success. Ultimately, though, you have to figure out which market segment you think you can win over in a profitable way.

OPEN FOR BUSINESS IN THE REAL WORLD

You have so many ideas for new products, you really don't know where to begin. You really favor your creative and artistic side, but are coming around to the realities of "business" now that you're deep into your Business course and this textbook. But rather than open your own store where you have to pay rent and sit there all day waiting for people to come in, it finally hits you that you can go into a jewelry and crafts wholesale business. You scour the Internet for some small boutiques in a town selling handmade crafts by local artisans, and you hit the road to begin your market research. The secondary data proved that there's a market for what you want to do, now you have to gather some primary data to see if people will like your styles and sell them.

There are several nice bracelets and necklaces that you've made for family and friends over the years, so you go ask to borrow them back for a bit. "Samples" in hand, you enter a medium-sized shop and talk to the owner. You explain how everyone loves your work and that you always get positive feedback from your "focus groups," friends commenting to your relatives about how cool and unique your designs are. The owner is impressed and proposes a test market in the store. If you prepare an assortment of jewelry, they will be displayed in the store on consignment. If at least 1/3 of the items are sold during the first month, then the owner will place an actual order for a dozen necklace/bracelet pairs of each style and color.

A month later, 1/2 of your items sold to rave reviews! You're excited, but you haven't been sitting still. During that time, you've been working up new designs, showing them to friends, and refining the distinctive look that identifies your jewelry. You're ready to supply the store with your products, and armed with this success, you approach a second store on the other side of the town.

Chapter Summary

You have to figure out what customers want before you can be successful at product development and design. Market research is vital for collecting and analyzing data for good decision-making before you develop or introduce new products or features. Collecting secondary data first can help you determine if you have a good idea that hasn't been done before spending money on primary data, collecting survey responses or conducting focus groups, or rolling out a test market.

Market segmentation can help you decide on a mass market or niche market approach. You can divide and market to people based on demographics, geography, occasions, benefits, behavior, or psychographics. Concept testing can get your products into the hands of consumers early to help refine your efforts. You need to focus on utilization, since customers often find new and unusual ways to use things. Packaging can help you highlight this, as well as provide a means of distinctiveness. Adapting products to local tastes via distributed product development can also increase your chances of success.

Pricing strategies can help you decide if you can make enough money to "break even" on your product or feature. You can price based on cost plus, targeted return, value based, or psychological pricing. Skimming can help you get the most profit selling to early adopters; penetration can increase sales to get a large installed base or discourage competitors; dynamic pricing lets you change prices in real time based on a customer's history and buying habits.

Successful products go through all stages of the product life cycle: introduction, growth, maturity, and decline. Introduction is a question mark, but with great potential if it can cross the chasm into growth. Growth is a star, with high growth and high profits if you have few competitors. Maturity denotes cash cow products, which you can milk for revenue. A marketing push might extend this phase, but a manufacturing focus can help cut costs and increase profit margins somewhat even as competitors enter and eventually push profits towards zero. Products in decline are dogs that you should consider discontinuing or selling off if you don't have another reason to keep them around. The BCG Matrix gives you a visual way to see the relative amount and size of products in each phase.

Product development and design requires good planning so that you can take advantage of consumer trends identified via your market research. You must, though, be sure to manage the process so that you don't have product slippage delaying introductions or scope creep that makes them too expensive or cumbersome when released. New products are more about good ideas, whereas new features are more targeted to feedback. Finally, keep in mind that even though new products and features are glamorous to work on and introduce, their profits are front-loaded and often short-lived. New process introductions, on the other hand, start off slow but have the potential to show increasing profits for a long period of time since they aren't as easily imitated.

Review Questions

1. What is the first step in the Market Research process? Even before you begin conducting any type of market research, what should you have in mind?
2. List three types of primary data and three types of secondary data. Which should you do first?
3. What are the six ways that you can segment the market when trying to choose a target market to pursue with your product development?
4. Explain why packaging is so important in the potential success of any new product development effort once it appears on the shelf.
5. Of the four main pricing methods, which one allows you to consider all fixed costs and variable costs? Which one might help you make your product appear less expensive? How and why?
6. Which of the pricing objectives is more about selling the most units? Which one is about generating the most profit? How might you be able to do both at the same time?
7. In the Product Life Cycle model, which stage presents the most difficult challenges to overcome? Why?
8. Which stage of the Product Life Cycle presents the greatest opportunity for sustained profits to last over a long period of time? How might you prolong that even more?
9. Why do you focus on marketing your products more so than cutting costs in the Introduction and Growth stages of the Product Life Cycle?
10. Why do you focus on manufacturing your products and finding ways to cut costs in the Maturity and Decline stages of the Product Life Cycle?
11. In which quadrant of the BCG Matrix should you want most of your products? Why?
12. What are two potential problems that can occur with any product development effort, whether for a new product or new feature? How can you overcome these?

Discussion Questions

13. How would you go about overcoming path dependency issues when introducing new products? Come up with some specific industries or product categories that you use frequently and lay out some specific recommendations to get people to switch.
14. Which market research step do you think is the most important for ensuring that you get usable data for developing products? Explain and defend your position.
15. What are some of the best ways to come up with new uses for the existing products? Are these viable product development options? How can you encourage this?

16. Where would you put each of the following Apple products on the Product Life Cycle: iPod, iPad, iPhone, Apple TV? Do you think Apple Watch has an advantage compared with other new product introductions? Is it possible for a product to skip any of the phases? Explain your response.

17. Do you agree with the implication in the chapter that process development has the potential to be better than product development? How can you encourage your product development people to pursue avenues that are better for the company rather than what they're interested in?

Key Terms

- BCG Maxtrix (Boston Consulting Group Matrix
- Behavior
- Benefits
- brainstorm
- brand
- break even
- Break Even Point (BEP)
- business intelligence
- Cash Cow
- commercialization
- concept testing
- Cost Plus
- Decline
- Demography
- distinctiveness
- distributed product development
- Dog
- dynamic pricing
- early adopters
- Fixed Costs (FC)
- focus group
- Geography
- Growth
- Introduction
- market research
- market segment
- mass market
- Maturity
- niche market
- Occasions
- Packaging
- path dependency
- penetration
- Pricing Objectives
- primary data
- Product Adaptation
- Product Life Cycle
- product screening
- project slippage
- prototype
- Psychographics
- Psychological Pricing
- Question Mark
- Research and Development (R&D)
- Return on Investment (ROI)
- scope creep
- secondary data
- skimming
- Star
- Targeted Return
- test market
- type
- utilization
- Value Based
- Variable Costs (VC)

Entrepreneurship

LEARNING OBJECTIVES

1. Explain what an entrepreneur is and what it takes to be one.
2. Discuss considerations when starting a business or buying a franchise.
3. Detail how differentiation is important in your marketing plan and business plan.
4. Discuss the pros and cons of various ways to fund your business.
5. Explain some other resources that might help get your business started.

OPENING STORY

Entrepreneurship is a combination of vision, risk-taking, and luck. Mobile game company Rovio was founded in 2003, but it wasn't until after near collapse in 2009 that they would have a runaway success: Angry Birds. They were close to bankruptcy after having created 51 different titles that sold millions of copies, . . . but for other game publishers. Such is the life of a developer: create a game, but turn over most of the rights for future sales and merchandising to the publisher who contracts your work.

> **Entrepreneurship** is the risking of time and money by a business owner to set up and operate a for profit business.

© OlegDoroshin/Shutterstock, Inc.

To save the company, the founders felt that they had to create the perfect game. They "had developed 51 titles before *Angry Birds*. Some of them had sold in the millions for third parties such as Namco and EA, so they decided to create their own, original intellectual property." The right combination of persistence, marketing, and luck came together to make Angry Birds the runaway success that it was. The company felt that devoting time to make the perfect game would minimize the need for luck. Upon its release, Angry Birds had 150,000 downloads and boasts 75 million users today. Their unique free play model with in- app purchases was a huge hit. Cross-over licensing made lots of money, too, but they're now looking for their next hit that isn't Angry Birds related.

(Source: http://www.wired.co.uk/magazine/archive/2011/04/features/how-rovio-made-angry-birds-a-winner)

INTRODUCTION

So, you really want to start a business. If you are going to have a successful business, you should treat yourself as an expense as quickly as possible—pay yourself. Above all else, always keep good records of anything and everything you do. That will keep you out of trouble (just check with your lawyer about how long to keep everything). We're here to help you with some of the insight and assistance you'll need using the concepts contained throughout this textbook. In fact, we'll revisit some of the issues you need to consider as you move forward with your plan. Keep in mind that not everyone is cut out to be an entrepreneur. Let's see if you think you're ready.

WHAT IS AN ENTREPRENEUR?

Entrepreneurs people who risk their time and money to start a business.

An **entrepreneur** is a person who risks time and money to start a business venture or make money on his/her own. Time and money are two distinct yet related risks that you must assume if you choose this path rather than working for someone else. Remember the opportunity cost that we discussed in the Economics chapter? The time you must devote to your entrepreneurial endeavor is the time that you must take away from leisure or from work that might earn you a paycheck at a regular job. That's where part of the monetary risk comes from as well. In addition to whatever money you must invest to make and sell your products or advertise your services, you also won't be making money from a job to pay your personal expenses for food and rent if you devote full-time hours and effort to starting your business venture.

© Lightspring/Shutterstock, Inc.

Sometimes people try to start a business on the side while they keep their regular job or take a part-time job and then only devote full-time hours to an entrepreneurial venture once they've proven to themselves that they can make money on their own. This might work for some types of businesses (such as if you are making custom jewelry to sell wholesale to another store owner), but not for other types of businesses (such as if you are opening your own retail store). Keep that in mind as we explore other points you need to consider about becoming an entrepreneur.

Characteristics of an Entrepreneur

One of the first things you should understand about entrepreneurship is that there's risk involved. In fact, it's part of the definition! Thus, one of the first characteristics that an entrepreneur must have is the **willingness to take on risk**. You must be okay with uncertainty, and consider that if you have a family, then your significant other should be aware of the risks as well. If they're supportive, then that's great; if they are hesitant, then that can add to your stress as you deal with the inherent uncertainty that comes with a new business.

Perhaps the most important characteristic, though, is a **passion for the business chosen**. People who decide to become entrepreneurs often do it for the challenge of accomplishment or to take advantage of an opportunity they see, but only passion can get you to keep working hard when things don't go as planned right away. Your primary reason for starting a business should not be that you want to get rich. "According to Bloomberg, 8 out of 10 entrepreneurs who start businesses fail within the first 18 months." (http://www.forbes.com/sites/ericwagner/2013/09/12/five-reasons-8-out-of-10-businesses-fail/) Passion is what can keep you going. It takes more than just an idea to be a successful entrepreneur; you must also have good planning and realization to be a success.

Other important characteristics include **high energy** because long hours are often required, **belief in oneself** because any salesperson knows that many more people will tell you "no" than say "yes," and **discipline** because no one else will be telling you what to do or when to do it. The independence is nice when you're creating your own schedule, but it can also make you feel guilty when you are devoting time to things other than your business. Only you can decide the right balance, but make sure that you actually have a balance. We said that starting your new business venture can be stressful; it can also be stressful if you don't take a little time for yourself or completely ignore your family.

Risk   uncertainty about the future, especially about the possibility of loss.

Passion   zeal or energy that someone has, especially for the challenge of accomplishment.

© Andrey_Popov/Shutterstock, Inc.

© eltoro69/Shutterstock, Inc.

Other Types of Entrepreneurs

If you're not sure you want the responsibilities—and the stress—of being a "regular" entrepreneur, then there are a few other options. Rather than go all out and try to start a large business or one with multiple locations, some people might suggest going the route of being a **micropreneur**. The thought here is that if you stay small, then there's less stress and more time for a balance in your personal life. This is not always the case, however, since most of the duties remain the same. One answer might be to **delegate** more duties to other people, but a "regular" entrepreneur can do that as well.

The only real alternative is being an **intrapreneur**, where you can still have the creative freedom to work on projects, but within the safer environment of a large company that can provide you with resources—and a regular paycheck. It's not as glamorous and you probably won't get to share in profits to the same extent

Micropreneur   person starting a business who chooses to stay small, opting for less stress and more time for a balance in personal life.

Delegate   to assign duties to other people.

Intrapreneur   person with the creative freedom to work on projects, but within the safer environment of a large company that can provide resources—and a regular pay check.

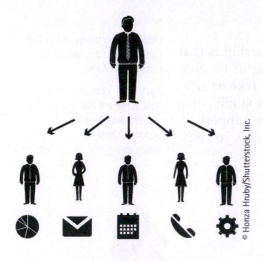

© Honza Hruby/Shutterstock, Inc.

as if you were on your own, but you've also minimized the two big risks of being an entrepreneur. You're making money from your "job," and you have resources to get things done.

For the rest of this chapter, though, we are going to assume that you are going out on your own to start or run a business. We'll discuss some of the different ways you can do that. It's very different to start a business from scratch, compared to buying an existing business. You can open a company in a new field where you are unfamiliar, or you can go off on your own after you've worked for another company for awhile to learn the industry. If you got laid off, perhaps you can leverage your knowledge or experience or contacts into some type of business venture or a consulting contract. You can always consider buying a franchise if you are careful to select a good one.

© Lightspring/Shutterstock, Inc.

STARTING YOUR BUSINESS

Before you actually start to do any business activities, you should carefully review the Business Law chapter. You must comply with numerous laws, depending on what type of business you want to go into. There are a number of decisions you need to make about how you will structure your business. The more contact that you will have with the public for your products or services, then the more important it is that you establish your business as a corporation or LLC to give you some liability protection. Sole proprietorships may work for some small side businesses that don't

© Marlon Lopez MMG1 Design/Shutterstock, Inc.

produce things or where people don't visit your location, but you are assuming some additional risks that really aren't necessary. Basic legal advice is not very expensive and there are online tools to help you as well. Similarly, a partnership may make sense for a few types of businesses, perhaps a collaborative creative business, but again there are downsides that can be avoided with proper planning. You should get a lawyer involved with this also.

Some of the other business alternatives really *require* that you get legal advice. Taking over an existing business or buying a franchise both need an experienced eye to review documents and make recommendations. When you buy a business, keep in mind that you are buying the assets *and* the liabilities. The assets that a company owns can be tangible (buildings, equipment, etc.) or intangible (patents, trademarks, customer lists), but it takes an expert to determine what some of these are worth. If a business has something that makes it unique, such as a proprietary manufacturing process, two people could value that "asset" very differently. Accountants are very useful here.

More importantly, though, you are buying the liabilities of the company as well. This is not just about buying its debts; it's very easy to see who the company owes money to. What takes much more **due diligence** research into the company's past involves potential liability from lawsuits for defects or negligence or other wrongdoing. When you are buying a company, you are also buying these potential problems and possible future litigation. Attorneys are very useful here. You don't want to get too excited about the company's revenue stream or profits, and overlook issues that may cause customers to stop buying from you in the future for some reason.

© Andrey_Popov/Shutterstock, Inc.

Buying a Franchise

A **franchise** is a business where the small business owner ("**franchisee**") pays a fee to a larger corporation ("**franchisor**") for the right to sell that company's branded products or services in a given territory. The franchisee typically pays an up-front buy-in fee as well as an ongoing **royalty** percentage of sales. Typically, the franchisee must also agree to follow all rules of the franchisor, which may require purchases of stock or materials as well as exclusions on other activities. In exchange for this, the franchisor provides management expertise to the new owner and may also provide advertising or marketing materials. Some franchisors also provide financing assistance.

It's best if you thoroughly investigate any franchise opportunity. Some are excellent, some are not. You may have the chance to turn your franchise into a legitimate business which can be resold in the future (usually with approval of the franchisor), but other times, you are not doing much more than buying yourself a job. The best franchises typically require large cash outlays, and the franchisor checks that the franchisee has liquid assets to sustain the business. Entrepreneur.com says that the total Investment for a McDonald's franchise is $1,000,708–$2,335,146, (depending on location, equipment levels purchased, etc.) and the new owner must have liquid cash available of $750,000. This is on top of the $45,000 franchise fee up front and the ongoing royalty that must be paid off the top from gross sales.

(http://www.entrepreneur.com/franchises/mcdonalds/282570-0.html)

Due diligence research into the past of a person or company, verifying the accuracy of information presented and also especially looking for issues that involves potential liability from lawsuits for defects or negligence or other wrong-doing.

Franchise a business where the small business owner ("**franchisee**") pays a fee to a larger corporation ("**franchisor**") for the right to sell that company's branded products or services in a given territory.

Franchisee a person who buys and runs a franchise business in exchange for paying fee(s).

Franchisor a business that licenses the right to a franchisee, allowing that person to sell the company's branded products or services in a given territory.

Royalty a percentage of sales, usually paid as a licensing fee for use of another company's products, intellectual property (such as patents or trademarks), and so on.

© Vytautas Kielaitis/Shutterstock, Inc.

Obviously, McDonald's is a very high-end, in-demand franchise, so they can ask for a lot. At the other end of the spectrum are hundreds of opportunities to buy into everything from cleaning businesses to staffing companies to learning centers. The up-front fees and requirements vary, but be sure what you are buying with your money. Some franchisors promise management help that is not much more than a copied training manual, while others promise advertising that never materializes. Talk with current franchise owners, and always get legal advice.

Business plan a written document that states a business' goals and how they will be achieved with details about your marketing, finance, management, and so on.

MARKETING YOUR BUSINESS

This is actually the most important part of getting your business going. If you recall what you studied in the Marketing chapter, that is a good start. It's crucial that you have a plan to go after a certain market, and in a way that differentiates your product or service from the competition. What can help formulate that for you is putting together a **business plan**. Your business plan is a written document that states your business goals and how you will achieve them, with details about your marketing, finances, management, and so on.

© Marlon Lopez MMG1 Design/Shutterstock, Inc.

As much as a marketing plan will help sell your products or services, a good business plan will help sell your business to investors or banks. Even if you start out small without a need for outside capital, it's still a good exercise to assemble a business plan so that you can see your strategy in writing. There are numerous software packages that can make the job easier. To help ensure that you think of everything, it will create the plan by asking you questions about your product or service, the target market you will go after, general information about the industry, specific information about your competitors, and much more.

You will give historical financial data if the business is a going concern, and future projections for sales and cash flow as you see the business growing and succeeding. Don't stress out about the actual numbers you include. They should be realistic and defensible, but two investors or two accountants can look at the same figures and have completely different opinions; one might think the projections are too low and conservative, another might think those same numbers are too high and unrealistic. Regardless of the numbers, the most important part of the business plan to an investor or the bank is the management team. They

© Digital Storm/Shutterstock, Inc.

want to see all about you and the other people you have involved, if they've been successful before in the industry, or are good at sales, or if they've run successful marketing campaigns in the past. People are what matters most to the success of any business.

Why Differentiating Your Business Is Important

There are a few different ways that you can set yourself apart from the competition. You must have at least one; but the more you have, the better chance you have of success. We've discussed all of the marketing angles in the marketing chapter, so you should review that as you are deciding how best to move forward with your business. We won't repeat those here, but we will focus on a few key areas. One crucial mistake that some entrepreneurs make is presenting a business plan or marketing strategy that assumes they have no competitors. This can disqualify you immediately in the eyes of many investors. Nothing is so new that there's not at least a remote competitor, even if it's just the old industry you're going to "overtake." They won't sit still while you take their business away, so you have to address that. At the very least, your customers will have to take dollars from somewhere else or forego some other expenditure in order to spend money with you. Acknowledge that.

© iQoncept/Shutterstock, Inc.

Also understand that you *must* create value, in the eyes of customers and also in the eyes of investors, banks, and so on. Anyone who you want to believe in your business or help your business must be convinced that you can do something better than anyone else. Successful businesses have found a profitable niche or are very customer-focused in a way that competitors aren't. You must know how to articulate this clearly and succinctly. If you can't explain why you're different or better in a few sentences, then it will be hard to convince others.

Elevator pitch   a 30-s or 1-min summation about why someone should want to do business with a company or an individual. (The name comes from imagining that a person gets lucky one day and rides the same elevator as an important potential client or a key new investor.)

People talk about preparing an "**elevator pitch**." This is a 30 s or 1 min summation about why someone should want to do business with you. The name comes from imagining that you get lucky one day and ride the same elevator as an important potential client or a key new investor. Could you win him or her over in that amount of time or at least get them interested enough during the elevator ride for them to want to hear more about your business? You need to refine your message until you can recite it effortlessly. This is also an area where your passion will hopefully show through because that sends a powerful message as well.

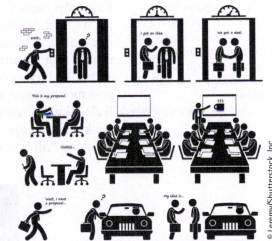

© Leremy/Shutterstock, Inc.

FINANCING YOUR BUSINESS

Every business has to have some money to get started, but obviously some need much more than others. Perhaps, if it's a very small business, you can start it with money you've saved over the years. Some of the most successful businesses are those started by people who gained experience and knowledge at their job before venturing off on their own in the same field. Or, maybe you are taking over the business where you worked because the owner wants to retire. In that case, he or she might actually do the financing for you since coming into a large sum of money would have tax consequences for them. Instead, they agree to take payments from the profits as a way for you to buy the business.

© bikeriderlondon/Shutterstock, Inc.

If that's not enough, then you need to look elsewhere. One of the top reasons for business failure is not enough capital. You need money to pay the rent, utilities, and wages while you wait for sales to start bringing in cash flow from your idea. Poor cash management can doom a business also. Sales are easier to get if you give generous credit terms, but if everyone gets 90 days to pay, how do you pay your bills in the current month? If you give out too much credit to others or you use too much credit yourself obligating you to large monthly debt service payments, then your business can fail quite easily—even if you have a product people like and want.

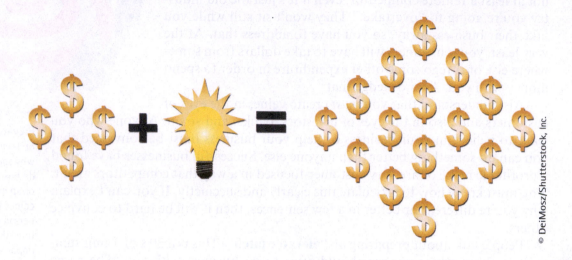

Sources of Capital

Capital is money invested in a business and used to buy assets or fund operations. As we said, if you can self-finance with your own money, then that takes away one potential distraction, at least at the outset. You may be tempted to borrow money from family and friends, but be very cautious when doing so. You understand the high potential failure rate of businesses, but does your Aunt? She gives you money expecting to get it back, but if you can't, then you would probably feel awkward when you need to see her every holiday. If you actually do pay her back with interest, she may feel it's not enough because of the huge success you're enjoying "all because of her."

Capital is money or the things money can buy, like machines and buildings, which are used in the production of goods and services. The initial money used to start an investment.

If you decide to look for outside help for funding, beware of scams advertising help in finding you funds in exchange for a fee. Nothing wrong with paying a commission, but do it on a contingency basis after the money is raised.

"Application fees" up front to people who will find you funding sources rarely lead to results. Be skeptical. If you are going to attempt to raise money on your own, be sure that you talk to a lawyer before selling stock to anyone. There are numerous regulations in place and strict rules that must be followed to **register** your securities before selling them. The idea is that the government does not want scam artists preying on retired people and getting their life savings in exchange for lavish promises. Thus, selling unregistered securities is a serious offense that can lead to criminal prosecution.

Professional investors are a legitimate source, but it can be hard to get money from them. **Angel investors** are private individuals with a high net worth who are looking for promising investments that have tremendous growth potential. Traditionally, these were doctors or accountants looking for someplace to put some of their money. It is getting harder to reach these people, however, because they've employed gatekeepers who deny access to them since public information makes them easy targets to be hounded by so many "opportunities." Furthermore, many of these individuals have banded together and now operate closer to venture capitalists. **Venture capital** firms are professional organizations formed specifically to make high-risk, high-reward investments in various industries. In addition to investment dollars, many also offer management expertise. This also means that some of them may want to become more involved with your company, sometimes on a day-to-day basis but at the very least with a seat on your Board of Directors.

© Sergey Nivens/Shutterstock, Inc.

© Mark Van Scyoc/Shutterstock, Inc.

Two more funding sources may be of use to you in certain situations. First, there's the Small Business Administration (SBA), which gets involved making **SBA loans** possible to small businesses. Keep in mind, though, that these loans are still made by a bank, so even with government backing they're still stricter about requirements to qualify. Established businesses with a track record have a chance, but you will not get an SBA loan for an unproven idea with no sales history. The more likely scenario would be a small business with $1 million in sales the past few years looking for expansion capital with a plan to double their sales. The last possibility is **crowd funding**, which is just starting to evolve with new government regulations that will change this process. Previously at sites like

Register   submitting formal paperwork with various governmental bodies, especially prior to the sale of securities. (This is a requirement at the federal level by the SEC and by various state regulatory bodies.)

Angel investors   private individuals with a high net worth who are looking for promising investments that have tremendous growth potential. (Traditionally, these were doctors or accountants looking for some place to put some of their money.)

Venture capital   professional organizations formed specifically to make high-risk, high-reward investments in various industries. (In addition to investment dollars, many also offer management expertise.)

SBA loans   loan guarantees put in play by Small Business Administration to help small businesses. (Keep in mind though, that these loans are still made by a bank, so even with government backing they're still more strict about requirements to qualify.)

Crowd funding   process whereby people interested in a product can pledge money to get it developed and then receive the item when finished. (Essentially, these people are pre-ordering. Look for more changes in the future though.)

KickStarter.com, people interested in a product would pledge money to get it developed and then receive the item when finished. Essentially, they were pre-ordering. New rules will allow money to be taken for other reasons, with equity shares allowed to change hands. Watch developments here for exciting new possibilities.

RESOURCES THAT MIGHT HELP YOU

As you try to move forward with your business, there are some resources that might be able to provide you with different types of assistance. **Service Corps Of Retired Executives (SCORE)** is a volunteer organization with thousands of locations across the country providing free in-person counseling. Obviously, the advice can be hit or miss depending on if the person you meet has experience in your particular industry; however, there are some universal principles of business these mentors can discuss with you. They also have How-to Resources, Tools, and Templates available on their website at www.Score.org.

Service Corps Of Retired Executives (SCORE) a volunteer organization with thousands of locations across the country providing free in-person counseling. They also have How-to Resources, Tools, and Templates available on their web site at www. Score.org.

© Pressmaster/Shutterstock, Inc.

Enterprise zones places designated by local government with low or abated taxes in those areas to encourage development there.

Incubators business help provided by a larger corporation (or government entity) designed to provide low-cost space, available services, management help, and other types of advice to companies who are just getting started.

Seed money small amounts of initial capital provided to further the work being done by a small company.

In the public sector, there is government assistance in the form of tax breaks, which you can explore. It's best to check with your state or local jurisdiction, but it's common for there to be designated **enterprise zones** that have low or abated taxes in certain areas to encourage development in those places. Other incentives are also available from various government entities and agencies for bringing technology to the area, utilizing resources, or providing jobs to communities or certain groups of people.

In the private sector, there are some large companies who have set up **incubators** to provide low-cost space, available services, management help, and other types of advice to companies who are just getting started. Often times the start-ups must be in the same industry as the larger company for businesses to be able to take advantage of this carved out space. The idea is that the large corporation wants to encourage research that might lead to advances. Sometimes even **seed money** is provided in small amounts to further the work being done by the small company and grow the idea.

Note that for some, but not all, of these resources you must be classified as a "small business." That's not so much about actual size or even number of employees. The SBA defines a **small business** as "small" if it's independently owned (meaning not part of a larger corporation) and not dominant in its industry (meaning relative size, not absolute).

© world of vector/Shutterstock, Inc.

OPEN FOR BUSINESS: ENTREPRENEURSHIP IN THE REAL WORLD

You have some big plans and big ideas, but you decide you'll put those off for a year or two. Lack of funds is a problem you're not quite sure how to overcome just yet, but you want to venture off on your own and work for yourself. You finally settle on the business you've discovered has the lowest barriers to entry, the cheapest initial investment: a lawn care business. You figure you can get started with your truck and a decent lawnmower. Once you've proved to yourself it will work, you'll buy a little better tractor. Your plan is to use some of the profits from the summer to buy a snow plow blade to put on your truck so that you can keep busy all year round.

You decide to put some goals down in writing. It won't be a bulky business plan just yet, but you will go through and talk about how your service will be different and better, who you see as competitors, risks to your model, and then put together some financial projections. Those are actually pretty hard to do: Sales will be dramatically different depending on what the weather is like in the winter. Even in the summer, if we don't get enough rain, the grass won't grow so fast, or if we get too much rain, you really can't cut the grass driving through mud. You decide to create two sets of numbers: your real estimate, based on last year's weather, and one alternative scenario for a scarce winter.

You write everything down and put it aside. If you hit your projections, you can maybe hire one person part-time to help. But you really want to be cautious because you know that running out of money is one of the fastest ways to kill a business. You've got a little bit saved, and you figure only to do cash business for the first month or so. But you have your eye on that nice office building down the street. If you can get their business, you'd agree to invoice them in 30 days as long as they're the only one getting credit. You decide you'll go onto Score.org to see if you can get some more ideas to thrive.

Chapter Summary

An entrepreneur risks time and money to start a business venture, so he/she must have a willingness to take on risk, a passion for the business chosen, high energy, belief in oneself, and discipline. A micropreneur stays small, with more time for balance in personal life; an intrapreneur has creative freedom to work on projects within the safer environment of a large company that can provide resources and a regular paycheck.

Your business should be structured to limit liability. Get legal advice if buying a business or franchise. When you buy a business, you're buying the assets and the liabilities, plus potential future litigation, so due diligence is needed to research the company's past. With a franchise business, the small business owner ("franchisee") pays a fee up-front to a larger corporation ("franchisor") for the right to sell that company's branded products or services in a given territory, as well as pay an ongoing royalty percentage of sales, plus other requirements.

It's crucial that you have a plan to go after a certain market, and in a way that differentiates your product or service from the competition. Put together a business plan so that you have a written document that states your business goals and how you will achieve them, with details about your marketing, finances, management, and so on. But the most important part of the business plan to an investor or bank is the experience of the management team.

You must create value, in the eyes of customers and investors, banks, and so on. Successful businesses find a profitable market niche and must know how to articulate this clearly and succinctly. Practice an "elevator pitch" stating in a minute or less why someone should want to do business with you. It's a critical mistake to assume you have no competitors; others will eventually emulate you, plus you are competing for consumer dollars no matter what.

Every business needs money to get started, but if you can't self-finance, be careful about borrowing from family or friends. Capital used to buy assets or for operations might be obtained from angel investors (individuals) or from venture capitalists (firms). SBA Loans are a possibility for established businesses; crowd funding might be an option to sell product pre-orders. Do not sell unregistered securities since that's a serious offense. Other advice might be available from SCORE, government agencies touting enterprise zones, or incubators that may be willing to provide space, advice, and some seed money. Make sure you pay yourself with your new venture, and always keep good records.

Review Questions

1. What risks does an entrepreneur take when starting a business?
2. List some characteristics of successful entrepreneurs, and state why each of them is important.
3. State what should be your primary reason for starting a business and what should not be your primary reason for starting a business. Why?
4. Which business form is best for an entrepreneur? Explain.
5. Explain what's purchased when someone buys a business. Why should an attorney be brought in to look at the deal?
6. What are some of the pros and cons of buying a franchise?
7. List what's contained in a business plan. Why is it important to put one together?
8. Explain what it means to differentiate your business. Why is this important?
9. What is one of the top reasons for business failure? Why?
10. Explain the difference between Angel Investors and Venture Capital firms.

Discussion Questions

11. What are some ways that an entrepreneur can do a better job of balancing family life, personal time, and working?
12. Do you see a franchise as a real business opportunity or buying a job? Upon what are you basing your opinion and what might change your perception of this?
13. How would you address the issue of creating projections when you're new to an industry and obviously can't know the future? Do you think it's best to go high or low? Explain.
14. Since an elevator pitch is obviously limited in scope, what points do you think should definitely be included?
15. How can you address the issue of competitors in a comprehensive way while still making it clear that you have a definite place in the market?

Key Terms

- Angel investors
- business plan
- Capital
- crowd funding
- delegate
- due diligence
- elevator pitch
- enterprise zones
- entrepreneur
- entrepreneurship
- franchise
- franchisee
- franchisor
- incubators
- intrapreneur
- micropreneur
- passion
- register
- risk
- royalty
- SBA loans
- seed money
- Service Corps Of Retired Executives (SCORE)
- small business
- Small Business Administration (SBA)
- Venture capital

14

Information Technology and E-Business

LEARNING OBJECTIVES

1. Describe what makes up an information system.
2. Discuss ethics in regard to information technology.
3. Explain the requirements for and the difficulties associated with protecting information technology.
4. Detail how to prevent and/or recover from loss of information.
5. Explain how e-business is like and different from traditional business.

© Northfoto/Shutterstock, Inc.

OPENING STORY

On Wednesday, December 18, 2013, Target Inc. reported they were investigating a massive breach of security that may have led to loss of customer's credit and debit card information for about 40 million shoppers (Fairchild, 2013). The customers used their cards during the Christmas shopping season, so the number was especially large.

© Arina P Habich/Shutterstock, Inc.

Unfortunately, this was not the first massive information loss, nor was it the last. In 2007, TJ Maxx stores lost the data on 90 million cards. In October of 2012, Nationwide Insurance lost information on 1.1 million insurance customers (Tam, 2012). On March 2, 2014, credit card numbers used at Denton, Texas–based Sally Beauty Inc., stores went on sale at an illegal site that sells stolen information. Some of the banks that originally issued the cards bought them back as a less expensive alternative to whatever else they would have to do (Sally, 2014). These security breaches are very expensive for the companies affected, as well as potentially very dangerous and expensive for the customers whose information is stolen.

INTRODUCTION

The 2001 recession and stock market crash were primarily related to what became known as the Dot Com Bubble. Leading up to the bubble bursting was a new way of doing business, on the Internet. Thousands of start-up companies were born into a new environment, conducting business online instead of having a brick-and-mortar fixed establishment. These companies could have potentially global reach with instant communications from a single site or possibly from no site at all.

Many wondered if this was the beginning of a rapid cultural shift with traditional businesses failing as their customers quit going to the store in favor of reaching the store while sitting at the kitchen table, through their computer. The perception was that it was a huge competitive battle between the new innovative companies and the old stagnant firms. Who would we choose: the e-businesses or the brick-and-mortar companies?

Then it occurred to someone, somewhere, that being traditional did not preclude being innovative. Brick-and-mortar business everywhere opened e-business departments and we had Walmart.com, Sears.com, Penny.com, and everything else.com and gone was the innovative advantage of the start-up companies. Most of them failed, many without ever producing a product for sale. Fifteen years later, the cultural change may be occurring and we are going to the store from our kitchen table more frequently every year, but it is with the same companies we shop when we do go to the store.

E-business and information technology have brought tremendous change and along with it great risk as criminals prowl the Internet like they used to prowl the alley. Thinking about the enormous change that has taken place in the last 20 years, it is hard to imagine what will happen in the next 20 years.

© Radu Bercan/Shutterstock, Inc.

INFORMATION AND DATA

Businesses need information on how they are doing, on what they can do differently, and on the potential results of alternative courses of action. Some questions businesses need to answer are relatively simple, such as, how are sales this year compared to last year, or last month, or the same month last year. Others are much more complex: how do sales in the northeast region among 18–24 year olds compare to the same age group in the southeast region. In March 2014, McDonald's, the world's largest restaurant chain, reported a drop in sales of 0.3% for worldwide sales for stores open over 13 months and 1.4% for U.S. same store sales (Hill, 2014). Although this may not seem like a large drop, it is very troubling for McDonald's. The quick acquisition and analysis, along with the detail of the information to determine this, points out the value of information technology.

> **Data** is a compilation of facts and figures.
>
> **Information** is useful correlated data that can inform or allow decision making.
>
> **Information system** way to collect the data and archive it and compare it or manipulate it to provide ready access to decision makers when they need it.

To make the report, McDonald's Inc. had to collect a lot of data and use it to derive information. **Data** is a compilation of facts and figures. Determining the sales figures from the days, weeks, months, and years is gathering data. To compare it nationwide and worldwide to support purposeful conclusions or decisions is information. **Information** is useful knowledge drawn from the study of the data. Companies usually will have some sort of **information system**. An information system is a way to collect the data and archive it and compare it or manipulate it to provide ready access to decision-makers when they need it. In the past, organizations might have sales figures, accounting information, and human resource data, all stored in separate files or systems. With modern technology, it is possible to have all of the information available on the same system.

© jannoon028/Shutterstock, Inc.

© Kendall Hunt Publishing Company

THE COMPONENTS OF AN INFORMATION SYSTEM

A small business with a simple set of data may elect to keep everything on paper, in file folders, located in file cabinets and available to physically retrieve as needed. The volume of data for most businesses along with the need to correlate it with other data sets forces most companies to rely on computer-based information systems

The four components of a computer-based information system—computer hardware, specialized computer software, networks or communications, and data management—work together to turn raw data into useful information. **Computer hardware** can consist of desktop and laptop computers, notebooks, and often today, tablets or smart cell phones. Each of these is a physical component that gives the user access into the network. Something needs to make the devices run and that is **software**. There is a wide variety of commercially available systems software; QuickBooks for accounting, Kronos for Human Resources, BambooHR specializing in small business, and many others to handle vehicle fleet operations, work scheduling, equipment management, training plans, and almost any aspect of business operations. The **network** or **Intranet** ties the various subsystems into an integrated whole using telecommunications. All this is managed by a **database managers** or **network specialists**, overseen by the **Chief Information Officer** or CIO.

> **Computer hardware** can consist of desk top and lap top computers, notebooks, and often today, tablets or smart cell phones. Each of these is a physical component that gives the user access into the network.
>
> **Intranet or network** ties the various sub-systems into an integrated whole using telecommunications.
>
> **Database managers or network specialists** work with and manage the information technology system in the company.
>
> **Chief Information Officer (CIO)** senior IT person in the company.

© Dragon Images/Shutterstock, Inc.

Computer Hardware are the physical parts of an information technology system. These can be input devices, mass storage, processing devices, or output devices. Desktop or laptop computers, hand-held devices like tablets or smartphones, mainframe computers, servers, printers, routers, and other tangible devices link people into the system. More and more, people are also seeing a change in what constitutes a computer. Cash registers, which used to be stand-alone devices to add up a customer's bill, are now links to accounting and inventory control. Where climate control is important, refrigeration units that used to simply maintain the temperature now report the status of the climate. There are numerous examples of previous stand-alone systems being integrated into an overall system that combines data on the overall process.

Computer hardware can consist of desk top and lap top computers, notebooks, and often today, tablets or smart cell phones. Each of these is a physical component that gives the user access into the network.

Computer software provides the instructions for the hardware to perform its function.

Computer Software provides the instructions for the hardware to perform its function. Computers need an operating system to drive the basic function of the computer itself. Aside from that, the computing device needs some functional guidance to allow it to perform a useful function. Word processing, for instance, is performed by the computer using software for that purpose. Other common business software includes database programs, spreadsheet programs, some of which can be found in comprehensive office programs, desktop publishing and presentation software, and planning programs.

© cherezoff/Shutterstock, Inc.

Computer Networks link computers and computing devices to allow sharing of information, documents, and communications. A company might install a **Local Area Network or LAN** to link the various computers in a single facility or area. If a company is spread into several locations, they might need to connect to a **Wide Area Network, or WAN**, which uses telephone, fiber-optic cable, satellites, or some other communications methods to connect in an almost limitless area. Connection through either a LAN or WAN has become much easier through the use of WiFi, (wireless fidelity) or hotspot, which wirelessly connects users to a system using WiFi routers covering a small area. This limits the need to run cables and gives the ability to quickly expand the connections.

An **Intranet** is a network that is designed like the Internet itself, but provides secure access to the organization only or other authorized users by way of passwords. A **firewall** or security system is established to limit access into the Intranet, while also allowing access from within the system to the outside, broader Internet. A **Virtual Private Network (VNP)** is a way to design an Intranet, but using the Internet. This links people in different physical locations, even worldwide, through software to set up a system much like an Intranet. The VPN connects two or more points on the Internet securely.

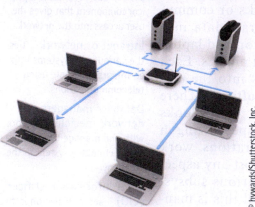

© hywards/Shutterstock, Inc.

© sheelamohanachandran2010/Shutterstock, Inc.

Computer networks link computers and computing devices to allow sharing of information, documents, and communications.

Local Area Network (LAN) link the various computers in a single facility or area.

Wide Area Network (WAN) uses telephone, fiber optic cable, satellites, or some other communication methods to connect in an almost limitless area.

Firewall or security system limits access into the internet.

Virtual Private Network (VPN) way to design an Intranet, but using the Internet to link people in different physical locations, even worldwide.

Data Management or database management is the task of controlling the other three parts of the information system. This involves controlling and safeguarding the information itself and managing the resources used in the IT system. Data managers must ensure that the correct information is collected, at the right time, manipulated into useful information, and distributed to the right people for their use in making decision or tracking progress. Data managers must keep up with the existing and emerging technologies and predict the future trends in the industry. They must do this while also remaining on budget.

INFORMATION SYSTEM TYPES

Information Systems come in various types that serve different functions. Two broad information systems types include Operational Support Systems and **Management Support Systems**. **Operational Support Systems** provide a flow of data in the daily operations of a company. A common example of this type of system is a **Point-of-Sale Terminal or POS**. A POS acts like a cash register from the perspective of a customer, but it includes card and check readers that allow information on the sale itself, the inventory item, and the financial transaction to be sent to both internal and external users. The transaction is processed and money collected as either cash or noncash while simultaneously, the information on the particular item is reported to inventory control, so the company can keep track on how many are on hand. If the order point is reached, either a resupply order can be flagged to that part of the management or even an automatic resupply order can be generated. At the same time, if the payment is noncash, in the form of a check, credit card, or debit card, the financial transaction is recorded and the actual collection process is begun to move the money into the company's account. Another type of Operational Support System is a **Process Control System**, which tracks the flow of product or work throughout a process. An example of this is the way packages are now tracked by various package

© dotshock/Shutterstock, Inc.

© Zern Liew/Shutterstock, Inc.

Management support system   help make decision making easier by providing information in the form of reports and or graphs that are easy to read and encapsulate necessary information.

Operational support systems   provide a flow of data in the daily operations of a company.

Point-of-sale terminal or POS   acts like a cash register from the perspective of a customer, but they include card and check readers that allow information on the sale itself, the inventory item, and the financial transaction to be sent to both internal and external users.

Process control system   tracks the flow of product or work throughout a process.

Management information system or decision support system   provide reports to several levels of management within the organization.

Executive support system   designed to provide reports and graph information in summary form to upper levels of management.

delivery services. Using a barcode, the package is scanned at each delivery or exchange point, so both the company and the customer can determine its location and delivery time.

Management Support Systems help make decision-making easier by providing information in the form of reports and/or graphs that are easy to read and encapsulate necessary information. These may come under several names such as a **Management Information System or Decision Support System** that provide reports to several levels of management within the organization. Some systems like an **Executive Support System** are designed to provide similar information to upper levels of management.

Enterprise Resource Planning (ERP) Software is a system or package of integrated business software that combines many of these management information systems into a packaged set of software that shares information and provides many decision-making applications.

THE ETHICAL ASPECTS OF INFORMATION TECHNOLOGY

Rapid changes in technology have brought enormous benefits to society, but the dark side to that technology may be the loss of personal privacy and the exposure to identify theft. As the opening story pointed out, security breaches have left millions vulnerable to the theft of their credit or debit card information, bank account information, and in some cases, complete identify theft. Companies find it to their advantage to collect as much information as possible on their clients to use it for sales and marketing, but they then incur a moral and legal responsibility to protect that information on behalf of those clients.

© Benoit Daoust/Shutterstock, Inc.

HIPPA   Health Information Portability and Accountability Act.

FERPA   Family Educational and Privacy Act.

In some cases, laws have not kept up with technological changes, thus making it difficult to enforce ethical behavior. **HIPPA** (Health Information Portability and Accountability Act) laws were enacted to protect private medical information from being released to anyone who does not have a specific requirement to have it. So, a person's medical information cannot be released even to family and friends without the patient's permission. It can, however, be released to medical billing companies and insurance companies that need it in the performance of their duties. **FERPA** (The Family Educational and Privacy Act) laws offer similar protection for your educational records.

Businesses, however, find it very beneficial to collect and use as much information on their clients as they can. By knowing their customers' buying habits along with where they live, where they shop, what they earn, their age and gender, and much more information, the companies can tailor their sales pitch to be more successful. Not only that, but they can sell that information to companies that specialize in market data. These companies, like InfoUSA in Omaha, NE, collect customer information from many sources and correlate the data, package it, and sell it to businesses around the world.

Customer information is valuable, but keeping it secure is important. Existing laws require companies to notify clients about what information they collect and share and to whom they share. Although customers can have some say in what is distributed, it requires action on the part of the customer. If companies violate the law or their own practices, they may be liable to customers who have lost their privacy or identity.

In addition to keeping client and partner information secure from those that would commit computer crimes, they must also keep it secure from those that would commit vandalism in a modern computer-driven world. Vandalism in the form of computer viruses, Trojans, and worms, grouped together as Malware can damage computer networks and cause the loss of valuable information.

Not only is it important to protect the information a business has collected, it is also part of the legal responsibility. Although it will be discussed in greater detail in both the law and accounting chapters, the Sarbanes–Oxley (SARBO) law passed in 2002 requires corporations to verify and certify the correctness of their information and to retain records in the event of future investigations.

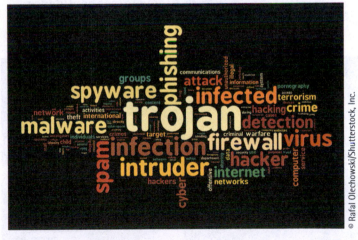

Recovering from Data Loss

There are many things, some natural, some not, which can cause disastrous loss of data for modern companies. In addition to **e-crime**, the deliberate theft or destruction of a company's Information, there are also natural disasters such as fires, floods, hurricanes, and tornadoes. Each of these has caused the physical destruction of computer hardware and communications systems that has led to a loss of data.

E-crime   the deliberate theft or destruction of a company's information.

Companies are exploring a variety of ways to prevent the loss of data or recover from it should it occur. In the early days of IT, companies kept a paper copy of nearly everything. Even after paper copies were no longer used or needed, companies held onto files of paper to back up their data in the event

of a catastrophic loss. Of course, a catastrophic loss was just as likely to affect the paper as it was to computers. Early methods of mass storage encouraged this because computers did crash and floppy disks and flash drives failed often enough that a dual system was thought necessary.

Information backup has become a commonplace method to prevent loss of data. Just as in the early days of computing, users were told to frequently save their work in case the computer crashed, now company employees are told to frequently back up valuable information to avoid loss due to system failure or disaster. Systems are also designed to automatically back up the information at periodic times, such as nightly after the business closes. This can be done either on-site or off-site. In addition to backing up the information to mass storage devices, many companies are using cloud computing to automatically store the information off-site in an area that is protected, but also readily accessible from almost anywhere. **Cloud computing** uses off-site mass storage servers that provide access and security.

Since almost every company deals with information and information technology in some form, every company should have a disaster recovery plan; a plan that can be rapidly set in motion to reduce the severity of a data loss, recover the data as soon as possible, and get the company up and running as quickly as possible to maintain or restore customer confidence.

Electronic Business

Electronic Business or E-Business is the conduct of business or enterprise online. In many ways, it is no different than the normal conduct of business in a traditional setting, sometimes referred to as a brick-and-mortar establishment. The resources of the company are applied in a way to satisfy the customers and accomplish organizational goals. The actual operation of the business may be very different in that suppliers, retailers, and customers may act without ever seeing each other.

Cloud computing uses off-site mass storage servers that provide access and security.

The few years leading up to the dotcom bust and recession of 2001 was an interesting time for American commerce. There appeared to be a contest between the traditional brick and mortar companies and the new upstart e-businesses. Who would dominate in the coming years? Would the American consumer change their mind and stop going to the mall and shop online instead. Were we on the verge of a great cultural shift in how we shop? The Nasdaq, the stock index that represents most high-tech companies, saw record highs as stock prices rose quickly as people invested in the new companies that were going to take on and perhaps defeat the companies we have known for years. Suddenly, it became obvious that a company did not have to choose between brick and mortar and online. The dot-com companies with no history collapsed and the traditional companies entered the e-business environment. Of course, a few of the dotcoms survived; notably Amazon, Netflix, and PayPal. For now, e-business and traditional business are not in conflict, but operate together and in complementary ways. Solely, e-businesses have become more active in the business-to-business (B2B) model and to a lesser extent in the business-to-consumer (B2C) model.

© szefei/Shutterstock, Inc.

How are e-business operations different? The most obvious difference is the lack of personal contact with the customer and the fact that a physical store is not necessary for businesses to welcome those customers. Other ways e-businesses differ are the necessity to keep up with current technologies and the need and sometimes difficulty to market to the customers.

E-business Marketing   Every business must find a way to connect with their potential customers. E-business tends not to use newspaper inserts, billboards, mailings, and radio and television advertisements. Instead, they use similar audio and visual ads in the online mediums such as Google, Facebook, and Yahoo. They pay to advertise where they believe their customer is more likely to be looking, the online environment.

© Kheng Guan Toh/Shutterstock, Inc.

To take advantage of this online advertisement potential, they need a web presence. It is much easier for an online company or the online component of a traditional company to operate 24/7, that is, 24 hr a day and 7 days a week. To do so, however, they need a 24/7 web presence. They need people and/or computers that are up and operating all the time. Many small companies may outsource this function to another e-business that specializes in providing online services to online companies.

© Roobcio/Shutterstock, Inc.

Employee Monitoring   Any business can run into the difficulty of worrying about the actions of their employees. Is the plumber working in a customer's home going to steal the jewelry they see left in a bathroom? Is the worker in another building going to spend his hours shopping online, surfing the Net, responding to Facebook posts, or worse yet, conducting their own business using the company's time and computer? Is the remote call center employee working at home going to spend their working hours doing laundry?

© Amir Kalijikovic/Shutterstock, Inc.

The courts have confirmed that companies have the right to ensure that their employees are actively engaged in the company's business. That means the company may, without the employee's permission, listen to phone calls, install surveillance cameras, and monitor computer use. Although they may do this without the employee's permission, they do have to inform the worker that monitoring is done. They are also required to stop listening to a phone call as soon as they realize it is a personal call, even if personal calls are not allowed at work. Surveillance cameras are never allowed in restrooms or dressing rooms.

© sevenke/Shutterstock, Inc.

New laws affect technological approaches to the public. Although they are not solely created for e-business, the use of technology has brought new ways for businesses and individuals to take advantage of people.

The **Children's Online Privacy Protection act (COPPA)**; this act requires anyone collecting personal information from a child under the age of 13 to comply with strict Federal Trade Commission (FTC) guidelines. The act requires the companies to notify parents that they do collect information and have a verifiable consent from the parents for doing so.

CAN-SPAM; it is a law to protect people from harassing or deceptive emails that can flood a person's inbox. The law requires a company to indicate who the email is from and have a subject line that accurately lets the recipient know what the email concerns. The law also requires the sender to provide an obvious link to opt out of receiving any future emails and then drop the recipient's address within 10 days.

COPPA (Children's Online Privacy Protection Act) a law to protect children under 13 from online predators.

"CAN-SPAM" rule national rule providing establishment of a list of consumer provided email addresses that cannot receive unsolicited emails, thus designed to prevent marketers from sending emails in bulk to random people in the hopes of obtaining business or other responses.

OPEN FOR BUSINESS IN THE REAL WORLD

It is difficult to predict what Information Technology will look like in the future and what it will do. Two emerging technologies, at the time this chapter was written, are smart-chip cards and smartphone payment systems. The Smart Chip Card, also known as an EMV card, includes information on the person who is supposed to be using it. This helps reduce fraud because the information is visible to the person accepting the card, but not to the person using it. EMV cards are in use already in Europe, but not yet widely available in the United States (Smart-Chip, 2014). In spite of the commonly held beliefs, the incidents of financial fraud are declining over time as technologies to prevent them improve. Just 6 cents of every $100 spent electronically is fraudulent, which is about half of what it was in the mid-1990s (Smart-chip, 2014).

A second emerging technology is Smartphone payment systems. Using a credit card or debit card in a store sets off a

© Kamira/Shutterstock, Inc.

complicated communication system that verifies that the money is present in the account for the debit card and account is open and there is room on the card in the case of credit cards. Money is actually moved in end-of-day transactions by the handling agencies and credit card companies, each of which collects some of the fee that is charged for the process. By removing the physical card from the process and substituting a cell phone, both the convenience and security can improve. However, to get to that point, the many companies getting into the business of creating applications for phones will need to agree on and standardize terms and software language to allow common use. The producers of the new apps also want a cut of the fees, or possibly access to information on users, which they can then sell as marketing information (The future, 2014). The way we pay, and even money itself, is changing rapidly and the information technology to keep up with the changes will present challenges for the foreseeable future. Businesses will need to decide if they want to become early adopters of changing technology or wait until the bugs are worked out. They will also need to decide how much money they can devote to the changes and at what pace they can make those changes in their operational processes.

© Mmaxer/Shutterstock, Inc.

Chapter Summary

Information technology is a rapidly changing and vitally important aspect of almost any modern business. Gathering data and turning that data into useful information and then putting that into the right hands and the right format for decision-making—this is the essence of information technology.

Cell phones became available in the late 1970s. Since then, the devices have retained the name, but have expanded enormously in their capability to the point that phone calls are sometimes only a minor feature, still part of the features.

Review Questions

1. How are data and information different?
2. What is an information system?
3. What are the four components of a computer-based information system?
4. What is the job of database managers or network specialists in a firm?
5. What are the different types of hardware that make up Information Technology?
6. What are the different types of software that Information Technology uses?
7. How is an Operational Support System different from a Management Support System?
8. What are some examples of Operations Support Systems
9. How have computer networks eased the information flow in large organizations?
10. How does a Smart Chip Card protect against fraudulent use of a credit card?
11. Is it legal for an employer to listen to the worker's phone calls or monitor their computer use? What limitations are there?

Discussion Questions

12. How have rapid changes in technology changed Information Technology
13. How can companies protect the information they collect from competitors and from those that mean to do harm?
14. How will changing methods of payment change the way businesses conduct operations in the future?
15. What future computing advances will drive changes in information technology?
16. How is conducting business online different from conducting business in a traditional setting? How are they the same?

Key Terms

- CAN-SPAM
- Chief Information Officer
- Cloud computing
- Computer hardware
- Computer Networks
- Computer Software
- Children's Online Privacy Protection act (COPPA)
- Data
- database managers or network specialists
- e-crime
- Executive Support System
- FERPA

- firewall HIPPA
- information
- information system
- Intranet or network
- Local Area Network or LAN
- Management Information System or Decision Support System
- Management Support Systems
- Operational Support Systems
- Point-of-Sale Terminal or POS
- Process Control System
- Virtual Private Network (VNP)
- Wide Area Network, or WAN

Works Cited

Fairchild, C. (2013). *Target security breach likely to be 'highly sophisticated organized crime'*. Retrieved from CNNMoney, http://tech.fortune.cnn.com/2013/12/19/target-security-breach-likely-to-be-highly-sophisticated-organized-crime

Hill, C. (2014). *McDonald's may soon be more like Chipotle*. Retrieved from Marketwatch, http://finance.yahoo.com/news/mcdonald-may-soon-more-chipotle-132358604.html

Sally Beauty Inc. (2014). Sally Beauty Hit by Credit Card Breach. Retrieved from http://krebsonsecurity.com/2014/03/sally-beauty-hit-by-credit-card-breach/

Smart-Chip. (2014). *Smart-chip cards safer but hardly foolproof*. Omaha World Herald, April 29, 2914, from the Atlanta Journal-Constitution.

Tam, D. (2012). *Hackers steal customer info from insurance provider Nationwide*. Retrieved from http://news.cnet.com/8301-1009_3-57557408-83/hackers-steal-customers-info-from-insurance-provider-nationwide/#!

The future of money. (2014). Omaha World Herald, April 29, 2014, from the Atlanta Journal-Constitution.

5

BUSINESS CONTROL

CHAPTER

15

Accounting

LEARNING OBJECTIVES

1. Explain the importance of accounting.
2. Identify the users of accounting information.
3. Explain the rules that govern accounting.
4. Describe the accounting equation and functions of the accounting cycle.
5. Prepare an income statement, a statement of owner's equity, a balance sheet, and a statement of cash flows.

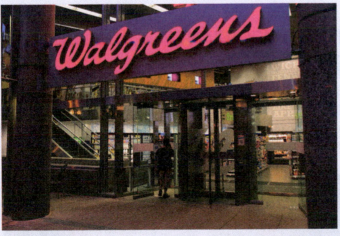

© Tupungato/Shutterstock, Inc.

OPENING STORY

As the nation's largest drugstore chain operating more than 8,300 drugstores in all 50 states, the District of Columbia, Puerto Rico, and the U.S. Virgin Islands, Walgreens Company grew larger on December 31, 2014 when it reorganized Walgreens into a holding company and merged with Alliance Boots, a multinational pharmacy-led health and beauty group. Alliance Boots, headquartered in Bern, Switzerland, and a presence

© Tupungato/Shutterstock, Inc.

© Martin Good/Shutterstock, Inc.

in over 27 countries, had two core business activities—pharmacy-led health and beauty retailing and pharmaceutical wholesaling and distribution. This strategic partnership, which was launched in 2012, merged into the world's first global pharmacy-led, health, and wellbeing enterprise. Walgreens will now be known as Walgreens Boots Alliance.

In fiscal year 2014, Walgreens reported sales of over $76 billion, as reported in its annual report. Walgreens vision is "to be America's most loved pharmacy-led health, wellbeing, and beauty enterprise. Each day, in communities across America, more than 8 million customers interact with Walgreens using the most convenient, multichannel access to consumer goods and services and trusted, cost-effective pharmacy, health and wellness services and advice" (Walgreens, 2014).

Consequently, Walgreens is considered successful from several perspectives—customers, investors, and creditors. What makes them successful? How is this determined?

EXPLAIN THE IMPORTANCE OF ACCOUNTING

Customers evaluate Walgreens' success through the vast selection of the products they sell and the scope of their pharmacy services. Investors, creditors, and management measure Walgreens' success in financial terms by evaluating its financial statements.

© Artkwin/Shutterstock, Inc.

Key Financial Highlights (in millions)

	2014	2013	2012
Net sales	$76,392	$72,217	$71,633
Net earnings	2,031	2,450	2,127
Total assets	37,182	35,481	33,462
Total liabilities	16,621	16,027	15,226

Information in the above-mentioned Key Financial Highlights is common analytical measures of the financial performance of Walgreens and most companies.

Walgreens accountants are qualified professionals whose responsibility is to accurately reflect the business activities so users of the financial statements are confident that information fairly presents the financial performance of the company. Accounting transforms business transactions through the accounting process and generates the data into financial statements.

Hence, the study of accounting is important regardless of one's educational journey. Accounting knowledge is essential for anyone aspiring to understand, interpret, and analyze financial data.

> **Accounting** information system that measures the business activities in financial terms, analyzes, classifies, summarizes, processes the information into reports (i.e., financial statements), and communicates it to decision makers.

> Walgreen's first quarter sales in 2015 increased 6.7% compared with fourth quarter 2014?

Did you know?

© totallyPic.com/Shutterstock, Inc.

ACCOUNTING OVERVIEW

Introduction

Accounting professionals focus on the preparation of the financial reports that users of accounting information evaluate to make intelligent decisions. Knowledge of accounting is important, whether or not you plan a career in accounting because of its usefulness in evaluating financial information for decision-making purposes.

Accounting is the language of business, and it is fun! It is the information system that measures the business activities in financial terms, analyzes, classifies, summarizes, processes the information into reports (i.e., financial statements), and communicates it to decision makers. The role of accounting is to supply the information that links business activities and decision makers to help them make sound decisions.

We find accounting prevalent in the opening vignette. Walgreens interpreted the financial statements of Alliance Boots as a viable entity to enter into a strategic partnership, and then, made the business decision to eventually merge with the company. Walgreens managers, employees, investors, and creditors (also referred to as **stakeholders**) all have a direct or indirect interest in the financial health of Walgreens and depend on the financial statements for decision making purposes.

> **Stakeholders** Walgreens managers, employees, investors, and creditors (also referred to as stakeholders) all have a direct or indirect interest in the financial health of Walgreens and depend on the financial statements for decision-making purposes.

Income Cash Expense
Budget Revenue Credit
Accounting
Debit Assets Payable
Ledger Cost
Balance Sheet Report

© Dusit/Shutterstock, Inc.

Profitability   ability to earn a satisfactory income.

What information can be captured from Walgreens financial statements? How can management use this information? What process would investors and creditors use to compare Walgreens with other companies in the industry?

© Dirk Ercken/Shutterstock, Inc.

The answers to all of these questions can be found in the financial statements. Walgreens management, the investors, and creditors must have an understanding of accounting to effectively use the financial statements to evaluate the financial performance of Walgreens or any business.

We know many big companies like Walgreens are successful. What about the small business owner—can she or he run a successful business? The answer is a resounding Yes! Although **profitability**, measuring a company's ability to yield a financial profit is not guaranteed, nonetheless, knowledge of accounting will help managers, employees, investors, creditors, and students make wise business decisions. The key is understanding accounting.

COMPLIANCE LAW

Today, due to the scandals of Enron, WorldCom, and other corporations related to questionable accounting practices and failure of the external auditors to adhere to appropriate auditing standards, new federal regulations were passed by Congress that reformed the accounting industry and the way businesses report their financial information to the public.

The **Sarbanes-Oxley Act of 2002** (often shortened to SOX or Sarbox), also known as the "Public Company Accounting Reform and Investor Protection Act," put greater emphasis on corporate accountability. Specifically, SOX is designed to restore public confidence in corporate financial reporting and the integrity and trust that was damaged in the corporate scandals. Public companies must have financial information that users can trust to be accurate and not misleading.

To help ensure the financial information is accurate, the Sarbanes-Oxley Act is legislation passed by the U.S. Congress to protect shareholders and the general public from accounting errors and fraudulent practices in the enterprise, as well as improve the accuracy of corporate disclosures as follows (http://www.soxlaw.com/index.htm):

Sarbanes-Oxley act   is legislation passed by the U.S. Congress to protect shareholders and the general public from accounting errors and fraudulent practices in the enterprise, as well as improve the accuracy of corporate disclosures.

Securities and Exchange Commission (SEC)   the governmental agency that has the legal power to enforce accounting standards for public companies whose securities are traded in the United States financial markets.

- Public Company Accounting Oversight Board—The **SEC (Securities and Exchange Commission)** is required to police the accounting industry by providing independent oversight of public accounting firms providing audit services.
- Auditor Independence—establishes standards for external auditor independence and limits conflicts of interest. Accounting firms are prohibited from providing both consulting and auditing services to the same clients.
- Corporate Responsibility—The chief executive and financial officers are required to certify and approve the integrity of their company's financial reports quarterly and are subject to criminal penalties for violations of the reporting requirements. The Chief Executive Officer should sign the corporate tax return.
- Enhanced Financial Disclosures—enhanced reporting requirements for financial transactions, including off-balance-sheet transactions and stock transactions. Additionally, the Act mandates effective internal control procedures, accurate disclosures, and timely reporting of material changes in the company's financial condition.

- Corporate and Criminal Fraud Accountability—Auditors and accountants can be imprisoned for up to 20 years for manipulation, destruction or alteration of financial records, interference with investigations, and willful violations of the securities laws. Additionally, the Act provides added protection for whistle-blowers who report violations of the Sarbanes-Oxley Act.
- Studies and Reports—Public corporations are required to change its auditing firm every 5 years. Auditors must maintain financial records and their working papers for 5 years.

July 30, 2002 [H.R. 3763]

Sarbanes-Oxley Act of 2002. Corporate responsibility. 15 USC 7201 note.

© Ellen McKnight/Shutterstock, Inc.

While compliance of the requirements of the Sarbanes-Oxley Act is expensive and time-consuming for accounting firms and companies, the legislation has restored public confidence and trust in the financial reporting of public corporations. It is impossible to effectively manage a business without accurate financial information. Consequently, knowledge of accounting is vital for the firm's accountants supplying the information and to decision makers who rely on the financial information.

ACCOUNTING PROFESSIONALS

Accountants work in the public or private sector. **Private accountants** work for a specific company. They generally perform their responsibilities in one of many accounting services—general accounting, budgeting, taxes, cost accounting, forensic accounting, or internal auditing.

Public accountants work independently of a particular company and hire their services to perform accounting duties. They may be self-employed or work for an accounting firm. Accountants can be **Certified Public Accountants (CPA)**, a licensed accountant who serves the general public and has passed a national accounting exam prepared by the **American Institute for Certified Public Accountants (AICPA)** and meet the state requirements for education and experience. The AICPA is the professional organization for CPA's and contributes to the development of accounting practices.

Financial and Management Accounting

Accounting is separated into two major areas—financial accounting and managerial accounting. Both provide relevant information about the company's performance, which is communicated to decision makers but are distinguished by the types of reports generated.

Managerial accounting focuses on the preparation of documents, such as short- and long-term budgets, cost reports, incremental analysis for capital purchase decisions for use by people inside the company—managers and

Private accountants accounts who work for a specific company. They generally perform their responsibilities in one of many accounting services – general accounting, budgeting, taxes, cost accounting, forensic accounting or internal auditing.

Public accountants work independently of a particular company and hire their services to perform accounting duties. They may be self-employed or work for an accounting firm.

Certified Public Accountant (CPA) licensed accountant who serves the general public and has passed a national accounting exam.

American Institute for Certified Public Accountants (AICPA) professional organization for CPA's and contributes to the development of accounting practices.

Managerial accounting focuses on the preparation of documents, such as short- and long-term budgets, cost reports, and incremental analysis for capital purchase decisions for use by people inside the company.

© Andrey_Popov/Shutterstock, Inc.

Internal users people inside the company—managers and employees—who use make informed decisions to achieve the company's goals and are charged with making the company profitable.

employees—to assist them in making informed decisions to achieve the company's goals and effectively perform their jobs. **Internal users (decision makers)** use the financial statements in setting short-term goals and strategic goals and are charged with making the company profitable. Hence, they need to evaluate such decisions as establishing the price of the product, keeping costs down, and whether to purchase long-term assets. For example, senior management may set a goal "to increase revenue 10% over the previous year."

© Andresr/Shutterstock, Inc.

The internal documents generated are flexible, can include future-oriented information, and are of interest only to the managers and employees. Because management accounting reports are for internal use only, they don't need to adhere to **generally accepted accounting principles (GAAP)** and are driven by the needs of the managers and employees.

Financial accounting generates financial statements that summarize the financial performance of the firm. **External users** (decision makers)—investors, creditors, governments, and customers—rely on these reports—the income statement, balance sheet, statement of stockholder's equity (owner's equity), and the statement of cash flow in evaluating the profit-

Generally Accepted Accounting Principles (GAAP) the rules, guidelines, and standards used by accountants in the preparation of any financial statements.

Financial accounting generates financial statements in accordance with generally accepted accounting principles that summarize the financial performance of the business.

External users investors, creditors, federal government, and customers—rely on the financial statements in evaluating the profitability and liquidity of the business.

ability and liquidity of the business. External users want to know *if the business would be a good investment* or *if a loan should be made.* Consequently, they use the financial statements to compute profitability and solvency ratios to determine if the firm is a good risk. Investors give money to the firm in exchange for stock with the expectation of increasing the stock value and/or receiving dividends.

Creditors evaluate the financial statement to determine if the company is "capable" of repaying its debt plus interest if they decide to loan the firm money or extend credit for inventory. Hence, it is important that the financial statements are reliable since many people depend on its accuracy to make sound business decisions. The financial statements must follow GAAP. Why is this important? Why go through the trouble? It is essential because the public—external users—depend on companies to adhere to proper accounting procedures and regulations in issuing financial statements in order for them

© mindscanner/Shutterstock, Inc.

to make informed decisions. Moreover, the expectation is that the financial information will be presented on a consistent basis with previous years. For example, Berkshire Hathaway, Inc., headquartered in Omaha, NE, reported one-time charges against earnings of $1.3 billion in 2013. As a result, earnings in 2014 will be significantly higher. On the surface one may be concern, but further review of the 2013 Annual Report and the Letter to Stockholders, reveal that Berkshire acquired a major interest in H.J. Heinz company in 2013. This charge against earnings was a result of the purchase and restructuring of H.J. Heinz's. If Berkshire Hathaway failed to adhere to GAAP in reporting this charge, the 2014 financial statements would be misleading and inconsistent with the previous year.

IDENTIFY THE USERS OF ACCOUNTING INFORMATION

The primary users of accounting information are categorized as external or internal decision makers. Investors, creditors, government agencies, and the Internal Revenue Services are external decision makers who would be interested in using the accounting information to answer questions such as:

© Duncan Andison/Shutterstock, Inc.

- Is the business profitable?
- Should I invest in this business?
- If we decide to loan this business money, can it repay us?

Internal decision makers include the owner(s), managers, and employees. They evaluate the financial information to make decisions regarding:

- Is this a sustainable business in which I can build a career?
- Should we purchase an existing building or construct a new building due to the significant growth of the company?
- If we increase the sales price of the product 10% what will be the breakeven point in sales volume?

Did you know?
© totallyPic.com/Shutterstock, Inc.

> Walgreen's cash flow from operations for fiscal year 2014 was $4.2 billion? The company paid $1.0 billion in cash dividends to its shareholders?

Non-financial information is also important as it explains the goals and future direction of the business. For example, the 2014 Walgreens Annual Report mentioned that the company launched a national campaign in collaboration with Blue Cross Blue Shield to educate consumers about the new health care reform law and provide them with information about insurance options as a result of the Affordable Care Act.

The **annual report** is a summary of a company's activities and financial performance for the fiscal year. The annual reports include the audited financial statements, which report the results of the company's operations for the

Annual report summary of a company's activities and financial performance for the fiscal year.

© maxuser/Shutterstock, Inc.

year—the income statement, the stockholder's equity statement (the statement of owner's equity for sole proprietors), the balance sheet, and the statement of cash flows—and the Notes to the Financial Statements. Not only will the annual report share the highlights of the year but also management includes a letter to the shareholders addressing important financial and non-financial information. The annual report is valuable because of the comprehensive material it contains for people who rely on the information to make informed decisions such as the potential for growth, investing opportunities, or whether to extend credit.

Companies like Walgreens, and smaller businesses, use accounting to provide information needed to the decision makers. Individuals use accounting knowledge to build wealth and plan their future financial needs. For example, basic accounting knowledge can help you determine how much money you need to save or invest to have a comfortable nest egg in retirement? Regardless of your educational major or life status, everyone should have a basic understanding of accounting.

Public companies like Walgreens operate under the auspices of the SEC and are required to have their financial statements audited by an external accounting firm, which employs CPA's.

© totallyPic.com/Shutterstock, Inc.

EXPLAIN THE RULES THAT GOVERN ACCOUNTING

The accounting industry has specific guidelines and principles that govern the accepted practices. These regulations are established by governing organizations that have developed the specific concepts and principles to be followed by accountants.

GOVERNING ORGANIZATIONS

Financial Accounting Standards Board (FASB) the governing organization that develops and issues rules for *generally accepted accounting principles* and standards in the United States.

The **Financial Accounting Standards Board (FASB)** is the governing organization that develops and issues rules for GAAP and standards in the United States. An independent, privately funded organization, the FASB is charged with issuing *Statements of Financial Accounting Standards.*

The SEC is the governmental agency that has the legal power to enforce accounting standards for public companies whose securities are traded in the U. S. financial markets. The FASB works under the SEC and has been given the authority to develop the accounting standards for the accounting industry. Many organizations contribute to formulating GAAP; however, the primary responsibility rests with the SEC.

Audit official independent examination and verification of accounts, records, and financial statements.

An **audit is** an official independent examination and verification of accounts, records, and financial statements. The purpose of an audit is to provide confidence to stakeholders that the financial statements are not materially misstated and that the financial statements are prepared in accordance with GAAP, a set of principles and concepts accepted in the accounting industry for reporting financial information.

Though an audit can't guarantee that the company's financial records are 100% accurate, the auditor can make a determination, after conducting the audit using established auditing procedures, that the financial statements, on the whole, are presented fairly. The opinion in the audit report will contain the following commonly used statement:

In our opinion, the financial statements of XYZ, Inc. present fairly, in all material respects for the year ended December 31, 2014. . . in conformity with GAAP.

The independence of the auditing firm gives credence to the validity of the financial statements. Hence, the users of the company's financial information are more likely to trust and use it for their decision-making purposes.

© Dusit/Shutterstock, Inc.

ACCOUNTING MEASUREMENTS, CONCEPTS, AND PRINCIPLES

There are four measurement issues that accountants must answer in accounting:

1. What is measured?
2. When should the business transaction be recorded?
3. What value should be place on the business transaction?
4. How to classify the items of a business transaction?

These questions must be addressed and form the foundation for establishing accepted guidelines in the accounting industry. Today's accountants formulate these measurement issues into generally accepted accounting practices. Accounting uses money to measure the impact of business transactions.

Assume on July 16, 2014, a computer manufacturing plant produced 100 computers at a cost of $1,000 each. ***What is being measured is the cost of 100 computers,*** not the size or weight of the computers. The general journal will record this transaction on July 16, 2014 (**when to record**) for $100,000 (**value placed on the transaction**) in the Computers account (**how to classify**).

Entity concept requires that the business activities must be separate from the owner's personal transactions and all other entities.

Cost principle (historical cost) stipulates that assets and services are recorded at their actual cost—what you paid for it.

CONCEPTS, PRINCIPLES, AND ASSUMPTIONS

Each business, as a separate and distinct entity, is the most basic assumption in accounting. The entity concept requires that the business activities must be separate from the owner's personal transactions and from all other entities.

The cost principle (historical cost) stipulates that assets and services are recorded at their actual cost—what you paid for them. The receipt is the documented proof of the cost. It doesn't matter that the market value of the acquired asset or service may be higher. For example, assume that Ocean Julia Williams, of Williams Accounting Service, purchased a building for $100,000 with an appraised market value of $200,000; the building will be recorded at the $100,000 "bargain" price. The local government property taxes may be assessed on the

© iQoncept/Shutterstock, Inc.

Lower of cost or market if the market value of the inventory is less than cost, an adjustment must be recorded to bring the inventory down to market value.

Conservatism principle requires when uncertainties exist in regards to accounting procedures, the procedure which will least likely overstate assets or income must be applied.

Going concern assumption accountants assume that the business (entity) will remain in operation for the foreseeable future.

Reliability concept assumes that the user of financial information can trust that the reports are useful, accurate, and credible.

Consistency principle mandates that businesses must use the same accounting procedures and methods from year to year.

Stable monetary unit assumption requires that the amounts reported in the financial statements remain stable and not adjusted for inflation.

International Financial Reporting Standards (IFRS) a set of global accounting standards that are comprehensive, high quality, understandable, enforceable, and globally accepted.

market value, but that is separate from recording the cost at the purchase price. If the market value continues to rise, the cost principle necessitates that the asset cost remains on the books at $100,000 for the useful life of the asset. If the asset is eventually sold, the gain or loss will be based on the actual cost.

The exception to the cost principle is that inventory is reported at the **lower of cost or market (LCM).** That is, if the market value of the inventory is less than cost, an adjustment must be recorded to bring the inventory down to market value. This adjustment is required in accordance with the **conservatism principle**, which requires when the accountant has doubts or faces uncertainties in regards to accounting procedures, he or she must choose the procedure that will least likely overstate assets or income. In other words, accountants must abide by the adage, "anticipate no gains but account for all probable losses."

Under the **going concern assumption**, accountants assume that the business (entity) will remain in operation for the foreseeable future. In other words, the intention is that when the business commences operations, it doesn't intend to close.

Financial data that is verifiable and can be confirmed/validated by an independent observer is said to be reliable. The **reliability concept** assumes that the user of financial information can trust that the reports are useful, accurate, and credible.

The **consistency principle** mandates that businesses must use the same accounting procedures and methods from year to year. If a method is changed, the business is required to report this information in the Notes to the Financial Statements. The purpose is to prevent misleading financial statements. For example, assume a company's operating income increased. One's initial thought is the company either had increased revenues or had lower expenses. After further review of the financial statements, neither occurred but the company changed the costing of inventory methods, resulting in a lower cost of goods sold for the year. Without disclosing this change in accounting method, stakeholders may incorrectly assume the company performed better in terms of increased sales or lower expenses. Consequently, GAAP requires consistency reporting of financial statements to prevent this type of misleading perception.

U.S. GAAP dictates businesses to use dollars as the method of recording transactions because it is the medium of exchange in the United States. Furthermore, the **stable monetary unit assumption** requires that the amounts reported in the financial statements remain stable and not adjusted for inflation.

The **International Financial Reporting Standards (IFRS)** are a set of global accounting standards published by the International Accounting Standards Board, an independent, non-for-profit organization. IFRS's purpose is to develop standards that are comprehensive, high quality, understandable, enforceable, and globally accepted.

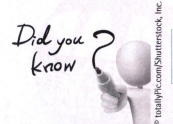

© totallyPic.com/Shutterstock, Inc.

Did you know?

The ultimate goal for U.S. companies is to endorse IFRS by 2015 or 2016.

Accounting equation shows the relationship among assets, liabilities, and owner's equity. It is written as: Assets = Liabilities + Owner's Equity.

DESCRIBE THE ACCOUNTING EQUATION AND THE FUNCTIONS OF ACCOUNTING CYCLE

The **accounting equation** is the financial position of the company showing the relationship between economic resources and equities. Economic resources are the assets of the business (what the business owns). The equities of the business are the liabilities and the owner's equity.

The **financial position** (the accounting equation) refers to the resources that belong to the company (assets), and the creditors' equities (liabilities) and owner's equities against those resources at a specific point in time. The accounting equation is the basic tool of accounting and forms the basis for the accounting process. The relationship between assets, liabilities, and equity is written as a simple equation:

Assets = Liabilities + Owner's equity

REMEMBER, the accounting equation must always balance   The left side, the assets, must **ALWAYS** equal the sum of the right side, the liabilities, and owner's equity. Double-entry bookkeeping is used to record the firms' business transactions that impact the accounting equation. Every transaction affects the financial position of the company. All business transactions impact at least two accounts of the firm and keep the accounting equation in balance.

Assets are economic resources, which the company owns—cash, inventory, accounts receivable, or equipment. Think of assets of anything of value to the company. Although human resources (people) are valuable to the company (the company probably can't effectively function without its employees), they are not considered assets because the company does not own people. Assets can be in physical form—equipment, land, building, and nonphysical form (intangible)—patents, copyrights, trademarks, or natural resources—oil, minerals.

© Krasimira Nevenova/Shutterstock, Inc.

Liabilities are the obligations (debts) that the business owes to others (creditors)—accounts payable, notes payable, or unearned revenue. Liabilities are also referred to as creditor's equities because they are claims against the assets. These obligations are incurred as the result of receiving assets in exchange for the promise to repay the debt in the future with the company's cash, transfer of assets or exchange to provide services. Liabilities have priority of repayment, by law, over the owner's equity claims. That is, if the company failed to pay its bills and filed for bankruptcy (or is forced into bankruptcy), the company's assets would be sold and used to pay debtors claims before any residual money, if any, went to the owner. Hence, if there were not enough assets to fully pay the liabilities, the owner would have no residual equity.

Owner's equity is the excess of assets over liabilities. It represents the owner's claims, or residual interest, to the remaining assets after paying the debts (liabilities). Equity is also referred to as the company's net worth/net assets because it is the balance after the creditors' claims.

To compute the owner's equity, the accounting equation can be rewritten as follows:

Owner's Equity = Assets − Liabilities

There are four types of transactions that affect owner's equity: revenues, owner's investments, expenses, and owner's withdrawals.

Revenue, which increases owner's equity, is income received from the sale of goods or delivering services to customers during the normal course of the company's business activities.

Financial position   refers to the resources that belong to the company (assets), and the creditors' equities (liabilities) and owner's equities against those resources at a specific point in time.

Assets   economic resources which the company own such as cash, inventory, accounts receivable, and equipment.

Liabilities   the obligations (debts) that the business owes to others (creditors) such as accounts payable, notes payable, unearned revenue. Owner's equity is the excess of assets over liabilities. It represents the owner's claims, or residual interest, to the remaining assets after paying the debts (liabilities).

Owner's equity   is the excess of assets over liabilities. It represents the owner's claims, or residual interest, to the remaining assets after paying the debts (liabilities).

Revenue   is income received from the sale of goods or delivering services to customers during the normal course of the company's business activities.

Expense decreases owner's equity. It is money paid or the cost incurred in the sale or delivery of goods and services during the normal operation of business activities. Another way of putting it, expenses is the cost of doing business.

Owner's Capital (owner's investment) is the owner's contribution to the business in the form of cash or other assets, such as equipment or land. Capital increases owner's equity.

Owner's Withdrawals are payments the owner takes from the business for personal use. They are not a business expense but a reduction, usually taken as cash but the withdrawal can be non-cash assets, in the owner's capital. Withdrawals, also referred to as drawings, decrease owner's equity.

Assume the following information: Ocean Julia Williams, CPA, worked for an accounting firm for the past 10 years. Last year, her salary was $40,000. Williams' strong desire to be her own boss finally materialized. Although she knew it would be a struggle the first year, Williams resigned from her job and opened her own business—Williams Accounting Service on January 1, 2014, with an original investment of $50,000.

After her initial investment, the Cash (an asset) account was increased $50,000 and the Capital (owner's equity) account was increased $50,000. Thus, the left side, $50,000 equals the right side, $50,000.

Assets	=	Liabilities	+	Owner's equity
Cash	=			Capital
Jan. 1 $50,000	=			$50,000

Williams later purchased, on February 1, 2015, $500 in supplies on credit. The Supplies account (asset) is increased $500 and Accounts Payable (liabilities) is increased $500. Hence, the accounting equation is in balance under the double-entry bookkeeping system as follows:

Assets	=	Liabilities	+	Owner's equity
Cash + Supplies	=	Accounts Payable	+	Owner's equity
Beg. Bal. $50,000	=			$50,000
Feb. 1		+$500	=	+ $500

After this transaction, the accounting equation will look like this:

Assets	=	Liabilities	+	Owner's equity
$50,500	=	$500	+	$50,000
$50,500	=	$50,500		

Williams Accounting Service has $50,500 in total assets of cash and supplies and liabilities and owner's equity total $50,500. It is important to remember that each business transaction impacts the accounting equation and MUST balance after recording the transaction in the General Journal.

THE ACCOUNTING CYCLE

The process from the initial recognition of a business transaction (e.g., purchasing supplies on account) through preparing the financial statements is referred to as the **accounting cycle**. A complete set of records will make it possible for the users of the financial information to tell where the money is coming from and where it is going.

A **transaction** is any business activity that impacts the financial position (accounting equation) of the company and can be measured reliably (a monetary amount can be assigned to the transaction). For example, purchasing land, buying supplies, performing a service that generates revenue or paying the monthly insurance on the building are transactions that are recorded in the financial records.

Transaction any business activity that impacts the financial position (accounting equation) of the company and can be measured reliability.

Other types of activities, such as hiring an employee or placing an order that has not been delivered, are considered business events and not recordable at that time because there is no exchange of value. However, the day the employee is paid or the order is received, the accountant will journalize the transaction. Additionally, personal transactions of the owner are not recorded on the company's books. The entity concept requires the separation of personal and business transactions.

Journalizing is the process of recording every business transaction in a journal. Transactions are recorded in specialized journals for specific transactions, such as the cash receipts journal, or in the general journal, for typical transactions. The **general journal** is the book of original entry to record business transactions in chronological order.

Journalizing process of recording every business transaction in a journal.

General journal book of original entry to record business transactions in chronological order.

The **accounting cycle is a five-step process** to transform financial data into the company's financial statements: (i) analyze source documents, (ii) record transactions in the journal, (iii) post transactions, (iv) prepare the trial balance, and (v) prepare the financial statements. The following functions are performed in the accounting cycle:

Analyze Source Documents: The documented proof is found in the *source documents*, such as receipts, sales invoices, or other documents that show the dollar amount in the transaction. The accountant analyzes business transactions from the source document to determine the classification of the accounts affected, whether the account increased or decreased and the proper accounting period. The analysis answers the questions: What happened? How was the financial position affected?

Record Transactions in the Journal: Each transaction is journalized in a journal and classified appropriately—office supplies account for all supplies that are non-inventoriable. You wouldn't record the monthly rent expense in the insurance expense account. An accounting system may have specialized journals for all the major types of transactions in addition to the general journal. The advantage of the specialized journals is to categorize the frequent transactions by types. For example, a business that makes frequent purchases and earns daily sales may have a sales journal, a purchase journal, and a cash disbursement journal, listing all the checks written. It's easier to find detailed information about specific sales in the sales journal, thus, it's common for companies to have these specialized journals.

Post Transactions: After the transactions are recorded in the general journal and special journals, the amounts of each account are posted to the **general ledger**. The general ledger is a collection of all the individual accounts used by a business to form a book. Each ledger will show the balance of that account. The accountant also journalizes and post adjusting and closing entries. Necessary adjusting entries are made to the accounts at the end of the fiscal year to ensure all revenues and expenses are properly accounted for in the current accounting period. Closing entries are journal entries made after all adjusting entries are posted.

General ledger collection of all the individual accounts used by a business to form a book.

Trial balance listing of the general ledger balance of all the company's accounts.

Prepare the Trial Balance: A **trial balance** is a listing of the general ledger balance of all the company's accounts. The primary purpose of a trial balance is to ensure debits = credits; it doesn't ensure that the individual balances are correct. Account balances in error are usually the result of recording to the wrong account or forgetting to record a transaction. Despite these errors, the trial balance will still be in balance.

Usually, the trial balance is prepared several times during the accounting cycle before preparing the financial statements—before and after the recording the adjusting entries and after the closing entries. In addition to ensuring the debits = the credits, the accountant also takes a cursory look at the trial balance for any unusual account balance. For example, the accountant recalls purchasing $5,000 in supplies in the last month of the fiscal year but the Supplies account balance is only $1,000. The trial balance debits and credits equal, but a review of the general journal during that month indicated that the debit was recorded in error to Equipment account.

Prepare the Financial Statements: After making this correction and the accountant is satisfied the accounts are accurate, the financial statements are now ready to prepare. The four major financial statements are the income statement, statement of owner's equity (stockholder's equity for corporations), balance sheet, and statement of cash flows.

"T"-account visual form of a general ledger account that resembles the capital letter "T."

A **"T" account** is a visual form of a general ledger account. It is appropriately named because it resembles the capital letter "T." There are three parts to the "T" account: (i) the top of the "T" identifies the account name of the asset, the liability, or owner's equity account; (ii) the left side is the debit side; and (iii) the right side, is the credit side. Many accountants use it as a tool for analyzing transactions in the double-entry accounting system.

Title of Account	
Left side	Right side
Debit	Credit

Any entry on the left side will be recorded in the journal as a "debit." All entries on the right side of the "T" account are recorded in the journal as a "credit." Using the previous example of Williams Accounting Service and the financial data from the accounting equation, we can show the transactions in the following "T" accounts.

Assets	**=**	**Liabilities**	**+**	**Owner's equity**
Cash + Supplies	=	Accounts Payable	+	Owner's equity
$50,000 + $500	=	+500		$50,000

Cash				Capital	
1/1/14	50,000			50,000	1/1/14
Balance	50,000			50,000	Balance

Williams later purchased, on February 1, 2014, $500 in supplies on credit.:

	Supplies			Accounts Payable	
2/1	500			500	2/1
Balance	500			500	Balance

PREPARE AN INCOME STATEMENT, A STATEMENT OF OWNER'S EQUITY, A BALANCE SHEET, AND A STATEMENT OF CASH FLOW

The firm's financial statements are the end products in the completion of the accounting cycle process. They are the means of communicating to the decision makers the financial information that occurred during the fiscal year of the company. The financial statements provide the essential information needed for the internal and external users—investors, creditors, management, the government, and other users—to interpret in order to make sound business decisions such as evaluating the firms profitability, the ability to repay their debts when due, (**solvency**), and the firm's future sustainability. They are the formal documents generated after recording the business transactions.

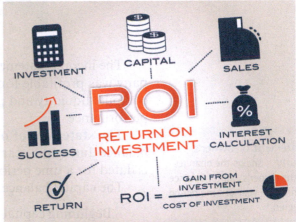

© Tureffelpix/Shutterstock, Inc.

When decision makers analyze the income statement, they use several ratios to analyze the financial performance of a company.

> **What percent did Walgreens 2014 sales increase over 2013 sales using the data from the opening vignette?**
>
> Answer: 5.8%

The four major financial statements listed in the order of preparation are

1. Income Statement
2. Statement of Owner's Equity
3. Balance Sheet
4. Statement of Cash Flows

Was the firm profitable? What were the revenues for the fiscal year? What were the major costs? These are questions that can be answered by evaluating the firm's income statement. The **fiscal year** covers the 12-month accounting period a company uses to report its financial activities.

The **income statement** (also called Profit and Loss Statement) summarizes for the fiscal year the firm's performance in terms of generating revenues and incurring expenses. If the revenues exceed the expenses, the firm reports net income. If the expenses exceed revenues, a net loss occurred. The Income statement reflects this information for a specific time period, that is, "For the Year Ended December 31, 2014."

Income statement summarizes for the fiscal year the firm's performance in terms of generating revenues and incurring expenses.

$$\text{Net Revenues} - \text{Expenses} = \text{Net Income (Net Loss)}$$

© mphotoz/Shutterstock, Inc.

The income statement is the first statement prepared and will reveal if a company was profitable for the year. Furthermore, the income statement is used to compute liquidity and profitability ratios as a means of evaluating the financial performance.

The statement of owner's equity shows the changes in the owner's capital balance during the year or time period covered. The statement of owner's equity is dated for a time period, that is, "For the year ended December 31, 2014."

The capital balance is computed as follows:

> Beginning capital balance
> + Investments
> + Net Income (or minus Net Loss)
> − Withdrawals
> = Ending Capital balance

The balance sheet (also referred to as the statement of financial position) reports the financial position of the business as of a specific date. Imagine when you take a picture, the click freezes the object at that moment in time. The balance sheet is the snap shot of the business on that date. Whereas, the other financial statements cover a time period, the balance sheet is dated for a specific date, that is, December 31, 2014.

The Statement of Cash Flows shows the cash inflows and outflows. The statement of cash flows reflects the liquidity of the business. Transactions that affected cash are categorized by operating activities—the day-to-day operating transactions of the business, investing activities—the purchase and sale of the long-term assets and financing activities—and transactions affecting long-term debt and equity. Review of the cash flow statement will disclose how cash was received and spent during the months of the fiscal year. The Statement of Cash Flows accumulates the monthly cash transactions and the statement is dated for a time period, that is, "For the year ended December 31, 2014."

SAMPLE FINANCIAL STATEMENTS

Each statement relates to each other. The net income from the Income Statement flows to the Statement of Owner's Equity. The ending capital balance in the Statement of Owner's equity is the balance on the equity side of the Balance Sheet.

Statement of owner's equity   shows the changes in the owner's capital balance during the year or time period covered.

Balance sheet   shows the financial position of the business as of a specific date.

Statement of cash flows shows the cash inflows and outflows—all cash only transactions.

Williams Accounting Service
Income Statement
For the Year Ended December 31, 2014

Fees earned (Revenues)		$75,000
Operating expenses:		
Advertising expense	$ 2,500	
Supplies expense	$ 1,500	
Rent expense	$12,000	
Total operating expenses		$16,000
Net income		**$59,000**

Williams Accounting Service
Statement of Owner's Equity
For the Year Ended December 31, 2014

Ocean Julia Williams, Capital, January 1, 2014		$ 0
Investment	$50,000	
Net income for the year	$59,000	
Less withdrawals	$20,000	
Increase in owner's equity		$89,000
Ocean Julia Williams, Capital, December 31, 2014		**$89,000**

Williams Accounting Service
Balance Sheet
December 31, 2014

Assets		Liabilities	
Cash	$77,500	Accounts payable	$ 1,000
Accounts receivable	$ 5,000	Mortgage payable	$100,000
Supplies	$ 1,500		
Computer equipment	$ 6,000	Owner's Equity	
Building	$100,000	Ocean Julia Williams, capital	$ 89,000
Total assets	$190,000	Total liabilities and Owner's equity	$190,000

OPEN FOR BUSINESS IN THE REAL WORLD

Although it is commonly known that Enron was the firm that brought down the former Big Five accounting firm Arthur Andersen, in actuality, they caused their own demise. Greed and the relentless focus on profits were the reasons for its collapse. The SEC regarded Arthur Andersen as a "serial offender," and following Enron's collapse and the public's outcry to hold Andersen accountable, the SEC was determined to make an example out of Andersen (Smith and Quirk, 2004). In June 2002, Arthur Andersen was the first accounting firm to be convicted of obstruction of justice—a felony. How did this happen? The legal reason is Andersen destroyed documents and impeded the SEC's imminent investigation into their auditing relationship with Enron. However, the back-story finds that Andersen violated several accounting and ethical standards.

Arthur Andersen failed to adhere to the reliability concept, which assumes that the user of the financial information can trust that the reports are useful, accurate, and credible. During their audit of Enron, Andersen was aware that Enron was not following GAAP, yet failed to disclose these inaccuracies in their audit report. Enron was so powerful that suggestions to implement required accounting procedures went ignored by Enron's accountants. Consequently, the giant in the utility industry "flexed its muscles" against any advised accounting changes because their intention was to inflate assets and understate liabilities. Furthermore, since the auditing and consulting fees received by Enron were significant, the accounting firm turned its head, so as not to lose this big client.

Another problem was that Andersen failed the "independent external auditor" test. Enron had been a client of Arthur Andersen since 1986. Over the succeeding years, Andersen became closely involved with Enron on matters other than the yearly audit. (For example, Andersen hired the internal auditors from Enron and opened an office in the Enron's Houston headquarters.) How can you be an independent auditor when you attend your client's staff meetings as if you were an employee? There was a perceived and actual conflict of interest. Arthur Andersen's fall from grace was orchestrated by their failure to enforce GAAP and greed.

Chapter Summary

Accounting professionals focus on the preparation of the financial reports to help users of accounting information make intelligent decisions. Knowledge of accounting is important to understand and interpret financial statements. Internal and external users find this information valuable for different reasons, but nonetheless, accounting is the foundation that transforms the financial transactions into the financial reports. The accounting industry has specific guidelines and principles that govern the accepted practices. These regulations are established by governing organizations that have developed the specific concepts and principles to be followed by accountants.

You learned in this chapter the importance of accounting, the different users of the accounting information, the rules that govern accounting, in what way the accounting equation impacts the financial statements, how to perform the basic functions of accounting and how to prepare the four major financial statements. There is much more to accounting but after reading this chapter, you have a basic foundation and understanding of accounting.

© Gustavo Frazao/Shutterstock, Inc.

Review Questions

1. What is accounting important?
2. What is accounting?
3. Describe the two major areas of accounting.
4. What is the legislation, and briefly describe the sections, passed by Congress to improve the accuracy of public companies financial statements?
5. Explain the types of accountants and the certification available for accountants.
6. Distinguish and identify the users of financial information.
7. What is the accounting equation and what is another name for it?
8. Describe each of the parts of the accounting equation.
9. What are the four types of transactions that affect owner's equity?
10. Briefly describe the five step process of the accounting cycle.
11. How do you calculate net income? When would a net loss occur?
12. List and describe each of the four financial statements.
13. What are the concepts, principles, and assumptions of accounting?
14. Describe the "T" account.

Discussion Questions

15. Do you think the passage of the Sarbanes-Oxley Act restored public confidence and trust in the corporate financial reporting and integrity of the accounting industry?
16. As an investor what type of information—financial and non-financial—would you want to know before investing in a business?
17. Identify other transactions you think would occur in Williams Accounting Service during the year?
18. What can a small business owner do to help ensure his or her success for a sustainable, profitable business?

Key Terms

- accounting
- accounting cycle
- accounting equation
- American Institute for Certified Public Accountants (AICPA)
- annual report
- assets
- audit
- Balance Sheet
- Certified Public Accountant
- conservatism principle
- consistency principle
- cost principle
- entity concept
- expense
- external users
- financial accounting
- Financial Accounting Standards Board (FASB)
- financial position
- generally accepted accounting principles (GAAP)
- general journal
- general ledger
- going concern assumption
- income statement
- internal users
- International Financial Reporting Standards (IFRS)
- journalizing

- liabilities
- lower of cost or market
- managerial accounting
- owner's capital
- owner's equity
- owner's withdrawal (drawing)
- private accountants
- profitability
- public accountants
- reliability concept
- revenue
- Sarbanes-Oxley Act
- Securities and Exchange Commission (SEC)
- stable monetary unit assumption
- stakeholders
- statement of cash flows
- statement of owner's equity
- T-account
- transaction
- trial balance

Works Cited

Berkshire Hathaway, Inc. *Letter to Stockholders*. Retrieved January 25, 2015, from http://www.berkshire-hathaway.com/letters/2013ltr.pdf

Sarbanes-Oxley Act of 2002. Retrieved November 29, 2014, from http://www.soxlaw.com/index.htm

Smith, N. C. & Quirk, M. (2004). From grace to disgrace: The rise & fall of Arthur Andersen. *Journal of Business Ethics Education, 1(1)*, 91–130. London Business School. Nelson Journals Publishing.

Walgreens 2014 Annual Report. Retrieved November 29, 2014, from http://investor.walgreensbootsalliance.com/annuals-proxies.cfm?c=wag&arArchive=Archive

16

Financial Management

LEARNING OBJECTIVES

1. Understand the functions of money in business.
2. Explain the importance of the financial banking system.
3. Discuss financial markets and investments.
4. Explore the global impact on the financial system.
5. Explain the role of strategic planning in financial management.

© Thomas Barrat/Shutterstock, Inc.

OPENING STORY

First National Bank, headquartered in Omaha, NE, is a sixth-generation family-owned business founded in 1857 by two brothers—Herman and Augustus Kountze. It is one of the largest family-owned holding companies in the United States and has become the largest privately owned bank holding company in the United States. With locations in Nebraska, Colorado, Illinois, Iowa, Kansas, South Dakota, and Texas, First National Bank has over $17 billion in managed assets and nearly 5,000 employees.

© Oleksiy Mark/Shutterstock, Inc.

For more than 150 years, First National Bank has maintained its commitment to helping build strong communities. They proudly boast that "Though our founders were engaged in the rough-and-tumble business of the pioneers, they created an innovative and forward-looking organization. Many people over many generations did that with their hard work, dedication, and vision. But a local bank that understands and embraces the community's vision can make a big difference, and we are proud of our commitment to these principles" (FNB 2015).

First National Bank was among the first banks to issue credit cards and one of only four banks to issue all four credit card networks: Visa, MasterCard, Discover, and American Express.

The Kountze brothers envisioned that their bank would succeed and have a positive impact on the communities they served.

The bank's success story can be attributed to its effective and efficient management of their financial resources. Their executive management team includes people responsible for various financial management functions including investments, buildings and finance, corporate banking, and wealth management. In this chapter, we focus on the financial functions of organizations, how businesses efficiently manage their financial resources, identifying ways to accomplish the company's goals and strategic planning.

INTRODUCTION

All business activities, employed by First National Bank, Walgreens Boots Alliance, and other large and small companies require financial resources. Whether selling inventory, purchasing supplies, hiring employees, or buying equipment, business must possess the financial capital to engage in these normal business activities to remain open for business. If the business doesn't have the immediate funds available, they may have to strategize ways to raise the money to satisfy these needs perhaps through issuing bonds payable or common stock, taking out a bank loan or increasing the sales price of their merchandise, all of which are financial management functions of an organization. In this chapter, we focus on the financial functions of organizations, how businesses efficiently manage their financial resources, identifying ways to accomplish the company's goals and strategic planning.

© Erlo Brown/Shutterstock, Inc.

Financial management is the process of engaging in activities to obtain money to effectively and efficiently use those funds to achieve the goals and objectives of the business. For many businesses, the **financial manager** develops and manages the financial plan for the business and is responsible for identifying ways to secure needed capital.

UNDERSTANDING THE FUNCTIONS OF MONEY IN BUSINESS

In Chapter 4, we learned how Walgreens interacts with nearly 8 million customers annually to provide cost-effective pharmacy, health and wellness services, and advice. These customers enter their local Walgreens store to request a product or a service and in exchange give the respective Walgreens employees metal coins, paper bills, a plastic credit card, or a smartphone, thus with a touch, swipe, or exchange, the customer and Walgreens have participated in a modernized barter system. In this illustration, **money** has acted as the common medium for exchange.

Financial management the process of engaging in activities to obtain money to effectively and efficiently use it to achieve the goals and objectives of the business.

Financial manager develops and manages the financial plan for the business and is responsible for identifying ways for securing needed capital.

Money anything society agrees to accept in the purchasing of products, services, or resources.

© Twin Design/Shutterstock, Inc.

Functions of Money

Money, as a **medium for exchange**, is anything society agrees to accept in the purchasing of products, services, or resources. The **function of money** in business is to serve as a medium of exchange for products, goods, and services, a common measurement for value and the accumulation of wealth.

Suppose you develop a cold. In deciding whether you can afford to buy cough drops, a cough suppressant medicine, and honey to place inside your tea from your local Walgreens, you check your bank account. Because you work and were recently paid, you have the money to afford such purchases. In this example, several functions of money are visible. First, you have determined the value of your labor by participating in the labor market. Money is utilized as a common

© Svetlana Lukienko/Shutterstock, Inc.

© Studio_G/Shutterstock, Inc.

denominator for the purposes of measuring value. Whether we purchase goods or services or accept money for our labor, we agree that the amount of money exchanged represents a mutually agreed upon fair value for such an exchange. Thus, **money is a measure of value**. Money, as a measure of value, helps us use a common measuring stick, especially in terms of the pricing. If a common measuring stick were not used to help determine value, then you would have difficulty in comparing products.

Another element of the function of money is the **accumulation of wealth.** In the previous illustration assume that you need to decide between various brands of cough drops. The price of the product that will be used to satisfy an exchange helps you compare the value of each cough drop product and thus determine your buying decision. If a common measuring stick were not used to help determine value, then you would have difficulty in comparing products. Furthermore, you have determined that a function of money is being able to store it and later use for exchange. The accumulation of wealth is a by-product of this function of money. It is important to note, however, that when choosing to take advantage of the accumulation of wealth, the value of the money may change due to inflation or deflation, which is covered in the economics chapter.

Explain the Importance of the Financial Banking System

In the previous example, you have agreed on a value of your labor in exchange for money or a paycheck. Once you are paid, you decide to store your money in a banking institution rather than placing your hard earned money under your mattress. What exactly is a banking institution? How does the banking system interact with the money?

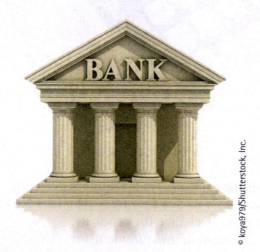

© koya979/Shutterstock, Inc.

THE FINANCIAL SYSTEM

It is money that provides the needed capital for businesses to effectively operate. Additionally, the government and individuals may need to raise money to implement their programs or personal needs. Or, these same parties may have excess cash available and decide to save it (e.g., store it). These decisions of raising or saving money are elements of the financial system. The **financial system** is the process of the flow of money from the savers to the borrowers.

Everyone participates in the financial system—individuals, government, businesses, financial markets, and financial institutions. The **financial institutions**

Financial system   the process of the flow of money from the saves to the borrowers.

are one of the most important components of the financial system as they are the intermediary for transferring funds from the people who save money to those who want to borrow money. Financial institutions include banks, credit unions, life insurance companies, mutual funds, investment houses, and pension funds.

© dabldy/Shutterstock, Inc.

Thrift Institutions and Commercial Banks

Thrift institutions are financial institutions that generate revenue mostly through the savings of its customer. Common thrift institutions are savings and loan associations, mutual savings banks, and credit unions. Historically, thrift institutions differed from commercial banks. Thrift institutions focused more on savings and offering small loans for residential home ownership; many times, they did not offer other financial services, such as checking accounts. Commercial banks, on the other hand, were typically larger, offered various loans products, and primarily held ownership as a stock corporation; this often differed from thrift institutions, which commonly held mutual ownership with their depositors and borrowers. Though competition and other variables have no longer distinguished the lines between thrift institutions and commercial banks because both now offer very similar products and have similar profitable agendas, still laws and regulations in many states emphasize different regulatory oversight to these historically different financial institutions.

Thrift institutions financial institutions that generate revenue through customer's savings.

Commercial banks are financial institutions within the overall financial system, and as such they are in the business of receiving deposits and lending money. Profiting through the management of this flow of money from saver to borrower is the primary responsibility of banks and their means of making profits. This excess profit allows banks to better enhance the customer experience, which in turn, encourages customers to become stronger participants in saving and borrowing.

Commercial banks financial institution that receives deposits and lends money.

The Banking System

When customers store their money in a bank, they are depositing money. The bank now has a reserve of money that it will use for its own profitable purposes of exchange. Banks exchange these deposits of money through the process of lending, such as giving loans or issuing credit cards. In the lending process, a bank will offer to lend its customer a certain sum of money. The customer receives the **principal**— the amount of money that the bank loans—and in return, the customer contractually promises to pay back the principal plus interest. **Interest** is the additional amount of money the bank charges at a particular rate for loaning money and is the primary mechanism by which banks earn profit. In order to generate revenue, the bank allocates loan payments first to satisfy the interest due on the loan, then to any late fees assessed, and finally to the principle balance.

© ra2studio/Shutterstock, Inc.

Principal the amount of money that the bank loans.

Interest the bank's charge at a particular rate for loaning the customer money.

The amount of interest due at any time is based on the remaining amount of the principle. To reduce the total amount paid on a loan or owed on a credit card at a quicker rate, it is advantageous for the customer to pay more than the minimum amount due on the loan or credit card statement each month and on time. Besides, more of your payment will be applied to the principle amount.

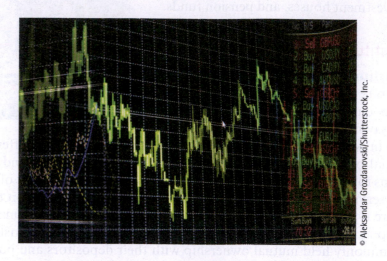

© Aleksandar Grozdanovski/Shutterstock, Inc.

As a result of the economic downturn in 2008, financial institutions were negatively impacted since individuals and businesses sought fewer loans. Moreover, many who had loans were not making the payments and thus defaulted. A loan in default means the customer has failed to satisfy the legal contractual obligations of repaying the loan. An unpaid loan translates into reduced profits for financial institutions. Without these profits, financial institutions suffer and may fail.

Compounding Interest, APR, and APY

Annual Percentage Yield (APY) includes intra-year compound interest.

Annual Percentage Rate (APR) does not take into account compound interest and is the summation of the interest rate charged over a period of time also called the periodic rate.

The rate of interest is a financial tool used by the bank to help customers and itself profit off of money. Remember, in order for a bank to have money to lend, customers must deposit their money into a bank for storage. A bank will entice the customer to deposit money into its own financial banking institution over another bank by offering a competitive interest rate on deposits. Just as you pay interest on a loan, the bank pays you interest on deposited money. A bank remains profitable by maintaining the difference in interest they pay you verses the interest they charge others through loans.

© Nadin3d/Shutterstock, Inc.

When shopping for a loan and/or savings account, read the fine print. Banks will offer different compounding periods. **Compounding** is earning interest on previous interest. In a loan, frequent compounding of interest negatively impacts the customer because it results in higher payments. Conversely, frequent compounding of interest in interest-bearing accounts positively impacts the customer because the earned interest is reinvested back into the principle amount. Consequently, a larger amount of money is earning interest.

Compounding impacts the interest rate and total amount of interest. The **APY, annual percentage yield**, includes intra-year compound interest, whereas the **APR, annual percentage rate**, does not take into account compound interest.

APR is the summation of the interest rate charged over a period of time; this period of time is called the **periodic rate**. Financial institutions can compound interest monthly, quarterly (every 3-months), or semi-annually (every 6-months).

Assume your credit card company charges you 12% APR on all purchases, equating to a periodic interest rate of 1% each month for 12 months. However, the fine print may state a 12.68% APY, which is the rate you will be charged if you carry a balance for a year on that same credit card. In this illustration, the 12.68% APY takes into account interest compounded monthly. When financial institutions offer you a loan, they will quote the APR, which is the lower rate. Likewise, if you are looking for a savings account, the institution will quote you the APY, which is a higher rate.

Periodic rate   the summation of the interest rate charged over a period of time.

Interest-Bearing Accounts

Having an interest-bearing account is considered an investment because you are earning extra money on your deposited principal amount. Interest bearing deposit accounts are typically called **savings accounts**. In some cases, banking institutions may offer interest bearing checking accounts for high balanced accounts. **Money-market accounts (MMA)** are a hybrid savings-checking account. These accounts do not typically require as high a minimum balance as an interest-bearing checking account but may require a higher balance than a regular savings account. Additionally, MMA pay a higher interest rate than a savings account and allow limited withdrawals without penalty. A certificate of deposit (CD) is also a readily available banking product that banks use to entice customers to deposit their money. **CDs** are known as a timed deposit because when you purchase a CD, it typically requires a longer time commitment in storing your money; however, in return for this longer timed deposit, the interest rates on CDs are higher than a regular savings account. There are penalties if you break the timed commitment and choose to withdraw your money from the CD.

© Champiofoto/Shutterstock, Inc.

CDs are considered less liquid than other interest-bearing accounts because CDs have increased restrictions for withdrawal when compared with the other aforementioned accounts. **Liquidity** is based on the ability to quickly convert assets into useable cash with little or no loss in value. A checking account is the most liquid because it has little to no restrictions on withdrawals. In fact, a checking account is considered a **demand deposit** because customers can demand their money back at any time. However, withdrawal restrictions may apply to savings accounts. MMA fall between savings accounts and CDs because these accounts typically have monthly limits on withdrawals. All of these accounts are insured by the Federal Deposit Insurance Corporation (FDIC).

Money-Market Accounts (MMA)   hybrid savings-checking account.

Liquidity   the ability to quickly convert assets into useable cash with little or no loss in value.

FDIC and Federal Reserve System

During the Great Depression, a number of financial institutions failed, and as a result, customers lost all their deposited savings. Soon, citizens lost confidence in the financial system and no longer wanted to store their money in banks nor thrift institutions. In response to this panic and lack of confidence, Congress created the **Federal Deposit Insurance Corporation (FDIC)** in 1933 to restore public confidence in the U.S. financial banking industry. At an FDIC insured institution, each depositor's account is insured up to $250,000. The NCUA (National Credit Union Association) insures deposits in credit unions to the same amount.

Federal Deposit Insurance Corporation (FDIC)   promotes public confidence by insuring customer deposits in banks and thrift institutions up to $250,000 per deposit per customer.

According to the FDIC, there were 6,487 FDIC-insured commercial banks and thrifts institutions in the United States as of February 12, 2015 with assets of over $15 trillion and deposits exceeding $11 trillion. Interestingly, the current number of banks is down from over 12,000 twenty years ago. Since the start of FDIC insurance, no depositor has lost a single cent of insured funds as a result of a financial institution's failure. Remember, banks fail when it does not generate enough revenue to meet obligations to its creditors or depositors.

The FDIC insures checking accounts, negotiable order of withdrawal (NOW) accounts, savings accounts, MMA, certificates of deposit, cashier's checks, money orders, and other official items issued by a bank. However, the FDIC insurance does not cover stocks, bonds, mutual funds, life insurance policies, annuities, municipal securities, nor safe deposit boxes, and their contents.

All U.S. financial institutions that are insured by the FDIC must be part of the Federal Reserve System. The **Federal Reserve System**, often referred to as the Fed, is the central bank of the United States and is responsible for regulating the banking industry. As in the creation of the FDIC, it was a panic within the financial institutions during the 1913s that led Congress to pass the Federal Reserve Act, which created the Federal Reserve System with the primary responsibility of overseeing and creating stability in the U.S. financial systems. A group of seven people, known as the board of governors, comprise the governing body. The board of governors includes a chairperson and a vice chair, both are appointed by the President of the United States of America and confirmed by the United States Senate. Like other banks, the Federal Reserve operates by generating its own revenues through interest earned on Treasury securities and fees collected through financial services transactions, including loans.

© YamabikaY/Shutterstock, Inc.

The Federal Reserve System has several functions; two primary responsibilities are known as its dual mandate. This **dual mandate** of the Federal Reserve System is to manage a monetary policy that maximizes employment and prevents inflation (and deflation) within the prices of goods and services. How does the Fed manage this dual mandate? Through increasing and decreasing the supply of money in the economy; this is the Fed's monetary policy. If the Fed increases the supply of money, it increases the demand for goods and services, which, in turn, increases the demand for the employees who produce those goods and services. In this way, the Fed's monetary policy may have positively impacted employment. If economic activity results in lower unemployment, generally at about 5% or less annually, then the goal of full employment is achieved.

The other part of this dual mandate is to ensure price stability in goods and services. If the Fed's monetary policy causes a stronger demand for goods and services, then the result tends to push employee wages and other costs higher. This greater demand for workers and increased cost for materials to produce goods and service reflect in higher prices. As long as these higher prices are kept in check, generally at no more than 3% annual inflation, then the goal of price stability is achieved.

A central bank's **monetary policy** can influence the inflation or deflation of prices because monetary policy affects the flow and availability of money and impacts interest rates. For example, when monetary policy is less constrictive, the **Federal funds rate**—the rate financial institutions use to charge each other for loans—is low. A low Federal funds rate translates into lower short- and long-term interest rates for the typical banking customer. That's because a lower Fed

Federal reserve system the central bank of the United States responsible for regulating the banking industry.

Monetary policy the government's means of controlling the supply and cost of money. Can influence the inflation or deflation of prices because it affects the flow and availability of money.

Federal funds rate the rate financial institutions use to charge each other loans.

funds rate induces banks to lower the **Prime Rate**: the interest rate banks charge their best customers. Since all bank rates are based on the Prime Rate, this means that it becomes cheaper to borrow, thus households are more willing to buy goods and services and may even be more likely to secure mortgages, car loans, or credit cards. We already learned this increase in demand increases the cost of production, and the cost of production has an impact on inflation.

Prime rate   the interest rate banks charge their best customers.

Conversely, a more constrictive monetary policy increases the Federal funds rate; making it more costly for banks to borrow from one another. In turn, the banks increase the Prime Rate and thus charge a higher interest rate for both consumer and business loans. Because the cost to borrow is higher, money supply is slowed. As a result, business and households do not borrow or expand their businesses, economic growth is slowed and demand decreases, which reflects in lower prices.

Wait! Aren't lower prices a good thing? Not if declining prices persist. Remember, businesses operate because of profits. They are able to pay employees and pay creditors because of these profits. If declining prices continue over a long period, profits fall, employment and incomes fall, defaults on loans by companies and individuals increases, and businesses close. To fight deflation, the Fed increases the flow of money, but this increase has to be tempered so as not to cause inflation. The dual mandate of the Federal Reserve System is its most difficult responsibility to manage.

DISCUSS FINANCIAL MARKETS AND INVESTMENTS

Now that you've secured a well-paying job, you're faced with a choice to invest a portion of your income. Investments are a way to put money to work for you. **Investing** is a way to commit money to an organization with the expectation of obtaining a profit. As previously discussed, a bank will offer you a variety of saving account products that will pay you interest for storing, or investing, your money in their particular institution. This type of investment has no risk because your original **capital**—the initial money used to start the investment—will not lose value and in fact, you will earn interest. However, rather than earning low rates of return via low interest rates, another option to earn money on your investment is to invest in the financial market. Investing in the financial markets is more risky because you can lose your initial capital investment rather than earning a profit.

Investing   a way to commit money to venture with the expectation of obtaining a profit.

Capital   is money or the things money can buy, like machines and buildings, which are used in the production of goods and services. The initial money used to start an investment.

Financial market   the means of exchange in which financial securities, such as stocks and bonds, metals, and agricultural goods, can be traded at a particular value.

IPO   first time offerings of a security are called initial public offerings.

Glass Steagall act of 1933 prohibited banks from owning full-service brokerage firms.

Financial Services Modernization Banking Act of 1999   this allowed banks to establish one-stop financial services where customers can buy and sell securities and purchase insurance coverage.

The **financial market** is the term used to indicate the means of exchange in which financial securities, such as stocks and bonds, or commodities including metals and agricultural goods, can be traded at a particular value. Individuals or institutions can participate in trading as investors. Institutional investors are pension funds, insurance companies, mutual funds, banks, or any other organizations that trade large quantities of securities. Investing can be done in either the primary or secondary market. In the primary market, investors purchase financial securities directly from the issuer of the security. Investment banking organizations typically act on behalf of the corporations who are issuing the security for the first time. First time offerings of a security are called initial public offerings **(IPO)**. IPOs issued through investment banking organization or direct sales of securities directly from the corporation to stockholders are all part of the primary market.

It is through the issuance of IPOs that businesses raise capital. The secondary market exists for those securities that were originally sold through the primary market. The secondary market is the most common market for investors to trade between themselves existing financial securities. The company does not receive any of the money traded in the secondary market. If you buy General Motors stock on the market, the current owner of the stock gets the money, not General Motors.

In May 2012, the social networking company Facebook went public with its IPO. This public offering was the biggest IPO in the technology sector. The initial stock price for Facebook was $38 per share. As of February 2015, the stock price was $75.86. Throughout the IPO process and even now, financial analysts speculate on Facebook's ability to raise revenue and remain profitable, despite the increasing stock price.

To enter the financial market, an investor must use a licensed broker. Financial institutions compete for the business of customers by offering investment options through licensed brokers. This is in addition to offering loans, checking and high-yielding savings accounts, including CDs, credit cards, and a host of online banking options. But this was not always the case because of the **Glass Steagall Act of 1933**, which prohibited banks from owning full-service brokerage firms. But the **Financial Services Modernization Banking Act of 1999**, which repealed the 1933 act, now allows banks to establish one-stop financial services where customers can bank in the traditional manner as well as buy and sell securities and purchase insurance coverage. Many banks now employ licensed brokers to help customers invest in the financial market.

To purchase stocks, bonds, and other investments, you must work through a licensed representative, called a **stockbroker** or account executive. In turn, the stockbroker will buy or sell securities for you at a fee, called a commission. With the advent of online brokerage firms, many customers self-direct their own investments. However, the online brokerage firm, still acts as the intermediary to the markets (and collects a fee for using its stock trading platform), even though the customer is the one directing the trade.

The two largest stock exchanges are the **NYSE** (New York Stock Exchange) and The **NASDAQ** (National Association of Securities Dealers Automated Quotation). The main difference between the two exchanges (though other differences exist) is how stocks are traded. Stocks traded on the NYSE are traded in a face-to-face format directly on the trading floor in an open auction while the NASDAQ operates in a computerized intranet format rather than the trading floor model. In the wake of technological advancements, the NYSE uses technology to satisfy most trades, but not all. The NYSE and NASDAQ are only two of many local and global stock exchanges.

Stockbroker   a licensed representative buys or sells securities for you at a commission.

NYSE   New York Stock Exchange.

NASDAQ   National Association of Securities Dealers Automated Quotation.

© Vacclav/Shutterstock, Inc.

TYPES OF INVESTMENTS

There are various investment types. Bonds, stocks, and mutual funds are common. **Bonds** are a type of investment based on debt. With a bond, you are lending out your money to a company or government. As with a financial institution who

Bonds   an investment of lending money for a specific length of receiving interest over the time period and principal paid at the end of the investment period.

Volatility   fluctuating prices that could cause you to lose some or all of your investment.

lends money through a loan, you too, generate revenue by agreeing to receive interest on the money you used to buy the bond. In the end of the investment period, you receive the amount you lent plus interest. Bonds are relatively safe, especially those issued by governments, and therefore, the potential return is low.

Compared to bonds, stocks provide relatively high potential returns because of their **volatility**; fluctuating prices could cause you to lose some or all of your investment. Stocks are purchased in either the primary or secondary market. The price is set by a supply and demand model. The basic premise of purchasing stocks is "buy low, sell high," meaning buy the stock at a low price, and then sell it high before the price of the stock falls. The

© Robert Brown Stock/Shutterstock, Inc.

Capital gain profit from selling stock at a price about the cost.

Stock become part owner of the business, which entitles you to participate in and vote at shareholders' meetings, and potential to receive dividends.

Common stock is the most common form of shares, equity in a corporation that includes voting dividends rights.

Dividends profits that the company allocates to its shareholders.

Preferred stock a much less used form of equity ownership that lies somewhere between stock and bonds in how they work. Equity in a corporation with preferential status to receive dividends over common stockholders.

difference is your profit, or **capital gain**. Because stock prices rise and fall daily, you might buy a stock at a low price and that same stock might continue to fall to a lower price. If you sell the stock at the new lower price, you have lost your initial investment. There is no guarantee you will profit by buying and selling stocks.

Purchasing a **stock**, or equity, means you become part owner of the business. If you buy **common stock**, you are invited to participate and vote at shareholders' meetings, and you can receive **dividends**, which are profits that the company allocates to its shareholders. Note, not all companies pay dividends. If you buy **preferred stock**, you receive dividends ahead of others, but you do not have voting rights.

Mutual funds are a collection of stocks and bonds. When you invest in mutual funds, you are paying a professional manager to select specific investments for you with a specific focus. For example, mutual funds can focus on large company stocks, small company stocks, mid-sized company stocks, stocks of foreign companies, bonds, or much more.

EXPLORE THE IMPACT OF A GLOBAL FINANCIAL SYSTEM

Financial institutions continue to increase their global exposure as our world becomes more and more connected. This exposure gives U.S. banks access to a larger market; thereby increasing customers who seek to save money, receive loans and purchase other financial services, which leads to increased profits. Though U.S. banks are increasing their global exposure, it is still banks in Europe, Great Britain, and Asia that maintain some of the largest total assets in the world.

© siiixth/Shutterstock, Inc.

Earlier we discussed how the U.S. Federal Reserve System controls the flow of money through its monetary policy. Similarly, other countries have a central banking system, like that of the Fed, which controls each countries' monetary policies. Because of a globalized financial system, the impact of one country's monetary policy can reverberate throughout the globe by way of other countries altering their own monetary policy. As a result, global economic prosperity or decline could occur due to the monetary policies of several countries. For example, many foreign countries borrow money from U.S. institutions. If the U.S. Federal Reserve lowers its Federal fund rate, interest rates will decrease; thereby making it cheaper for these foreign countries to borrow money. Again, when banks lend money, they profit off of the interest. More profitable U.S. banks equates to a healthier U.S. economy.

The same practice works for the Central Bank of Japan. If U.S. interest rates fall, the Central Bank of Japan might alter their monetary policy so as to lower the cost of borrowing in its own country. As countries begin to increase the flow of money by lowering rates, global economic demand for goods and services increases; thereby, creating an opportunity for global economic growth, but also the opportunity for increased prices, inflation, globally. Truly, we live in a globalized economy.

EXPLAIN THE ROLE OF STRATEGIC PLANNING IN FINANCIAL MANAGEMENT

The fundamental success of an organization, whether a small or large business, is driven by its ability to effectively manage its financial resources, capitalize on its core competencies, and make sound business decisions. Increasingly, there has been a targeted focus on how businesses can avoid failure and ultimately achieve sustained economic success. The Small Business Administration (2005) reported that approximately half of new businesses fail within their first 5 years of operation. Moreover, small businesses are failing at a higher rate than larger businesses. The reasons cited for small business failures are associated with poor management, finances, and failure to employ strategic planning (Christopher, 1998).

© mindscanner/Shutterstock, Inc.

DESCRIBE STRATEGIC PLANNING

When the owner of a shoe store in Omaha, NE, (a participant in a research study investigating strategic planning in small businesses), went to a local bank to get a loan to expand his business, the bank asked for his written strategic plan in addition to the business plan and financial reports. Baffled, the owner responded that he doesn't have anything in writing, but in his mind, he knows the amount of daily sales he must generate to make a profit, as he had been in business for 3 years; besides, who would know this information better than he. Furthermore, the entrepreneur owner stated that his goal for next year is to add additional items to his product line and that he had a long-term plan in mind. Why would a bank ask for a strategic plan? How is the strategic planning process incorporated into financial management?

© chillchill_lanla/Shutterstock, Inc.

© Ivelin Radkov/Shutterstock, Inc.

First of all, understand that a lender or investor would expect to see a Business Plan as well as a Strategic Plan. Sound financial management is important for both of those and thus to get a better understanding of the business there are typically three Financial Statements necessary in developing a business plan or expansion plan for the future. There's critical financial numbers and information presented in those Financials which we discussed in the Accounting chapter. The Balance Sheet shows a company's assets and liabilities . . . what it owns and what it owes. The Income Statement shows revenue and expenses, providing a way to determine profitability.

And the Cash Flow Statement shows money coming in and going out each month to demonstrate that you can pay your bills. This will help the lender or investor or business know if it can pay back any loan it might take out. These financials will also indicate if the business can afford to carry out the strategic plan with money generated internally from operations or if the company will have to seek outside funds to grow.

As defined earlier, financial management is the process of engaging in activities to obtain money to effectively and efficiently use it to achieve the goals and objectives of the business. One activity that has proven to be effective is **strategic planning**, a disciplined process of decision making that sets in motion action plans and resource allocation to achieve company goals and objectives. Whereas strategy is a plan of action, strategic planning is an intentional management tool that implores **strategic thinking** about being proactive, not reactive, to creating value and vision for the organization. It is the way people think about the future direction of their business and how they are going to achieve that direction.

Any business should know who they are, their goals for the future and how they plan to accomplish them. The strategic planning process builds upon the mission statement and spells out a company's who, what, when, where, and how into a long-term document that specifically articulates goals and action plans to be successful.

Strategic planning   the longest range and largest scope planning that looks out several years and is supported by the tactical plans. A disciplined process of decision making that sets in motion action plans and resource allocation to achieve company goals and objectives.

Strategic thinking   being proactive, not reactive, to creating value and vision for the organization.

Strategic Management
High quality modern classic design concept illustrations InfoGraphics

© pixome/Shutterstock, Inc.

THE STRATEGIC PLANNING PROCESS

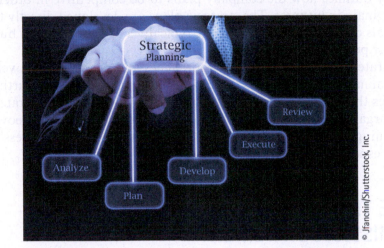

The **strategic-planning process** is the development of an accountability system that provides a written plan to the following questions:

1. Who are we?
2. Where do we want to be?
3. What are our core competencies and resources?
4. When do we want to meet our goals?
5. How do we get there?

The process helps an organization by providing a guideline to making strategic decisions about the direction for the firm and what activities are best. Moreover, the strategic plan gives the organization a sense of direction and focus on how best to utilize resources. As mentioned in Chapter 5, strategic planning is normally developed at the executive level of the organization but may include input from mid-level managers. Executives decide where the organization wants or needs to be in the future and then develops the strategic plan to get them there. An effective plan is embraced by all stakeholders and takes the active participation of the entire organization to be successful. Although strategic planning is common in large businesses, it is becoming more popular among small businesses.

Strategic planning models scenario models for outlining the strategic planning process.

There are several different **strategic planning models**—scenario models for outlining the strategic planning process. There is no one perfect strategic planning model for each organization, but typically it's a five-step process, which will address the above-mentioned questions. They include guidelines for basic strategic planning, goals, objectives, scenarios and how to strategize to achieve the goals. The strategic planning process outlines five distinct steps: (1) define the organization's vision and mission, (2) assess the organization's competitive position, (3) set organizational goals and objectives, (4) create strategies for attaining and sustaining a competitive advantage, and (5) develop an action plan for implementing the strategies.

Once all the components are developed and put together, a strategic plan provides a framework for articulating the vision and decision making. Although a strategic plan does not guarantee

Strategic plan A written, living document that specifically outlines how the company plans to be competitive in order to successfully remain in business.

success for the business, a good **strategic plan** is a written, living document that specifically outlines how the company plans to be competitive in order to successfully remain in business. The strategic plans are developed directly from the overall goals of the organization and are typically a 3- to 5-year plan but maybe for a longer period of time.

The strategic plan identifies new approaches and directions for overcoming and/or eliminating the obstacles to achieving the vision or goal. Furthermore, it translates the vision and mission into action tasks. The written strategic plan can help organizations improve efficiency and accountability. Moreover, strategic planning is ultimately about effective allocation of the business' limited resources, especially its money.

DEFINE THE ORGANIZATION'S VISION AND MISSION STATEMENT

Vision statement a clear, inspirational and compelling broad statement about what the company aspires to be, their values, purpose, and future direction.

Mission statement a formal, clear statement that describes the organization's purpose, their reason for existing, the product and customers.

The first step in the strategic planning process is to describe the vision statement and translate it into developing the organization's mission statement. The **vision statement** is a clear, inspirational and compelling broad statement about what the company aspires to be, their values, purpose, and future direction. It is the big picture of what a company wants to achieve and is generally a one line statement. For example, Walgreen's vision statement is "To be America's most loved pharmacy-led health, wellbeing, and beauty enterprise." The **mission statement**—a formal, clear statement that describes the organization's purpose, their reason for existing, the product and customers—should be brief, but not too narrow or too broad. In effect, the mission statement tells how the company will achieve their vision.

An effective mission statement keeps the organization focused on their purpose and why they are in existence. Although a mission statement should be short, a statement such as "We will make the top quality product for our customers," is too broad

and, really, this statement is given for any company. The mission and vision statements are the organization's guiding light that keeps it focused and moving in the right direction. The vision statement is what the organization wants to pursue, whereas the mission statement describes what the organization wants to accomplish. The following examples illustrate mission statements:

Mission statement of the Sickle Cell Association

- To enable individuals with sickle cell anemia to live lives to the extent possible unhampered and uncompromised by their sickle cell conditions.
- To increase the knowledge and understanding of sickle cell disease as a health problem through professional standards of administration, health care, public relations, and fundraising.

Mission statement of Starbucks

- To inspire and nurture the human spirit—one person, one cup, and one neighborhood at a time.

Mission Statement of First National Bank

- To build and maintain long-term relationships by delivering a superior customer experience through simplicity, efficiency and engaged employees while driving profitability and long-term growth.

ASSESS THE ORGANIZATION'S COMPETITIVE POSITION

© box912/Shutterstock, Inc.

Once the mission statement is developed, the next step is to assess the organization's competitive position in the industry by conducting a situational analysis of its internal and external environment. The procedure to accomplish this task is to prepare an **SWOT analysis**. SWOT, an acronym for strengths, weaknesses, opportunities, and threats, is an assessment tool for identifying a company's capabilities and deficiencies—what they can control and its market opportunities and business threats—factors out of the organization's control. Environmental factors internal to the organization are classified as strengths (S) and weaknesses (W), whereas those factors external to the organization are identified as opportunities (O) and threats (T). Strengths and weaknesses evaluate the organization's capabilities, functional areas, products, employees, location, and all aspects in which they control. For example, name recognition, experienced employees, and quality products are strengths and weaknesses. Opportunities and threats include the booming economy (or recession), federal regulations which could hinder or prosper growth of firm, and social media.

SWOT analysis an assessment tool for identifying an organization's strengths, weaknesses, opportunities, and threats.

By understanding these four aspects of the environment, a business can create strategies, which leverages its strengths—competencies and capabilities—to capitalize on possible opportunities. Additionally, the SWOT analysis can pinpoint the weaknesses and focus on correcting or minimizing them and develop plans on deterring potential threats. When you know what's facing your business and take steps to act upon it, there is a better chance of success.

SET ORGANIZATIONAL GOALS AND OBJECTIVES

© totallyPic.com/Shutterstock, Inc.

The next step is to develop goals and objectives for the organization which will define the company's planned performance and future direction. The **goals** are the company's overall plans of what they want to achieve and should align with the vision statement. For example, the shoe store owner in the above-mentioned example may set a goal "To improve profitability." A company should not identify too many goals as it may become overwhelming and the company may lose focus.

Objectives are specific, concrete, quantifiable statements for achieving the goals. They state what is to be achieved and when the objective will be achieved. It is important that objectives are achievable, measurable, time sensitive, and realistic, particularly to the individual expected to be accountable for achieving the objective. To achieve the profitability goal, the objective could be "To increase sales by 15% over the next 3 years."

Objectives   specific, concrete, quantifiable statements for achieving the goals that are measurable, and time sensitive.

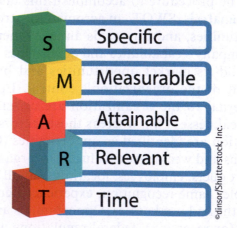

S	Specific
M	Measurable
A	Attainable
R	Relevant
T	Time

©dinsor/Shutterstock, Inc.

CREATE STRATEGIES FOR ATTAINING AND SUSTAINING A COMPETITIVE ADVANTAGE

Developing the goals and objectives, which aligns with the vision and mission statement, narrows the specific direction for the organization. It keeps the organization focused on carrying out its mission and striving to be a successful business. Next, in the strategic planning process, is to create specific strategies for realizing a competitive advantage in the industry and how to keep the advantage.

The underlying goal of creating strategies is to identify **competitive differentiation**—combining the company's strengths and seizing opportunities to develop approaches that set them apart from the competition. A hypothetical strategy for Walgreens may be to use its strength of locating stores on corners to collaborate with a new clinic, opening in space across the opposite corner and run by the largest hospital in the area, to establish the first partnership of its kind in offering reduced prescriptions and supplies.

Competitive differentiation combining the company's strengths and seizing opportunities to develop approaches that set them apart from the competition.

© Thinglass/Shutterstock, Inc.

DEVELOP AN ACTION PLAN FOR IMPLEMENTING THE STRATEGIES

After analysis of the environment, establishing goals and creating strategies for achieving the goals, the final step is to put the strategic plan into action and effective execution of the strategies. The **action plan** is the actual work performed to meet the goals and objectives. Implementing the strategies requires developing specific tactics that will give the business a competitive advantage in the marketplace. The entire organization comes together to put the proper systems in place to allocate the needed resources to support and carry out the strategies, such as designating specific dollars in the budget or empowering the middle manager to make definite decisions.

© Dusit/Shutterstock, Inc.

In our previous example, the entrepreneur shoe store owner established a goal to improve profitability. He plans to accomplish this by increasing sales 15% over the next 3 years. The action plan to increase sales in year one may be to form a focus group to determine the utility of his existing product lines and suggestions for adding to the product line. Furthermore, the focus group may reveal additional strategies to implement to be successful for this goal. In other words, the action plan should offer specific tactics to achieving the objectives and implementing the formalized strategic plan.

Action plan the actual work performed to meet the goals and objectives.

MONITORING THE STRATEGIC PLAN

Once the strategic plan has been developed, it is essential to monitor and evaluate the results. Additionally, the organization must refine the plan when the actual performance fails to meet expectations. Monitoring includes comparing results

© Artkwin/Shutterstock, Inc.

© iOoncept/Shutterstock, Inc.

with the budget and forecasts, reviewing financial goals, securing feedback, interviewing employees, sharing results with the focus group, and reviewing reports prepared by other departments.

If the focus group recommended adding a fluorescent line of color shoe strings, but the sales of the shoe strings didn't meet expectations during the first year, the owner must decide whether to change the pricing, continue selling the product, and monitor for an additional year or discontinue the fluorescent shoe string line altogether. Several years ago, Walgreens made the decision to gain a competitive advantage by relocating and opening new stores on corner lots. This strategic decision is ingrained in their motto, "At the Corner of Happy & Healthy." Location, location, location.

Regardless of the process, components, or other activities used in the strategic planning process, the consensus from the participants in the research study conducted in Omaha is that strategic planning is important and must be monitored regularly in order to ensure their competitive position in the industry. Several of the participants commented that the strategic plan kept them focused and on track. The strongest advice given from the participants was to develop a strategic plan, conduct an SWOT analysis, and monitor the plan regularly. All of these activities, according to the participants, help the owner gain knowledge and be successful in their business (Williams, 2008).

OPEN FOR BUSINESS IN THE REAL WORLD

Self-directed Goals to Investing.

Creating a successful business requires a plan, sticking to the plan, and evaluating the plan. This insight is applicable to your personal financial management. Critical success in your personal financial management plan exists when you make a plan, stick to the plan, and constantly evaluate the plan. Investments are an important part of this plan. Whether you are an institutional investor or a fledgling personal investor, are investing a percentage of your monthly income, you should consider setting these goals for yourself.

1. Before beginning an investment program learn to balance your budget. Do not spend more than you make. This overspending only leads to more debt.

2. Pay yourself first. Many people will spend nearly all of their income on expenses; thereby, leaving little for savings. Make a commitment to save a certain percentage or amount of your income, and then whatever is remaining, use to pay your monthly bills and expenses. Consider religious and philanthropic organizations as well. A socially conscious investor also considers these institutions as an investment in our society.

3. Always, participate in employer-sponsored retirement programs, especially if the employer will match your contributions. 401 (k) or 403(b) retirement

accounts are a long-term investment in your future. If an employer matches your contribution, the match is typically up to a certain percentage. Always contribute up to this percentage.

4. When you receive tax refunds or other unexpected gifts, invest them. If you are budgeting, then this extra money is outside of your budget; so invest it.

© Tashatuvango/Shutterstock, Inc.

Chapter Summary

Financial management is the process of engaging in activities to obtain money to effectively and efficiently use it to achieve the goals and objectives of the business. This chapter focused on the financial aspect of a company—planning and managing their money effectively, raising money when needed, and identifying ways to accomplish the company's goals through financial management. Money, as a medium for exchange, is anything society agrees to accept in the purchasing of products, services, or resources. The function of money in business is to serve as a medium of exchange for products, goods and services, a common measurement for value, and the accumulation of wealth.

The financial institutions are a critical component in the financial system, which is the flow of money from the savers to the borrowers. Everyone participates in the financial system—individuals, government, businesses, financial markets, and financial institutions. The financial market is the term used to indicate the means of exchange in which financial securities, such as stocks and bonds, or commodities, including metals and agricultural goods, can be traded at a particular value. Individuals or institutions can participate in trading as investors.

Congress created the FDIC in 1933 to restore public confidence in the U.S. financial banking industry. At an FDIC insured institution, each depositor's account is insured up to $250,000. All U.S. financial institutions that are insured by the FDIC must be part of the Federal Reserve System. The Federal Reserve System, often referred to as the Fed, is the central bank of the United States and is responsible for regulating the banking industry. The Federal Reserve System has several functions; two primary responsibilities are known as its dual mandate. This dual mandate of the Federal Reserve System is to manage a monetary policy that maximizes employment and prevents inflation and deflation within the prices of goods and services.

The strategic planning process outlines five distinct steps: (i) defining the organization's vision and mission, (ii) assessing the organization's competitive position, (iii) setting organizational goals and objectives, (iv) creating strategies for attaining and sustaining a competitive advantage, and (v) developing an action plan for implementing the strategies. Regardless, of the size of the business, it is important to develop financial plans and regularly evaluate the financial stability of the business.

Review Questions

1. Describe the functions of money.
2. Define the financial market and give an example of a transaction which occurs in the financial market.
3. Briefly describe the financial system and the functions of financial institutions.
4. Distinguish between annual percentage rate (APR) and annual percentage yield (APY).
5. Explain the dual mandate of the Federal Reserve System in regards to its monetary policy.
6. Distinguish thrift institutions and commercial banks.
7. What are the types of interest-bearing accounts and explain each?
8. Explain the difference between a primary financial market and a secondary financial market.
9. Describe the steps in the strategic planning process.
10. What are the reasons, from research studies, for the failure of businesses?
11. Define and describe an SWOT analysis.
12. Compare and contrast goals and objectives.

Discussion Questions

13. What is financial management? Why is it important?
14. Give an example of a transaction processed through the banking system?
15. Why is a strategic plan important?
16. Using the strategic planning process steps, develop a strategic plan for a non-profit organization or your college/university.
17. Go to the web site of the Board of Governors of the Federal Reserve System (http://www.federalreserve.gov/) and the FDIC (http://www.federalreserve.gov/). Review and discuss some recent developments found on the web sites.
18. Is it more profitable to invest in stocks or bonds? Explain your position.

Key Terms

- action plan
- annual percentage rate (APR)
- annual percentage yield (APY)
- Bonds
- capital
- capital gain Commercial banks
- common stock
- competitive differentiation
- dividends
- dual mandate Federal Deposit Insurance Corporation (FDIC)
- Federal funds rate
- Federal Reserve System
- Financial management
- financial manager
- financial market
- Financial Services Modernization Banking Act of 1999
- financial system
- Glass Steagall Act of 1933
- goals
- Interest
- Investing
- IPO
- Liquidity
- mission statement
- monetary policy
- Money-market accounts (MMA)
- money NASDAQ NYSE
- Objectives

- periodic rate
- preferred stock
- principal
- Prime rate
- savings accounts
- stock
- stockbroker
- storing money

- strategic plan
- strategic planning
- strategic planning models
- strategic thinking
- SWOT analysis
- Thrift institutions volatility
- vision statement

References

Business Dictionary. Retrieved February 12, 2015, from http://www.businessdictionary.com/definition/liquidity.html#ixzz3S0VZcg1x

Christopher, J. (1998). Minority business formation and survival: Evidence on business performance and viability. *Review of Black Political Economy*, *16(1)*, 37–68.

FDIC. Retrieved February 13, 2015, from https://www2.fdic.gov/idasp/index.asp

First National Bank. Retrieved February 12, 2015, from https://www.firstnational.com/site/about-us/company/index.fhtml

Small Business Administration. (2005). *U.S. Census Bureau news*. Retrieved February 14, 2015, from https://www.sba.gov/about-sba/what_we_do/mission

Source: Kapoor, J. R., Dlabay, L. R., & Hughes, R. J. (2004). *Personal Finance*, 7th ed. Burr Ridge, IL: Irwin-McGraw-Hill, p. 421.

Williams, I. R. (2008, August). Strategic Planning in Small Businesses: A Phenomenological Study Investigating the Role, Challenges, and Best Practices of Strategic Planning. Dissertation.

CHAPTER
17

Risk Management

LEARNING OBJECTIVES

1. Identity the primary causes of business failure.
2. Explain the different types of insurance.
3. Explain risk.
4. Identify the sources of risk.

© Dirk Ercken/Shutterstock, Inc.

OPENING STORY

Borders Book Stores opened in Ann Arbor Michigan in 1971. They expanded their operation to every state to over 1,200 stores including Waldenbooks. In 2011, however, they announced they were closing their remaining 399 stores and going out of business (Ovide, 2011). Meanwhile their chief competitor, Barnes and Noble is continuing to do well. What went wrong with Borders? Several reports have been written to analyze their decline. Most center around two factors, poor decision making by senior management and failure to keep up with emerging technologies. Borders started selling music CDs about them time people stopped buying them because they wanted iPods. The company started selling e-books and e-book readers well after the competition has established their brands. They were in too much debt and had too many stores. The last time they made a profit was 2006.

After 40 years of operations, they were gone. The analysts agree the company failed to recognize and manage the risk to the company.

INTRODUCTION

Many people start a business and many will fail. No one starts a business thinking they will fail, but it happens anyway. The long-term risk of failure is great, with only about 25% of new business ventures lasting 15 years and around 50% failing in the first five years. The rates of failure vary considerably depending on when a business opens and the industry in which they operate. One study that tracked start-up businesses from 1992 to 2002 found that only 29% survived that 10-year period (Shane, 2008).

Not only is there variation in the risk of failure, there is considerable variation in the cause. The three most common reasons cited for failure are poor management, inadequate financing, and going into business for the wrong reasons.

Managing risk involves understanding the sources of risk and the steps to either avoid it or mitigate its impact.

What is risk? **Risk** is uncertainty about the future, specifically about failure, loss, or injury. When someone starts a business, they run the risk or uncertainty of losing their investment or possibly their personal assets because of mistakes they make. Risk will occur in business; it is a natural part of business and life. Many people ignore risk, but a better alternative is to recognize it and understand it. After that, you can try to avoid risk or reduce it, accept it, or share it.

Risk uncertainty about the future, especially about the possibility of loss.

SOURCES OF RISK

Risk is constantly prevalent in the business world but comes primarily from four sources; poor management, the **legal/regulatory environment**, competition, and unlimited liability, which may result in law suits.

Legal/regulatory environment the body of laws and regulations in which a company operates.

Poor Management

One of us (Williams) was teaching a business class at a college in Iowa a few years back. When going around the first day and asking students what their goals were; one student replied she was trying to learn enough about business to fire her husband. Once the laughter died down, she made her point. She and her husband owned an electrician business in Council Bluffs, Iowa. Her husband was an excellent electrician and having worked for another company for years, decided to open his own company believing he knew all he needed to know about the industry. What his wife said was that he knew all he needed to know about being an electrician but very little about running a business.

The skills an electrician needs include understanding the flow of electrons, wattage and voltage, electrical fixture design, construction, local code requirements, safety issues, and many more specifics about the business. The skills a business manager must have include accounting, cash flow, scheduling, regulation compliance, labor laws, payroll, tax law, human resource management, reporting requirements,

and many more specifics about business operations. There are not a lot of common items on the two lists. Being the best in the business does not prepare one to be the best business manager.

Managing a business is not just about telling workers what to do. Every aspect of the business operation requires careful management and each function brings challenges. If good employees are recruited and retained, the human resource aspect can even be the least problematic.

It is difficult for any one person to know everything there is to know about running a business. However, there is help available. College curriculum and continuing education courses along with written material can be studied to learn basics. Staff with particular expertise can be hired, consultants may be engaged, experts may be retained, and government organizations offer advice and assistance.

Following is a partial list of functional areas that must be considered by any manager.

Personnel	Do you have established procedures to recruit, hire, train, and evaluate employees?
Communications	Do you have a web site, email, fax, cell phones, radios, and service on all of them to provide internal and external communications?
Accounting	Do you have accounting expertise or an accountant on staff or retainer to provide bookkeeping and tax preparation services?
Finance	Do you have adequate capital and cash flow to continue the enterprise and weather difficult times?
Processes	Do you have internal processes established and laid out in clearly understood form?
Organizational structure	Have you created an organizational structure that facilitates operations
Compliance and reporting	Do you understand the various government regulations with which you must comply and the periodic reports that must be made?
Competitive environment	Do you understand the competitive environment in which you operate; have you realistically evaluated the competition and your own business?
Marketing	Do you have a plan for marketing, including pricing, promotion, product, and placement?

Legal/Regulatory Environment

On January 1, 2015, new laws went into effect in every state in the country. Minimum wage laws were changed, tax laws, employee health care insurance changes, and even traffic law changes will impact many businesses. US codified law runs to thousands of pages and businesses are expected to comply with those laws, even if they are not aware of them. The Legal/Regulatory Environment is the body of laws and regulations in which a company operates. Local, state, and federal laws may all affect businesses.

Each year, many businesses fail to comply with regulations or laws and face fines because of it or are forced to make costly corrections because of errors. The auto industry faced record recalls in 2014 to fix problems in design of various components of automobiles. Sometimes, these defects do not show up for years, like in the case of the air bag problem facing several manufacturers. United Airlines is faced with a fine for leaving off a single washer off a bolt in a landing gear assembly and negative publicity because of one flight attendants actions regarding a special needs child. Fisher Brand Nuts recalled much of their product from two production runs because of possible salmonella contamination. Many food products have been recalled for similar contamination, such as the chorizo, recently recalled by the San Antonio company Garcia Foods that makes store brands for grocery stores. Native Oilfield Services, Inc. faced lawsuits from a group of current and former employees because of underpayment of overtime wage. Computer Sciences Corporation paid $150 million in fines imposed by the Securities and Exchange Commission because of their accounting practices.

Numerous government agencies provide oversight to ensure compliance with regulations in the interest of public safety and consumer or investor protection. Almost every industry establishes standards of performance and compliance. Failure to meet the standards can result in imposed fines or even shut down of a company. Even when an enterprise meets appropriate standards, that compliance can be expensive. Many companies hire a compliance officer just to ensure their operations do not violate any oversight agency's policies. Smaller companies may also use a consultant or another business to conduct compliance audits, if they cannot afford a full-time compliance officer.

Competitive Environment

Few businesses enjoy a monopoly in the market place. Even when they do, it is usually a regulated monopoly such as a utility. The competition then, brings risk of failure simply due to being outcompeted. Walmart has been accused of driving many small enterprises out of business when they move into an area. Many industries also reach a point of market saturation, where the local area has all the businesses of that type that it can support. As additional similar businesses enter the competition, the customer base is spread out among those companies. Even a firm that is adequately run can suffer if there are too few customers being attracted by too many businesses. For example, restaurants often fail, not because they do not offer good food at good value, but simply because there too many other restaurants in the market. It is vital for any enterprise to thoroughly understand the competition. In a saturated market, if one more business enters, one must go because there will not be enough customers to support them all.

Market share   the division or percentage of the marketplace each business serves.

The division of the customer base is known as **market share**. Although the size of the customer base changes with population growth and new technologies and products, at any given time, it represents a fixed group every competitor is trying to attract. Increasing the market share improves a company's position. How is the competition doing? Are they attracting more customers than you? If so, what are they doing differently? Is your pricing and customer support the best it can be? Could you lower your costs somewhere and use that to lower your price? Could a technology upgrade improve your position? Are your marketing activities improving your business? Have you chosen the right price point and targeted the right market segment? All of these questions need to be asked and continuously reasked as the company operates.

© Dusit/Shutterstock, Inc.

Unlimited Liability

Firms are held liable for their actions. If they cause injury, or in failing to act, allow injury to occur, they may be held accountable for that injury. In Chapter 2, we discussed the liability an owner faces based on the business actions. Owner's liability may be limited by the form or ownership. For instance, an owner of a corporation has liability limited to the extent of the investment in that corporation. The business itself, however, can still have unlimited liability. In other words, a business may be sued for more than it is worth.

There are many examples of businesses being sued because of the actions of a single employee or by people outside their direct control. In 1994, McDonalds Inc. was sued and lost a case in which a woman bought hot coffee from a restaurant and spilled it on her lap, causing third degree burns. The interesting part of this case from the perspective of this chapter is that the woman did not buy the coffee from McDonalds Inc. but from a privately owned franchise. The corporation was brought into lawsuit, however, because they specified standards by which the franchises must operate.

In 2000, Ford Motor Company was sued for their use of tires made by Firestone Inc. that were falling apart as people drove and cause accidents and injuries. Again, the actions of one company had an impact on another. A company may make a mistake and subject itself to debilitating lawsuits. However, they could also be subject to lawsuits from the actions of other people or companies, as well. A company that fails to shovel snow off the walk in front of their establishment may be sued for damages if someone falls. A firm whose driver causes an accident while on business may also be held liable.

DEALING WITH RISK

The techniques to reduce risk vary depending on the source of that risk. The goal, however, is the same; avoid risk, or reduce it, accept it, or share it. The first step in reducing risk is to recognize and identify it. A business must constantly evaluate their exposure to risk and one way to do that is to conduct an **SWOT Analysis**. SWOT or Strengths, Weaknesses, Opportunity, and Threats are a formal means of doing that evaluation.

SWOT Strength, Weaknesses, Opportunities, and Threats.

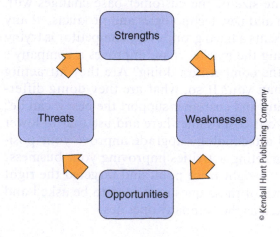

Strengths are areas where the company is strong or better than the competition. The strengths of an enterprise might be its highly trained staff or existing market share. Perhaps the organization has strong supply partners or long-term contracts. Maybe the company owns patents or copyrights that give it a competitive advantage. Understanding the strengths is important so those can be leveraged for gain in the future.

Weaknesses are those areas where the company is suffering or perhaps is at a disadvantage to competitors in the industry. Weaknesses need to be realistically identified so they can be dealt with. It is easy to underestimate weaknesses. If a company is not willing to acknowledge them, it will be difficult to correct them. Weaknesses might be clients that are leaving due to poor customer service or an inexperienced sales staff that is not closing sales at the necessary rate. Weaknesses could be dated technology or operating in an area with restrictive regulations or excessive taxes.

Opportunities represent areas a company can take advantage of a new or changing situation. A new area might be opening up that will offer potential growth chances. Customer dissatisfaction with a competitor may give your company the opportunity to grow its market share.

Threats are areas in which there is potential danger to the firm. A new competitor opening up, or changing technologies that will leave your company behind are certainly threats. Changes in the local laws or regulations can also bring threats to the company.

An SWOT analysis should be done regularly to keep the company aware of the results. A careful appraisal of the elements of the analysis can help reduce the tendency to act on intuition and instead act on facts. Fact-based or evidence-based decision making is far superior to deciding based on opinion or feelings. As noted above, once the analysis is done the company can more easily identify the risks and make decisions to avoid, reduce, accept, or share those risks.

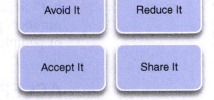

© Kendal Hunt Publishing Company

AVOIDING RISK

Poor management is a leading cause of business failure. This is true regardless of the size of a business. However, a small business, one that is often owned and operated by a single owner/manager must depend on that person having a broad range of expertise. One way to avoid risk is to gain the knowledge, expertise, or experience necessary to make good management decisions. Since that may or may not be possible, another way is to hire or engage people that already have it. A business may hire experts in various fields, such as a corporate attorney or

© iQoncept/Shutterstock, Inc.

accountant. A firm may also use consultants who are experts in risk management to steer them away from risky business practices.

One way to try to avoid risk is to address it in contracts or agreements. A common practice in schools is to have a hold harmless agreement signed by parents, who then agree not to pursue claims if their child is injured in a sporting event for instance. Companies also have similar agreements for newly hired employees, who often must sign an agreement to accept Workmen's Compensation and in doing so, give up their right to file a lawsuit in the event of work place accidents. Businesses who engage in potentially dangerous activities such as a shooting range, ski slope, or dirt bike course have similar agreements to avoid the risk by having the participant assume it themselves.

All of these methods are a way of acknowledging that risk is present and trying to get someone else to accept it for themselves. All of these methods also have limited success. Although someone may agree not to sue in the case of injury, which does not actually preclude them from doing so.

REDUCING RISK

Risk may be reduced through careful operations, sound practices, and conscious efforts to recognize dangerous situations and address problems before they occur. Many organizations have safety officers and regular safety training. Periodic safety or risk inspections may also be used to reduce incidents. Signage and frequent reminders may be used as well. In construction trades, there are "hard hat" areas or eye protection policies. Many transportation firms have phone numbers printed on their vehicles to allow motorists to report driving violations or compliance of their drivers.

ACCEPTING RISK

In some industries, the companies must simply accept that risk exists, may not be avoided, and must be factored in. In spite of careful and thorough training in parachute operations, the U.S. Army uses a casualty forecast figure to estimate the number of injuries that will occur on a mass tactical parachute drop. Trucking companies use a formula to try and predict the number of accidents and the budget impact, based on the expected miles over the coming forecast period.

SHARING RISK

Although risk can be shared through contractual agreement with business partners, the most common form of risk sharing is through insurance. Insurance companies agree to assume part of the risk in exchange for payment in the form of premiums. In a common example, most states require automobile drivers to insure their vehicle. All drivers then pay a premium from which the insurance company earns a profit and also affords to make claim payments to drivers who have accidents. The drivers are able to contract with the insurance company to share the risk of accidents, at least financially.

© TFoxFoto/Shutterstock, Inc.

For an individual or a company to insure against loss, they must have an insurable interest. A company can insure their buildings against a fire that would cause a loss of capital but cannot insure a building down the street that belongs to another firm. In other words, they cannot enrich themselves by randomly buying insurance on some other company's assets. In the same way, you cannot buy a life insurance policy to cover the death of an elderly neighbor that you expect do die in the next few years. That neighbor could, however, insure their own life, at their own expense and name you as the benefactor.

For something to be insured, it must be subject to pure risk and that pure risk must be insurable risk. **Pure risk** is risk in only one direction. It is a pure risk if there in only one possible outcome; loss of the asset or not. You insure against loss only, not against or for gain. To insure an asset against pure risk, it must meet the following requirements that make it an **insurable risk**:

1. It must have a predictable chance of loss
2. The value of the loss must be measureable
3. The loss must be accidental
4. The asset's risk must be over a fixed area.

BUSINESS INSURANCE

PROPERTY INSURANCE
PRODUCT LIABILITY INSURANCE
PROFESSIONAL LIABILITY INSURANCE
COMMERCIAL AUTO INSURANCE
TRIP BUSINESS INSURANCE
WORKERS' COMPENSATION INSURANCE
CASUALTY INSURANCE
HEALTH INSURANCE
BUSINESS INTERRUPTION INSURANCE

© arka38/Shutterstock, Inc.

Pure risk   a risk for which there is only one possibility; the loss of the insured asset.

Insurable risk   for an asset to be insurable, it must have a predictable loss possibility, have a measurable value, the lost must be accidental, and in a fixed geographical area.

© nasirkhan/Shutterstock, Inc.

Insurance comes in many types and is used by both individuals and companies in much the same way and for the same purpose. Just as a person should and in most states must, insure their vehicle, companies face the same regulations. Some states do allow a person or a company to self-insure; that is isolate a certain amount of money, for instance $100,000 in a savings account that must be kept there for possible accident claims. A company with capital and cash flow may be in a better position than an individual to do this. Although the money still belongs to the company, it cannot be accessed, so a firm may not want to deny themselves the use of their capital for other uses besides self-insurance.

Automobile insurance itself covers several forms, notably collision repair, medical costs, and liability for causation.

Automobile insurance insures against loss due to collusion as well as the potential medical costs and liability that may arises from an accident.

HEALTH CARE—A SPECIAL CASE

Families and individuals usually want to have medical insurance coverage. Now with the Affordable Care Act, individuals are required by law to have some form of coverage. For many that coverage is provided as a form of employee benefit. For years, companies have provided employee family and individual health care insurance as an incentive to make them competitive at drawing the best workforce. The Affordable Care Act now requires it of companies with 50 or more employees.

Providing for the health care of the workforce is more than just a benefit, however. It is an important factor in risk management. The employees are the most important asset in many organizations. Keeping them healthy and productive means continued operation of the enterprise. In recent years, companies have found preventative measures such as wellness programs have kept the workers at their jobs and even those that get sick, spend less time away.

Health care insurance cover medical expenses of employees and sometimes their families.

Health care insurance provided by companies is very expensive and without regard to the law, there must be a financial reward for having the program. Companies only tend to be more productive if they have a healthy work force, they also have greater retention and better success at recruiting excellent workers, if they have good employee benefits.

Many companies face the risk of loss of key executives or subject matter experts through death. Death of an important part of the company, particularly the owner, can cause loss of the business. Companies help share this risk by insuring the life of owners and key executives. The insurance policy cannot prevent loss of expertise and experience but can help with the financial burden of that loss.

© T33kid/Shutterstock, Inc.

Hazard Insurance covers individuals and organizations against a variety of potential risk classes. A company can buy a fire policy or a flood policy, or wind damage, and so on, but it is more cost effective to buy general hazard insurance that protects against a variety of potential risks.

Hazard insurance covers individuals and organizations against a variety of potential risk classes such as fire, flood, wind damage, or earthquake.

© intoit/Shutterstock, Inc.

© FeyginFoto/Shutterstock, Inc.

Business insurance covers a company from the loss of business associated with the loss of assets or the interruption of business. It is a common practice for farmers to purchase crop insurance that provides a financial payback if there is no rain and the crops fail. This same type of insurance may protect a firm from destructive events such as hurricanes or tornadoes or even from employee theft.

Business insurance insures against loss of business activities or interruption of commerce.

Liability Insurance covers potential loss from law suits brought by business partners or customers or even by casual people who are near the place of business. For instance, in Omaha, Nebraska, in 2007, a worker cut down a tree on the property of an apartment building. The tree was old and in danger of falling during a storm, so the owner told his worker to cut it down. As he did so, the tree fell into the street and crushed a passing car and injured the driver. The resulting lawsuit was for actions that caused damage to personal property and personal injury.

© IvelinRadkov/Shutterstock, Inc.

Companies, who produce a product, must do so exercising care that the product, when used properly and as intended, will not cause injury. Not only that, but also companies must anticipate problems. Baby product companies that used to produce playpens with mesh sides did not anticipate babies falling and hooking a button in the mesh. Several babies chocked when this happened. Companies that produced folding baby strollers also had to anticipate that after months of wear the locking mechanism might wear out and allow the stroller to fold up with the infant inside.

OPEN FOR BUSINESS IN THE REAL WORLD

The sad fact is that most businesses will fail. Even businesses that have existed for a long time are at constant risk. Pontiac was an automobile brand for over a hundred years and Pan American Airlines was a leader in their industry. Montgomery Ward was a major retail department store. All are gone and the root cause is a failure on the part of management to recognize and deal with the ever-present risk to the company. The market place is constantly changing and businesses must change with it. That change is a risk in itself because the processes used today will not meet the demands of the market place in the future. There is an old adage; No one plans to fail, but many fail to plan.

Sometimes, success itself can breed failure. When a company comes to believe it has developed the perfect approach, the perfect process, it can become stagnant because they fail to recognize the need to evolve.

Chapter Summary

Virtually, every aspect of our lives involves risk. In business, the risk comes from four primary sources: poor management, the legal/regulatory environment, competition, and unlimited liability. Poor management risk is caused by the many functional areas with which a manager must deal, often without adequate knowledge in all areas. Legal/regulatory environment risk comes from the constantly changing body of laws and ordnances with which companies must comply. Competitive risk comes from the challenges brought by other companies in the same or similar industry. Unlimited liability creates risk by placing everything the owner owns at risk in the conduct of enterprise.

Companies can reduce risk by doing a careful SWOT analysis to evaluate their Strengths, Weaknesses, Opportunities, and Threats. Careful analysis and objective review of the environment allows firms to foresee risk and deal with it.

Risk can be avoided, reduced, accepted, or shared. Risk can be avoided by recognizing the threats and making adjustments to the business's plans or procedures. Risk can be reduced by careful operations and sound practices. Risk can be accepted and planned for when other options are not possible. Risk can be shared through insurance or partnership agreements.

Review Questions

1. What is risk and why is it some important to businesses?
2. What is market share?
3. What does it mean to self-insure?
4. Why can't you insure your elderly neighbor's life?
5. What is risk sharing?
6. What is meant by accepting risk?
7. What are the broad factors that lead to Border's Bookstore's closing?
8. What is the likelihood of a start-up business lasting 10 years?
9. What is the Legal/Regulatory Environment?
10. How can an SWOT analysis protect a company from risk?
11. How is a Weakness different from a Threat?
12. How is a Strength different from an Opportunity?

Discussion Questions

13. What kinds of business insurance policies are similar to what an individual would purchase for themselves and what kinds are unique to businesses?
14. Discuss the sources of risk
15. Discuss the techniques to reduce or deal with risk

Class Exercise

16. Select an organization, perhaps the one for which you work, or your college and do your own SWOT analysis of the enterprise.
    a. What Strengths, Weaknesses, Opportunities, and Threats did you identify?
    b. Do you think the organization is aware of them?
    c. What steps would you take to take advantage of the strengths and opportunities?
    d. What steps would you take to reduce the risk of the weaknesses and threats?

Key Terms

- Automobile insurance
- insurable risk
- Business insurance
- Hazard insurance
- Health care insurance
- legal/regulatory environment
- market share
- Pure risk
- Risk
- SWOT

Works Cited

Ovide, S. (2011, February 16). *Borders Books Bankruptcy: List of Closing Stores*. Retrieved January 27, 2015, from http://www.huffingtonpost.com/2011/02/16/borders-books-bankruptcy_n_824143.html

Shane, S. (2008, April 28). *Startup Failure Rates—The REAL Numbers*. Retrieved November 11, 2014, from http://smallbiztrends.com/2008/04/startup-failurerates.html

CHAPTER
18

Are You Open for Business?

LEARNING OBJECTIVES

1. Explain the steps to success in business.
2. Explain how customer service is so vital to success.
3. Identify causes of stress in the workplace.

© FooTToo/Shutterstock, Inc.

OPENING STORY

In 1955, General Motors board chairman Charlie Wilson said "What's good for General Motors is good for America" (Hewison, 2008). His point was that the car company was the expert on automobiles and they were in the best position to determine what Americans should and would drive. Besides, a large powerful company such as General Motors had the expertise to develop the cars that would lead the automotive world. Mr. Wilson was very wrong. Since that time, the company has been passed by Toyota as the world's largest, introduced an electric car in 1996 when gas was $1.28 a gallon and cancelled it in 2002 when gas was $4.00, and went into bankruptcy in 2008 while their chief American rival, Ford, managed to avoid any government involvement.

What was General Motor's mistake; not recognizing that it is the consumer that will determine what they want to drive, not GM. The company has had to discard several car companies, such as Olds-mobile and Pontiac, and regroup. Only when you understand the market, the industry, the customer, and yourself, are you really open for business.

© Linda Parton/Shutterstock, Inc.

INTRODUCTION

© LDprod/Shutterstock, Inc.

In a very real sense, we are all in business. Whether you own a business, work for someone else, work for a nonprofit, or are a self-employed independent contractor, you are conducting business. In every enterprise, you are working with and for a revenue stream and operating with expenses within a budget. Regardless of your role, you have not only the responsibility for doing your job but also the responsibility of helping to achieve the organizational goals and furthering the success of the firm. Working toward those goals requires knowledge and skills along with an attitude of personal accountability.

Succeeding also requires understanding customers, their needs, and what motivates them to want what you have to offer. It is way more complicated than just opening the door to let the customers in. They must want to come in and you must understand why or how to reach them and convince them if they do not.

SUCCEEDING IN BUSINESS

Whether you are the owner, executive, or middle manager, succeeding requires understanding the environment in which you operate. Entrepreneurs take the risk by putting their time and money into the enterprise from the start. Intrepreneurs take the risk by putting their time and careers into the company as an employee. Risk taking inside the company by managers is just as important for success as the risk taking by the owners. Keys to success include understanding your role, understanding the goals, hard work, and mental toughness.

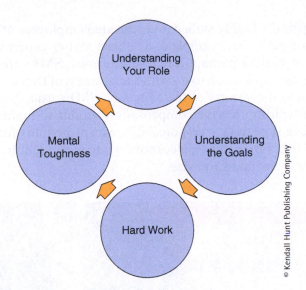

© Kendall Hunt Publishing Company

Understanding Your Role

Chapter 7 shows the organizational structure and the organization chart, which denotes the levels of management and chain of command. This gives a lot of information on the various functions of the company's management. A person's role in the company has a lot to do with where they are assigned and their assigned duties. In addition, workers must understand the expectations of their working relationships.

The employees are divided into three primary groups; the workers, the managers, and the **subject matter experts (SMEs)**.

Subject Matter Experts (SMEs)   typically highly skilled and educated employees with special skills needed by the company.

© Chuck Rausin/Shutterstock, Inc.

The **workers**, sometimes called individual contributors, have an assigned function with no supervisory responsibility. Workers may be relatively unskilled or highly skilled. They may perform mostly repetitive tasks or he or she may do something different every day. Workers may have a boss nearby and operate under close supervision or may be independent with little apparent supervision. The worker's role is primarily that of completing their assigned functions effectively and efficiently.

Workers   (sometimes called individual contributors) are people who have an assigned function with no supervisory responsibility.

SMEs are typically highly skilled and educated employees with special skills needed by the company. An example of a subject matter expert would be a corporate attorney, a pilot, or perhaps a college professor. **SME**s are skilled in fields that may or may not have much to do with the business of the company, but their role is important to the success of the company. SMEs usually operate without supervision and typically receive compensation similar to managers. SMEs do not normally have supervisory responsibility except perhaps for someone that works in their office. For instance, a corporate attorney might have a legal assistant, which he or she would supervise.

© Jerry Sliwowski/Shutterstock, Inc.

The subject matter expert's role is to provide their knowledge and experience at potentially several layers of management. Furthermore, they are expected to prevent business mistakes or improve operations by make suggestions based on their unique perspective. Companies may have these experts as part of their staff, keep them on retainer, or outsource their services as needed. For instance, business consultants are sometimes hire when a company runs into a particular problem or when a unique opportunity presents itself.

Managers are the decision makers of the company. There are often several layers of managers, which range from foreman; directly supervising the workers, to executives that make decisions for the overall company. Large companies may have many layers of middle managers between these two extremes. As noted in Chapter 5, there are many functions and assets in a company that need to be managed. Middle managers have direct reports, that is, people for whom they are the direct supervisors and for whom they perform an annual performance report or evaluation. Direct supervisors are also responsible for the actions of their subordinates. If someone that works for you messes up and costs the company money, then you, as their supervisor, may get into just as much trouble as the subordinate.

© Robert Kneschke/Shutterstock, Inc.

Managers   decision makers of the company. There are often several layers of managers, which range from foreman who directly supervise the workers, to executives who make decisions for the overall company.

This aspect of business —being liable for the mistakes or actions of others—is a crucial element in being a manager. The managers' role is not only to accomplish the organizational goals but also to do so through the efforts of others as well as himself or herself. Obviously, there is a limit on how much control over workers any manager has. Managers must thoroughly understand the functions for which they are responsible so they can properly supervise the work. They must also understand the people who work for them and the techniques of effective supervision.

Understanding the Goals

Lewis Carroll said "If you don't know where you are going, any road will get you there" (Think, 2015). To effectively manage, a person must know both where they are heading and where they are at the start. Companies will frequently publish sales goals or production target numbers. This gives the company a target to meet or surpass. However, it is important to understand not only the overall goal but also how each section and person must contribute to it. Not only that, it is important to realize achieving a sales goal may not be enough. A company can usually increase their sales by lowering price but that may reduce profit even as the sales goal is accomplished.

It's obvious that a sales manager plays a key role in reaching the company's sales goals. Another manager may have nothing to do with sales, but yet his or her actions may be vital for the success of the company. That is why once goals are established for the company, each level of management must break those goals down into unit-specific goals that then lead to actions to accomplish them. While one unit may try to increase sales, another unit might be responsible for holding down costs. Production targets may be met, but if the shipping department cannot get the products to the customer, the goals are not met. Every part of the company contributes to the overall success and it is necessary for each unit in the company to understand how they contribute, what their role is, and how it fits in the firm.

© Tuan_Azizi/Shutterstock, Inc.

To understand the starting point, companies use **control**; that is tracking the current position relative to the goals. Controlling work and production requires the manager to understand the work processes and how each step can be measured for quality. If a company waits until the end of a production process to do quality control checks, they may wind up discarding products. If quality is built in, by controlling the process to eliminate rejections at each step, production runs more smoothly, more quickly, and at less cost.

Control   tracking the current position relative to the goals.

Hard Work

"Hard work is the reward for hard work." This quote, which comes from many sources, reflects an understanding of the reward for working hard to apply oneself to the task of managing a business. For most people, there is a direct relationship between how hard they work and how much they succeed. It is important to understand that hard work does not always mean back-breaking physical labor. Hard work may mean sitting in an office

some people dream of **SUCCESS,** while others wake up and **work hard** at it.

© Mihai Maxim/Shutterstock, Inc.

© Vladimir Melnikov/Shutterstock, Inc.

all day, attending meetings, spending the day on the phone, crunching numbers, or checking results. When moving into management positions, the work becomes more mental and less physical. Although mental work may not have the impact on the body, there is frequently more stress with mental work than with physical efforts.

Especially when it comes to working hours, people that start their own business or go into management positions frequently wind up working far more hours than simply putting an eight hour shift working for someone else. Chapter 6 discussed different types of compensation. Most of the time, managers earn salaries and sometimes bonuses as their form of compensation. Receiving a salary has the benefit of providing a standard rate of pay regardless of the hours worked. Therefore, working fewer than 40 hs does not reduce the pay. However, working more than 40 hr also does

© Tom Wang/Shutterstock, Inc.

not increase the pay. Many managers working long hours are disappointed with their compensation when viewed as an hourly rate. One type of compensation not mentioned in Chapter 6 was profit. For the business owner, the pay is simply the profit of the company, in the case of proprietorships and partnerships. The profit may be great or nonexistent. Many owners will work long hours and earn nothing at all, especially in the beginning of their start-up.

Business managers at all levels are responsible for the success of the unit, section, or department he or she manages. If the success means doing more, then it is frequently the manager that must do more because with if hourly paid workers, work longer hours then that means higher labor costs. For a salaried manager, working longer hours does not mean higher labor costs.

Mental Toughness

© VisRad/Shutterstock, Inc.

Managers may have to be tough on the outside, but they certainly must be tough on the inside. Chapter 5 discussed different leadership styles, but in every case, the style must lead to accomplishing the business goals. Sometimes, business decisions are not clear, easy, or nice. Workers may need to be laid off because the business does not support the staff on board. Sometimes, people will need to be fired for wrong doing or poor performance; and these may be people you know well and respect.

© baranq/Shutterstock, Inc.

Both hiring and firing decisions are critical and tough. Many businesses boast that their people are their most important asset. In a company discussion about a new hire, this was amended to "The right people are our greatest asset. The wrong person may be our biggest liability" (Management Blog, 2015). Businesses need people to do work, and getting the right people to do it is important, difficult, and expensive. Business interview and selection processes are not very effective. One study by Price Waterhouse Coopers showed that about 25% of newly hired managers are fired or leave voluntarily within the first year (Erb, 2010). The standard interview in which several candidates are asked the same questions may in fact be one of the poorest ways to make hiring decisions. Whether a person will be productive over years is very difficult to determine in a 30- to 45-min interview.

© Andrey_Popov/Shutterstock, Inc.

Hiring decisions are not only difficult, they are also expensive. Recruiting and screening takes time and resources. Interviewing, selecting, and orienting newly hired people do as well. Management hiring typically costs a company between 8% and 20% of the person's first year salary (Erb, 2010). There are a variety of techniques to improve the process such as working interviews, probation periods, and personality tests. The more put into the process, however, the more expensive it is and results are still far from perfect.

© Lisa F. Young/Shutterstock, Inc.

Letting people go for low performance or wrong-doing is also a difficult task that can be emotionally draining for everyone involved. Not only that but lawsuits for wrong termination are fairly common. Most states are **employment at will** states, in which a person retains their position only at the will of the responsible manager. In other words, a person may be fired for any reason, or no reason, as long as it is not because they are in a protected group. There are legal exceptions, however, and careful documentation is very important. It is probably a good idea to keep records of every employee transgression. Sometimes what appear to be minor variations will eventually add up to large problems. Being a few minutes late a couple of time is not bad, but if that becomes a couple of times a week because nothing is done, it become a major problem. If small mistakes are not noted, there could be an implied approval of behaviors. That is not to say that every small mistake should result in counseling, but simply that a small not be made, for instance of someone being five minutes late for work. If it becomes necessary later to discuss it with the employee, it is far better to say "you have been late 6 times in the last two months", than to say "you have been late a lot lately."

> **Employment at will**   states in which a person retains their position only at the will of the responsible manager. In other words, a person may be fired for any reason, or no reason, as long as it is not because they are in a protected group.

© carpe89/Shutterstock, Inc.

Dealing with stress is another important aspect of mental toughness. Stress can be emotionally draining and can also have a physical impact on the body. **Stress** is "the psychological and physical state that results when the resources of the individual are not sufficient to cope with the demands and pressures of the situation" (Michie, 2002).

> **Stress**   psychological and physical state that results when the resources of the individual are not sufficient to cope with the demands and pressures of the situation.

Stress comes from many sources including:

1. Work overload
2. Poor working conditions
3. Time pressure
4. Physical danger
5. Role ambiguity or conflict
6. Office politics
7. Lack of job security

People may have many negative responses to stress including depression, irritability, fatigue, and anxiety. Positive responses to stress are also possible, such as motivation, heightened activity, and productivity. How a person acts under stress is very individualistic. Prolonged exposure to stress can cause physical symptoms such as headaches, depression, heart palpitations, and changes in mental and physical health.

© barang/Shutterstock, Inc.

Stressful situations are common at work. It is the ability to deal with stress or to operate under stressful environments that may determine success. Not everyone is cut out to be a manager even if they want to be one.

Successfully dealing with stress depends on the causes, but general techniques include getting plenty of rest, eating a healthy diet, exercise, and most importantly, addressing problems as soon as they develop instead of waiting for them to grow.

Another aspect of mental toughness is the ability to think on one's feet. Decision making is a deliberative process that employs distinct steps of gathering and evaluating information, careful study, making the decision, and following up to see how things are working. All that is fine when there is time for the process. Unfortunately, in business, sometimes decisions must be made on the spot with little or no time for checking facts. Experience brings with it the background for quick decision making.

Related to thinking on one's feet is the willingness and ability to live with the decisions. No matter how good a person is, sometimes he or she will get it wrong. There are many careers where these decisions can mean life or death. In business, most of the time it is about money, but it can also be the life or death of a contract or even a business.

People will make mistakes and businesses should be realistic about it. If a company is a "one mistake" place of work, they will stifle decision making as well as get rid of a lot of talented people. Basketball coach John Wooten said "If you're not making mistakes, then you're not doing anything" (Dachis, 2011). Managers who have become afraid of making mistakes because they see the negative consequences of errors will stop making decisions. If a person waits long enough to decide, sometimes the correct decision becomes obvious. However, waiting too long usually means waiting too long for it to do any good. If managers are not afraid of making mistakes, they will be more aggressive about making decisions. Although mistakes are not good, they are a learning opportunity.

© Ribah/Shutterstock, Inc.

CUSTOMER SERVICE

In an earlier chapter, we described value as a combination of price and quality. There is another element, however; customer service. **Customer service** is treating a customer the way they want to be treated. When people shop, they want value, and good customer service is part of that value.

Business owners and managers are in business to make a profit, not to satisfy customer needs. It does a company no good to spend all their potential profit making sure that the client is completely satisfied. Are this and the previous paragraph in conflict then? No, they are not. In any competitive industry, the customer will decide for himself or herself, what they value most. Some will look for the lowest price, some will look for the best quality, and some will look for the best customer service. Many will determine for themselves, what combination of those three are most important.

One way to provide customer depends on location and the convenience if offers. This can be done in many ways. For example, Enterprise Rental Car Company, picks up customers wherever they are instead of insisting the customer get to them to rent a car. This service is very useful for auto body shops that can partner with Enterprise to provide convenience for their customers.

Customer service   treating a customer the way they want to be treated.

© 360b/Shutterstock, Inc.

Many banks offer branches with later hours in grocery stores. The United Services Automobile Association (USAA) is an insurance company with legendary service that insures its customers, worldwide. Safelite Auto Glass will bring their automobile window repair and replacement business to wherever the customer is located, while the customer is at work, or even a grocery store parking lot.

Another customer service factor is offering money back guarantees or low price guarantees on merchandise or services. It is more expensive to attract new customers than it is to retain existing ones. Retaining customers provides a steady cash flow and saves money.

Customer service is to base it on time or speed. For example, Gallery Furniture in Houston has a reputation of delivering furniture the same day it is purchased. Even if you buy furniture right at closing time, they will deliver it in the middle of the night if necessary. As they say "Buy it tonight, sleep on it tonight." Other companies offer 24-hr service or 24-hr operating hours. For instance, 24-hr Fitness operates around the clock to provide a fitness center whenever a customer wants. Many businesses offer on-line transactions and technical support as their means of being "always open" to service the customer's needs.

© Maridav/Shutterstock, Inc.

Sometimes, good customer service is simply a smiling face or a cheerful attitude. When customers have a problem, they want a solution, but they also want that solution without an argument or hassle. Customers want to sense their business is appreciated. Many businesses frequently tell customers their business is valued. Simply saying so is part of getting that message across. However, after saying it, the business person then needs to show it in their deeds. Many businesses are now allowing customer service people to offer discounts or credits to appease clients with discounts or lower prices when a problem cannot be resolved or even when it is resolved but with considerable hassle delay.

© dotshock/Shutterstock, Inc.

Important to good customer service is understanding just who your customers are. It may seem natural to think of customers as external to the organization, but it may not be obvious who the customer really is. Research for instance has shown that men's underwear is normally bought, not by men, but by their wives or girlfriends. Women's underwear is bought by women, but so is men's underwear. However, there are times when the customer is internal. For instance, the accounting department's customers are the business executives. The accounting department rarely sees or deals with external customers. Their products are the financial reports produced for the business decision makers.

Customer feedback is a valuable source on how the product or service and the customer service are working. Companies can do telephone, email, or mailed surveys to gauge customer satisfaction. In general, if a product is sold and the customer is unhappy with the quality, he or she will return it. However, with a service, it usually cannot be returned. In those instances, the customer will probably not return—and will likely tell friends and others about the bad experience. Businesses that do not track their customer satisfaction will not know what is causing declining sales. Knowledge is power. If problems can be discovered and addressed quickly, losses can be minimized.

OPEN FOR BUSINESS IN THE REAL WORLD

A credit union in Omaha, Nebraska, was trying to expand their customer base and decided to open a new branch in an area they were not serving and to renovate the main branch to make it more attractive to their clients. Credit unions are different from banks in that they are not for profits and depositors are referred to as members because in a sense, the organization is member owned.

The year the credit union opened the new branch, the city had a record number of bank robberies and the new branch was built in an area of high crime. As a result, the credit union installed increased security that included a double-door system that allowed only one person into the lobby at a time and the second door would not open until the first one closed. An entering customer was briefly locked between two doors and people coming together had to enter separately. The credit union thought that the additional security would both help prevent robberies and give added confidence to their depositors. They were later unsettled to discover few people wanted to do business there because the customers felt like they were treated as criminals.

The credit union was proud of its renovation and pristine appearance at the main branch. However, members were much less impressed. Since credit unions are non-profit, net operating excess is returned to the members, or in this instance, spent on a nice work place for the employees instead of returned to the depositors in the form of higher interest on deposits and lower interest on loans.

In both cases, the credit union failed to appreciate the reaction of customers to their decisions.

Chapter Summary

Succeeding in business, whether an owner, manager, or subject matter expert, requires people to understand their role in accomplishing the mission of the company. They must also understand those goals and how their efforts fit into the big picture. Managers must be prepared to work hard as well. When people move into management, they tend to move away from physical work and toward mental work. This move often means working more hours and dealing with more problems. Success also requires mental toughness. This involves dealing with making difficult decision such as hiring and firing and dealing with stress that is common in all levels of management.

Succeeding also involves understanding the value of customer service. Customer service is about giving recognized value to customers. This can be done through time and speed, through convenient locations, through technical support, through low price guarantees, or through happy employees.

For all of this, knowledge is key. Customer satisfaction must be gauged to determine how the company is doing.

Review Questions

1. In your own words, define customer service
2. What are the keys to success in business?
3. What are some different ways to provide customer service?
4. How is time and speed a customer service factor?
5. What is an SME?
6. What are the three types of workers in a company?
7. If additional work is necessary, can't a manager just make a worker do it?
8. What percentage of business hires could be described as failures?
9. What are some sources of stress at work?
10. How can stress at work affect you physically?
11. What is meant by "thinking on your feet"?
12. What is meant by a "One mistake" company?

Discussion Questions

13. Discuss how understanding your role in the company, contributes to the overall success of the firm.
14. How is understanding your role in the business important to accomplishing the mission?
15. How do the roles differ among the three types of workers?
16. Why do managers put in more hours than hourly workers?
17. Discuss some ways of dealing with stress.

Key Terms

- control
- Customer service
- employment at will
- managers
- Stress
- subject matter experts, SMEs
- workers

Works Cited

Dachis, A. (2011, July 21). *Lifehacker*. Retrieved May 10, 2015, from http://lifehacker.com/5823441/if-youre-not-making-mistakes-then-youre-not-doing-anything

Erb, M. (2010, September 8). *Finding the Right Kind of People for your Workplace*. Retrieved May 10, 2015, from http://www.entrepreneur.com/article/217277.

Hewison, A. (2008, June 27). *INO.com Traders Blog*. Retrieved March 7, 2015, from http://www.ino.com/blog/2008/06/what-is-good-for-general-motors-is-good-for-america/#.VPtzHtE5BMs.

Management Blog. (2015). Retrieved May 10, 2015, from http://managementblog.org/2013/05/17/why-people-are-not-our-most-important-assett/

Michie, S. (2002). *The Causes and Management of Stress at Work*. Retrieved May 10, 2015, from http://oem.bmj.com/content/59/1/67.long

Thinkexist.com, Lewis Carroll quotes. Retrieved May 9, 2015, from http://thinkexist.com/quotation/if-you-don-t-know-where-you-are-going-any-road/533751.html

GLOSSARY

3PL (Third Party Logistics)   outside firms that provide various services to customers in support of supply chain management functions. 3PL functions usually include transportation, warehousing, storage, and materials handling, and can also include inventory management, order fulfillment, and customer service.

Absolute advantage   when one country (or a very few countries) enjoy a virtual monopoly on production of a specific product, ingredient, or resource.

Accept (or acceptance)   when the other party receives and agrees with what was offered by the other party and thus intends to enter a contract.

Accounting   information system that measures the business activities in financial terms, analyzes, classifies, summarizes, processes the information into reports (i.e., financial statements), and communicates it to decision makers.

Accounting cycle   process from the initial recognition of a business transaction (i.e., purchasing supplies on account) through preparing the financial statements.

Accounting equation   shows the relationship among assets, liabilities, and owner's equity. It is written as   Assets = Liabilities + Owner's Equity.

Action Plan   the actual work performed to meet the goals and objectives.

Actual product   is able to fulfill a customer's wants/desires, and thus, your product is seen as different from your competitors. (The second level of Total Product Concept; also called **expected product.)**

Affirmative action   provisions in the law to encourage and promote equal opportunity for all protected classes.

Affordable Care Act (ACA)   federal law that says employers with 50 or more full-time employees (defined as working 30+ hr per week) must provide a certain level of paid health care coverage for their employees.

"Age of majority"   when someone is no longer considered a minor (varies by state, but is usually 18 years of age).

American Institute for Certified Public Accountants (AICPA)   professional organization for CPA's and contributes to the development of accounting practices.

Americans with Disabilities Act (ADA)   federal law that prohibits discrimination against people with disabilities and requires that you provide "reasonable accommodations" so that the applicant/employee can perform the duties of the job.

Angel investors   private individuals with a high net worth who are looking for promising investments that have tremendous growth potential. (Traditionally, these were doctors or accountants looking for some place to put some of their money.)

Annual Percentage Rate (APR)   does not take into account compound interest and is the summation of the interest rate charged over a period of time also called the **periodic rate.**

Annual Percentage Yield (APY)   includes intra-year compound interest.

Annual report   summary of a company's activities and financial performance for the fiscal year.

Anticompetitive   ways that businesses conspire to harm consumers via actions that distort competitive forces in the marketplace.

Antitrust laws   the government's regulatory authority and police power to stop abuses by businesses and protect consumers.

APR   See Annual Percentage Rate.

APY   See Annual Percentage Yield.

ASEAN (Association of Southeast Asian Nations)   trading bloc formed to ease the movement of goods and labor across borders.

Assembly line   using interchangeable parts, automation or robotics, and rapid production.

Assets   economic resources which the company own such as cash, inventory, accounts receivable, and equipment.

Assign   legally giving your rights and obligations in a contract to another party.

Audit   official independent examination and verification of accounts, records, and financial statements.

Augmented product   additional things provided like a quality guarantee, an extended warranty, free installation, or easy financing to help make your product irresistible to those unsure of which product to finally select. (The third level of Total Product Concept.)

Authoritative style   of leadership; one in which the leader makes the decision, with or without checking with anyone.

Automobile insurance   insures against loss due to collusion as well as the potential medical costs and liability that may arises from an accident.

"Bait and switch"   when a business advertises a product at a very low price to lure customers, but in reality has no intention of selling the advertised product—or may not even have it—instead trying to push something more expensive on consumers who respond to the ad.

Balance of payment   the difference between all money coming into a country and out of a country.

Balance of trade   the total value of all exports of a country compared to its imports.

Balance sheet   shows the financial position of the business as of a specific date.

Bankruptcy   situation where companies or individuals owe more money than they are worth and cannot continue making payments on their debts.

Bar-code scanning   technology that provides information on where goods are in the flow from raw materials to finished products if items are scanned by electronic readers.

Barriers to entry   obstacles that can keep firms out of any market, such as government regulations or patents.

BCG Matrix (Boston Consulting Group Matrix)   chart that visually represents products which are "high market share" and "high market growth" during the Product Life Cycle in a way so that people can actually compare all of the products at the same time.

Behavior   dividing potential customers by their buying habits, spending patterns, and other similar factors.

Benefits   non-monetary compensation. Dividing people by what they want most from the product, such as convenience, quality, thrift, or luxury.

Biodegradable   when the "entire product or package will completely break down and return to nature within a reasonably short period of time after customary disposal" . . . which is defined by the FTC to be within one year.

Bill of lading   an additional document given from the seller to the shipper of the goods showing details of the shipment, such as description, quantity, destination, and conditions of transport.

"birdy back"   transportation technology that allows cargo containers to be loaded onto airplane transports.

Bonded   you have deposited a certain amount of money with a recognized authority which will pay out cash to any of your customers in the event that you are not able to complete a job as promised, in this way ensuring that the customer is "made whole" and not left with unfinished repair work.

Bonds   an investment of lending money for a specific length of receiving interest over the time period and principal paid at the end of the investment period.

Bonus   special pay for certain circumstances.

Brainstorm   throwing out ideas at others in the group until something silly is refined into something that seems worthwhile.

Brand   distinctive name or other characteristic of a product.

Breach of contract   if one side fails to perform as promised in a contract.

Break even   the level of sales that must occur for the company to realize any profits.

Break even point (BEP)   the number of units of product that must be sold to realize any profits.

Bribe   any money or other incentive given to an individual to influence his or her behavior.

BRIC   the emerging economies of Brazil, Russia, India, and China.

Bundle   including something extra in a package, usually an additional item or sample to increase value.

Bureau of Worker's Compensation (BWC)   programs at the federal and state level to assist employees who may be injured on the job by offering compensation and care.

Business   is an organized effort intended to earn a profit.

Business cycles   general swings in business activity, moving from Expansion to Peak to Contraction and Tough during different phases of the cycle, then repeating.

Business insurance   insures against loss of business activities or interruption of commerce.

Business intelligence   information obtained by looking on the internet, scouring industry publications, attending trade shows, reading corporate annual reports, and pursuing other avenues of data collection.

Business law   the study of the regulations and rules companies must follow to comply with various federal, state, and local statutes put in place by governments at all levels.

Business plan   a written document that states a business' goals and how they will be achieved with details about your marketing, finance, management, and so on.

Business Process Outsourcing (BPO)   new cross-functional approach for outsourcing alliances, with an emphasis on horizontal integration across your organization and all of these partners, which leads to efficiency, competitive advantage, and strategic market opportunities not available alone.

Business-to-Business (B2B)   the industrial market and all the businesses (and individuals) that buy products to re-sell, as components for making goods, or for other business uses.

Business-to-Consumer (B2C)   the consumer market and all individuals and households that buy products for personal use.

"CAN-SPAM" Rule   national rule providing establishment of a list of consumer provided email addresses that cannot receive unsolicited emails, thus designed to prevent marketers from sending emails in bulk to random people in the hopes of obtaining business or other responses.

Capacity   legal ability to enter a contract because a person is not a minor nor mentally ill.

Capital   is money or the things money can buy, like machines and buildings, which are used in the production of goods and services. The initial money used to start an investment.

Capital gain   profit from selling stock at a price about the cost.

Capitalist economic system   when private people own and control the resources and other means of production, making individual decisions about what to make and how much to produce.

Cash cow   BCG matrix quadrant that is equivalent to product life cycle "Maturity."

Certified public accountant (CPA)   licensed accountant who serves the general public and has passed a national accounting exam.

Chain of Command   the flow of authority within the organizations.

Chapter 7   a liquidation bankruptcy, where a trustee is appointed to sell off your assets and use that money to satisfy creditors to whatever extent possible.

Chapter 11   a reorganization bankruptcy, which stops any creditor actions while the business submits a repayment plan to the court within 120 days. (This can be voluntary or as a response from an attempted forced bankruptcy.)

Chapter 13   a bankruptcy that allows for an adjustment of debts, where a person who still has a regular income might decide to enter a payment plan to get out debt after certain amounts have been reduced via the court's bankruptcy proceedings.

Chief Information Officer (CIO)   senior IT person in the company.

Child labor   worker defined under FLSA as anyone under the age of 14 and thus they may not work (except on farms or when self-employed, such as models or delivering papers).

Civil Rights Act of 1964   law that prohibits discrimination on the basis of race, color, religion, sex or national origin for employment, education, and access to public facilities (including businesses).

Clayton Act   law that prevents companies from joining forces in circumstances where doing so would limit competition or consumer choice.

Cloud computing   uses off-site mass storage servers that provide access and security.

Code of ethics   guideline for an organization's staff to follow and help understand what are right and wrong behaviors.

Collusion   businesses working together to set prices higher than they otherwise could by simply reacting to market forces.

Colonial Period   was a time of small towns with a few small businesses and mostly agriculture.

Commercial banks   financial institution that receives deposits and lends money.

Commercialization   final product phase such that it's ready to be sold.

Common market   when a regional group of countries agree to coordinate laws and trading rules, have no internal tariffs, and have common external tariffs, if necessary.

Common stock   is the most common form of shares, equity in a corporation that includes voting dividends rights.

Commission   pay based on a percentage of sales.

Communist economic system   when the government owns the resources and decides how to allocate them, with a central authority making all production decisions for the entire economy.

Communication   informing and motivating customers, raising their awareness of your products or services and the reasons that yours are better.

Comparative advantage   concept where each country should make and sell goods that it produces more efficientlyand then buy the other goods and services it needs from other countries.

Compensation   pay for work.

Compensatory damages   an amount determined by the court to make up for any losses incurred by the injured party.

Competitive advantage   being able to deliver products or services that have better features or at a lower cost than other companies so you can charge a lower price.

Competitive differentiation   combining the company's strengths and seizing opportunities to develop approaches that set them apart from the competition.

Competitive firm   company without market power because it has output that is small compared to the entire marketplace, and as such, its output decisions do not have a significant impact on market prices.

Compliance-based ethics   approach by firms, government agencies, and regulators alike to prevent unlawful or unethical behavior.

Computer hardware   can consist of desk top and lap top computers, notebooks, and often today, tablets or smart cell phones. Each of these is a physical component that gives the user access into the network.

Computer networks   link computers and computing devices to allow sharing of information, documents, and communications.

Computer software   provides the instructions for the hardware to perform its function.

Concept testing   where consumers are shown products at various stages of completion so that companies can get feedback to hone their approach.

Conflict of interest   action taken that benefits someone that might not have benefited had someone else taken the action.

Conglomerate merger   When companies that have little relationship or common interest combine forces.

Consideration   something of value given by the parties for entering into the contract.

Conservatism principle   requires when uncertainties exist in regards to accounting procedures, the procedure which will least likely overstate assets or income must be applied.

Consistency principle   mandates that businesses must use the same accounting procedures and methods from year to year.

Consumer Price Index (CPI)   government index that measures the fixed cost of a market basket of goods and services used by consumers (such as food, transportation, energy, andhousing).

Contingency Planning   what planning is done to anticipate problems and the actions to take when they occur.

Contract   a legally binding agreement or promise.

Contract manufacturing   when additional facilities are hired to produce goods for you and put your name or brand on them.

Control   tracking the current position relative to the goals.

Convenience   having your products and services available where (and when) your customers need them.

Convenience good   product consumers can readily buy on impulse (such as candy).

Cooperatives   or Co-ops as they are sometimes called, are actually separate businesses, but act as a single business in cooperation with each other.

Copeland Anti–Kickback Act   the specific law that applies to federally funded projects for construction of other public works.

COPPA (Children's Online Privacy Protection Act)   a law to protect children under 13 from online predators.

Copyright   printed matter, software, and so on, that is protected under the law from unauthorized duplication since it was designated as such by the owner placing a "©" on the matter. (Full protection under the law is only guaranteed by registration with appropriate U.S. government agency.)

Core product   basic product function that fulfills a customer's needs. (The first level of Total Product Concept.)

Corporate responsibility   acting in the best interest of society.

Corporation   a business that is incorporated and is separate from its owners.

Corrective action   a series of actions taken to improve substandard performance.

Cost   the expense you incur to make something.

Cost Inflation   increases in prices are passed along to consumers (e.g., businesses raising prices to customers to recoup the money spent on rising gas prices).

Cost, Insurance, Freight (CIF)   shipping designation meaning that the seller will be responsible for the cost of insurance and freight charges to deliver the goods to a port city the buyer designates, usually on the coast of the home country or where buyer need the goods to be sent (e.g., CIF and L.A.).

Cost plus   pricing method that takes the actual total costs incurred to make the product and then adds a profit margin.

Cost principle   (historical cost) stipulates that assets and services are recorded at their actual cost—what you paid for it.

Cross-functional team   where members from different departments come together for a period of time.

Crowd funding   process whereby people interested in a product can pledge money to get it developed and then receive the item when finished. (Essentially, these people are pre-ordering. Look for more changes in the future though.)

Custom production   the method by which companies produce similar products but which are specifically designed and produced to meet customer-driven needs.

Customer-focused   finding out and then fulfilling customers' needs, wants/desires, and expectations.

Customer Service   treating a customer the way they want to be treated.

Customer Relationship Management (CRM)   business discipline that says businesses should learn as much as possible about their customers, then direct all of the companies' efforts and resources toward satisfying what the customers want.

Cycle time   the time needed to complete production of an item or produce output from the time the order is received until the item can be shipped to the customer.

Cyclical unemployment   when people are out of work caused by a downturn in the business cycle.

Damages   money paid by the party responsible for the breach to the injured party.

Data   is a compilation of facts and figures.

Database Managers or Network Specialists   work with and manage the information technology system in the company.

Decline   the fourth stage of the Product life Cycle when products no longer enjoy high market share or growth potential, and profits are now hard to come by. New entrants try to chase some profits at the end of the Maturity stage, but more players in the market have driven down economic profit at or near zero. (BCG Matrix equivalent is "Dog.")

Delegate   to assign duties to other people.

Delegated leadership   also known as Laissez Faire or free-rein leadership, is a style that moves the decision making and leadership down the levels of management.

Demand   the willingness and *ability* to buy something at a given price.

Demand curve   economics graph showing the amount of a particular good or service people would desire to buy at various prices.

Demand inflation   too much money chasing too few goods (e.g., businesses charging more for an item that is very popular but in short supply).

Demand schedule   a chart listing the survey results of asking lots of people how much they would be willing (and able) to buy at various prices, used to construct a demand curve line.

Demography   dividing people by gender, age, race, income levels, household size, and many other personal characteristics.

Determinants of demand   events or situations that have the power to shift the demand curve and affect prices in the marketplace (e.g., the total number of buyers in the marketplace, the income level of people involved, substitutes that are available, expectations buyers have, and tastes or desires of buyers in the marketplace).

Determinants of supply   events or situations that have the power to shift the supply curve and affect prices or quantities in the marketplace (e.g., the total number of sellers in the marketplace, the cost of inputs or factors of production, technological advances, substitutes that are available, expectations in the marketplace, and taxes or subsidies for businesses).

Development   broader, overall skills that help make a person more valuable in general.

Discharged   when a debt is cancelled and does not survive the bankruptcy. (Some debts, such as federal student loans, cannot be discharged and thus are still owed.)

Discounting   receiving less than face value.

Distribution channels   using various marketing intermediaries to get products from the manufacturer or producer to the consumer or end user.

Distribution warehouse   a facility designed for short-term storage such that finished goods, components, parts, raw materials, and so on, can be redirected easily to their final destination.

Distinctiveness   any product design element that contributes to making a product unique to set it apart from the competition and then using that product design or feature as a path to differentiation.

Distributed product development   where regional managers are permitted to sell authorized variations of established products. These variations would be based on local preferences.

Diversity   differences that exist in race, gender, culture age, national origin, and many other groupings.

Dividends   profits that the company allocates to its shareholders.

"Do Not Call" Registry   national list established where consumers can submit phone numbers which telemarketers are prohibited from calling under any circumstances, or risk facing a fine and other penalties.

Dog   BCG Matrix quadrant that is equivalent to product life cycle "Decline."

Drop ship   selling products in other markets, such that they are sent directly to your customers from the manufacturer, instead of bringing items all the way to the United States for processing, repackaging, and sending the goods off again to a foreign land.

Dual mandate   manage a monetary policy within the Federal Reserve System that maximizes employment and maintains the stability of prices for goods and services.

Due diligence   research into the past of a person or company, verifying the accuracy of information presented and also especially looking for issues that involves potential liability from lawsuits for defects or negligence or other wrong-doing.

Dumping   when products are sold in a foreign country for a lower price than they are sold in the domestic market.

Dynamic pricing   using info from databases and cookies to offer different prices to people based on preferences and past buying habits.

Early adopters   people who want to be first to buy new products to get the latest technology and will often help spread the word.

e-crime   the deliberate theft or destruction of a company's information.

Economic growth   expansion or increase in business activity, important for a country to grow and prosper, increase the wealth of citizens and businesses, and create jobs for a growing population.

Economic profit   the minimum amount of money needed to stay in business.

Economics   the study of the allocation of resources.

Effective communication   moves the right message through the right channels at the right speed.

Elevator pitch   a 30-s or 1-min summation about why someone should want to do business with a company or an individual. (The name comes from imagining that a person gets lucky one day and rides the same elevator as an important potential client or a key new investor.)

Employee benefits   additional compensation to entice workers to join the company and keep morale high while they work there, including things such as sick leave, vacation time, health insurance, retirement programs, and more.

Employee Stock Option Plans (ESOP)   these plans give employees of the company the opportunity to buy stock in the company, often at a discount.

Employment at will   states in which a person retains their position only at the will of the responsible manager. In other words, a person may be fired for any reason, or no reason, as long as it is not because they are in a protected group.

Empowerment   responsibility and authority in the hands of workers so they can use their own judgment to accomplish assigned tasks.

Enterprise zones   places designated by local government with low or abated taxes in those areas to encourage development there.

Entity concept   requires that the business activities must be separate from the owner's personal transactions and all other entities.

Entrepreneurs   people who risk their time and money to start a business.

Entrepreneurship   is the risking of time and money by a business owner to set up and operate a for profit business.

Enterprise Resource Planning (ERP)   software that allows companies to integrate business functions using shared data at every stage of production, helping everyone share in the information flow.

Environmental Protection Agency's (EPA)   federal, state, and local agencies that establish rules with regard to land usage, waste disposal, pollution, and handling of hazardous materials.

Equal Employment Opportunity Act (EEOA) law that applies to private employers, state and local governments, educational institutions, employment agencies, and labor organizations. (The provisions of EEOA added "disability" and "age" to the list of protected classes covered by original Civil Rights Act.)

Equal Employment Opportunity Commission (EEOC) agency established by EEOA to investigate and enforce alleged violations.

Equilibrium point where supply and curve and demand curve intersect and supply equals demand at the equilibrium quantity (Qe) and the equilibrium price (Pe).

Ethical behavior how you act when no one is watching.

Ethical dilemma when options are not clear-cut from an ethical perspective.

Ethical reasoning the process of assessing facts and acting with the best intentions.

Ethics doing the right thing.

Ethnocentricity trying to replicate things in a foreign country the same way you do them domestically because you think that you know what's best or that your culture is superior.

European Union (EU) common market formed by various European countries.

Exchange rate the price of one country's currency relative to another country's currency.

Exclusive a retail distribution strategy where companies will decide on only one location per area (e.g., vehicles or luxury watches).

Executive coaching conducted with senior executives where there is a belief that fine-tuned management skills are necessary.

Executive support system designed to provide reports and graph information in summary form to upper levels of management.

Expected product is able to fulfill a customer's wants/desires, and thus your product is seen as different from your competitors. (The second level of Total Product Concept; also called **actual product**.)

Expenses money paid or the cost incurred in the sale or delivery of goods and services during the normal operation of business activities. Another way of putting it, expenses is the cost of doing business.

Export selling goods to a foreign country.

Exporting products sold outside of the United States, by selling and shipping them directly to customers, trading companies, or other entities overseas.

Express contract contract that clearly spells out the terms and obligations of each person or entity.

Express warranty guarantee offered (usually in writing) from a seller to prospective buyers, spelling out any guarantees or policies you have with regard to repairing or replacing the product or parts for a specified period of time.

External users investors, creditors, federal government, and customers—rely on the financial statements in evaluating the profitability and liquidity of the business.

Externalities items that have costs (or benefits) to third parties, and not to the people who produce or consume them, and thus we cannot rely on the market because people will overproduce goods where they retain the benefit but the cost is shifted to other people (e.g., pollution).

Face value the amount written on the note, check, and so on.

Factor person or business who will discount the value of the money owed based on credit risk, industry, and any conditions in the purchase order since the factor typically assumes all risks of return, and so on.

Factors of Production   Land/Natural Resources, Labor, Capital, and Knowledge/Entrepreneurship; the factors necessary for the production of any good or service.

Factor mobility   factors of production move to where they can be utilized best (so for example, labor-intensive production moves to countries with large pools of low-cost labor and capital intensive production moves to countries with more capital).

Factors of production   all of the inputs necessary to make a good or provide a service. There are four basic categories used   land/resources, labor, capital, and knowledge/entrepreneurship.

Fair Labor Standards Act of 1938 (FLSA)   federal law that prohibits discrimination in pay and has been amended over the years to address additional topics such as minimum wage, overtime pay, child labor laws, and other issues.

Family and Medical Leave Act (FMLA)   federal law which provides 12 weeks of unpaid leave for workers, during which time employers must keep an employee's job open.

Favorable balance of payments   when more money is coming in to a country.

Federal Deposit Insurance Corporation (FDIC)   promotes public confidence by insuring customer deposits in banks and thrift institutions up to $250,000 per deposit per customer.

Federal funds rate   the rate financial institutions use to charge each other loans.

Federal Reserve Board ("The Fed")   agency responsible for implementing U.S. monetary policy and regulating commercial banks, among other things.

Federal Reserve System   the central bank of the United States responsible for regulating the banking industry.

Federal Tax Identification Number (TIN)   tax number assigned by the IRS to your business that is a corporation, LLC, or other entity that is separate from you personally. (This is also sometimes called an Employer Identification Number . . . EIN.)

Federal Trade Commission (FTC)   an agency of the U.S. federal government charged with monitoring business and advertising activity, since the public good depends on honest and true claims. The FTC's mission is to promote competition, protect consumers from anti-competitive mergers, and stop other unfair business practices.

Federal Trade Commission Act   law which set up the FTC as an agency watchdog to study industries, monitor behavior, establish ongoing rules, and engage in enforcement.

FERPA   Family Educational and Privacy Act.

Financial accounting   generates financial statements in accordance with generally accepted accounting principles that summarize the financial performance of the business.

Financial Accounting Standards Board (FASB)   the governing organization that develops and issues rules for *generally accepted accounting principles* and standards in the United States.

Financial management   the process of engaging in activities to obtain money to effectively and efficiently use it to achieve the goals and objectives of the business.

Financial manager   develops and manages the financial plan for the business and is responsible for identifying ways for securing needed capital.

Financial market   the means of exchange in which financial securities, such as stocks and bonds, metals, and agricultural goods, can be traded at a particular value.

Financial position   refers to the resources that belong to the company (assets), and the creditors' equities (liabilities) and owner's equities against those resources at a specific point in time.

Financial Services Modernization Banking Act of 1999   this allowed banks to establish one-stop financial services where customers can buy and sell securities and purchase insurance coverage.

Financial system   the process of the flow of money from the saves to the borrowers.

Firewall   or security system limits access into the internet.

Fiscal policy   the government's plan for spending, taxation, and debt management.

"Fishy back"   transportation technology that allows cargo containers to be loaded onto ocean vessels.

Fixed costs (FC)   those costs that *DO NOT* change no matter how many units are sold. (Fixed costs include things such as rent, equipment, executive salaries, and any R&D money.)

Fixed position layout   type of design is used for operations in a building or facility in which there is no movement of the product.

Flat organization   a relatively short and wide organizational chart.

Flexible production   method by which companies use advanced robotics and computer software to build different products on the same assembly line.

Flextime   a system of required hours with flexible hours around them.

Focus group   when a group of potential customers are brought into a room where they are shown product concepts or perhaps a finished prototype.

Foreign Corrupt Practices Act   law that specifically prohibits any U.S. citizen or other person acting on behalf of a U.S. company in a foreign country from offering anything of value (cash or non-cash items) to a foreign public official to obtain business, retain business, or direct business to specific entities or further to have that official perform duties inconsistent with local laws.

Foreign Direct Investment (FDI)   when a company has a physical presence in another country, from a simple branch office on foreign soil from which a sales force operates, to a large manufacturing facility making product for the locals to buy.

Foreign distributors   companies who sign on to represent a product in a foreign market and may actually purchase a small amount of product to have it readily available to ship to customers.

Form I-9, Employment Eligibility Verification   federal form to verify that each new employee is legally eligible to work in the United States.

Form utility   when you change the form of materials into something, consumers or businesses can use. (Sometimes services use the term **task utility**.)

Four "P's" of Marketing   Product, Price, Place, Promotion.

"Four Tigers"   the economies of Hong Kohn, Taiwan, South Korea, and Singapore.

Franchise   a business where the small business owner ("**franchisee**") pays a fee to a larger corporation ("**franchisor**") for the right to sell that company's branded products or services in a given territory.

Franchise agreement   a special arrangement with a popular service or product where you license the name, your business know-how, and so on, to a foreign company who will sell your product or service in another market in exchange for a percentage of the profits, but you maintain control over final say for the marketing and other aspects of the business.

Franchisee   a person who buys and runs a franchise business in exchange for paying fee(s).

Franchisor   a business that licenses the right to a franchisee, allowing that person to sell the company's branded products or services in a given territory.

Freedom of choice   right that allow individuals to decide for themselves what they want to do for a living and to start and own their own business if that is their choice, derived from a basic right in the legal system of the U.S.

Free on Board (FOB)   shipping designation meaning that the seller will only deliver the goods to a terminal from which the goods can be shipped out of the seller's home country (e.g., FOB and Taiwan).

Free trade   the movement of goods and services across international borders without economic of political barriers.

Freight forwarder   transportation specialist that combines many small shipments into one larger shipment that can fill a standard ocean container.

Frictional unemployment   when someone is out of work if they have leave one job and are looking for another.

Full employment   economic goal of having most citizens who want a job able to find one, with about 5% unemployment as an acceptable rate for those job seekers in a state of flux in their circumstances.

Functional structure   is one that is set up so people doing the same type of job are in divisions working together.

GATT, the General Agreement on Tariffs and Trade   agreement that serves as a framework to promote free trade among member countries. All signatories agree to reduce trade restrictions and work to eliminate tariffs or quotas for most goods.

General journal   book of original entry to record business transactions in chronological order.

General ledger   collection of all the individual accounts used by a business to form a book.

General Partnership   In a general partnership, all partnerships have full ownership and authority.

Generally Accepted Accounting Principles (GAAP)   the rules, guidelines, and standards used by accountants in the preparation of any financial statements.

Geographic structure   aligns people based on physical location instead of function.

Geography   dividing potential customers by physical location, such as region of the country, or maybe group potential markets by city population size.

Glass Steagall Act of 1933   prohibited banks from owning full-service brokerage firms.

Global supply chain   movement of raw materials, parts & components, and finished goods throughout all stages or production, distribution, and sale of products (or services) around the world.

Goals   the company's overall plans of what they want to achieve.

Going concern assumption   accountants assume that the business (entity) will remain in operation for the foreseeable future.

Going Private   An individual or small group buying the shares of a corporation and returning it to a privately held company.

Going Public   A corporation offering shares of stock to the public for the first time.

Golden rule   do onto others as you would have them do onto you or treat others as they would want you to treat them.

Goods   are tangible things we can hold or see.

Gross Domestic Product (GDP)   measurement of growth which is the total market value of all goods and services produced in the country.

Growth   the second stage of the Product Life Cycle when products have made the leap into general acceptance by the public and are now enjoying tremendous sales. Market share is high and profits are good if the product is in a fast-growing industry. Not every product is able to "cross the chasm" from Introduction to Growth. (BCG Matrix equivalent is "Star.")

H–1B specialty visas   U.S. entrance documents available for certain highly skilled occupations.

Hazard insurance   covers individuals and organizations against a variety of potential risk classes such as fire, flood, wind damage, or earthquake.

Health care insurance   cover medical expenses of employees and sometimes their families.

HIPPA   Health Information Portability and Accountability Act.

Horizontal integration   several firms working together to share resources at the same stage of production, such as partnering with a foreign trading company.

Horizontal merger   When competing companies working at the same level in the industry combine forces.

Hostile Environment   sexual harassment situation where lewd conduct or remarks are tolerated or encouraged.

Hostile Takeover   When a company is acquired or forced to merge, against the wishes of the current owners or managers.

Human Resource Functions   Forecasting, recruiting, selection, training and developing, retain and motivate, appraise, and corrective action.

Immigration and Nationality Act (INA)   federal law that allows you to hire foreign workers on a temporary or permanent basis for certain types of work.

Implied contract   contract where the actions of the parties are interpreted by custom or aw to obligate them.

Implied warranty   guarantee given by law from a seller to the buyer that the product (or service) can be used for its intended purpose.

Import   buying goods from a foreign country.

Inbound logistics   any raw materials, parts, goods, and so on, that you receive into your facility for the purpose of using, modifying, storing, or distributing those items.

Income Statement   summarizes for the fiscal year the firm's performance in terms of generating revenues and incurring expenses.

Incubators   business help provided by a larger corporation (or government entity) designed to provide low-cost space, available services, management help, and other types of advice to companies who are just getting started.

Independent Contractors   A company that consists of a single person.

Industrial Entrepreneurs   Individual risk takers who started business enterprises in the late 1800s that continued advances in technology which increased demand from consumers and brought opportunities for large business to develop, especially in steel, oil and automobiles.

Industrial Revolution   an era beginning in the middle of the 1700s which changed the nature of work as business owners brought together groups of unskilled or semi-skilled workers to mass produce consumer goods.

Initial Public Offering   The first offering of a typically large number of shares of stock to the public.

Inflation   measurement of prices which shows the general increase in the overall level of prices for goods or services.

Information   is useful correlated data that can inform or allow decision making.

Information system   way to collect the data and archive it and compare it or manipulate it to provide ready access to decision makers when they need it.

Information utility   gives point-of-sale marketing materials to businesses or consumers to help close the sale (e.g., brochures, displays, and samples).

Interest   the bank's charge at a particular rate for loaning the customer money.

Intrapreneur   person with the creative freedom to work on projects, but within the safer environment of a large company that can provide resources—and a regular pay check.

Introduction   the first stage of the Product Life Cycle when products are made available to the public. Companies try their best to market these new products, but it takes a special kind of attention to nurture these—and often more direct contact with potential users. At this stage, companies are spending lots of money trying to realize the product's full potential. (BCG Matrix equivalent is "Question Mark.")

Insolvent   state of a company (or individual) when it owes out more money than it has in assets or income.

Insurable risk   for an asset to be insurable, it must have a predictable loss possibility, have a measurable value, the lost must be accidental, and in a fixed geographical area.

Insured   an additional protection for yourself and your company should anyone be injured while you are working on an assignment, a job, or any other contracted work such that the insurance company will pay out any valid claims resulting from covered incidents.

Integrity-based ethics   approach where an organization communicates its guiding principles and values and has a culture of supporting ethically responsible behavior.

Intellectual Property (IP)   copyrights, trademarks, and patents owned as intangible assets and covered by specific laws.

Intensive   retail distribution strategy where companies will sell to anyone and try to be everywhere (e.g., candy or beverages).

Intermediaries   middlemen who assist in the movement of goods and add value by providing transportation, storage, and other services.

Intermodal   using a combination of shipping methods (water/ocean, train/rail, truck/over-the-road, and air) both because of where goods are located or need to go and also to obtain the best total shipping price.

Internal users   people inside the company—managers and employees—who use make informed decisions to achieve the company's goals and are charged with making the company profitable.

International Financial Reporting Standards (IFRS)   a set of global accounting standards that are comprehensive, high quality, understandable, enforceable, and globally accepted.

Intranet or network   ties the various sub-systems into an integrated whole using telecommunications.

Investing   a way to commit money to venture with the expectation of obtaining a profit.

Invisible hand   the constant, automatic adjustments of quantity and price balancing supply and demand as hoards of individual people and companies act in their own self-interest as they compete in the marketplace.

IPO   first time offerings of a security are called initial public offerings.

Job description   describes the key duties of the role the new hire will perform.

Job specifications   shows the critical and preferred skills necessary to succeed and therefore necessary for the search for candidates.

Joint Ventures   A combining of separate businesses is a Joint Venture, which combines the activities of two or more businesses acting as a single company for a specific project or period of time. A formal arrangement where two or more companies work together for a common purpose, with each performing a defined role, such as to share technology, spread risk for research and development (R&D), or focus on specializations.

Journalizing   process of recording every business transaction in a journal.

Just-in-time systems   inventory method used so that components, materials, and even finished goods are received just as needed for production and distribution.

Kickback   any money (or other thing of value) paid to an individual or a business in exchange for granting a contract, placing an order, and so on.

Knowledge   The skill required as a factor of production to maximize innovation and efficiently use the other factors of production to increase output or productivity.

Knowledge/Entrepreneurship   The most important factor of production, since it combines skill with risk-taking to maximize innovation and efficiently use the other factors of production to increase output or productivity.

Labor   is the human physical or mental effort used in the production of goods and services.

Labor unions   organized labor groups that work to protect the rights of workers.

Land   A factor of production which concerns use of space, real estate, and the natural resources contained below the earth.

Lawful   legal purpose for a contract.

Lay off   a large-scale termination of employees for causes other than their individual performance.

Leadership   motivating people, the human resources, to want to achieve those organizational goals.

Legal/regulatory environment   the body of laws and regulations in which a company operates.

Letter of credit   document whereby an international bank releases money from buyer's account to the seller once it has been confirmed that all conditions of the sale have been fulfilled.

Liabilities   the obligations (debts) that the business owes to others (creditors) such as accounts payable, notes payable, unearned revenue.

Liability   when each party is responsible for fulfilling his or her pledge(s) under the contract. The obligations (debts) that the business owes to others (creditors) such as accounts payable, notes payable, unearned revenue.

Liable   when it's determined that a responsible party is at fault for an injury, breach of contract, and so on.

License   the state's acknowledgment that you have demonstrated a minimum level of competence either through passing a test, providing educational credentials, or in any number of other ways that vary by state and/or by profession.

Licensing   contractually allowing foreign manufacturers to make and distribute your products in their local market in exchange for paying a royalty.

Limited Liability Company   A type of ownership that limits the liability of the owner to the amount of his or her investment.

Limited Partnerships   In a limited partnership, the business has one or more General Partners who have unlimited liability and one or more limited partners who have a liability equal to their investment.

Line authority   is operational or functional authority; that is, authority that is directly in line with the operation or function of the organization.

Liquidated damages   an amount agreed to beforehand and written into the contract.

Liquidity   the ability to quickly convert assets into useable cash with little or no loss in value.

Local Area Network (LAN)   link the various computers in a single facility or area.

Lockout   baring the employees from working is a similar tool, used to deny employees the right to work.

Logistics   planning, coordinating, managing, and controlling the movement of all aspects of goods (or services), including all related information flows during the entire process.

Lower of cost or market   if the market value of the inventory is less than cost, an adjustment must be recorded to bring the inventory down to market value.

Macroeconomics   the aggregate economic activity of all people and businesses in the entire country as a whole.

Management   the accomplishment of organizational goals, using the resources available.

Management information system or Decision Support System   provide reports to several levels of management within the organization.

Management support system   help make decision making easier by providing information in the form of reports and or graphs that are easy to read and encapsulate necessary information.

Managerial accounting   focuses on the preparation of documents, such as short- and long-term budgets, cost reports, and incremental analysis for capital purchase decisions for use by people inside the company.

Managers   decision makers of the company. There are often several layers of managers, which range from foreman who directly supervise the workers, to executives who make decisions for the overall company.

Market   any place where goods are bought and sold (thus, a market can be as broad as an entire industry or as narrow as that for a particular product or service).

Market demand   curve on a graph that shows the total of all individual demands in the marketplace for this good or service.

Market mechanism   situation where prices and quantities signal desired output and resource allocation to producers, with all people and businesses acting in their own best interests to maximize their position and that acts as the "invisible hand" that keeps the market at equilibrium.

Market power   the ability to set prices or quantities on their own either.

Market research   collecting and analyzing information for good decision making before you develop and introduce products (and also collecting and analyzing feedback afterwards as well).

Market segment   dividing potential customers into groups with the same characteristics.

Market share   the division or percentage of the marketplace each business serves.

Market supply   the sum of all supplier intentions at various price points.

Marketing   any activity that informs or promotes your products and services in a way that helps you sell to your customers and end users.

Marketing era   an era from about the 1950s – 1990s which focused on the consumer to understand buying habits and what consumers wanted, as Marketing became a science with scientific studies on consumer buying behavior to determine how the buying decision making process works.

Marketing mix   a combination of strategies and messages designed to influence consumer behavior.

Marketing utilities   ways that products (or services) are made more "useful" to customers or end users.

Mass market   an attempt to sell to everyone.

Mass-produce   The use of machines introduced during the Industrial Revolution, which allowed for greater productivity since groups of unskilled or semi-skilled workers could be trained to work the machines that produced individual parts that could be assembled into a complete product, rather than the older production methods of relying on a skilled craftsman to produce one entire item independently.

Mass production   the method by which companies produce large quantities of identical or very similar products.

Master Limited Partnerships   Master Limited Partnerships are a special type of business that is actually a partnership of businesses.

Material breach   when something important in a contract was not done as promised.

Materials handling   items that are moved around inside a warehouse, factory, and so on.

Matrix structure   has more of a grid-like pattern and lines of authority leading from and to different directions.

Maturity   the third stage of the Product Life Cycle when products have maintained their leadership and high market share from the Growth stage, but growth has slowed. Sustained high sales volumes mean that economies of scale can be reached. (BCG Matrix equivalent is "Cash Cow.")

"Meeting of the minds"   when "offer" and "acceptance" has occurred, and thus, a legally binding contract was formed (as long as there was genuine mutual assent, with no fraud, deceit, duress, undue influence, or mistake).

Merger   When two or more companies combine operations.

Microeconomics   the individual economic activity of people and businesses in particular markets.

Micropreneur   person starting a business who chooses to stay small, opting for less stress and more time for a balance in personal life.

Minimum wage   the lowest hourly wage that must be paid to most workers (although some occupations are exempt, such as restaurant workers who receive tips).

Mission statement   a formal, clear statement that describes the organization's purpose, their reason for existing, the product and customers.

Mixed economy   when there is mostly private ownership of businesses and resources, but some level of government involvement in certain aspects of the economy for various reasons.

Monetary policy   the government's means of controlling the supply and cost of money. Can influence the inflation or deflation of prices because it affects the flow and availability of money.

Money   anything society agrees to accept in the purchasing of products, services, or resources.

Money–market accounts (MMA)   hybrid savings-checking account.

Monopolistic competition   market situation when there are a number of providers who produce similar goods but enjoy tremendous brand loyalty that allows them some market power.

Monopoly   when one company or entity is the sole provider of certain products or services, and thus is able to charge any price.

Multinational company   a business that has operations or functions in more than one country.

Multiplier effect   when spending by individuals, businesses or government is larger than the initial expenditure, since the person receiving the dollar will often go out and spend it as well, thus $1 of spending contributes more than $1 of economic activity.

NAFTA (North American Fee Trade Agreement)   treaty whereby Canada, the United States, and Mexico agreed to reduce and eliminate barriers for everything from transportation to food.

NASDAQ   National Association of Securities Dealers Automated Quotation.

Natural monopolies   situation that exists where it is impractical for competing firms to supply a good or service because of high fixed costs for infrastructure or other structural reasons.

Natural resources   the resources that come from nature that are involved in the production of goods or services.

Negotiable instruments   documents which guarantee payment of a stated amount of money over time or on a specific date, such as promissory notes, checks, etc.

Niche market   a small and profitable, but currently under-served, place or method to sell something.

Nominal GDP   measure of economic growth or output that only states the raw number.

Non-economic trade barriers   more subtle, indirect trade barriers that can effectively restrain trade without direct costs imposed by governments (such as requiring redesigned packaging for imports).

Non-Profit Organizations   operate and are organized like businesses, but do not create net operating profits above expenses, or if they do, those funds are returned to the public.

NYSE   New York Stock Exchange.

Objectives   specific, concrete, quantifiable statements for achieving the goals that are measurable, and time sensitive.

Occasions   dividing the target market by life stage, life events, or other celebrations.

Occupational Safety and Health Act (OSH Act)   federal law that deals with unsafe working conditions by establishing safety rules and standards.

Occupational Safety and Health Administration (OSHA)   federal agency under the Department of Labor that makes employers responsible for providing a safe workplace.

OEM (Original Equipment Manufacturing)   when you agree to purchase an entire production run from a contract manufacturing company as the "cost" of them letting you put your name on the products they make.

Offers   when something of value is given by one party to entice another party to enter a contract. (This can even be just a "promise.")

Oligopoly   competitive situation when there are several large firms that dominate a market and thus the firms are able to have some market power by virtue of their size and their control of a large percentage of the market share in a particular industry.

Open market operations   when The Fed acts as an agent of the U.S. Treasury, selling and buying Treasury securities (bonds).

Operational Planning   planning that is usually short term and narrow in scope.

Operational Support Systems   provide a flow of data in the daily operations of a company.

Operations Planning   the process of creating an effective strategy to convert or transform resources into goods or services (often to "reduce time to market").

Opportunity cost   the lost chance of not having something because you decided to choose or do something else, such as deciding between using resources for different activities.

Organizational chart   depicts the levels of management, the lines of communication, line and staff authority, and the division of effort.

Organizational culture   a sort of personality that establishes the way things work in that company.

Outbound logistics   any raw materials, parts, goods, and so on, that you send out of your facility, primarily for distributing those items to your customers.

Outsourcing   when other businesses are utilized or contracted to perform various functions for your business.

Owner's Capital (owner's investment)   is the owner's contribution to the business in the form of cash or other assets, such as equipment or land.

Owner's equity is the excess of assets over liabilities. It represents the owner's claims, or residual interest, to the remaining assets after paying the debts (liabilities).

Owner's withdrawal (drawing) payments the owner takes from the business for personal use.

Packaging something that protects your product during shipping and can also help you sell the benefits of buying from you.

Paid overtime required payment equal to 1½ times the wage rate when hourly workers and non-salaried employees work in excess of a full-time week (generally 40 hr).

Participative leadership also known as democratic leadership is a style that employs group input and sometimes group decision making.

Partnership A business that is owned by more than one person and is not incorporated.

Passion zeal or energy that someone has, especially for the challenge of accomplishment.

Patents formal protection under the law for products' functionality ("utility patent") or appearance ("design patent") which have been filed and granted such protection by the U.S. Patent & Trademark Office. Companies are granted a monopoly on producing a new product that is deemed sufficiently innovative to be protected from competition for and exclusive period of time.

Path dependency when people are reluctant to change the way they've always done things even if a new product or other alternative is better.

"Pay-as-you-go-tax" tax concept that means you must pay the tax as income is earned using quarterly filings of estimated taxes.

Penetration a pricing objective where prices are kept low in an effort to maximize units sold. (This works best when a company can produce high volumes and wants to attract customers to establish a large installed user base, gain market share, or discourage competitors from entering the space.)

People anyone who works for your company, ultimately sales people for your product or service.

Perfect competition situation that exists in a marketplace where no one buyer or seller can control prices or output for a good or service.

Perfectly competitive market where products are essentially the same so that no one buyer or seller can change the market price of a good or service.

Performing when both sides fulfill and contract as promised and do what they agreed to do.

Performance Appraisal evaluating the effectiveness with which employees meet stated goals and objectives.

Performance Management Improving employee performance and company results.

Periodic rate the summation of the interest rate charged over a period of time.

"pick and pack" when individual customer orders are received into a warehouse and personnel "pick" the listed items from inventory and "pack" them together for shipment to the buyer.

"piggy back" transportation technology that allows special intermodal containers to be lifted from a boat and placed directly onto flatbed train cars or onto special truck frames so that the goods can be hauled via rail or roads without having to be unloaded until the reach their final destination.

Place where and how you make your products and services available for purchase.

Place utility making products available where consumers or businesses need them.

Point-of-Sale Terminal or POS acts like a cash register from the perspective of a customer, but they include card and check readers that allow information on the sale itself, the inventory item, and the financial transaction to be sent to both internal and external users.

Positioning   deciding which target market you want to reach with your products and then pursuing that market segment based on demographics, geography, benefits; dividing the market into groups to reach the ideal prospective customers for your product or service.

Possession utility   makes it easier for services to be purchased and goods to transfer ownership.

Power of attorney   where another person can legally sign for someone else.

Piece work   compensation based on production.

Preferred Stock   a much less used form of equity ownership that lies somewhere between stock and bonds in how they work. Equity in a corporation with preferential status to receive dividends over common stockholders.

Price   what you charge customers for your good or service.

Price leader   when the largest player in an oligopoly market attempts to raise prices to see if other firms in the market will follow.

Price stability   economic goal of having modest inflation to prevent prices from rising (or falling) too quickly or unpredictably, with about 3% inflation considered an acceptable rate so that individuals and businesses can plan and grow.

Price taker   a firm that must accept the equilibrium price dictated by market forces.

Pricing objectives   strategies that help businesses reach their goals, either by setting their prices to maximize profits or by setting their prices to maximize units sold.

Primary data   any information or responses you collect yourself. (This can be done in any number of ways, from surveys to focus groups to test markets.)

Prime rate   the interest rate banks charge their best customers.

Principal   the amount of money that the bank loans.

Private account   work for a specific company. They generally perform their responsibilities in one of many accounting services—general accounting, budgeting, taxes, cost accounting, forensic accounting, or internal auditing.

Private accountants   accounts who work for a specific company. They generally perform their responsibilities in one of many accounting services – general accounting, budgeting, taxes, cost accounting, forensic accounting or internal auditing.

Private property   things that an individual owns, derived from a basic right in the legal system of the U.S. which says that people have the right to own things, including the fruits of their labor or profits from a business.

Process Control System   tracks the flow of product or work throughout a process.

Process layout   the process layout designs the movement of people and materials through a process that may or may not all take place in the same location.

Procurement   sourcing materials or parts.

Producer Price Index (PPI)   government index that measures the price level of typical inputs used by a variety of businesses.

Product   the good or service you sell, along with whatever enhancements you include with it.

Product adaptation   different variations of an existing product to better meet the needs of one or more market segments so that the company can have products in as many niches as feasible.

Product differentiation   what makes your product (or service) unique from others (and hopefully better) in the eyes of your customers. (This can be because of features, quality, or brand.)

Product layout   type of layout is most associated with assembling a product in an assembly line process such as building an automobile.

Product life cycle   the stages that a successful product goes through introduction, growth, maturity, and decline. (Different types of products go through their life cycle at much different speeds, with consumer electronics and other tech products going through the fastest.)

Product line   a group of related products offered by the same company.

Product mix   a combination of all the product lines offered by a single source.

Production era   an era from 1880 - 1950s when companies focused on mass production of consumer goods using lots of labor as well as machines to drive down price and drive up the quantity of goods produced, rather than focusing on what consumers wanted.

Production possibilities curve   economics graph representing the maximum output that can be generated from all of the inputs available.

Product screening   where products are rigorously evaluated for market sales potential and how well they fit with the current product line or product mix being offered by the company.

Productivity   the amount of output generated from given inputs.

Profit   is the left over revenue after expenses have been deducted.

Profitability   ability to earn a satisfactory income.

Project slippage   when deadlines are missed and can delay product (hurting "newness" factor).

Promotion   how you make your product or service attractive to potential buyers to generate sales (now or in the future).

Promotion mix   the right combination of traditional advertising, promotions, and publicity. (A successful mix will also include personal selling, word-of-mouth, and various other "official" and "un-official" marketing and promotion activities.)

Prototype   a finished sample of a product that is not in production yet.

Psychographics   dividing the target market by what psychological criteria are important to them; their values, attitudes, or even a quest for the "cool" factor.

Psychological pricing   pricing method that considers consumer reaction most of all. (A high price might be chosen for image or prestige, but more likely a company is trying to make products appear less expensive, for example, by going just below a price threshold such as charging a price of $29.99.)

Public accountants   work independently of a particular company and hire their services to perform accounting duties. They may be self-employed or work for an accounting firm.

Public goods   items that benefit more than one person, and consumption by one person does not exclude others from using that item (e.g., the roads or the military).

Publicity   strategy to inform the media about your new product or service.

Pull marketing   marketing directed toward consumers, getting them to go into stores and buy your product off of retail shelves—or request it if they don't see it.

Punitive damages   an amount is imposed by the court as a penalty against the breaching party to discourage similar behavior in the future.

Purchase orders   contractual agreement between buyer and seller stating quantities bought and conditions of sale.

Pure risk   a risk for which there is only one possibility; the loss of the insured asset.

Push marketing   marketing directed toward businesses, convincing wholesalers, and retailers to stock and sell your product.

Quantitative easing The Fed policy that puts additional money into circulation to try and stimulate economic activity.

Question mark BCG Matrix quadrant that is equivalent to product life cycle "Introduction."

Quid pro quo sexual harassment situation where someone feels compelled to consent to sexual conduct to protect his or her job or be awarded a promotion.

Quotas limits imposed by governments on the quantity of goods that can be brought into the country.

Real GDP measure of economic growth or output that is adjusted for inflation.

Recession two consecutive quarters of declining GDP.

Recycled "materials that have been recovered or diverted from the waste stream during the manufacturing process or after consumer use."

Register submitting formal paperwork with various governmental bodies, especially prior to the sale of securities. (This is a requirement at the federal level by the SEC and by various state regulatory bodies.)

Relationship era an era from 1990s - present, when companies focused consumers to understand their buying habits, with an intent to establish and maintain long term, close relationships between suppliers, producers, transporters, and customers.

Release a signed waiver that absolves liability.

Reliability concept assumes that the user of financial information can trust that the reports are useful, accurate, and credible.

Research and Development (R&D) spending time and resources to learn about customers and the market and then using the info to create new products, features, processes, and so on.

Retailer marketing intermediary that places goods on store shelves so that they are available for consumers to examine, compare, and purchase individual units.

Return on investment (ROI) the profit that is ultimately received from creating a new product.

Revenue is income received from the sale of goods or delivering services to customers during the normal course of the company's business activities.

Reverse logistics when items are sent from customers back to you or other partners in your supply chain for various reasons.

Retail layout the purpose is to provide ease of flow of the customer in a logical way that allows the customer to find the products they want.

Retirement plan plans that provide pay after he or she leaves the company.

Return on Investment (ROI) productivity increases to offset the costs incurred.

RFID tags (Radio Frequency Identification tags) technology that sends out a constant radio signal to computers that can provide precise, up-to-the-minute location status reports to all parties via ERP or other software.

RFP (Request for Proposal) formal process to monitor and evaluate supplier relationships.

Risk uncertainty about the future, especially about the possibility of loss.

Royalty a percentage of sales, usually paid as a licensing fee for use of another company's products, intellectual property (such as patents or trademarks), and so on.

Sarbanes-Oxley Act (Sarbox) federal law passed to govern certain behaviors of public corporations in response to several accounting scandals. (For example, the CEO and CFO must now individually and personally certify all financial statements.)

Salary   A set pay, typically annually or perhaps monthly for a particular job, with little association with the number of hours worked.

Sarbanes–Oxley Act   is legislation passed by the U.S. Congress to protect shareholders and the general public from accounting errors and fraudulent practices in the enterprise, as well as improve the accuracy of corporate disclosures.

Savings accounts   interest bearing deposit accounts.

SBA   Small Business Administration. Government agency set up to help small business.

SBA loans   loan guarantees put in play by Small Business Administration to help small businesses. (Keep in mind though, that these loans are still made by a bank, so even with government backing they're still more strict about requirements to qualify.)

S–Corporation   A corporation that offers limited liability to the owners while also having single taxation.

Scope creep   when the parameters of the product keep expanding, often making the final product that is created to expensive.

SCORE   The Service Corp of Retire Executives.

Secondary data   any information that is examined which was already compiled by other people.

Securities and Exchange Commission (SEC)   the governmental agency that has the legal power to enforce accounting standards for public companies whose securities are traded in the United States financial markets.

Seed money   small amounts of initial capital provided to further the work being done by a small company.

Selective   a retail distribution strategy where companies will choose a preferred group of stores (e.g., appliances or brand-name clothing).

Self-employment tax   a tax equal to about 15% of your earnings, paid by individuals who do not work for a company, to replace the Social Security FICA taxes on a regular paycheck. If you work for someone else, that 15% is split between you and your employer.

Services   are things we do for other people or businesses, which are not tangible.

Service Corps of Retired Executives (SCORE)   a volunteer organization with thousands of locations across the country providing free in-person counseling. They also have How-to Resources, Tools, and Templates available on their web site at www.Score.org.

Service utility   provides additional value to keep customers happy with their purchase (e.g., training, service after the sale).

Severable   when a court decides or a contract clearly states that certain parts can be cut out from a contract without changing the rest of the contract.

Sexual harassment   unwanted sexual advances, obscene remarks, or anything of a sexual nature that can make others feel uncomfortable in the workplace.

Shareholders   People who purchase shares of stock in publically traded corporations.

Sherman Antitrust Act   law that prohibits companies from conspiring together to restrain trade, which would in effect raise prices for consumers because of lesser competition in the marketplace.

Skimming   a pricing objective where prices are kept high in an effort to maximize profits. (This works best when a product is new and has few direct competitive substitutes since these customers are typically less price sensitive when either or both of these conditions are met.)

Small business   companies defined by the Small Business Administration (SBA) as being independently owned (meaning not part of a larger corporation) and not dominant in its industry (meaning relative size, not absolute).

SMART goals that are Specific, Measurable, Attainable, Relevant, and Time-bound.

Socialist economic system when the government controls the resources and means of production (taxing away excess business profits, and sometimes owning the larger or important businesses).

Sole Proprietorship A business that is owned and usually operated by a single person and is not incorporated.

Span of control how many people work for a particular manager.

Specific performance one possible remedy for a breach of contract, where the court will order the breaching party to perform as promised.

Stable monetary unit assumption requires that the amounts reported in the financial statements remain stable and not adjusted for inflation.

Staff authority advisory authority.

Stakeholders Walgreens managers, employees, investors, and creditors (also referred to as stakeholders) all have a direct or indirect interest in the financial health of Walgreens and depend on the financial statements for decision-making purposes.

Standards OSHA's guidelines and rules to assure safe and healthful workplaces.

Star BCG Matrix quadrant equivalent to product life cycle "Growth."

Statement of Cash Flows shows the cash inflows and outflows—all cash only transactions.

Statement of Owner's Equity shows the changes in the owner's capital balance during the year or time period covered.

Statute of frauds law that requires certain contracts to be in writing and signed in order to be enforceable.

Stock become part owner of the business, which entitles you to participate in and vote at shareholders' meetings, and potential to receive **dividends**.

Stockbroker a licensed representative buys or sells securities for you at a commission.

Storage warehouse large building where finished goods, components, parts, raw materials, and so on are kept for long term until they are needed.

Storing money a function of money that helps produce the accumulation of wealth and creates an opportunity to exchange money at a later date. Also called saving money.

Strategic alliance long-term partnership in a foreign market between your company and one of the partnerships you've established via your supply chain (or through other means).

Strategic Plan A written, living document that specifically outlines how the company plans to be competitive in order to successfully remain in business.

Strategic planning the longest range and largest scope planning that looks out several years and is supported by the tactical plans. A disciplined process of decision making that sets in motion action plans and resource allocation to achieve company goals and objectives.

Strategic planning models scenario models for outlining the strategic planning process.

Strategic thinking being proactive, not reactive, to creating value and vision for the organization.

Stress psychological and physical state that results when the resources of the individual are not sufficient to cope with the demands and pressures of the situation.

Strike a work stoppage or walkout by the employees.

Strong currency when a country's currency can be exchanged for *more* of a foreign currency, thus making foreign imports cheaper and making exports expensive.

Structural unemployment   when someone is out of work if they have stopped working while they go back to school or get training for a new career.

Subject Matter Experts (SMEs)   typically highly skilled and educated employees with special skills needed by the company.

Subsidy   government payments to producers (especially farmers) so that their goods (agricultural products) can be sold more cheaply than comparable foreign products (food).

Substantial performance   when most of the promises in a contract are fulfilled and only a few minor things were not done.

"Substantial presence"   jurisdictions where you are determined as doing business for tax purposes, meaning you must collect text and forward those monies to the proper authorities. (Usually, it just means a physical presence, but even a warehouse used by a third party logistics provider could subject you to tax collection rules.)

Succession Planning   The process of identifying people who have demonstrated value to the company and the potential for promotion to higher levels.

Supply   the willingness *and ability* to sell something at a given price.

Supply and demand   law of economics that says for all products, goods, and services when supply exceeds demand, prices will fall and when demand exceeds supply, prices will rise.

Supply chain   movement that begins with raw materials (from suppliers) and ends with the final end-users (your customers) for the product or service.

Supply chain management (SCM)   efficiently planning and coordinating the movement of your goods through all stages of manufacture, from raw materials to finished product in the hands of your buyer.

Supply curve   economics graph showing the amount of a particular good or service that companies or individuals would produce and sell at various prices.

Supply schedule   a chart listing the survey results of asking lots of businesses how much they would be willing (and able) to make and sell at various prices, used to construct a supply curve line.

Sustainability   is the pursuit of strategies that contribute to long-term preservation of natural resources. Reduction of pollution and emissions and recycling.

Sustainable   delivering your unique value proposition to your customers consistently and ideally in a way that can't be copied by competitors.

SWOT   Strength, Weaknesses, Opportunities, and Threats.

SWOT analysis   an assessment tool for identifying an organization's strengths, weaknesses, opportunities, and threats.

"T"-account   visual form of a general ledger account that resembles the capital letter "T."

Tactical Planning   mid-range planning done to cover the 3- to 6-month period that supports the strategic plan and is supported by the operational plan.

Taft–Hartley Act   Further amended the Wagner Act.

Tall organization   many layers of management and small spans of control.

Targeted return   pricing method where its first decided what total ROI is expected on the investment, then divide that number of units expected to sell. (This gives the per unit "profit" that must be added to the cost of making the goods.)

Tariff   import tax levied by governments on products coming into their country.

Task utility   when your labor produces something consumers or businesses can use. (For manufacturers use the term **form utility**.)

Teamwork   working together to achieve a common purpose of goal.

Teamwork structure   creates teams with multi-disciplinary members that work together.

Telemarketing Sales Rule   FTC rule that covers things such as prohibiting unsolicited "cold calls" to consumers where a prior relationship does not exist, requiring immediate disclosures of certain facts, and warning against misrepresentations.

Test market   a rollout for new products in a few locations, perhaps supplying a medium-sized city or two, in order to see consumer reaction and sales data in real time under real market conditions.

Third Party Logistics (3PL)   outside firms that provide various services to customers in support of supply chain management functions. 3PL functions usually include transportation, warehousing, storage, and materials handling but can also include inventory management, order fulfillment, and customer service.

Thrift institutions   financial institutions that generate revenue through customer's savings.

Time utility   making products available when consumers or businesses need them.

Time value of money   concept which says that a dollar promised to you next year is worth less than one you can have today.

Timely training   is necessary to ensure employees have the tools and skills to perform and compete in a rapidly changing competitive environment.

Total cost of outsourcing (TCO)   a comprehensive list of all things you must price into your business model, which includes the normal costs businesses see as well as the hidden costs of outsourcing (thus more than just the cost of workers' wages).

Total product concept   all three levels of your product that contribute to its essence; core product, actual/expected product, and augmented product.

Total product offer (TPO)   everything a customer evaluates when deciding to buy something.

Trade deficit   when a country's imports exceed its exports.

Trade protectionism   the use of government regulations to alter market prices, either by limiting imports or some other means.

Trade surplus   when a country's exports exceed its imports.

Trademark   name, design, or trade dress protection afforded by law to physical products if designated as protected by placing a small "™" on your physical product names, symbols, and so on, or a small "SM" as "servicemark" for service-related protection claims. (Once Federal protection is granted a ® can be used instead.)

Tradeoff   having more of one thing and less of another (e.g., working more means less time for leisure).

Trading bloc   when a country's enter into arrangements to ensure the free flow of goods.

Trading companies   companies who sign on to represent a product in a foreign market and include sales information materials in presentation to their customers.

Training   specific job skill related to education.

Transaction   any business activity that impacts the financial position (accounting equation) of the company and can be measured reliability.

Transactional Leadership   is said to be more mission oriented, focusing on the job at hand with personal considerations secondary.

Transformational Leadership   is more focused on the people and their motives and desires.

Transparency   having a policy of openness and availability.

Trial balance   listing of the general ledger balance of all the company's accounts.

Truth–In–Lending Act   federal law which states that a business cannot simply advertise a low monthly payment to entice consumers without making additional disclosures about the other costs of obtaining the money, conditions of the loan, and credit terms.

Type   one way to group products that are similar by same kind.

Unemployment rate   government measure of jobs in the economy by calculating the proportion of people seeking a job who can't find one.

Unenforceable   when a contract cannot be upheld because it is vaguely worded, can't be proven or is for something illegal.

Unfavorable balance of payments   when more money is going out of a country.

Uniform Commercial Code (UCC)   rules and guidelines for businesses to follow in various detailed transactions and adopted by most states in order to make business transactions go smoothly.

Uniformed Services Employment and Reemployment Rights Act (USERRA)   law that protects the jobs of anyone who voluntarily or involuntarily leaves an employment position for military service, meaning they get their job back upon return.

Utility   the usefulness of something; the ability to satisfy a want or need.

Utilization   all the ways that customers might use a product.

Valid   something that it is legal and enforceable.

Value   the work or usefulness of something. Also, a good quality at a fair price.

Value based   pricing method where the price charged is equal to the perceived value of the customers. (Typically what competitors are charging is considered as well.)

Value chain   every business or entity that comes into contact with your good or service and is considered part of your supply chain (because they add "value" at various stages).

Varied costs (VC)   those costs which *DO* change depending on how many units are sold. (Variable costs include things such as parts or materials or ingredients and labor for hourly workers.)

Venture capital   professional organizations formed specifically to make high-risk, high-reward investments in various industries. (In addition to investment dollars, many also offer management expertise.)

Vertical integration   combining business functions at various stages of production, such as buying from a parts supplier.

Vertical merger   When companies operating at different levels in an industry combine forces.

Viral marketing   getting people to share a message (perhaps in the form of a video) that doesn't seem like a commercial.

Virtual Private Network (VPN)   way to design an Intranet, but using the Internet to link people in different physical locations, even worldwide.

Virtual structure   uses technology to link people, who may not be physically together in a work group.

Vision statement   a clear, inspirational and compelling broad statement about what the company aspires to be, their values, purpose, and future direction.

Void   when a contract is not valid or enforceable.

Voidable   when a minor may choose to cancel a contract.

Volatility   fluctuating prices that could cause you to lose some or all of your investment.

W-4 Form, Employee's Withholding Allowance Certificate   federal tax form used to determine how much income tax are withhold from each employee's paycheck.

Wage   Compensation based on an hourly pay.

Wagner Act   the national legislations that for the first time, officially recognized the right of workers to organize a union and use it to bargain collectively.

Weak currency   when a country's currency can be exchanged for *less* of a foreign currency, thus making foreign imports expensive and making exports cheap.

Website   internet presence that allows customers to find your products, inquire about them, and place orders.

Whistleblowers   people who come forward with allegations of misconduct to the authorities, stakeholders, or the press.

Whistleblower Protection Act of 1989   Protects whistleblowers that work in government or for companies doing business with the government.

Wholesaler   marketing intermediary that takes delivery of goods, stores them, and breaks them into smaller lots.

Wide Area Network (WAN)   uses telephone, fiber optic cable, satellites, or some other communication methods to connect in an almost limitless area.

Work Opportunity Tax Credit (WOTC)   tax incentive program for hiring certain groups of people, such as qualified military veterans or disabled people.

Workers   (sometimes called individual contributors) are people who have an assigned function with no supervisory responsibility.

World Trade Organization (WTO)   international body established by GATT to provide rules and procedures for mediating disputes between those member countries.

INDEX

CPSIA information can be obtained at www.ICGtesting.com
Printed in the USA
LVOW02s2310050715

444628LV00013B/4/P